LANGUAGE ACQUISITION

LANGUAGE ACQUISITION

A Functionalistic Perspective

John R. Muma

5341 Industrial Oaks Boulevard
Austin, Texas 78735

Copyright © 1986 by PRO-ED, Inc.

All rights reserved. No part of this book
may be reproduced in any form or by any means
without the prior written permission of the publisher.

Printed in the United States of America

Library of Congress Cataloging-in-Publication Data

Muma, John R., 1938-
  Language acquisition.

  Bibliography: p.
  Includes indexes.
  1. Language acquisition. I. Title.
P118.M78   1986   401'.9   86-4868
ISBN-0-89079-114-7

pro·ed

5341 Industrial Oaks Boulevard
Austin, Texas 78735

10 9 8 7 6 5 4 3 2   87 88 89 90 91

To Taylor Diane Muma—"Pooh"

CONTENTS

Foreword	xi
Preface	xv
1. The Quests	1
Two Issues: Cognition and Communication	1
Functionalism	3
Descriptive and Explanatory Evidence	4
The Framework	5

Part 1: Philosophical-Theoretical-Operational Perspectives

2. Philosophies	11
A Wedding: Rationalism and Empiricism	12
Inside Out and Outside In	14
Some Philosophical Views	19
Cognitive Bases	23
Generative Semantics	28
Interpretative Semantics	30
Intention	31
Stages of Development	32
The Four Big Issues	34
Summary	36

viii Contents

3. **Social Commerce: The Coin of the Realm** 37
   Anatomy of the Coin of the Realm 37
   Trafficking Information 39
   Intent 45
   Proposition: Explicit Content 52
   Presupposition: Implicit Content 60
   Summary 60

4. **Methodologies: "Outside"** 62
   Three Major Periods 63
   Chomskian Revolution 65
   Developmental Profiles 69
   Language Sampling 72
   Productivity 75
   Summary 76

5. **Methodologies: "Inside"** 78
   Active Versus Passive Learning 78
   LAD and LAS 79
   The Child's Task: Hypothesis Testing 81
   Attendant Principles 83
   Impelled Learning 89
   Competing Influences but Narrowly Focused Learning .. 95
   The Other Side of the Moon 96
   Individual Differences and Strategies 98
   Summary 100

Part 2: Chronological Perspectives of Language Acquisition

6. **Emergence of Symbolic Capacities** 105
   Camera, Action 105
   Sensorimotor Achievements 107
   Tools 109
   Sensorimotor Achievements: Rekindling the Fire 110
   Cognitive Distancing 113
   Gestures: Protosymbolic Behavior 115
   Onset of Symbolism 116
   Protopragmatics 118
   Humor and Symbolic Play 120
   Early Phonology 127
   Summary 128

7.	**Conventionalization: Indicative**	129
	Identification, Predication, Attribution	129
	Categorization	132
	Word Functions: Two Main Views	139
	Word Learning: The First Word?	142
	Word Learning: Overextension	143
	Perceptual or Functional Attributes	144
	Early Phonology Revisited	148
	Summary	153
8.	**Conventionalization: Predication and Early Formalization**	154
	Budding Grammatical Relations	154
	Grammatical Functions: Core Structures	166
	Functionalism	173
	Cognitive Functions: Operators of Reference	175
	The Three Bears	177
	The Envelope Please	178
	The Formal Grammatical Arena	181
	Brown's Five Stages	182
	Fourteen Morphemes	183
	Summary	188
9.	**Assistance**	190
	LAS Revisited	190
	Some Possible Pitfalls	197
	Saving Grace	199
	Hearty or Fragile	202
	Socio-Emotional Aspects	203
	Peer Influences	208
	Summary	211
10.	**Subsequent Formalization: Attribution**	213
	Mean Length of Utterance (MLU)	213
	Sequence	215
	Modulations of Meaning	215
	Loci of Learning	217
	Specific Grammatical Systems	223
	Summary	230
11.	**Late Formalization and Metalinguistics**	232
	Complex Grammatical Constructions and Subtleties	232
	Verbal Shift at 7 Years?	237

x Contents

  Adeptness 239
  Contingent Query: A Structural Consequence 247
  Indirect Speech Acts 248
  Metalinguistics 249
  Summary 257

Part 3: Issues in Application

12. Applications: Assessment 261
  Construct Validity 261
  Psychometric Versus Descriptive Approaches 263
  The Psychometric Mentality at Work 269
  Descriptive Procedures 272
  Some Psycholinguistic Models: Products of Description ... 273
  Summary 274

13. Applications: Intervention 276
  Communicative Payoff 276
  Viability of Normal Language Acquisition Principles 285
  Further Observations of the Intervention Literature 287
  Expansion and Replacement Principles 290
  Ten Techniques 291
  Input Status 298
  Three Basic Intervention Components 299
  Metalinguistics and Play 301
  Summary 302

14. Epilogue 303

 References 307

 Author Index 341

 Subject Index 351

FOREWORD

It is possible to speak of the modern era in the study of language acquisition as beginning around 1957. At that time, two notable events occurred. One was the publication of Berko's classic study on children's acquisition of English morphology. That work represented the beginning of a renewed interest in the careful observation of children's language. It was followed shortly thereafter by the longitudinal studies of Roger Brown, Martin Braine, and Susan Ervin and Wick Miller. This research has led to a rich collection of observations on children's language, many based on spontaneous language samples.

The second event was within the discipline of linguistics. With the publication of *Syntactic Structures,* Noam Chomsky initiated a new paradigm referred to as Transformational Grammar. Chomsky stressed the need to develop a *theory* of language, not just a descriptive account. He distinguished between competence (the speaker's internal grammar) and performance (the events which occur when people speak and listen). Moreover, he discussed the importance of language acquisition in his theory. Any theory of language would need to be able to account for how the child was able to acquire the grammar of any particular language.

At first glance, one would think that these two events would contribute to each other in their search for new insights into language and language acquisition. This, however, has not been the case. The first sign of disagreement occurred in 1963 at what probably was the first conference on language acquisition, held in Dedham, Massachusetts. At that meeting Roger Brown, Wick Miller, and Susan Ervin presented some early findings from the spontaneous language samples of their subjects. Their method has characterized much of the research in this field. It consists of observing the language of children for the purpose of discerning patterns in their acquisition. Chomsky was asked to respond to their papers at the meeting, and his response was quite critical of their approach to the study of children's language. In particular, he felt that the study of children's spontaneous language samples was unlikely to yield valuable information on children's linguistic competence.

In subsequent years, these two events have led to two very different views on the acquisition of language by children. Chomsky's own views have become more explicit as time has passed. He has developed what can be referred to as a nativist view of language acquisition. This view has the following characteristics: (1) The structure of language is modular, that is, it has its own unique formal properties, distinct from those of other domains such as cognition and perception. (2) These properties are innate, part of a unique faculty commonly referred to as the language acquisition device. (3) Acquisition can be conceptually viewed as instantaneous, in the sense that these properties will appear in the child in their adult state, with virtually no change over time. The child's language may change over time only in the sense that the properties of language in the child's language acquisition device may mature at different times, or the child's input may not trigger certain properties until relatively late in the acquisition process.

Those who have followed in the footsteps of Roger Brown have developed very different views of language acquisition. Perhaps the most widespread of these theories is FUNCTIONALISM. Developed by psychologists Elizabeth Bates and Brian MacWhinney, functionalism opposes Chomsky's nativism in many ways. We can contrast its characteristics with the three given above for nativism: (1) Language is not modular, but instead is under the influence of other cognitive systems. Linguistic structures, therefore, can be understood by examining their role in representing cognition. (2) Language structure is not innate, but results from the interaction of several psychological factors that may change over time. (3) Development is gradual and may go through stages before the adult state of knowledge is achieved.

It is the viewpoint of functionalism that John Muma has selected to follow in this introductory text on language acquisition. Because functionalism is a new and developing theory, most of this literature is still in the form of research articles. In the present text, Muma integrates this diverse literature and provides an overview of the functionalist approach to the study of language acquisition. He presents the arguments in its favor, and discusses and critiques the nativist position. The bulk of the text concentrates on the details of the functionalist perspective. It is important to understand the context from which this book has emerged: I would not be surprised if the debate on nativism versus functionalism becomes an even more central issue in the years ahead.

The developments of the last 30 years took root in the area of normal language acquisition. It is a period, however, in which rapid progress has also been made in the field of language disorders. It did not take researchers in language disorders very long to see the relevance of the new work in normal acquisition for their own field. Two obvious trends have emerged. First, the language of disordered children has been studied with the same methods being used for normal children. Paula Menyuk pioneered this kind of research; her example has been followed by other researchers who carried out a wide range of studies. The second trend is to take the findings from normal language acquisition and apply them to the intervention of language disordered children. This may take the form of specific suggestions for the analysis of the child's language, the development of programs, and even specific materials. For example, Lois Bloom and Margaret Lahey have discussed how one might apply the results of Bloom's research on syntactic-semantic development of normal children to the intervention of children with delayed language.

This second trend is a major motivation behind John Muma's text. He is interested not only in introducing the reader to functionalism, but also in showing the relevance the theory has for language intervention. His book is based upon a strong belief that the functionalist theoretical orientation will provide insights into the assessment and intervention of language delayed children.

In applying theoretical principles derived from research in normal acquisition to intervention with language-delayed children, there is always a risk: The practicing clinician may prematurely extract intervention practices from the theoretical orientation. This has been a continual problem in the area of language intervention, where a sincere concern for children has sometimes led to a premature acceptance of intervention proposals. Another problem is that clinicians may inaccurately conclude that theory is irrelevant to practice if specific proposals prove to be ineffective. At the outset, Muma argues that clinicians also need to be theoreticians, in the sense that they should never lose sight of the theory behind intervention suggestions. He feels (and I believe rightly so) that clinicians should not be mere technicians, but that they must continually be aware of, as well as evaluate, current theoretical work.

The years ahead should provide us with evidence for or against the viability of functionalism as a theory of acquisition, and thus as a basis for the intervention of language disordered children. As this unfolding takes place, it is clearly Muma's hope that practicing clinicians will not only follow these developments, but will participate in their examination and resolution.

David Ingram
University of British Columbia
October, 1985

PREFACE

Over the past three decades, a functionalistic orientation to the study of language acquisition and use has evolved. Functionalism, as contrasted to both structuralism and behaviorism, has roots extending back to the turn of the century, but it was largely due to Roger Brown's work on psycholinguistics, from the 1950s to the present, that gave an impetus to the emergence of functionalism. Indeed, his comment (Brown, 1956, p. 247) that language acquisition is "a process of cognitive socialization" has attained fuller meaning by the contemporary functionalistic views of language acquisition.

Functionalism received a major thrust forward with the publication of Werner and Kaplan's (1963) now classic book, *Symbol Formation*. More recently, various works by Bates, Bloom, Brown, Bruner, Greenfield, MacWhinney, Nelson, Wells, and others have defined a contemporary view of language acquisition from a decidedly functionalistic view.

Functionalism is indeed about cognitive socialization. It is a view of language acquisition and use that is decidedly vested in cognition on the one hand, and social commerce, on the other. In cognition, functionalism rests on the tenets of active learning and constructionism. In social commerce, functionalism rests on the tenet of intentions realized in various ways in various communicative contexts. It is a view of language acquisition and use that posits priorities for communicative *functions* over *forms*.

The traditional structuralistic and behavioristic views of language acquisition and use were oriented essentially toward verbal forms with little, if any, concern about verbal functions. Consequently, the traditional views of language in clinical assessment and intervention have been about verbal forms, such as words and sentences. The functionalistic view asserts that traditional clinical assessment and intervention should be reconsidered. It is hoped that this book will play a significant role in the reconsideration process.

Given the need to reconsider traditional clinical assessment and intervention of language, it is necessary to review language acquisition from a functionalistic perspective in order to discern which issues and principles are potentially relevant to clinical assessment and intervention. This book is an attempt to do just that. It not only reviews language acquisition from a functionalistic perspective, but it also highlights various issues and principles in functionalism that may have direct or indirect effects on clinical assessment and intervention.

This book is intended as an introduction. Consequently, various philosophical and theoretical issues are downplayed. The "applied" audience, for whom this book is intended, wants an introductory text that is washed of extensive detail and that highlights theoretical issues of potential use for applications. For this audience, too, a chronological organization is useful.

A note should be made about the use of gender. Solely for convenience, the male gender refers to the child learning language and the female gender refers to his mother. Such a convenience is necessary to eliminate the otherwise unwieldy use of both genders throughout, i.e., him/her and so on.

I wish to thank Doris Roye for typing the manuscript. She is so conscientious. And, I wish to thank Sue Motzer, Becky Crabtree and Janice Valdez for assistance in copy editing. Authors really appreciate such efforts.

1

THE QUESTS

Two Issues: Cognition and Communication

"As we come to know more about language in general and language development in particular, it becomes ever clearer that communication and knowledge of the world are intrinsic to the organization of human languages" (Greenfield & Smith, 1976, p. ix). Brown (1956, p. 247) said that language acquisition is "a process of cognitive socialization." Elsewhere, Brown (1977, p. 26) said, "If you concentrate on communicating, everything else will follow." These three quotes set the stage, in a sense, for this book.

Substantively, knowledge of the world (Bruner, 1981) and communication (Brown, 1977) are two overriding themes throughout. This means that the study of language acquisition centers on two major domains: *cognition* and *communication*. *Formal grammatical mechanisms* comprise the third major domain of language, which is subsumed by the other two. Inasmuch as cognition and communication are studied in the course of how they function in social commerce, the study of language acquisition is from a *functional* perspective.

> The three major domains of language acquisition are cognition and communication, which subsume formal grammatical systems.

The study of language acquisition is very much about *cognition*. Cognitive capacities such as sensorimotor skills, perceptual salience, cognitive tempo,

2 *Language Acquisition*

Table 1.1. The Cognitive Dimensions of Language

General Cognitive Capacities: Theory of the World

Substantive Cognitive Dimensions of Language: Intention, explicit content (semantic categories), implicit content (presupposition)

Encoding and Decoding Processes: Generative mental operations to encode (planning and execution) and decode (construction and utilization processes) messages

Metalinguistic: Reflections (thinking, commenting) about and play with language

cognitive distancing, and so on, have *general* relationships to language acquisition. Cognitive dimensions comprise the *substantive* aspects of language such as intention, explicit content (proposition: semantic categories) and implicit content (presupposition). Intention is the purpose of an utterance; explicit content refers to the basic ideas as they relate to each other in a sentence; implicit content refers to presumed information that is necessary in order for a message to work as intended. Schlesinger (1977) defined these two respective cognitive dimensions as the *interpretational problem* and the *categorization problem,* which the child needs to resolve. The study of language acquisition deals with cognitive *processes* that enable one to encode and decode messages. These are planning and execution processes in production and construction and utilization processes in comprehension (Clark & Clark, 1977). Metalinguistic skills comprise still another aspect of the cognitive bases of language. Table 1.1 outlines these cognitive dimensions of language, which are defined below. At this point it is necessary only to understand that language acquisition is based in cognition.

Communication is a generic term that encompasses various pragmatic activities for conducting social commerce. Early on, communication is achieved essentially without language, through pointing, crying, and selective sound production for "naming" objects, actions, and relationships. These protocommunicative efforts comprise a *pragmatic scaffold* (Bruner, 1981) for learning the formal grammatical mechanisms of language. A pragmatic scaffold is the routines of communication that afford the child opportunities to learn semantic, syntactic and phonological aspects of language.

In order to communicate knowledge of the world effectively and efficiently, social commerce must operate or *function* with formal conventional systems—*grammatical* systems. Thus, Brown's (1956, p. 247) statement that language acquisition is "a process of cognitive socialization..." not only identifies the two main dimensions of language—cognitive and communicative—but also subsumes the formal conventions for doing so - *grammatical mechanisms.*

Functionalism

Functionalism has dominated the psycholinguistic research over the past two decades. Both cognition and communication constitute the underlying motivations for language acquisition, and the actual grammatical structure (word learning, sentence learning, speech sound acquisition) serves both cognitive and communicative functions. This can be put another way: Language can function to facilitate thinking. Technically, this is known as the *mathetic function* of language. Language can also function to communicate intentions. This is known as the *pragmatic function* of language. The actual means (words, sentences, sound patterns) of carrying out these functions are the structures of language. Viewed from this perspective, the structure or form of language serves the functions of language. Thus, function has priority over form in language.

Function has priority over form in language.

In the psycholinguistic literature, the meaning of functionalism centers on *intentionality*. First, it is necessary to distinguish functionalism as espoused by behaviorism from functionalism espoused by contemporary psycholinguistics. The behaviorists, especially behavior modificationists, viewed functionalism as a functional analysis of various stimulus-response contingencies and reinforcement theory. The psycholinguistic literature, on the other hand, envisions functionalism as the realization of intentions in social commerce. The notion of the realization of intentions in social commerce is defined in Chapter 3. Here, it is necessary only to understand that functionalism deals with both the cognitive and the communicative aspects of language in the realization of intentions, and that this notion of functionalism should not be compared to functional analysis of behaviorists.

Second, the replacement of *intention* for *reinforcement* in the study of language acquisition has clearly placed contemporary psycholinguists within the purview of mentalism and outside the purview of behaviorism. As Bruner (1978a, p. viii) indicated, "the new approach to language has sparked a revolt against traditional 'cause-effect' psychology." Behaviorism is the study of observable behavior. Whereas mentalism rests on the disciplined use of inference, traditional behaviorism frowns on the use of inference.

More recently, neo-behaviorism has turned to the use of inference to keep pace with contemporary psycholinguistics. Such efforts, however, have not held up to the rigor that language acquisition theory seems to require. For instance, *learnability* theory (Bever, 1982) is beyond the purview of neo-behaviorism. In short, even the neo-behavioristic views have not kept pace with the contemporary psycholinguistic literature. Bruner (1981, p. 156) summarized this point as follows: "It was to Noam Chomsky's enormous credit that he boldly proclaimed that the old scarecrow had no clothes on." The "old scarecrow" is behaviorism and reinforcement theory. To say that they had "no clothes on" means that they lack substance. They are essentially procedural, and they lack explanatory force.

Indeed, eminent stimulus-response (S-R) theorists such as Deese, Palermo, Cofer, Krasner, and Jenkins have conceded that behaviorism is inadequate to deal with the complexities of language acquisition and use. "In principle, such S-R analyses of language behavior can never adequately account for the acquisition and maintenance of language" (Palermo, 1971, p. 152). He went on to assert that a paradigm shift has occurred in the field: The study of language acquisition is now tied so securely to intention that it has simply surpassed the boundaries of behaviorism, neo-behaviorism notwithstanding.

> Functionalism pertains to mentalistic capacities for the realization of intentions.

Given this paradigm shift toward a mentalistic view of contemporary psycholinguistics, the theoretical perspective of this book is a *functional* view of the realizations of communicative intentions. This view is in keeping with the major psycholinguistic scholars of language acquisition. In this regard, the book is highly influenced by the following scholars: Brown, Bruner, Bloom, Bowerman, Bates, MacWhinney, Greenfield, Schlesinger, Nelson, and Ingram.

Descriptive and Explanatory Evidence

The study of language acquisition can be approached from two basic perspectives (Ingram, in press). One perspective is a *descriptive* account of *what* is taking place. Efforts are made to observe and describe what children do as they attain various cognitive, linguistic, affective, social, and pragmatic skills in the course of language acquisition. This, in effect, is a serial description of the child's achievements in quest of an adult verbal capacity.

The second basic perspective is an *explanatory* account of *how* acquisition takes place. Descriptive accounts are used to formulate language learning principles, consistent with theoretical models, which need further substantiation and verification. Explanatory models are in quest of an understanding of language learning principles.

Both descriptive and explanatory approaches are molded by the methodologies used in sampling, observing, consolidating, analyzing, and reporting language acquisition behavior. Thus, different methodological approaches beget different substantive perspectives.

So what. What does it matter that *descriptive* evidence reflects the child's quest for an adult verbal capacity, *explanatory* evidence is a quest for the principles underlying language learning, and *methodological* approaches can substantively affect these quests? It matters a great deal because descriptive and explanatory evidence of language learning comprises the substantive base for how one goes about assessing and assisting language learning for normal preschool children, early school-aged children, and language-impaired children. Thus, the study of language acquisition is not only a matter of description and explanation with their attendant methodological issues, but it is also a quest for a substantive base for various applications.

The purpose of this book is to extract principles from current descriptive and explanatory evidence of language applications. Descriptive and explanatory evidence, with their attendant methodologies, not only provide a substantive base for understanding language acquisition, but comprise a substantive base for extracting principles for applications.

Given the many theoretical, methodological, substantive, and applied developments in the study of language acquisition over the past decade or so, it is necessary to glean these matters from a variety of diverse sources. In some instances, quotes have been used, whereas in other instances condensed paraphrases appear. In short, this book attempts to compile and integrate a large and scattered literature into a palatable and useful introduction.

The Framework

The book adopts the general language acquisition model proposed by Werner and Kaplan (1963). There are three motivations for doing so. First, the model lives. As a general framework, it is a reasonably good one in portraying major events in the course of the acquisition of formal language systems. Second, it has received fairly good substantiation from the study by Greenfield and Smith (1976). Third, it simply shows that some older notions remain relevant to the contemporary literature.

The basic model posits that the acquisition of grammatical capacities begins with *indicative* (labeling). This is followed by *predication* (commenting about actions or relationships) and then *attribution* (modification). In attribution, the child learns to modify noun phrases and verb phrases. The contemporary literature has a fair amount to say about what happens before, during, and after these accomplishments, especially in regard to functions (informativeness, intent, content) of language in social commerce. Therefore, the indicative-predication-attribution model is only convenient *within functionalism*.

Part 1 lays down the major philosophical and theoretical orientations of the contemporary psycholinguistic literature on language acquisition. These are mentalism and functionalism, respectively. Functionalism is defined from the perspective of *informativeness*; this is the information that is deemed most useful in a given context; such information will be coded in a message. The two views are operationalized first as methodologies of the researcher and then as presumed methodologies of the child.

Chapter 2 briefly discusses the major theoretical developments that have occurred in the recent history of psycholinguistics. Although philosophical considerations are downplayed in this book, some attention must be given to such issues because theory grounds empirical study, and both theory and empirical evidence comprise the substantive base of applications. Again, the basic theoretical orientation of the contemporary literature and of this book is *functionalism*. This can be stated more systematically. It is imperative that applied issues reflect a scholarly lineage. To this end, it is important to get a feel for the scholarly lineage throughout. This lineage is portrayed as follows:

Philosophical Base → Theoretical Base → Empirical Base → Applications

This book is based upon the philosophical notion of mentalism and the theoretical views of psycholinguistics in general and functionalism in particular. It summarizes a considerable empirical base, and in so doing many clinical applications are extracted.

Chapter 3 sets the *functionalistic* tone of the book. It is entitled: "Social Commerce: The Coin of the Realm." In a word, the coin of the realm is *informativeness* as it may be realized in various ways throughout the course of language acquisition. To *function* effectively in social commerce via communication, the child must resolve four major issues in language acquisition: pragmatic categories, cognitive categories, semantic categories, and grammatical categories.

Chapter 4 deals with "Outside" methodologies which are the procedures the researcher uses for studying language acquisition. These are contrasted to the "Inside" methodologies (Chapter 5) which are the ways in which the child presumably goes about learning language.

Part 2 (Chapters 6 to 11) presents a chronology of language acquisition. Chapter 6 discusses the emergence of symbolic capacities: perception, action, sensorimotor achievements, cognitive distancing, symbolization and tools, protopragmatics, humor, play, and early phonology.

Beginning with Chapter 7, the Werner and Kaplan model is used. This chapter deals with *indicative*, or labeling, which involves the difficult problems the child encounters when cognitive categories become referential categories. Accordingly, it is about word acquisition. Chapter 8 discusses *predication*, or commenting on actions and relationships. This chapter grapples with the difficult transitional period when the child's semantic categories become realized in formal grammatical categories and the child strives to deal with relational meaning.

Chapter 9 is a brief departure from the Werner and Kaplan model. It addresses the broad question of the nature of *assistance* the child may have in acquiring language. It raises different but complementary roles for parents and siblings in presumably assisting the child's language acquisition.

Chapter 10 deals with attribution or modification. This deals with the child's abilities to modify noun phrases and verb phrases. Chapter 11 focuses on the acquisition of relatively late formalization and metalinguistics. Here, children learn to be *adept* in playing the communication game; and, *metalinguistic* skills afford them capacities for learning to read and write.

In Part 3, two chapters deal with applications of the language acquisition literature. Chapter 12 deals with *assessment* principles and issues. Chapter 13 addresses *intervention* principles and issues. Finally, Chapter 14 is an epilogue.

In summary, this book is a quest for information on language acquisition from a *functional* perspective. This perspective is somewhat different from traditional perspectives of language acquisition. Thus, readers are asked to release themselves from many preconceptions and to view language acquisition from the perspective of the contemporary psycholinguistic literature, which has a decidedly *functionalistic* view. This view has considerable ramifications for the applied fields, many of which are highlighted throughout.

Part 1

Philosophical-Theoretical-Operational Perspectives

2

PHILOSOPHIES

Even though this book does not stress philosophical and theoretical issues, it is necessary to provide a philosophical-theoretical overview at first from an historical perspective and subsequently, in a selected manner, from a substantive perspective to underscore certain major issues. The philosophical-theoretical bases of inquiries into language acquisition constitute the *keystone* of this literature or of any scientific literature (Karmiloff-Smith & Inhelder, 1975). It is only fitting that an introduction to language acquisition should begin with an overview of some philosophical—theoretical perspectives.

> The philosophical-theoretical bases of inquiries into language acquisition constitute the keystone of this literature.

It is important to establish continuity between theoretical and empirical evidence because neither can stand alone. Moreover, theoretical advancements issue from preceding notions. As Bloom (1984, p. 221) said, "What we learn from our existing theories for building a better theory is more important than whether one or another theory is right or wrong (Kuhn, 1983)." Thus, an historical perspective of theory grounds the theoretical base. In turn, theory grounds the empirical base. Moreover, an overview of theory is mandated even in an introduction to language acquisition because, ultimately, theory comprises the substantive base for application issues—assessment and intervention.

> Theory grounds the empirical base.

The relevance of theory to practice was highlighted at the 1983 St. Paul Conference on education in speech-language pathology and audiology where it was strongly recommended that the theoretical and scientific base of graduate education should be strengthened. This recommendation was made to ward off "technicianship" and to encourage "clinicianship." *Technicianship* refers to an approach to the profession in which one merely follows the directives of an authority without examining the assumptions and the relevant theoretical and empirical evidence underlying them. Technicianship is patently weak. "Sound clinical practice should be based, in large part, on the relevant basic and applied research rather than on pronouncements by authorities, intuition, or dogma" (Ventry & Schiavetti, 1980, p. 3). *Clinicianship,* on the other hand, refers to a professional approach in which one is sufficiently trained to understand and appreciate the substantive value of theoretical and empirical evidence in deriving and revising application principles. Clinicianship is patently strong.

Ringel, Trachtman, and Prutting (1984), too, suggested the need to enhance the theoretical-empirical base of clinical activities. Basically, they indicated that the field of human communication sciences and disorders has not yet achieved scientific status because it lacks original theories and methodologies.

> Clinicians need to have a theoretical-empirical frame of reference.

A Wedding: Rationalism and Empiricism

Since the early 1900s, linguists and psycholinguists have held tenaciously to the conviction that only after the data are in can legitimate conclusions be made. That is, the strict empirical view posits that inference and conclusions can be made only on the basis of data; logic alone is insufficient. The empirical view has been vulnerable to "playing-it-close-to-the-vest" regarding the interpretation of data. This is sometimes cast as a motto for *objectivity,* such as "Let the data speak for themselves." Such views (e.g., Bloomfield, 1933) dominated the study of language until they were challenged successfully by Chomsky (1957).

Chomsky (1957, 1965, 1968, 1971, 1975) argued that, in language learning at least, various innate capacities underlie and govern the acquisition process; data about verbal performance are inadequate to account for such capacities. According to the rationalist view, it is necessary to turn to logical deduction for an understanding of innately driven language acquisition. Problems have been identified with the extreme versions of both empiricism and rationalism. The empiricists assert that logically deduced conclusions cannot be verified empirically. Stemmer (1971, 1973a, 1973b, 1978, 1981), though, has contended that many, if not most, of the logical premises posited by the rationalists are verifiable empirically. Messick (1980) pointed out that data are not useful until they have been interpretated—a subjective enterprise that must be constrained by discipline (Prutting, 1983). "Another way to put this is to note that data are *not* information; information is that which results from the interpretation of data" (Mitroff & Sagasti, 1978, p. 123). Or, as Kaplan (1964, p. 375) said, "What serves as evidence is the result of a process of interpretation—facts do *not* speak for themselves; nevertheless, facts must be given a hearing, or the scientific point to the process of interpretation is lost." As Messick (1980) put it, "Facts and rationale thus blend in this view of evidence ... "

Data are not evidence until they have been interpreted.

On the other hand, the rationalist view is vulnerable to excessive claims. Just because innate mechanisms may be operating, this does not mean that at least some data cannot be obtained. To be sure, inference is needed where data cannot go. For example, Chomsky's (1957) rationalist claims about Language Acquisition Device (LAD) were excessive to the point that not much was said about language acquisition principles and processes. Chomsky maintained that language acquisition occurs by innate or predispositional factors; consequently, environmental influences were considered minimal. LAD, which refers to this innate process, was thought to be so powerful that environmental influences were considered minimal. Environmental influences, however, were considered useful by many scholars in understanding language acquisition processes. Subsequently, the language acquisition literature has supported both innatist and environmental influences. Thus Bruner (1981) proposed that the concept of LAD be coupled with that of Language Assistance System (LAS). Bruner argued that language acquisition occurs with the assistance of others. The joining of LAD and LAS, in effect, couples rationalism and empiricism. The contemporary language acquisition literature reflects this synthesis.

Inference is needed where data cannot go.

In the final analysis, data are necessary, but they cannot speak for themselves; they must be interpreted (Messick, 1980). At the same time, many aspects of language acquisition are available only by inference and conjecture, guided by theoretical premises and constrained by scientific rigor. Data play a supporting role; and data are obtained in piecemeal fashion. In short, theory and data support each other in accounts of language acquisition. This relationship between rationalism and empiricism can be depicted as follows:

Empiricism ◄─────────► Rationalism
(Data)   (Theory)

> Data merely play a supporting role; data are obtained in piecemeal fashion.

Thus, the philosophy of language (rationalism) has become wedded to the psychology of language (empiricism). The great motivation behind this wedding is the potential for using both rationalism and empiricism to posit and then to substantiate or refute theories piece by piece. As a consequence of this synthesis, major strides have been made over the past decade in understanding language and language acquisition (Karmiloff-Smith & Inhelder, 1975). Palermo (1971) called it a scientific revolution. Bruner (1978a) discussed three characteristics of this merger:

> The first is that the new approach to language has sparked a revolt against traditional "cause-effect" psychology and raised deep questions about the adequacy of positivist theories. A central element in the revolt is the contrast between "caused" and "intended" behaviour, a matter that concerns several authors. Perhaps as a result of this revolt, it would be fair to say that psychology and philosophy are closer together in outlook (if not in method) than they have been in half a century. Perhaps it was the line of reasoning that stemmed from the later Wittgenstein and comes in a second generation from Austin, Searle, Strawson, and Grice that has made the liaison possible. A third trend is also discernible: the bridging of gaps that before were not so much empty as they were filled with corrosive dogmatism. The gaps between prelinguistic communication and language proper as the child develops, the gap between gesture and word, between holophrases and sentences, between chimps signing and man talking, between sign languages and spoken ones, between the structure of action and the structure of language. I think that the renewal of interest in language as an interactive, communicative system has made these "gaps" less like battlegrounds where one fights and dies for the uniqueness of man and more like unknown seas to be mapped. (p. viii)

> The study of language as a communicative system has: (a) replaced "cause-and-effect" with intentional behavior, (b) brought psychology and philosophy together, and (c) challenged "corrosive dogma."

Inside Out and Outside In

As for nativism and functionalism, they may be quarreling cousins. Bates and MacWhinney (1979) held that there are two competing hypotheses about the origins of grammar in child language. These are sometimes called the "inside-out" and the "outside-in" theories. The inside-out approach is the *nativist* position, which corresponds to Chomsky's (1957) LAD, whereas the outside-in approach is the *functionalist* position, which corresponds to Bruner's (1981) LAS.

Notice that *behaviorism* is not considered an outside-in approach, because it does not address basic issues about language functions. Some individuals now contend that *behaviorism* is alive-and-well because it has addressed the issue of *intention* in recent years. As Bruner (1978a) has indicated, however, the incorporation of intention in the so-called 'neo-behaviorism' movement actually converts behaviorism to mentalism.

The *inside-out* approach is based on the innatist view that the child possesses a priori structural knowledge of a language, not formal grammatical knowledge. This knowledge is a "given;" it is something that the child "knows" without experience. According to this view, a priori knowledge guides the child to look for formal properties of language, but it does not dictate the ways in which these properties become manifest. It is flexible. This approach led Bever (1982) to hypothesize that language is *learnable* only because it is inherently organized in terms of (or is the product of) a priori knowledge. Consequently, learning is thought to be an unfolding process in which the child discovers relevant aspects of language through appropriate contacts with it (Bever, 1982). "Certain innate clues about the range of possible human grammars" (Bates & MacWhinney, 1979, p. 168) serve to direct the course of language learning.

The inside-out approach views language acquisition as an unfolding of capacities as the result of a priori knowledge.

Bates and MacWhinney (1979, p. 168) adopted a narrow interpretation of Chomsky's (1957) syntactic theory saying, "This is, of course, a linguistic model, a theory of sentences rather than people." Chomsky's more recent writings indicate that a broader interpretation is more appropriate (Chomsky, 1965, 1971, 1975). The point to be made is that the broad interpretation of the innatist position is alive-and-well in contemporary psycholinguistic theory as evidenced by the following: bootstrap theory (Shatz, 1984), three bears theory (Gleitman and Wanner, 1982), and discovery theory (Bever, 1982). These are discussed in subsequent chapters.

Briefly, the broad interpretation of the nativist position is that the child has certain predisposing capacities that govern language acquisition. These predispositions enable the child to discover the structural nature of the particular language being learned; the child learns the specific grammatical mechanisms through actual exposure to the target language (Schlesinger, 1977). "He must begin with certain fundamental, deep-structure categories and use these as a beacon which will illuminate the entire grammar" (Bates & MacWhinney, 1979, p. 168).

> The broad interpretation of the innatist view, which holds that the child has certain predisposing capacities that guide language learning, is generally compatible with contemporary psycholinguistic theory.

The functionalist position is the *outside-in* approach. In this view, grammar is a secondary rather than a primary component of language, whereas both mathetic (thinking) and pragmatic (communicative) functions are primary. In functionalism, language acquisition is not considered to be governed by abstract categories; rather, the cognitive-social structure of discourse within social commerce and the various constraints especially of the speech channel are the primary determinants of language acquisition. In short, how and what the child strives to communicate in large measure determines the acquisition of language. This underscores Brown's (1977, p. 26) comment, "If you concentrate on communicating, everything else will follow." Bruner (1981) posited that the children themselves concentrate on communicating and eventually learn the semantic-syntactic-phonological nature of the particular language being learned.

> Verbal *functions* are primary; grammar is secondary.

The functional view of language acquisition indicates that the form or structure of language is derived from function. The functional view holds that the child functions pragmatically within a given context and uses pragmatic capacities as a scaffold for acquiring semantic-syntactic-phonological capacities (Bates, 1979; Bruner, 1981). Functionalists maintain that the relationship between form and function is indirect and complex: The child faces the continuing challenge of figuring out how to code or decode nonlinear meanings in linear ways. That is, the sentence is linear because it is a string of words, but the underlying notions, or meanings, are nonlinear. For the child learning language, the organization of words in a sentence is not merely a simple sequence of words; the child needs to learn the complex grammatical mechanisms for coding messages. One's native language provides formal grammatical mechanisms for coding messages; these formal mechanisms are semantic-syntactic-phonological devices for achieving presumed messages-of-best-fit (Muma, 1975a).

The following is a short discussion of the role of competing influences in coding messages. Even though the terminology may be difficult, please be assured that this topic is raised again below with a fuller discussion of terms. There are a number of competing influences that affect the emergent solutions (how a message will be coded). Bates and MacWhinney (1979) outlined the *competing influences* in terms of constraints: signal constraints, semantic constraints, and pragmatic constraints.

They identified four kinds of *signals*: lexical items (words), word order, morphological markers on lexical items, and intonation contours. These are used to convey *semantic* information: (a) reference to particular objects and actions, (b) reference to qualities and aspects of objects and actions, and (c) case relations between referents. These in turn are used *pragmatically* to deal with: intention, status relations between participants, felicity conditions or social contracts, given/new information, topicalization and focus, presupposition, etc. Given such competing influences, Bates and MacWhinney (1979) suggested three different principles by which message coding and its products (presumed messages of best fit), can be realized: "divide the spoils," "peaceful coexistence," and "implicational hierarchies."

> **There are competing influences for achieving presumed messages of best fit. These are signal constraints, semantic constraints, pragmatic constraints and new information.**

"Divide the spoils" refers to the principle that each aspect of the signal may serve only a certain function. In English, for example, word order, rather than morphological markers, express case roles, whereas morphological markers are used to modulate meanings (Brown, 1973a, 1973b). Thus, in English, word order tends to serve one function and morphological markers another.

"Peaceful coexistence" provides a direct contrast to the "divide the spoils" rule. "Peaceful coexistence" refers to the fact that a surface form can serve more than one underlying function. Bates and MacWhinney (1979) pointed out that in English, the surface form "subject," the semantic case role "agent" and the pragmatic role "topic" illustrate the principle of "peaceful coexistence" because the grammatical subject is also the semantic agent and the pragmatic topic. For example, "He" in the sentence *He is working* is the grammatical *subject,* the semantic *agent,* and the pragmatic *topic.*

I have observed a two-year, four-month-old girl who was well into syntax (seven or eight morpheme utterances were commonplace) who spontaneously repeated full sentences several times, even after appropriate communicative responses had been given. It is conceivable that this child was so engrossed in the considerations of peaceful coexistence that she had to re-experience the sentences several times to appreciate her achievements.

"Implicational hierarchies" refers to the fact that the inherent structure of language begets the formal grammatical structures of that language. Subject-verb-object languages, for instance, typically have noun modifiers before nouns rather than after nouns. Kuno (1973) argued that in most languages verbs and objects are clustered as natural units, although not necessarily in this order. The 'three bears' proposal (Gleitman & Wanner, 1982) is based upon such an assumption — predicate-argument-logical device. In this proposal, the predicate is the verb and the argument is the object noun phrase. Other arguments (noun phrases) such as the subject noun phrase may appear also.

18 Language Acquisition

Slobin (1977) discussed the competing pressures in coding messages in terms of clarity, processibility, efficiency, and expressivity. *Clarity* refers to the attempt to have a transparent relationship between intended meaning and its code. One can use too many or too few words; or use terms that are too simple or too complex. As Brown (1958a) indicated, the goal is to produce a message with the greatest *utility*. He (Brown, 1973b, p. 68) stated it this way, "A sentence well adapted to its function is, like a piece in a jigsaw puzzle, just the right size and shape to fit the opening left for it by local conditions and community understandings." Slobin (1973) observed that early utterances have more or less direct one-word to one-function relationships, whereas later utterances will demonstrate the peaceful coexistence principle (see also Bloom, 1973; Bowerman, 1973, 1976).

There are always competing pressures in coding messages; the task is to code the message of best fit.

Processibility "involves differences between alternative surface forms in relative demands on memory and perceptual clarity" (Bates & MacWhinney, 1979, p. 171). Topic-comment structure is organized for ease of processing. Topics, for example, are usually said first, followed by comments about the topics. This establishes a cognitive set (presuppositions) within which only certain information (implicatures) may follow. Moreover, new information is placed in positions where it is relatively easy to perceive, usually the predicate (verb, verb and object).

Ervin-Tripp (1973) and Slobin (1973) detailed how memory constraints operate in processing information, notable in this regard are primacy and recency functions. These functions show that in a linear string of words, the beginning (primacy) and ending (recency) are the most easily processed. Processibility must also consider the nature of the underlying hierarchical structure of sentences, such as left recursiveness and right recursiveness. An example of a left recursive sentence is, *The boy who wore the red cap* is a winner. An example of a right recursive sentence is: My boy is *the one who is wearing the red cap.* These constructions differ in mental processing.

Efficiency and *rapid processing* are pressures or constraints in message coding. On the one hand, it is desirable to be efficient by being as concise as possible, but a message can be *too* brief. Brevity and length are not the critical issues; what is critical is how the message fits into—or functions in—discourse. This, in turn, centers on informativeness, which is discussed in detail in Chapter 3.

In rapid production, Bates and MacWhinney (1979) suggested that phonological distinctions may become eroded thereby jeopardizing speech perception. In comprehension, a similar problem may occur in which the coded message is too slow or cumbersome so the listener "jumps the gun" by acting on the anticipated message rather than the actual message.

> A message can be rendered inefficient by excessive brevity or length; the important theory is how it fits into discourse.

Expressivity refers to the pressures to express both semantic and pragmatic content. Bates and MacWhinney (1979) defined expressivity as the attempt to encode *ideational content* (propositions about who or what is doing or relating to whom or what, where, and when), *social aspects* (issues of social commerce), and *rhetorical information* (given and new information; that is, informativeness). Expressivity usually translates into a pressure for increased grammatical complexity (Bates & MacWhinney, 1979). That is, the more fully an expression may be is the extent to which it becomes explicit. Increased explicitness usually means increased grammatical complexity.

> Codification should take the following into account: clarity, processibility, efficiency, and expressivity.

To summarize, the inside-out theory, which corresponds to Chomsky's (1957) LAD, holds that innate forces or predispositions govern language learning. The outside-in theory, which corresponds to Bruner's (1981) LAS, holds that nonverbal pragmatic functions provide a communicative lattice or scaffold upon which semantic-syntactic-phonological learning transpires. The inside-out theory focuses on learnability in terms of the inherent structure of language and contacts with language, whereas the outside-in theory focuses on communicative functions as a means for learning formal grammatical mechanisms. Both must face up to the competing pressures for arriving at the message of best fit. It should be pointed out that the inside-out and outside-in theories may be compatible; indeed, Bruner (1981) contends that they are complementary (see Chapter 5).

Some Philosophical Views

Reference

Philosophers have been interested in verbal behavior for a long time. The distinctions between competence and performance in language were raised in the mid-1800s. At the turn of the century, Frege (1892) and Russell (1905) debated theories of *reference*. Both turned to proper names and singular definite descriptions ("The boy"; "The big boy"; etc.) in their accounts of how things are referenced. Frege emphasized the role of *context* in providing intuitive or common *sense* meaning for reference. Russell, however, contended that a theory of reference should rely on *formal logic*. Russell's views dominated the theory of reference for about fifty years, until Strawson (1950, 1964) revived Frege's views, which by that time were compatible with the emerging views of pragmatics. Frege had made explicit provision for the role of *context* in discerning reference. Moreover, even though Frege did not discuss presupposition (presupposed or implied information) per se as an aspect of sense, both Strawson (1950, 1964) and Donnellan (1981) asserted that presupposition was implicit in Frege's notion of sense. Presupposition is a necessary aspect of reference because it frees meaning from a strictly logical or Russellian view.

Sense entails presuppositional context.

Kripke (1972) held that both the Frege and Russell theories of reference were inadequate. Implicit in Frege's notion of sense were two meanings (a theory of meaning and a theory of reference); Russell's requirements of formal logic were rudely and regularly violated in day-to-day reference. Kripke rejected a theory of meaning because it is grounded on a priori categories of truth; yet it is the context of use that determines meaning. He argued that a theory of reference should be broadened to extend well beyond proper names and singular definite descriptions to a cluster of alternative names that can be selectively used to *designate*, as opposed to define, reference. Consequently, Kripke proposed the *cluster concept theory of names,* which designates reference. Such a theory shows that terms within a cluster of possible terms are selectively used to fix or designate reference in a particular context. Kripke indicated that "a sort of mental ceremony" is used to select which of a cluster of terms is most useful in a particular context to designate a referent.

The cluster concept theory of names designates rather than defines, reference in context.

Brown (1958a) made a similar proposal when he argued that *utility* (most useful in a given context) is the primary reason for selecting a particular term to designate a reference in a given context. Dollard and Miller (1950) suggested that the term "learned distinctiveness" might be used to distinguish between two referents and that the term "learned equivalence" might be used to designate similarities. Thus, the word "glasses" stands for both a tall thin drinking glass and a short wide glass whereas the words "my glass" distinguish between two glasses that might otherwise be similar.

It is important to realize that words are *not* acquired essentially through formal definitions but through their designated use in context. Bruner (1981) called this acquisition process an *initial dubbing ceremony* in which the child is told that a particular referent is "ball," "apple," "juice," etc. Unless challenged, the child then uses the given term to designate similar referents. If challenged, the child either persists or reconciles the challenge by an appeal to an authoritative source.

Original word learning is accomplished by an initial dubbing ceremony.

Another referential distinction is that between referential and attributive reference (Donnellan, 1966). *Referentially*, "what is relevant is not what is true, but what is presupposed" (Stalnaker, 1972, p. 393). *Attributively*, "it is what is true that counts, not what is presupposed" (Stalnaker, 1972, p. 393). Thus, there is an inherent conflict between referential and attributive reference. Stalnaker called this conflict pragmatic ambiguity. Put another way, Stalnaker (1972, p. 374) said, "reference is a problem of pragmatics." (Pragmatics is the study of language in context.) Even so, he held that context and presupposition are used to reconcile pragmatic ambiguity.

These considerations about reference underscore the significance of *context* and *presupposition*. In so doing, the notions of verbal capacities extend well beyond words spoken to various notions of context, intention, and content or proposition as the product of one's mental construction of messages derived from one's own world (Piaget, 1952), possible worlds (Stalnaker, 1972), knowledge of the world (Bruner, 1981), or theory of the world (Palermo, 1982). These latter notions make it abundantly clear that cognition - broadly defined - comprises the bedrock of language.

Context

Context will be discussed in some detail later. At this point, it is necessary only to appreciate that context can be defined in many ways for many purposes. It is useful to consider communicative context from the perspectives of intention, reference (actual/presumed), and linguistic (semantic-syntactic-phonological) perspectives.

Wittgenstein (1953) has often been credited with defining *context* as the primary issue for pragmatics (Bar-Hillel, 1954; Montague, 1972). Pragmatics is the study of language in context. Wittgenstein's notion of indexical expression makes the point. Drawing upon Wittgenstein, Montague (1972, p. 142) defined indexical expression as follows: "An indexical word or sentence is one of which the reference cannot be determined without knowledge of the context of use." Macnamara (1972) and Wells (1974) proposed that knowledge of an event gives meaning to utterances about the event. This appears to be a rendition of the notion of indexical expression. These, in turn, seem to have been derived from Frege (1892) who emphasized that words are meaningless without context.

> An indexical expression is one in which meaning is derived from the context of its use.

Presupposition

Presupposition is the broad cognitive base from which one operates in formulating the content or propositional nature of a message. Presuppositions are drawn from one's knowledge of the world (Bruner, 1981) or theory of the world (Palermo, 1982). Stalnaker (1972) maintained that "presuppositions are propositions implicitly *supposed* before the relevant linguistic business is transacted" (p. 388). Further, Stalnaker (1972) said, "The set of all the presuppositions made by a person in a given context determines a class of possible worlds, the ones consistent with all the propositions. This class sets the boundaries of the linguistic situation" (p. 388). Hence, "shared presuppositions of the participants in a linguistic situation are perhaps the most important constituent of the context" (p. 389).

> Presupposition is the broad cognitive base from which the context and proposition of a message is derived.

Stalnaker (1972) distinguished between semantic and pragmatic presupposition; Bates (1976) added a further distinction concerning psychological presupposition. (See also Greenfield and Smith, 1976; Keenan, 1971.)

The following outline depicts these distinctions:

PRESUPPOSITION
(Knowledge of the world, theory of the world)

A. *Semantic Presupposition:* Explicit and implicit meaning of the utterance
   1. *Asserted meaning:* Stated or explicated information
   2. *Entailed meaning:* Information that must be true for an assertion to work
   3. *Presupposed meaning:* Unstated or implied information that is assumed in order for a message to work
B. *Pragmatic Presupposition:* Appropriate situational context for a message
C. *Psychological Presupposition:* Appropriate topic development or discourse for a message

Pragmatic presuppositions are the conditions that are appropriate for a given message. The felicity conditions (Austin, 1962) or cooperative principles (Clark & Clark, 1977; Grice, 1967) are pragmatic presuppositions. They are conversational assumptions:(a) to be informative but not too informative, (b) to be truthful, (c) to be relevant, and (d) to be clear, not ambiguous.

Psychological presupposition is the cognitive activity of relating sentences in contexts by the negotiation of topic-comment and given-new relationships between encoder and decoder. This pertains to topic development and the exchange of messages in discourse. The encoder produces or "dumps" a message-of-presumed-best-fit (Muma, 1975a), taking into account such things as intentions, reference, topic, codability, perspective of the decoder, and so forth. But, it may be necessary to "play" the *communication game* to negotiate the message-of-best-fit. Wells (1981) discussed a collaborative activity in implementing syntagmatic (turntaking moves) and paradigmatic (intentions) dimensions of discourse. It is useful to cite Brown (1973b, p. 68) again on this matter. "A sentence well adapted to its function is, like a piece in a jigsaw puzzle, just the right size and shape to fit the opening left for it by local conditions and community understandings." The following sentence illustrates these distinctions:

Sentence: John told his brother.

A. *Semantic Presupposition*: Agent Action Genitive Object
Asserted Meaning: Which Agent, what Action, which Possessive, which Object
Entailed Meaning: John has a brother
Presupposed Meaning: John exists, John can talk, etc.
B. *Pragmatic Presupposition*: The situation was such that someone should be informed that John had told his brother certain information.
C. *Psychological Presupposition*: Previous information had been given such that in the topic development or discourse exchange the information that John told his brother had become useful information.

Cognitive Bases

Given the philosophical considerations discussed above and elsewhere, it should be abundantly clear that language is inherently cognitive in nature. There is simply no choice. If one is to deal with language, one must also deal with cognition. The cognitive bases of language can be viewed from four perspectives. These perspectives are the *general*, or theory of the world, perspective, the *substantive* (implicit content, explicit content, and intent) perspective, the *process* perspective, and the *metalinguistic* perspective. To believe that one can deal with language without considering these cognitive perspectives is to make a serious error concerning the cognitive bases of language. Brown's (1956, p. 247) statement acknowledges that cognition is a major issue in language; language acquisition is "... a process of cognitive socialization."

The cognitive bases of language might be viewed from four perspectives: general, substantive, process, and metalinguistic.

Language and cognition have been viewed from several perspectives. Early on, the hypothesis of *linguistic determinism* (Sapir, 1921; Whorf, 1956), which held that one's language determines one's thoughts was widely accepted. Consequently, it was believed that samples of language could be used to ascertain thinking skills. On the surface this appears to be a legitimate notion. But, unfortunately, it is patently false simply because it rests on the unwarranted assumption that there is a one-to-one relationship or isomorphism between thought and language. It is only necessary to turn to the rather obvious principle that one referent can be expressed in many ways and one expression can have many referents to appreciate such falsity. If linguistic determinism were true, then this principle could not work. Yet, everyone knows that one referent such as "a man" can be expressed in many ways (e.g., *Jim, he, the man, someone, the man in the blue shirt, that man*, etc.)

Sinclair-de-Zwart (1969) also held that there is no direct relationship beween thought and language, although she asserted that there is an indirect relationship. Similarly, Goodson and Greenfield (1975) were unsuccessful in documenting mutual structures in language and play. Indeed, the psycholinguistic literature shows that the relationship between thought and language is not a direct one (Schlesinger, 1977; Wanner & Gleitman, 1982)

There is no direct relationship between thought and language.

Inasmuch as it was clear that isomorphism was not going to be substantiated, the search for cognitive underpinnings for language shifted into a two-pronged inquiry, cognitive precursors and substantive dimensions entailed in utterances. *Cognitive precursors* for language learning centered on Piagetian psychology. The crude notion of intelligence tests was simply inadequate (Wechsler, 1975). Piagetian psychology, on the other hand, was attractive for two reasons. First, it was the most highly elaborated and substantiated theory of cognition. It has been regarded as the gauge by which other cognitive theories are measured. Second, it is richly developed for the early stages of cognition—before the onset of language acquisition. It was hoped that such a theory would define the cognitive precursors for language acquisition.

Brown (1973b) and Bloom (1973) posited that children had to have at least a preliminary concept or prototype before they could learn a label for something (Bowerman, 1982; Nelson, 1974). This set the stage for concept formation as a precursor of words (Anglin, 1977). Again, the Piagetian sensorimotor skills seemed to offer a ready account of such early concepts, especially object permanence (awareness that objects exist even though they may not be present). Thus, a flurry of research set out to document cognitive precursors of language acquisition in terms of sensorimotor skills.

At first this avenue of research seemed promising, but problems soon developed (Ingram, 1978; Leonard, 1976; Moerk, 1975; Morehead & Morehead, 1974 Sinclair, 1970). As Mandler (1979, p. 374) put it, "the promissory note of sensorimotor development as the key to language acquisition has remained largely unpaid." One of the more perplexing problems is that object permanence does not show a unified function as a cognitive precursor to word learning. The theory indicates that the child should first learn about object permanence, then, cognizant of things about him (or displaced), he presumably strives to learn labels for these cognitive objects or concepts. Such a theory predicts that object permanence should be evidenced before the child learns words. And, this holds for many children, but there are some children with a limited repertoire of words who have not yet shown the cognitive skill of object permanence on formal tasks.

While this challenges the theory of cognitive precursors, it is not necessarily a telling blow, because there are methodological considerations about what is appropriate evidence of various sensorimotor skills (Donaldson, 1978) and of word knowledge for that matter (Miller, 1974). Should the tasks make "human sense" (Donaldson, 1978) or be tolerably artificial (Uzgiris & Hunt, 1975)? Does Stage 6 in the acquisition of object permanence provide appropriate evidence? Recently, studies of non-nominal expressions (Gopnik, 1981, 1982, 1984; Gopnik & Meltzoff, 1984) have raised a new view of the role of object permanence as a cognitive precursor to language learning. It appears that early words may function in two rather distinct ways—cognitive comments and communicative comments.

Piagetian sensorimotor skills may provide only an incomplete and partial appreciation of cognitive precursors for language learning.

Bates (1979) put a different perspective on the notion of cognitive precursors, raising the issues of analogy, deep homology, and local homology as alternative perspectives of cognitive precursors. In short, her data mainly supported local homology with only marginal support for deep homology and no support for analogy. Local homology refers to the fact that certain underlying cognitive precursors exist for some aspects of language learning but not other aspects and that different percursors exist for other aspects of language. That is, there is no single (deep) unifying cognitive precursor. Some are more pervasive than others. She then identified two major language learning implications of deep and local homology. These are *replacement* and *expansion*, respectively. Both were evidenced, but the latter was more strongly evidenced. In this way, Bates (1979, p. 6) contended that there is a *Great Borrowing* taking place in language acquisition in which "language is viewed as a parasitic system that builds its structure by raiding the software packages of prior or parallel cognitive capacities."

Language learning is characterized by replacement and expansion of the linguistic repertoire.

In addition to cognitive precursors, the cognitive bases of language may be viewed from a *substantive* perspective. Moreover, the mental capacities that provided the linguistic realization of messages encompass various encoding (planning and execution) and decoding (construction and utilization *processes* (Clark & Clark, 1977). And, metalinguistic skills comprise a fourth dimension of the cognitive bases of language. These skills are the abilities to reflect upon, and possibly play with, language itself.

Drawing upon E. Clark (1973a, 1973b, 1975, 1977) and Bowerman (1976), Rice (1983) maintained that there is an indirect relationship between nonlinguistic and linguistic knowledge. The so-called "mapping problem" is to map linguistic knowledge onto nonlinguistic knowledge in such a way that intended referents became conventional tender as the coin-of-the-realm of social commerce. Schlesinger (1977) said that the child is faced with a similar challenge in the *interpretation problem* (cognitive categorization) and the *categorization problem* (semantic categorization), which eventually becomes the grammatical problem. These are discussed below.

This raises a subtly complex issue: When and how does language knowledge become derived from worldly knowledge? For purposes of discussion, it is necessary to convert the question of worldly knowledge into *categorization*, and language knowledge needs to be confined to abstract *semantic knowledge* as opposed to other aspects of language knowledge such as formal rules of syntax, phonology, and pragmatic scripts. Admittedly, this is risky business but in the interest of establishing relationships between worldly knowledge and language knowledge, it is at least worth considering. Bloom (1970, 1973), Schlesinger (1974, 1977), Bowerman (1974, 1976) and Dore (1975) have recognized that it is necessary to do so. Bowerman (1976) summarized their positions as follows:

> Bloom (1973, p. 2), for example, distinguishes sharply between *semantic* knowledge, which she defines as involving the meaning of particular words

and of meaning relations between words, and *conceptual* knowledge, or underlying cognitive structures that the child uses to represent to himself the relations among persons, objects, and events in the world. Like Bloom, Dore (1975) argues against assigning linguistic significance to such nonlinguistic aspects of context as crying, gestures, etc. He recommends maintaining a clear distinction between "knowledge of language and knowledge of the world" to "prevent basing claims about the former on data about the latter" (p. 34). Similar arguments have been made by Bowerman (1974) about the need to make a clear distinction between the general conceptual knowledge that is reflected in a child's behavior at the time of speech and knowledge of the internal structure (i.e., semantic components) of words.

The matter of distinguishing semantic knowledge from cognitive knowledge is clearly a complex one and cannot be analyzed in detail here. However, the position I would advocate, in line with the sort of arguments made by Bloom (1970, 1973), Dore (1975), Schlesinger (1974) and Bowerman (1974b), is that the term "semantic" be reserved for cognitive knowledge that has demonstrably become linked to aspects of *language* for the child - i.e., that has begun to "make a difference, linguistically," to borrow Schlesinger's useful phrase (1974, p. 144). In other words, a concept that the child grasps at the nonlinguistic level achieves semantic significance only if (1) it has an effect on the way he selects a word to refer to a situation, or chooses an inflection and determines the class of words to which the inflection can be applied, or selects a word order or intonation pattern, or decides whether or not a particular operation can be performed (such as using a noncausative verb in a causative sense, see Bowerman, 1974), and so on, or, conversely, if (2) it governs the way in which he *understands* a word, inflection, word order, intonation pattern, etc. (pp. 108–109)

Categorization is central to cognition.

Virtually all cognitive activity involves and is dependent on the process of categorizing (Bruner, Goodnow & Austin, 1956, p. 246). The grouping of discriminably different stimuli into categories on the basis of shared features is an adaptive way of dealing with what would otherwise be an overwhelming array of unique experiences. (Bowerman, 1976, pp. 105–106)

Life in a world where nothing was the same would be intolerable. It is through . . . classification that the whole rich world of infinite variability shrinks to manipulable size. (Tyler, 1969, p. 7).

Virtually all cognitive activity involves and is dependent on categorization.

Categorization provides a *substantive* base for semantic knowledge of language. Roughly speaking, knowledge of the world—categorization—allows one to formulate ideas for social commerce. As Nelson (1973a, p. 21) put it, "Categorization of sound patterns and of objects and events in the real world is basic to learning a language." Lenneberg (1967, pp. 332-333) held that cognition, and specifically concept formation, is central to an understanding of meaning: "The abstractness underlying meanings in general... may best be understood by considering concept-formation the primary cognitive process, and naming (as well as acquiring a name) the secondary cognitive process." According to Brown (1956, p. 247), first language learning is "a process of cognitive socialization" involving "the coordination of speech categories with categories of the nonlinguistic world."

The speech categories are raw abstract notions about entities and relations (Greenfield & Smith, 1976). They provide the substantive base for deriving the semantic aspect of an utterance. Jointly, they comprise a *proposition*, or, in popular parlance, an idea cast into one sentence. The heart of a sentence is the propositional component of deep structure (Perfetti, 1972). It is these united notions, as a proposition, that are *intentionally* negotiated in social commerce. "People do many things with language, one of which is to express *propositions* for one reason or another, propositions being abstract objects representing truth conditions" (Stalnaker, 1972, p. 381). "One of the jobs of natural language is to express propositions" (Stalnaker, 1972, p. 383).

Propositions are informationally organized semantic notions or categories of social commerce.

In short, knowledge of the world constitutes a cognitive base for deriving an utterance via knowledge of the language. Figure 2.1 attempts to show that knowledge of the world is the basis for deriving an utterance via knowledge of the language.

Generative Semantics

In the early 1970s, the generative semantic movement attempted to describe, and hopefully to explain, the semantic basis of language. This in turn was thought to be helpful in defining the cognitive basis of language. This effort focused on the propositional (content) aspects of speech acts. Intentionality was assumed but not fully explicated. In a sense, the generative semantic movement attempted to delineate a repertoire of basic ideas in speech acts unencumbered by formal lexical, syntactic, and even phonological processes. Thus, the generative semantic movement held promise for delineating the brute cognitive

Figure 2.1. Knowledge of the world is the basis for deriving an utterance via knowledge of the language.

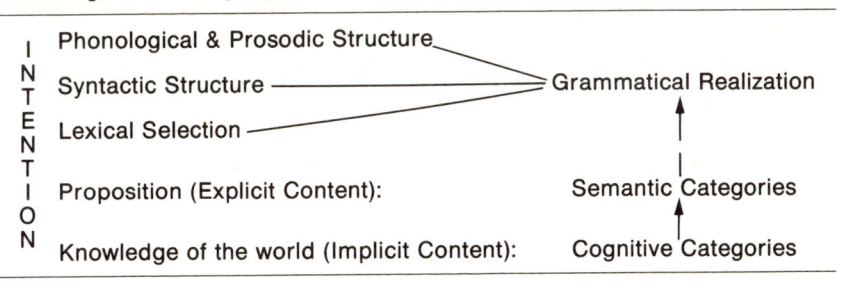

INTENTION		
	Phonological & Prosodic Structure	
	Syntactic Structure	Grammatical Realization
	Lexical Selection	↑
	Proposition (Explicit Content):	Semantic Categories
	Knowledge of the world (Implicit Content):	Cognitive Categories

base of language. Moreover, it was hoped that such delineations in language acquisition would help to identify developmental sequences within a cognitive orientation.

Fillmore (1968), Brown (1973b), Schlesinger (1971, 1974), Bloom (1970, 1973), Edwards (1973), Bowerman (1973), Braine (1976), Bloom, Lightbown, and Hood (1975), Lyons (1969), Leonard (1976), and Greenfield and Smith (1976) attempted to identify the basic cognitive notions entailed in early utterances by studying early semantic functions and relations. Leonard (1976) summarized these efforts in the progressive realization of relational distinctions. And, he (Leonard, 1983) and others (Duchan & Lund, 1979; Howe, 1976, 1981; Macrae, 1979) detailed some problems in knowing when to credit the child with knowledge of semantic relations. These problems pertained to how many and which semantic categories are truly psychologically real for the child. This, in turn, became a question of which criteria are needed to allow for legitimate inferences concerning one's semantic categories.

The Greenfield and Smith (1976) study was not only the most detailed study but it also yielded a somewhat robust developmental *sequence* for the emergence of semantic functions and relations entailed in utterances by two children. Roughly, they reported the following sequence: performatives, indicatives, volition, agent, action (pseudo-locatives, intransitive, transitive, state), object, dative, possessive, locative, and modification.

Utterance *content* has an acquisition sequence.

Slobin (1973) substantiated a language learning principle identified by Werner and Kaplan (1963) in terms of semantic functions and relations. The principle is that *new forms come in with old functions and new functions come in with old forms*. This principle is important for two reasons. First, it shows an intimate relationship between form and function. Second, it points out that an emerging semantic capacity is not merely a matter of the acquisition sequence of adding more and more semantic functions and relations; it is also a matter of an expanded repertoire of expression of these functions and combinations of these functions. Early on, each semantic notion and relation is expressed as a single word. As children become increasingly skilled, they are able to achieve a complex relationship between entailed meanings and their verbalizations.

New forms come in with old functions and new functions come in with old forms.

Even though the generative semantic movement shed new light on the cognitive bases of language, it was eventually replaced by interpretative semantics for four reasons. First, the "use" of various semantic categories, by themselves, led to a loss of confidence in accounting for early grammatical skill. Leonard (1983) attributed this loss of confidence to the following:

> When the child's word-combination rules transcend specific lexical items, they often embody meanings that are too narrow for the traditional semantic-relation categories ... Thus, these findings indicate that young children's two-word utterances may represent (1) memorization of a number of combinations into which particular words may enter, (2) productive rules applied only to specific words, (3) productive rules conveying meanings that cross lexical boundaries, but are narrower than traditional semantic relation categories, as well as (4) semantic relation rules of the traditional type. (p. 13)

Actually, Brown (1973b) had worried earlier that the generative semantic accounts may not adequately represent underlying semantic categories, cautioning that such accounts may only index procedures of inquiry into language acquisition rather than actual semantic categories of the child. It was only after considerations of *productivity* and *context* were taken into account that problems such as those cited by Leonard became evident.

Second, semantic cases apparently represent cognitive categories better than grammatical relations. It is relational meaning that is at the heart of semantics (Leonard, 1976). Perfetti (1972, p. 243) stated this problem as follows: "The main difficulty is that they represent cases as categories which they are not, rather than relationships, which they are."

Third, the generative semantic movement had not made sufficient provision for presupposition. Finally, the movement had not accounted for intention. Consequently, interpretative semantics replaced generative semantics.

Interpretative Semantics

Four years after he had ushered in the generative semantic movement, Fillmore (1968) was largely responsible for the replacement of generative semantics by interpretative semantics. He held that the delineation of semantic functions and relations is useful for defining the basic ideas of a proposition, but he also pointed out that such semantic ideas are merely products of an active dynamic underlying presuppositional structure, which is itself derived from knowledge of the world.

Interpretative semantics strives not only to account for semantic structure but also for the underlying presuppositional structure derived from knowledge of the world. Moreover, such efforts are placed within the structure of *intention* (Searle, 1975, 1977). Fillmore (1972, 1977) attempted to show that interpretative semantics addresses presuppositional, semantic and pragmatic structure. He used the internal and external contextualization analogy. According to Fillmore (1981, p. 14), *contextualization* refers to a text analysis of what "producers and interpreters of discourse are doing and what they are mentally experiencing." *Internal contextualization* then, determines "the set of worlds in which the discourse could play a role," and *external contextualization* refers to "possible worlds compatible with the message content of the discourse."

Internal contextualization pertains to "worldly knowledge" or presupposition; external contextualization pertains to how the expressed proposition fits into discourse.

Intention

Intention should be placed within the framework of speech act theory and given a preliminary definition. Austin (1962) and Searle (1969) placed the construct of intention in perspective with other major aspects of an utterance. Washed of technical jargon, they posited that a *speech act* is made up of the following: (a) utterance itself (words/sentence); (b) intention or intent; (c) proposition or explicit content with presupposition (implicit content); and (d) its effects on the listener. Moreover, speech acts are issued within social contracts or felicity conditions. While the basic notion of speech acts remains, Searle (1977) made a major revision whereby he identified the main types of speech acts and he tied intention to some related issues (purpose of the act, direction of fit between words and world, psychological state, etc.). His revised speech act types were summarized by Wells (1981):

Representatives: To have the encoder posit particular relationships. Thus, an encoder may say: "The boy is carrying a bucket." "He ran around the track." "Nobody asked a question." "She is here."

Directives: To get the decoder to do something. These can be direct or indirect *requests* for information or action. *Direct requests* for information are accomplished by the use of yes/no and wh- questions. "Is she going to the dance?" "Who bought the antique?" Direct requests for action are imperative statements: "Go outside." "Give it to me." "Stop!" *Indirect requests* for information and action are somewhat more difficult to illustrate. It is possible to make a statement that requests information. For example, a person who wants to know an address might say, "I'm sure he lives in the city." And, an indirect request for action could be expressed, "It is hot in the school." Such a statement could be an indirect request to turn the heat down.

Commissives: To commit the encoder to some future action. "I promise to pay you in two days." "If it doesn't rain, I'll go for a ride tomorrow."

Expressives: To express the psychological state of the encoder with respect to the proposition. "Ouch!" "I like it."

Declaratives: To bring about a new state of affairs. "I pronounce you man and wife." "I declare the game has ended." (p. 38)

As for psychological states, representatives deal with *beliefs*, directives with *wants*, commissives with *commitments*, expressives with *expressions*, and declaratives with *declarations*. These play different roles in realizing directions of fit between words and the world. For representatives, words match the world; for directives and commissives, the world matches words; for expressives, words evoke feelings; for declaratives, words create a state in the world.

Intention is the purpose of a speech act. It is tied to the direction of fit between words, world, and psychological state.

The literature on the acquisition of intentions is reviewed in Chapter 3. At this point, it is necessary only to appreciate that intention is a major dimension of speech acts and that intention is substantively related to one's theory of the world just as the propositional dimension is substantively related to one's theory of the world.

Stages of Development

Piaget delineated the following stages in cognitive development: sensorimotor stage, preoperational stage, concrete operations stage, and formal operations stage. Some neo-Piagetians have proposed an additional stage called dialectics (Riegel, 1975). In early language acquisition, Brown (1973a, 1973b) proposed five stages: basic semantic and relational functions; modulations of meaning; modalities of sentences; embeddedness; and coordination. In keeping with the contemporary interest in pragmatics, however, this notion of structural stages in language acquisition has been replaced by a functional perspective which is discussed below in terms of the "four big issues," or problems, that children face in acquiring language. Before discussing these, however, it is necessary to consider briefly what the *stage* perspective entails. First and foremost, this perspective asserts that acquisition is *discontinuous* (Gleitman & Wanner, 1982). Further, this view implies that learning is somehow different - qualitatively - from one stage to the next. Thus Gleitman (1981) characterized the stages theory of language acquisition as a metamorphosis, or tadpole-to-frog, hypothesis. Given these qualitative changes, the issue of *readiness* to handle such changes becomes important. From this perspective, readiness might be viewed in two ways: transitional phenomena and appropriate repertoire. Dore, Franklin, Miller and Ramer (1976, p. 13) delineated some *transitional phenomena* that pertain not only to cognitive and linguistic dimensions, but also to affective dimensions. They said, "Each major linguistic stage is preceded by a transitional phase which serves as a bridging device for the next major acquisition."

Schlesinger (1977) acknowledged that stages of learning occur in which cognitive development precedes language acquisition at least in so far as the child attains a minimal repertoire of knowledge for primitive utterances. Thereafter, there seems to be a crossover (Bloom, 1972) effect whereby cognition is a precursor to language acquisition and acquired language serves to structure cognition. Schlesinger (1977) put it this way:

> A modicum of cognitive development must precede any learning of language, because language remains meaningless unless referring to some already interpreted aspect of the environment. However, once some structuring of the environment has occurred and some primitive utterances can be understood in accordance with this structure, there is room for an influence of the form of these utterances on the child's cognitive development: they may direct him towards further interpreting events and states referred to. (p. 166)

Basically, if children have not achieved the necessary repertoire for launching new efforts, they are not ready to do so. Moreover, it should be emphasized that repertoire means two things: a sufficient range of knowledge and a sufficient range of varied exemplars within this range. These might be called "breadth and depth." For example, in grammatical acquisition children not only have to learn the range of the 14 different morphemes (Brown, 1973a, 1973b) in the modulations of meanings or the range of semantic relations (Greenfield & Smith, 1976) and their distinctions (Leonard, 1976), but they also must attain some degree of productive competence for these aspects before advancing to a new stage. This raises the issue of which criteria are most appropriate for crediting children with verbal competence. The Piagetian criteria of preparation, attainment, and consolidation are attractive to some psycholinguistic scholars (Brown, 1973b; Greenfield & Smith, 1976).

Further, the stages theory posits that predispositions or innate capacities are under maturational control. Bruner (1981) maintained that predispositions for language acquisition are realized by environmental influences. Indeed,

Schlesinger (1977) suggested that linguistic input may trigger learning, provided that an adequate repertoire is available. "For a distinction to emerge, a certain level of maturity is indispensable, and this leaves open the possibility that this distinction is triggered off by linguistic input" (Schlesinger, 1977, p. 164). The traditional language learning landmarks do not correspond to the concept of stages in language learning. These landmarks are the occurrence of the first word, first simple sentence, and so on. Even the well known mean length of utterance (MLU) is suspect as a viable index (Dale, 1980). And, of course, Brown (1973b) himself indicated that MLU has only a small range as an index of language acquisition, roughly 1.5 to 4.0 morphemes.

The Four Big Issues

The learner faces four major issues or problems in the course of language acquisition. Initially, the child is faced with the big issue of what Schlesinger (1977) called the *interpretation problem*. Progressive realization of this problem results in a working knowledge of the world (Bruner, 1981), theory of the world (Palermo, 1982), or possible world (Stalnaker, 1972). In grappling with this problem, the child strives to convert perceptions into categories, thereby reducing unlimited variability to a manageable size. Citing Tyler (1969, p. 7), Bowerman (1976) put it this way, "life in a world where nothing was the same would be intolerable. It is through . . . classification that the whole rich world of infinite variability shrinks to manipulable size." The child's knowledge of the world provides a substantive base for language acquisition. Greenfield and Smith (1976, p. 173) said, "What the child knows—world of his experience—is his basis for deciphering the unknown—adult language." The first big issue, then, is the *cognitive* problem of arriving at categories about one's world.

The second big problem the child faces is *semantics*. The child must learn to derive semantic categories which can be used selectively in language. The source for learning these semantic categories is the child's cognitive categories, but there is no direct correspondence between the two. Schlesinger (1977) contended that linguistic input is a primary means for collapsing cognitive categories into semantic categories. Schlesinger (1977, p. 160) said, "It is the linguistic input which shows the child whether or not to collapse these cognitively distinguishable relations into one." This second big issue of learning semantic categories is what Schlesinger (1977) called the *categorization problem* which is endemic to language itself:

> To function effectively, the child must attain certain cognitive skills which enable him to interpret what is going on in his environment. This interpretation problem can be solved without the aid of language; in fact its solution is itself a prerequisite for learning language. But language learning depends in addition on a categorization of objects and events, which is

needed solely for the purpose of speaking and understanding speech. It will be argued below that the categorization problem cannot be dealt with independently of language: its solution is part and parcel of the language learning process (p. 155).

The third big issue is *grammatical*. Somehow, the child must make a transition from *semantic categories* to grammatical categories. Bever (1982) posited that this is done through the use of *discovery* processes. Others have said that such acquisitions occur by *hypothesis testing* (Brown & Bellugi, 1964; Hirsh-Pasek, Treiman, & Schneiderman, 1984; Muma, 1978a). Whether by discovery or hypothesis testing, it appears that the acquisition of grammatical knowledge is governed somewhat by predispositional forces, which become tuned to one's native language. Schlesinger (1977, p. 159) suggested that linguistic input "imposes order on the many unique occurrences of objects, events and relations."

The fourth, and more generic, problem is how to conduct social commerce while also grappling with these three big issues. This is the *pragmatic dilemma*. Bruner (1981) posited that pragmatic capacities are evident early on, when they function as a scaffold for learning the semantic, syntactic, and phonological aspects of language. Children's use of a pragmatic scaffold is evident, for example, in "buildups," in which children express a sentence, but rather than resuming the topic, they actually disrupt social commerce momentarily while building up a particular construction. Similar behaviors are *spontaneous rehearsals* and their cousins, *spontaneous imitations*. Both involve brief disruptions of social commerce while addressing grammaticalness and possibly semantic categories. Still others include reductionism, pronominalization, interrogatives, and certainly metalinguistic activities all of which are discussed in subsequent chapters. In short, the three big issues (cognitive, semantic, and grammatical) are operationally realized from the standpoint of the fourth, more generic, issue, the pragmatic issue. These issues can be conceived of as categories (see Figure 2.2)

Figure 2.2. The four big issues.

Pragmatic Categories:

Grammatical Categories
↑
Semantic Categories
↑
Cognitive Categories

Summary

Philosophical considerations are critical to an understanding of language acquisition. An historical perspective grounds the contemporary theoretical base which is, in turn, the basis of empirical study. Neither can stand alone. Thus, philosophical-theoretical-empirical perspectives are needed for an understanding of language acquisition.

In recent years, rationalism (theorizing) and empiricism (data gathering) have joined forces in the study of language acquisition. Developments in the philosophy of language have contributed substantially to these efforts. The inside-out (nativism) and the outside-in (functionalism) approaches to the study of language acquisition both seem to offer major contributions, possibly complementary, to an understanding of language acquisition. In the philosophy of language, theoretical advances in the area of reference, presupposition, context, and intent have shed new light on how language is acquired.

Language is inherently cognitive. The cognitive bases of language can be viewed from four perspectives: general, substantive, process, and metalinguistic. The general cognitive base is the child's theory of the world. The substantive base pertains to the content (explicit and implicit) and intention. Generative semantics dealt basically with explicit content; whereas interpretative semantics addressed both explicit and implicit content. The process perspective refers to the mental capacities that enable the child to encode or decode messages. Metalinguistic skills are those whereby the child can reflect on and play with language itself.

The stages theory clearly holds a place in the study of language acquisition. From the stages perspective, language acquisition is conceived of as follows: It is a discontinuous process; each stage is qualitatively different; earlier stages serve as stepping stones to later ones; and each stage reflects innate predispositions, as well as linguistic input. The four big issues of language learning are cognitive categories, semantic categories, and grammatical categories, all of which operate within pragmatic categories.

3

SOCIAL COMMERCE: THE COIN OF THE REALM

The wedding of the philosophy of language to the psychology of language resulted in more enlightened and broadened views of language and language acquisition. Previously, the utterance itself was the focus of interest. The contemporary view extends to children's theory of the world (Palermo, 1982) which enables them to construct messages selectively about unknown or unanticipated information within the context of known or presumed information. Moreover, this view defines the motivation for dealing with such messages as the realization of *intentions* in social commerce. Brown (1956, p. 247) characterized the acquisition of these capacities as "a process of cognitive socialization."

The previous chapter presented the *cognitive bases of language* and the four big issues of language acquisition. This chapter draws upon these cognitive bases and issues to establish a *social commerce basis* of language and language acquisition. The two fundamental communicative *functions*, content and intent, have priority over structure, syntax and phonology.

Anatomy of the Coin of the Realm

The goal of social commerce is to transact social business. Such transactions can be physical, such as stealing a toy in infancy, or running a race in adolescence. Verbal interaction offers a great deal of flexibility and range of topics that could

38 Language Acquisition

not otherwise be achieved in social commerce. In terms of their scope and complexity of coding, physical, gestural, postural, and other nonverbal devices in the *code matrix* (co-occurring linguistic, nonlinguistic, paralinguistic messages) are penny-ante compared to formal grammatical devices, but they have sufficient weight in the balance of trade to tip the scales for a particular, usually indirect, message.

Whatever is done to *inform* in achieving communication constitutes the coin of the realm in social commerce. *Information* works as intended. Thus, *informativeness* is the key inserted into intention—the lock that opens communication. Brown (1977, p. 26) acknowledged that communication is crucial. He said, "If you concentrate on communicating, everything else will follow."

> Whatever is done to inform in achieving communication constitutes the coin of the realm in social commerce.

Early on, the coin of the realm is *informing* realized as a communicative point, a grasp, or a referential display. Soon the child operates symbolically and issues messages by producing performatives (prenaming behaviors such as pointing or noises for animals to designate a referent) and early words—*indicative* or *identification*. Thus, the child becomes a giver of signals (Bruner, 1981). The emergence of symbolic capacities and conventional words raises the denomination of the coin, allowing the child to enter into the domain of *predication* and then *attribution*. Werner and Kaplan (1963) proposed this model of language acquisition (see also Greenfield & Smith, 1976). In short, the model posits that identification (performatives or labels) is followed by predication (relational comments concerning actions and relationships with verbal nuclei implicit and explicit), which is followed by attribution (determiners, modulations, modifiers—word, phrase, clause).

In order to understand the functional aspects of *informativeness*, it is useful to provide a skeletal framework of an utterance in social commerce (see Figure 3.1).

An utterance has four dimensions: intention, proposition, presupposition, and perlocution. These are elaborated below. At this point, it is useful to denote them briefly. *Intention* is the purpose, or goal. *Informativeness* is the plan of action in social commerce, which is realized both explicitly and implicitly. The *proposition* is the explicit content or semantic functions and relations. The *presupposition* is the implicit content or presumed information that permits the explicit content to be understood. Note that there is a link between proposition and presupposition. This is because proposition is a subset of presupposition. What is placed in explicit content as opposed to residing in implicit content is a negotiable matter concerning *informativeness*. *Perlocution* refers to the effects of the locution or utterance on the listener.

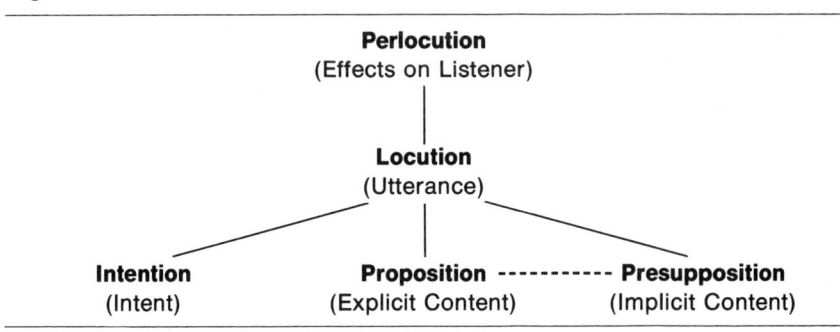

Figure 3.1. The skeletal framework of an utterance in social commerce.

```
                    Perlocution
                (Effects on Listener)
                        |
                    Locution
                   (Utterance)
              _____|_____
             /         |         \
       Intention   Proposition ------ Presupposition
        (Intent)  (Explicit Content)  (Implicit Content)
```

In social commerce, the speaker has certain intentions that will be realized as selected propositions derived from presuppositions. Many factors go into discerning the particular structure of *informativeness* as a message-of-best-fit (Muma, 1975a) or the coin of the realm in social commerce. Brown (1973b, p. 68) likened the process of finding the message-of-best-fit to working a puzzle. The message must be just the right size and shape to fit ongoing social commerce. He said, "A sentence well adapted to its function is, like a piece in a jigsaw puzzle, just the right size and shape to fit the opening left for it by local conditions and community understandings."

But, what if the message is not the-message-of-best-fit? Muma (1975a) suggested that two outcomes are possible. One is that the participants do not realize the failure of the message; both believe that they have communicated as intended when, in fact, they have not. The other is that at least one of the participants realizes the message failure, in which case he or she has the option of notifying other participants, in order to "play" the communication game in resolving such obstacles. Garvey (1975, 1977, 1979), Gallagher (1977, 1981), and Gallagher and Darnton (1978) have conducted a series of studies on these kinds of "play" skills, which they called "contingent queries." These are discussed below.

Trafficking Information

Another way to appreciate the *functional* as opposed to the structural significance of an utterance is to think in terms of trafficking information. Trafficking information refers to concise decisions about what information can be presumed or implied and what information should be coded. And furthermore, trafficking refers to the organization of information in topic development and discourse. Figure 3.2 uses an "iceberg analogy" to illustrate this point.

Consider first the theory of the world (Palermo, 1982) which is a repository of representational experiences. It can also be conceived of as the glacial source of the iceberg. The speaker draws upon this repository to formulate ideas in a hierarchy of presuppositions making decisions as to what must be expressed to realize a given intention in a particular context, and what can remain unexpressed as presupposition and implicature. Such decisions result in what is presumed to be informative. Presupposition is the base of the iceberg. The grammatical machinery (semantic-syntactic-phonological) is then set to work in generating an expression of the resultant proposition. The proposition is just below the surface as explicit content whereas syntax and phonology are on the surface for all to see.

The point is that the expressed sentence is a language action focusing on certain explicit relations that are set against a background of implicit relationships; implicitly and explicitly, this action centers on *informativeness*. In this characterization, the grammatical machinery employed in the generation of a sentence *functions* to highlight selectively particular aspects of information. The message itself is explicitly focused against a backdrop of implicit relationships. Viewed from this perspective, syntax and phonology do not stand alone; they are formal mechanisms for trafficking presumed information.

Furthermore, the iceberg must be freshly hewn from presuppositional history and must be amenable to revision as the expression collides with active implicature. That is to say, both encoder and decoder play active roles in negotiating what is informative. Old icebergs that have bounced around awhile in social commerce become "smoothies" shorn of a rich presupposition history—these are verbal cliches, formulaic utterances, or "frozen forms" in social commerce (MacWhinney, 1981).

This analogy is also helpful for understanding three of the cognitive bases of language—general, substantive, and process. The informational value of utterances, as either a direct or an indirect speech act, is essentially a propositional base derived from presuppositional history (substantive cognitive base). This, in turn, was cleaved from one's theory of the world (general cognitive base). Its actual semantic–syntactic–phonological structure is the result of what Clark and Clark (1977) described as planning and execution processes (production) and construction and utilization processes (comprehension).

Surely, this shows that language is heavily vested in cognition—social cognition (Craig, 1983). Referring to Schaffer (1979), Mandler (1979, p. 375) contended that cognitive growth itself is inherently social: "Cognitive growth occurs mainly in a social nexus." The theory of the world deals with *general* cognitive capacities that afford one an ideational perspective, that is, ideas, thoughts, concepts, schemas, and so forth. The propositional and intentional

Social Commerce 41

Figure 3.2. The New Iceberg Analogy of the presuppositional history underlying sentences.

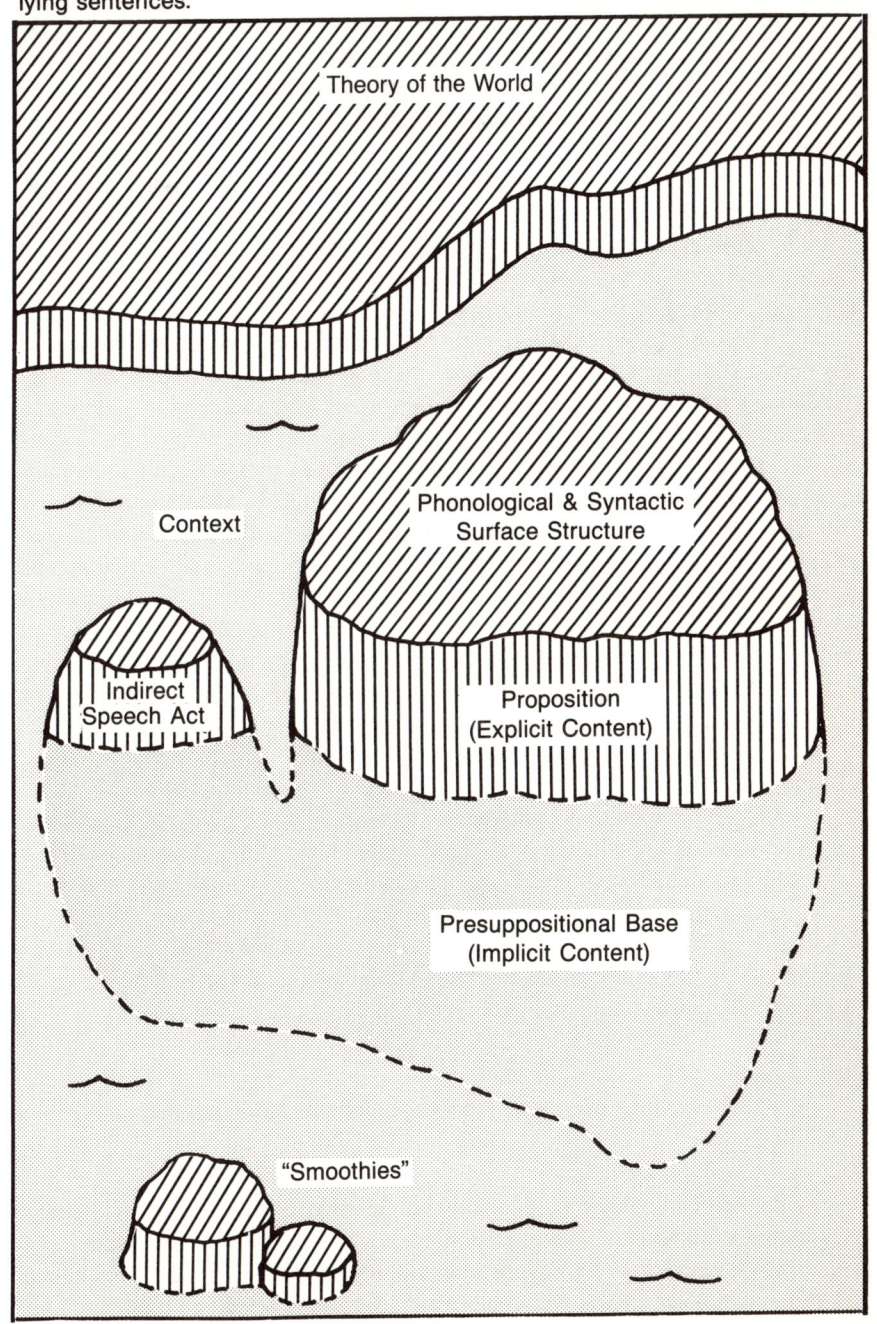

aspects are cognitive dimensions comprising the *substantive* basis of negotiated messages. The phonological and semantic–syntactic realizations are accomplished by the comprehension (construction and utilization) and production (planning and execution) *processes*, which are cognitive in nature. Thus, these cognitive bases of language are *general, substantive,* and *process*. However, when these seemingly independent domains operate in normal social commerce, they become inextricably related in what the participants are doing to negotiate messages: "Boundaries between psycholinguistic theory and general cognitive theory will be most difficult to draw when we try to characterize what a speaker is doing" (Miller, 1974, p. 412). These cognitive perspectives are a far cry from the old traditional notions of intelligence tests and the Sapir (1921) and Whorf (1956) hypothesis of linguistic determinism.

The iceberg analogy also provides for indirect speech acts, intentions, and for highly routinized messages. *Indirect speech acts* may have a different overt manifestation from direct speech acts yet share the same basic underlying propositional content and presuppositional base. Further, they can be implemented with the same felicity conditions or cooperation principles. *Intention*, though, is not well characterized by the iceberg analogy. It is represented here as the direction or course the iceberg may take. Pragmatically, the different kinds of speech acts taken in discourse comprise the intention of the speech act. Searle (1975, 1977) characterized these speech acts as representatives, directives, commissives, expressives, and declaratives. These intentions and associated psychological states are discussed below. At this point, it is necessary only to indicate that intention is a substantive dimension of the cognitive basis of language. It should also be emphasized that *intention* is crucial in another regard. It replaces *cause* and *effect* reinforcement theory in the psychology of language (Bruner, 1978a, 1981).

Highly routinized messages or frozen forms (*How come? You know. No kidding,* etc.) are depicted as "smoothies" in Figure 3.2. They are smooth on the surface structure because they are "fixed" utterances; little or no tampering is ever done to them. Moreover, their underlying proposition, speech act function, and associated presuppositions are time honored and noncreative. Thus, in the iceberg analogy such routinized utterances have been smoothed off by virtue of bobbing about in social commerce over time.

Trafficking *information* is the essence of functionalism.

Greenfield and Smith (1976) said that "sensitivity to information content is a point of structural continuity between the one-word stage and later grammatical speech" (p. 198). As to what is encoded, they said, "This principle of informativeness can generally explain which element is selected" (p. 184). They went on to say that *informativeness* pertains to uncertainty as understood from the perspective of information theory. "Uncertainty exists where there are possible alternatives" (p. 184). Greenfield (1980) said,

> I agree with Garner (1962) that the core value of the information concept for psychology is the notion that information is not a function of what does happen, but rather of what could have happened but did not. In the field of child language, this notion challenges us to discover implicit possibilities, as they exist for the chi ld, and to distinguish these from the actualities which, under the child's current circumstances, could be no other way. (p. 221)

Greenfield and Smith (1976) showed that the child's encoding of *volition* appears to be predicated on informativeness. "Positive volition (demand) is usually expressed by means of the Object, negative volition (rejection) by means of Volition, more specifically by the word *no*. Hence, the prediction from informativeness is borne out, uncertainty leads to verbal expression" (p. 185).

Uncertainty exists where there are possible alternatives.

Turning to the presuppositional cognitive base, Greenfield and Smith claimed that relative certainty-uncertainty is derived from presupposition:

> Specifically, we would like to argue for certainty-uncertainty as the perceptual-cognitive basis for the distinction between *presupposition* and *assertion* in language. But first it is necessary to define presupposition and assertion. The presuppositions of a sentence are "those conditions that the world must meet in order for the sentence to make literal sense" (Keenan, 1971, p. 45). Keenan distinguishes two kinds of presupposition, pragmatic and logical.
>   *Pragmatic presupposition* is the appropriate context for uttering a sentence. Presumably, then the *pragmatic assertion* would be the sentence itself. Although the presuppositions are not stated, a sentence makes no sense if they do not hold . . .
>   Pragmatic presuppositions are assumed rather than stated. This parallels the situation in single-word utterances: What, from the child's point of view, can be assumed is not stated, what cannot be taken for granted is given verbal expression. And it is the relatively certain element that is assumed, the relatively uncertain one that is stated: The former is the psychological basis for presupposition, the latter for assertion.
>   *Logical presupposition* is closely related to pragmatic presupposition, but involves a relation between sentences rather than between a sentence and its nonverbal context. One sentence presupposes another just in case the truth of the second sentence is a necessary condition for the truth or falsity of the

first. The major psychological relation between the two concepts of presupposition is that a pragmatic presupposition is represented nonverbally, whereas a logical presupposition is a linguistic form. (1976, pp. 185–186)

The uncertainty premise states that the Object in subject-verb-object or verb-object constructions is the most uncertain component. Thus, Object would be specified before its Action or State. Regarding only Action-Object or State-Object constructions, Greenfield and Smith (1976, p. 188) predicted the conditions of uncertainty under which a particular component would be encoded:

1. When the Object is securely in the child's possession while it is undergoing its process or State change, it becomes relatively certain and the child will first encode Action-State.
2. In such a situation, the only exception occurs when an adult question changes focus to the Object by presupposing its Action or State. Then the child will express Object rather than its Action-State.
3. When the Object is *not* in the child's possession, it becomes more uncertain and his first utterance will express the Object.
4. Once the most uncertain or informative element in the situation has been encoded, be it Object or Action-State, it becomes more certain and less informative. At this point then, if the child continues to encode the situation verbally, he will switch to expressing verbally the other aspect, heretofore unstated.

Informativeness deals with more information than the simple perception of the event. Olson (1970, p. 265) put it this way, "A word or an utterance, since it not only specifies the perceived referent but also the set of excluded alternatives, contains more information than the simple perception of the event itself."

By whatever means (gesture, word compositions, or grammatical relations), *codification* is the product of "pointing out" uncertain aspects of otherwise "known" (perceived, presumed) information. Thus, codification operates in social commerce to regulate participants' joint attention and action (Bruner, 1975a, 1975b) concerning uncertain referents. Brown and Gilman (1960) suggested that usage is based upon the social significance or utility (Brown, 1958a) of linguistic forms.

Codification is the product of "pointing out" uncertain aspects of otherwise "known" information.

Intent

Intent, or intention, is another conventional dimension of language. That is, as children learn various intentional functions of language, they become able to use language the way others use it. The notion of intention constitutes an especially important shift in perspective in the psycholinguistic literature because it links the philosophy of language to the psychology of language. Furthermore, it frees psycholinguistics from the cause-and-effect constraints of S-R psychology (Bruner, 1978a, 1981).

Intent is the reason or purpose for an utterance. Austin (1962) and Searle (1969) delineated basic verbal intentions; Searle (1977) then added three accompanying issues: purpose, direction of fit between word and world, and psychological state. Wells' (1981, p. 39) summary of these intentions is shown in Table 3.1.

Representatives commit the speaker to a conviction about something. *Directives* attempt to get the hearer to do something. *Commissives* commit the speaker to some future action. *Expressives* express the psychological state of the speaker. *Declaratives* seek to bring about a correspondence between the state of the proposition and state of affairs in the world.

Table 3.1. A Classification of Types of Speech Act (after Searle, 1977)

	Direction of fit	Psychological state	Example
Representatives	Words match world	Belief	*I've dried my hands now*
Directives	World match words	Want	*Put the top back on the washing basket*
Commissives	World match words	Intention	*Well I will play if you put the top on the basket*
Expressives	—	As expressed	*Thank goodness*
Declaratives	Words create state in world	—	*I declare the fete open*

From *Learning through interaction* (p. 39) by G. Wells, 1981, New York: Cambridge University Press. Reprinted by permission.

46 *Language Acquisition*

Halliday (1975) proposed a sequence for the emergence of intentions. This is depicted in Figure 3.3. In Phase I, Halliday (1975) identified seven early intents. *Instrumental* intention refers to the use of language as a tool to attain something. The child could point or say *cookie* to get a cookie. *Regulatory* intention refers to the use of language in order to regulate someone. The child could say *Mommy* in order to induce her to refrain from rubbing the towel so vigorously to dry the child's hair. *Interactional* intention refers to the use of language as a means of seeking interpersonal interaction. The child may say *Mommy* as a request for her to enter the child's activity. *Personal* intention refers to the use of language to express the child's individuality and self-awareness. The child may say *Jim* in order to identify himself. *Heuristic* intention refers to the

Figure 3.3. Halliday's proposed sequence of the emergence of intentions.

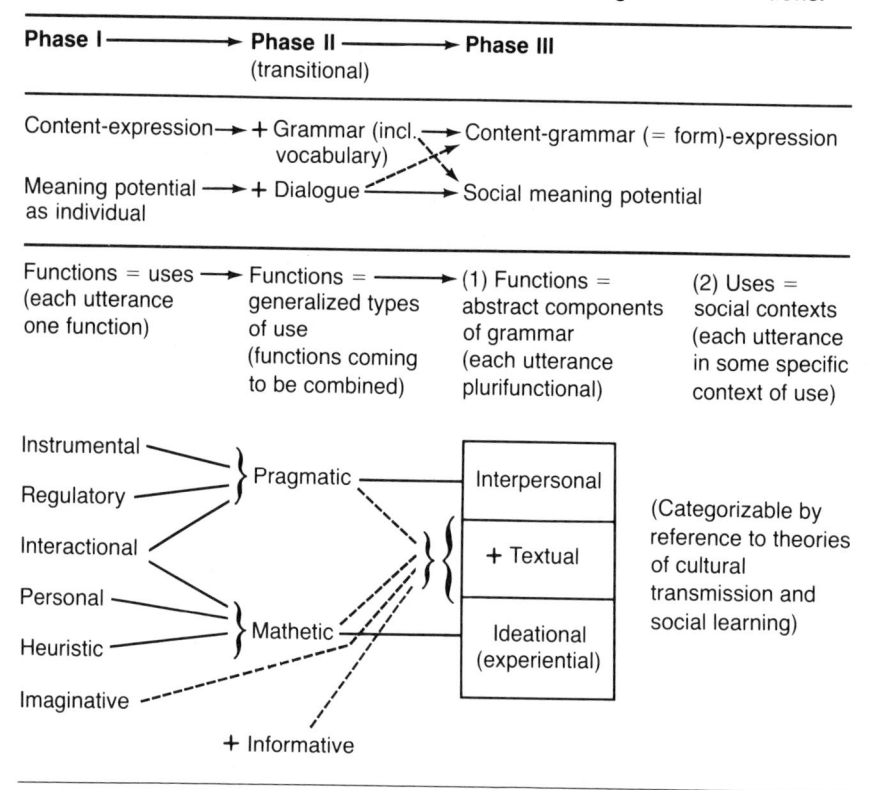

Phase I ⟶	Phase II ⟶ (transitional)	Phase III
Content-expression ⟶	+ Grammar (incl. vocabulary) ⟶	Content-grammar (= form)-expression
Meaning potential as individual ⟶	+ Dialogue ⟶	Social meaning potential

Functions = uses (each utterance one function) ⟶	Functions = generalized types of use (functions coming to be combined) ⟶	(1) Functions = abstract components of grammar (each utterance plurifunctional)	(2) Uses = social contexts (each utterance in some specific context of use)

Instrumental
Regulatory   } Pragmatic ⟶ Interpersonal
Interactional
                              + Textual
Personal
Heuristic   } Mathetic ⟶ Ideational (experiential)
Imaginative

+ Informative

(Categorizable by reference to theories of cultural transmission and social learning)

From *Foundations of language development: A multidisciplinary approach* (p. 260) by E. Lenneberg and E. Lenneberg (Eds.), 1975, New York: Academic Press. Reprinted by permission.

child's use of language for exploration and discovery. Thus, the child may say, "Tell me why," going beyond the original experience to ask about something or even to play with language. *Imaginative* intention refers to the child's use of language for pretending. The child may use language to reenact an event. The *informative* intention develops decidedly after the others; it refers to comments about something. Thus, the child may use *Oops* to tell someone that he or she had just spilled some juice. Just as with *content, intent* has a one word-one function relationship early on.

Language acquisition and use are intentional to achieve social commerce.

However, as the child moves into Phase II, content and intentional combinations can be combined. Halliday (1975) solved the problem of intentional combinations by positing only two basic intentions, pragmatic and mathetic. *Pragmatic* (communicative) intentions provide for interpersonal communication or true dialogue whereas *mathetic* (cognitive) intentions provide for intrapersonal communication or thinking. In its mathetic function, language can be used to advance thinking (Vygotsky, 1962). Gopnik (1981, p. 104) referred to this function when she posited that "children might actually use early language to solve cognitive problems." Bloom (1972) referred to the point at which children are able to use language in this way as "crossover." Initially cognition seems to be a precursor to language. However, after a certain repertoire of verbal capacities has been obtained, language may facilitate cognitive development, while cognitive development may continue to facilitate language development (Schlesinger, 1977). Thus there is a crossover functional relationship between language and cognition. Similarly, Vygotsky (1962) held that cognition and language first develop in parallel (actually language lagging behind cognition) but merge in early childhood. In keeping with Piaget, Karmiloff-Smith (1979, p. 7) argued against crossover: "Language is not considered to be dynamic in provoking change in thought structure." On the other hand, Gopnik (1981, p. 104) argued for such crossover functions. "There is an interaction between linguistic and cognitive development. Children use language to make cognitive advances, and these advances allow them to develop new linguistic structures."

By Phase III, the child's interpersonal (communicative) and ideational (thinking) intentions are adultlike (see also Searle, 1977; Wells, 1981). One particularly important change that occurs in Phase III is that intentions become textual in character. This means that the child can put several intentions in sequence to develop a conversational topic and can incorporate his or her intentions with those of another participant in dialogue to maintain a topic. Phase I intentions, in contrast, serve the speaker with essentially no dialogue considerations—except for the two-person sentence (Greenfield & Smith,

1976). Bloom (1970, 1973) called this "talk-to-attitude" as opposed to dialogue. Phase II intentions may initially and briefly consider other participants in dialogue, but these do not persist. Consequently, these speakers shift topics frequently, and they are often unaware of the dialogue problems this entails.

Bates (1979) indicated that early language learning is *context bound*; this is followed by *decontextualization*, then by *recontextualization*. Similarly, Bruner (1981) maintained that early language learning is formatted (corresponding to context bound), which affords the child opportunities to obtain rudimentary pragmatic skills while semantic–syntactic–phonological domains may be held in obeyance. Bruner did not specify a decontextualization stage, but his descriptions of semantic–syntactic–phonological learning, which are derived from a pragmatic scaffold, are consistent with decontextualization. Increasingly, decontextualization has been regarded as a major accomplishment in language acquisition (Zaporozhets & Elkonin, 1971) and as an episodic-semantic shift in memory (Nelson & Brown, 1978; Petry, 1977; Tulving, 1972). Bruner (1981) said that language learning then turns to the acquisition of cultural scripts (K. Nelson, 1981a; Nelson & Gruendel, 1979), which is what Bates meant by recontextualization. The point is that there is a general correspondence between Halliday's (1975) three phases in the acquisition of intentions and Bates' (1979) notions of context bound learning, decontextualization and recontextualization. These in turn relate to Bruner's notions of formatting and scaffolding as well as to Nelson's notion of scripts.

> Language acquisition is initially context bound, then decontextualized, and finally recontextualized.

Dore (1975) proposed a set of primitive speech acts: labeling, repeating, answering, requesting action, calling, greeting, protesting, and practicing. He held that this proposal distinguishes between referential and intentional meaning. According to Dore, *referential meaning* concerns the conceptual representation expressed by the word, whereas *intentional meaning* concerns the speaker's purpose for uttering the word. Dore's distinction between intentional and referential functions is essentially the same as the distinction made earlier between illocutionary (intentional) act and the propositional (explicit) content distinctions in the preliminary delineation of sentence components. Moreover, Halliday's (1975) three phases in the emergence of intention seems to be more comprehensive than Dore's intention; and, Greenfield and Smith's (1976) delineation of an acquisition sequence for semantic functions and relations is more detailed than Dore's referential functions. Chalkley (1982), on the other hand, regarded Dore's explications as more informative. Dore's discussion of the *referring* and *predicating* expressions that enter into grammatical categories (grammaticalization) and *emergence* are good arguments for language universals.

Bruner (1981, p. 155) held that *indicating* and *requesting* are two major early intentions. "Two of the great functions fulfilled through language by native speakers, even at a tender age are: indicating and requesting." Reeder (1980) showed that Offers are well established by 2½ years of age but Requests continue to develop between 2⅓ and 3 years of age. Bruner said, "I would like to speculate that there are probably four basic, innate communicative intentions that govern a great deal of the child's communication during the early acquisition of language" (Bruner, 1981, p. 162). These intentions were (a) *joint attention* to achieve and regulate joint attention with another; (b) *instrumental* to seek help in carrying out one's own goal-directed acts; (c) *affiliative* " ... the degree to which mother-infant pairs very rapidly fall into a pattern of reciprocal turn-taking under conditions of moderate activation. Each becomes active as the other becomes receptive—in terms of vocalization, gesture and expression. Turn-taking and joint arousal represent a kind of protoformat that will become socialized as a kind of carrier wave in communication" (Bruner, 1981, p. 163); and (d) *pretense* to pretend and to simulate, including drawing others into their pretense with evident delight.

Indicating and *requesting*, however, appear to be the two major early intentions (Bates, 1979; Bruner, 1981; Clark & Clark, 1977). *Indication* begins with pointing. This is followed soon after with a point and the vocalization *um*. Then, these may be combined (point + *um*). *Performatives* can be used for indication. Thus, the child may say *Moo* to name a cow. This is followed by true indicatives, which early on may be phonetically consistent forms (PCFs; Dore, 1975) or vocables (Ferguson, 1978). A PCF is a sound pattern that is specific to a particular referent, but the sound pattern does not correspond with a conventional word in the language. An example of a PCF is when the child calls chairs *ga* but does not call other things *ga*. Eventually, the child will use conventional labels or fragments ranging from vowel nuclei and open syllables to the full phonetic patterns in the realization of indicatives. Indicatives express assertion when the child places an emphatic stress on the label.

The acquisition of *requests* is somewhat different, beginning with reaching and grabbing. Then, reaching and grabbing may be accompanied by a general request word. This is followed by naming the object requested and making the request. Sometimes the name is accompanied by a volitional whine or "no." In early requests, the child may name either the speaker or listener in combination with the main content words. In assertions, however, the speaker or listener are rarely mentioned. "Requests for action took indirect forms, while requests for information took direct forms" (Wilkinson, Spinelli, & Chiang, 1984).

As the children obtain increased linguistic skill, they will elaborate both assertions and requests. From Searle's (1975, 1977) perspective, assertions are representatives and requests are directives. Primitive expressives such as *Hi* and *Oh-oh* for dismay occur infrequently. Neither promises (commissives) nor declarations appear at this stage.

Table 3.2. Communicative Functions Categories

Category	Definition	Example
Regulation		
Attention	An utterance that attempts to direct the attention of another person to an object or event.	*look,* as the child points to an object and looks up at the listener.
Request	An utterance that requests that another person do something for the child, or requests permission to do something.	*juice,* as the child holds out a glass to the mother.
Vocative	An utterance that calls another person to locate him or her or to request his or her presence.	*Mommy* (spoken loudly), as the child goes from room to room in search of mother.
Statement		
Naming	An utterance that makes reference to an object or person by name only.	*car,* as the child points to a car.
Description	An utterance that makes some statement, other than naming, about an object, action, or event.	*gone,* as the child arrives at the location where a desired object is usually found, but is unable to find it.
Information	An utterance that makes a statement about an event beyond the "here-and-now," excluding acts the child is about to perform.	*chick,* as the child looks at the visitor. The mother then comments "We saw some chicks at the farm yesterday, didn't we?"
Exchange		
Giving	An utterance spoken while giving or attempting to give an object to another person.	*here,* as the child hands a doll to the father.
Receiving	An utterance spoken while receiving an object from another person.	*thank you,* as the child takes the offered cookie.

Social Commerce 51

Table 3.2. *continued*

Category	Definition	Example
Personal		
Doing	An utterance describing an act the child is performing or has just performed.	*down*, after the child has just put a box of blocks on the floor.
Determination	An utterance specifying the child's intention to carry out some act immediately.	*out*, spoken immediately before standing up and walking toward the door.
Refusal	An utterance used to refuse an object or request to do something.	*no*, as the mother hands the child a hat to put on the doll.
Protest	A "high-pitched" utterance expressing the child's displeasure with an action by another person.	*don't!*, as the child's brother starts to take the play phone away from the child.
Conversation		
Imitation	An utterance that imitates all or part of a preceding adult utterance with no intervening utterance on the child's part.	*fish*, in response to the father's utterance "What a big fish."
Answer	An utterance spoken in response to a question (excluding imitations).	*shoe*, in response to the mother's question "What's this called?"
Follow-on	An utterance serving as a conversational response that is neither an imitation nor an answer.	*yeah*, in response to the visitor's comment "Let's see what's in the box."
Question	An utterance that requests information from another person.	*what's that?*, as the child looks first at a microphone, then at the visitor.

From *Language disorders in children* (pp. 8–10) by A. Holland (Ed.), 1983, San Diego: College-Hill. Reprinted by permission.

McShane (1980) did a longitudinal study of communicative functions as they became expressed lexically. The communicative functions appear in Table 3.2. These functions are regulation (attention, request, vocative), statement (naming, description, information), exchange (giving, receiving), personal (doing, determination, refusal, protest), and conversation (imitation, answer, follow-on, question). Over the age range of 12 to 24 months, the six children evidenced increased lexicalization of communicative functions. That is, they were increasingly able to use words rather than pointing to express their intentions. Requesting, naming, and answering were most frequently lexicalized. But these forms also had a variety of other functions for relatively limited lexicons. This is consistent with the principle that old forms take on new functions (Slobin, 1973).

In keeping with *informativeness* as the coin of the realm in social commerce, it is important to appreciate that *intention* is the motivating force or reason for conducting social business. Greenfield (1980, p. 217) made this point: "The role of situational structure is relative to the child's communicative intention. It is the child's communicative intention within which uncertainty or alternatives are perceived." She went on to draw a distinction between *salience* or *importance* as discerned by the child (Braine, 1974) and *uncertainty* or *informativeness* as a pragmatic issue upon which both encoder and decoder intentions are vested. As Greenfield (1980, p. 220) said, ". . . the locus of uncertainty becomes a relative certainty for linguistic realization."

Proposition: Explicit Content

Somehow children bring to bear certain basic ideas or propositions in dealing with messages. This means that they (a) somehow acquire some basic ideas about the *content* of messages, (b) begin to realize that these basic ideas are tacitly related to each other, and (c) begin to realize that these ideas can be manifested in a variety of forms. The basic ideas or semantic functions and relations comprise the semantic categories of language. Furthermore, these basic ideas are locally realized as children perceive the objects, actions, and relationships in events around them or concerning a topic.

The proposition or explicit content is comprised of semantic categories.

The notion of basic ideas as the semantic core of language learning is an aspect of the conventions of language—innate conventions, if you will. As the children learn the basic notions of language, they become aware of the potential array of propositional ideas that others use in verbal codes. This awareness to a certain extent "levels" their notions. That is, they consider topics and ideas in much the same way that others do. Indeed, the psycholinguistic literature in the early and mid-1970s focused on the identification of semantic functions and relations in early language learning (Bloom, 1970; Bowerman, 1973; Brown, 1973b; Chafe, 1970; Edwards, 1973; Fillmore, 1968; Greenfield & Smith, 1976; Ingram, 1971; Lyons, 1969; Schlesinger, 1971; etc.). This literature shows that early ideas coded in language are remarkably similar from child to child (see Leonard, 1976, for an excellent review of these and other approaches as well as a good discussion of semantic relations as they may be related to the acquisition of various sensorimotor skills).

Retherford, Schwartz and Chapman (1981, pp. 586–589) provided a composite of 15 semantic categories based upon Brown (1973b), Bloom (1973), Schlesinger (1971) and Greenfield and Smith (1976):

Action: A perceivable movement of activity engaged in by an agent (animate or inanimate).
Locative: The place where an object or action was located or towards which it moved.
Agent: The performer (animate or inanimate) of an action. Body parts and vehicles, when used in conjunction with action verbs, were coded *agent*.
Object: A person or thing (marked by the use of a noun or pronoun) that received the force of an action.
Demonstrative: The use of demonstrative pronouns or adjectives, *this, that, these, those,* and the words *there, right there, here, see,* when stated for the purpose of pointing out a particular referent.
Recurrence: A request for or comment on an additional instance or amount; the resumption of an event; or the reappearance of a person or object.
Possessor: A person or thing (marked by the use of a proper noun or pronoun) that an object was associated with or to which it belonged, at least temporarily.
Quantifier: A modifier that indicated amount or number of a person or object. Pre-articles and indefinite pronouns such as *a piece of, lots of, any, every,* and *each* were included.
Experiencer: Someone or something that underwent a given experience or mental state. Body parts, when used in conjunction with state verbs, were coded *experiencer*.
Recipient: One who received or was named as the recipient of an *object* (person or thing) from another.
Beneficiary: One who benefitted from or was named as the beneficiary of a specified action.
Comitative: One who accompanied or participated with an agent in carrying out a specified activity.
Created Object: Something created by a specific activity, for example, a *song* by singing, a *house* by building, a *picture* by drawing.
Instrument: Something which an *agent* used to carry out or complete a specified action.

State: A passive condition experienced by a person or object. This category implies involuntary behavior on the part of the *experiencer,* in contrast to voluntary action performed by an agent.

Examples of these appear in Table 3.3. Additionally, Retherford, Schwartz, and Chapman (1981) had five syntactic categories, seven routines, and seven conversational devices, all of which were observed in mother-child discourse with one- and two-year-old children. The syntactic categories were:

Entity (one-term utterances only): Any labeling of the present person or object regardless of the occurrence or nature of action being performed on or by it.

Entity (multi-term utterances only): The use of an appropriate label for a person or object in the absence of any action on it (with the exception of showing, pointing, touching, or grasping); or someone or something that caused or was the stimulus to the internal state specified by a state verb, or any object or person that was modified by a possessive form. (*Entity* was used to code a possession if it met either of the preceding criteria).

Negation: The expression of any of the following meanings with regard to someone or something, or an action or state: nonexistence, rejection, cessation, denial, disappearance.

Attribute: An adjectival description of the size, shape, or quality of an object or person; also, noun adjuncts that modified nouns for a similar purpose (e.g., *gingerbread* man). Excluded were the semantically coded categories of *recurrence* and *quantifier.*

Adverbial: Included in this category were the two subcategories of action/attribute and state/attribute.

Action/Attribute: A modifier of an action indicating time, manner, duration, distance, or frequency. (Direction or place of action was separately coded as *locative,* repetition as *recurrence.*)

State/Attribute: A modifier indicating time, manner, quality, or intensity of a state. (Retherford et al., 1981, p. 589)

The seven routines are presented as formats in Chapter 7, and the seven conversational devices appear in the section on early pragmatic scaffolding in Chapter 4. In brief, the routines and conversational devices are various pragmatic devices:

Routine: Stereotyped verbal games, subcategorized as questions about what the animal says; recitations of stories, songs, and nursery rhymes; counting or alphabet recitals; greetings; requests to say "X"; sounds accompanying pretend play, such as animal or car noises; and explicit naming routines.

Conversational Devices: Words and phrases that served to mark conversational boundaries. These included the subcategories of requests for attention; affirmation; positive evaluation; interjection; polite forms;

repetition requests; and accompaniments to action. (Rutherford et al., 1981, p. 590)

The Greenfield and Smith (1976) model of semantic functions and relations is especially useful because it gives a developmental sequence for the emergence of these basic ideas. Leonard (1976) integrated several approaches in support of successive distinctions presumably made to obtain semantic functions and relations. His results are compatible with the empirically derived sequences of Greenfield and Smith. Table 3.4 is an abridged version of the Greenfield and Smith sequence for the acquisition of semantic functions and relations.

Before reviewing the Greenfield and Smith (1976) acquisition sequence for semantic functions and relations, it is useful to review five basic assumptions that establish firm theoretical support for an adult deducing appropriate semantic sense from children's communicative efforts in context. These assumptions (Greenfield & Smith, 1976, pp. 44–45) are:

1. "We assume that the child distinguishes entities and relations. Entities are 'point-at-ables,' or things; relations are actions and states that cannot be pointed at but can be predicated of entities" (p. 44).
2. "We assume that the child distinguishes animate from inanimate entities" (p. 45).
3. "We assume that the child's gestures and orientation, particularly pointing and reaching, indicate important elements of the situation" (p. 45). Communicative pointing is assumed to be a realization of *indicative* whereas reaching is a realization of *volition*.
4. "We assume that the adult's experience with a given child's particular phonological system . . . can help the adult to make a valid judgment of what word the child is attempting to say" (p. 45).
5. "We assume that an element that phonetically resembles an adult vocabulary item also semantically resembles it" (p. 45).

In using these assumptions to "credit" the child for semantic functions and relations, Greenfield and Smith (1976) suggested that it is most propitious to make "the minimal possible inference." They suggested that "each function first appears in relation to perceived situational elements, and only later in relation to a linguistic representation of those elements" (p. 73).

The young child begins with *performatives*. Performatives were originally proposed by Austin (1962) who observed that certain utterances were events in themselves, such as "I proclaim . . . ," "I promise . . . ," "I pronounce . . . ," etc. The notion of performative in early child speech is similar to the adult form in principle but not in form. Greenfield and Smith (1976) defined early performative as an utterance that occurs as part of the child's actions "and has no meaning (or use) separate from it" (p. 50). "It is an act without information content . . . For this reason, it probably is more accurate to call them *pure* performatives" (p. 50). Thus, a motor noise accompanying the action of a car or truck is a performative; an animal noise such as a *moo* for a cow is a performative.

Table 3.3 Examples of 15 Semantic Roles Coded in Mother and Child Speech

Category	Utterance	Context
Action	M: Can you *play* a song?	M addressing C
	C: Mom *cook* some.	C gestures toward toy stove.
Locative	M: Flower *upstairs*.	In response to C request for a flower.
	C: Milk *in*.	C pulling cup away from M
	C: *Doctor*.	In response to M's question of where to take a broken doll.
	C: Jason *work*.	In response to M's question of where Jason is.
Agent	M: *I'll* cover you.	C pretending to sleep.
	C: *You* do it.	C holding wind-up toy out to M.
Object	M: Let's pick up your *blocks*.	M and C playing with blocks.
	C: Somebody ate the *cookies*.	M and C playing with toy tea set.
Demonstrative	M: *That* Santa Claus?	M looking at picture.
	C: *This* one.	C reaching for container.
Recurrence	M: *Another* bead.	M referring to beads C dropping in box.
	C: I *more* hat, mama.	C putting second hat through rungs of fence.
Possessor	M: Get *your* puzzle.	M walking towards puzzle.
	C: *My* fence fall down.	M and C playing with toy farm house.
Quantifier	M: There's sure *a lot of* mommies in that bus.	Referring to dolls C had put in toy bus.
	C: *Five* fingers.	C holding puppet's hand and tapping its fingers.
Experiencer	M: *I'd* like to see Ernie, please.	Referring to puppets C is playing with.
	C: *She* feels better.	C hands baby doll to M
Recipient	M: Can you sing ring-around-the-rosie *to her*?	M and C pretending 'grandma' is on toy telephone.
	C: Give *me*.	C putting beads in container.
Beneficiary	M: I already dumped it out for *you*.	M dumps puzzle and hands board to C.
	C: Do it for *me*.	C hands doll with untied shoe to M.
Comitative	M: Come *with mommie*.	M standing, extends hand.
	C: A go *mommie*.	M puts C in crib and starts to walk away.

Table 3.3. *continued*

Category	Definition	Context
Created Object	M: Can you draw an *apple*? C: Write *tummy*.	C playing with paper and crayons. Same as above.
Instrument	M: Don't you write on the sofa *with that green pen*.	C writing on sofa.
State	M: You *want* some milk? C: She *feels* better.	M and C playing with breakfast set. M kisses baby doll and hands to C.

From "Semantic roles and residual grammatical categories in mother and child speech: Who tunes into whom?" by K. Retherford, B. Schwartz, and R. Chapman, 1981, *Journal of Child Language, 8,* p. 287. Reprinted by permission.

Table 3.4. An Abridged Version of the Greenfield and Smith (1976) Sequence for the Acquisition of Semantic Functions and Relations

Functions	Performative Indicative Volition
Relations	Agent Action (protolocative, intransitive, transitive, state) Object Dative Possessive Locative Modification

How far can one carry this notion of performatives? Are nonspeech acts performatives? Are the following performatives: a communicative display, a facial expression, a communicative point, a communicative head nod, a tug on the arm, and so on? Performatives are important because they foretell indicatives or labels. Ninio and Bruner (1978) reported that before labels or indicatives the following "performatives" were used either to indicate a referent or to request a label for a referent: smiling, reaching, pointing, and babbling. Bates (1979) produced a similar list in what she regarded as a gestural complex (show, give, communicative point, ritual request). Both Ninio and Bruner (1978) and Bates (1979) pointed out that performatives are *replaced* by labels, but subsequently they may reappear in combination with labels.

Children's performative repertoire comprises their prenaming behaviors.

Indicatives, which are labels of entities, follow performatives. The distinction between animate and inanimate entities is potentially useful in the realization of subsequent semantic relations. Indeed, Schlesinger (1974) said that ego/non-ego and animate/inanimate distinctions are among the earliest to be made and are used to realize "agent" and "object" distinctions. *Volition* is expressed when the child can place stress or emphasis on a label, or can negate, usually coupling "no" to a label; this can also be done by shaking the head in a negative manner.

Agent is the identification of an instigator of action. *Action* itself has an acquisition sequence that begins with protolocatives whereby the child will say *Up* or *Down* to mean *Pick me up* or *Put me down* respectively. These do not denote location. This is followed by *intransitives* usually about the child's own actions; *transitives* ensue. Again, most early comments about actions refer to the child's own actions. Finally, *state predicates* are acquired. The following illustrates this sequence:

Protolocatives: *up, down*
Intransitives: *sleep, go, run*
Transitives: *hit, eat, drink*
State: *be* verbs, *know, like, have*

Bloom, Lifter, and Hafitz (1980) showed that these predicate categories attain inflections in distinctly different ways.

Object is the recipient of action. Again, the animate/inanimate distinction is important (Golinkoff & Harding, 1978; Greenfield & Smith, 1976). In early word combinations, object appears more frequently and more elaborately than agent (Brown, 1973b; Limber, 1976). This is probably because agents are usually implicated by context whereas objects are not. That is, most early utterances are extended actions (Greenfield & Smith, 1976) in which children themselves are the subject. Another reason is that objects appear in the recency portion (end or object noun phrase) of a sentence string so it is more easily perceived, stored, and reconstructed in recall (Muma, 1978a; Slobin, 1973). An important point about the appearance of objects is that this semantic relation is grounded in grammatical structure. Thus, its appearance provides evidence that the child has made the transition to semantic categories and may be ready to convert such categories into grammatical categories in the realization of the formal rules of grammar (Greenfield & Smith, 1976).

Dative, the indirect recipient of action, provides even stronger evidence that the child is prepared to deal with the formal grammatical machinery of language. *Possessive* is an indication of ownership, and this semantic relation, as well as locative and modification, is a qualifier of previously attained notions. *Locative* is an identification of place or location. *Modification* is a broad term that includes virtually any modifier—temporal, quantitative, and so on.

When portrayed as a list in an acquisition sequence, these semantic functions and relations are deceptively simple. A few key points need to be made. First, the sequence has been shown to be relatively robust for a few children—beyond the two children studied by Greenfield and Smith, but it should be further studied. However, it may have to be altered eventually. Second, the semantic functions and relations do not advance by discrete increments. Rather, they phase in gradually. This means that at any given moment the child may strongly evidence one or perhaps two semantic functions and relations with the adjacent ones marginally evident. Third, the three issues of *productive* capacity need to be considered. In *preparation,* a semantic function or relation occurs infrequently and is context bound. In *attainment,* a semantic funcțon or relation occurs frequently and is not context bound. In *consolidation,* these may appear in a variety of combinations. Consolidation, according to Sigel and Cocking,

> Must always involve at once an aspect of achievement of the recently acquired behavior and an aspect of preparation for the behavior of the following level. (Pinard & Laurendeau, 1969, p. 129)

> The period of consolidation is a period of synthesis, where the "recently acquired behavior" implies a plateau, however temporary, which serves as a stepping stone for subsequent behavior (1977, p. 222)

Fourth, with acquisition the various semantic functions and relations can be expressed in a variety of new ways and new combinations. Slobin (1973, p. 184) said, "New forms first express old functions, and new functions are first expressed by old forms." He added that the first functions of two-word utterances seem to be more explicit expressions of one-word utterances. Fifth, explicit content deals only with expressed semantic functions and relations. It must be recognized that while it may be possible to describe the child's repertoire of semantic functions and relations there is a great deal yet to be explained, such as presupposition, syntax, morphology, phonology, and pragmatics. As Fillmore (1972) noted, generative semantics is inadequate; it is necessary to consider interpretative semantics as well. Gleitman and Wanner (1982) stressed the need for a perspective that is more complete than semantics. They said, "There are many ways to say the same thing. So in this sense, too, it is massively overexuberant to hope that knowing meaning is tantamount to knowing language . . . As Bowerman . . . argues, the learner must eventually transcend his initial semantic-categorial organization of language to acquire certain grammatical categories and functions" (p. 14).

> New forms first express old functions, and new functions are first expressed by old forms.

Presupposition: Implicit Content

Presuppositions are those sets of information, or basic assumptions and premises, from which propositions, or utterances, are derived. This kind of knowledge, which is in a sense a kind of convention, affords the child a frame of reference (Wallace, 1972) from which messages can be negotiated between implied and explicated information. Greenfield (1980) said that it is necessary to consider implicit possibilities that exist for children as they code, or contemplate coding, a message. Chapter 2 discusses three distinctions concerning presuppositions: semantic, pragmatic, psychological.

> Presupposition or implicit content is the substrata from which propositions are derived.

In short, there is much more to language than the explicit content of an utterance. There is the phonological and syntactic structure of the utterance, its pragmatic determinants, the implicit content—presupposition and intention. These are all inextricably tied to cognition indirectly (such as sensorimotor skills), directly (content, intent), and in the formulation of messages (verbal processing capacity).

Summary

Social commerce operates to a large extent through communication. The coin of the realm of social commerce is *informativeness*. The act of informing, generically speaking, entails intention, proposition, presupposition, locution, and perlocution. *Intention* is the motivation or purpose for communicating. *Proposition* is explicit content (semantic categories) negotiated as a piece of *presupposition* (implicit content). Locution is the utterance itself (semantic-syntactic-phonological realization); and, perlocution refers to the effects of the utterance on the listener.

The message-of-best-fit is the product of encoder-decoder negotiations to be informative. Trafficking information underscores the functional bases of communication in social commerce. *Informativeness* is the key and *intention* the lock for opening the door to communication.

Language acquisition could be characterized in three stages: context bound, decontextualization, and recontextualization. Intentions are both mathetic (cognitive) and pragmatic (communicative). Bruner suggested that the two great early communicative intentions are *indicating* and *requesting*. He speculated that the four basic innate communicative intentions are (a) joint attention, (b) instrumental, (c) affiliative, and (d) pretense.

4

METHODOLOGIES: "OUTSIDE"

Methodologies might be considered from two perspectives, "Outside" and "Inside." The "Outside" perspective refers to the methodologies that researchers use to study language acquisition, whereas the "Inside" perspective refers to the methodologies the child uses in striving to acquire language. In a sense that researchers' methodologies are derived from observation about children's efforts to acquire language, there should be congruity between the two, but philosophical perspectives themselves differ; so, to a certain degree incongruity exists. The extent to which the child "calls the shots" in language acquisition and the extent to which the researchers' methodologies reveal the acquisition process is the extent to which congruity may be achieved. Cognizant of previous tendencies to label behavior rather than explain it and to take labels as explanations, Locke (1983) admonished that it would be desirable to inquire why a particular child evidences a particular behavior. He suggested such questions define an empirical trail—whether it leads into cognitive or physiological or social domains—and furthermore, the trail is one in which it must not be decided in advance where we want to go.

This chapter deals with the "Outside" perspective, giving an historical overview of the various methodologies used to study language acquisition in order to reveal how major methodological shifts accompanied major theoretical shifts.

Three Major Periods

The study of language acquisition has evidenced several major theoretical shifts in the last century. In the early period, diary studies recorded the language behavior of individuals. This was followed by the cross-sectional empirical movement, which attempted to quantify language behavior in an objective manner. This, in turn, was followed by the psycholinguistic movement, which involves the comprehensive study of single subjects and their emerging verbal capacities within an open, dynamic, functioning social system.

The *diary study period* began in the late 1800s and lasted until it was replaced by empiricism in the early 1900s. The early diary studies were remarkably detailed accounts of individual children as they acquired language. Occasional comments addressed the role of *context* in language learning, and to this extent these early diary studies anticipated the present functionalist movement. Moreover, these studies frequently included issues of cognition and dialogue in the study of language acquisition, thereby anticipating the cognitive and pragmatic thrusts of the past decade.

The primary drawback of these early diary studies is that they did not take into account facets of language learning such as implicit content (presupposition), explicit content (proposition), intent, and functional distinctions between given and new information. Moreover, the diary studies did not demonstrate a theoretical appreciation of verbal capacities, even though the competence/performance distinction had been made by de Saussure and vonHomboldt in the 1800s in regard to langue/parole, respectively (Chomsky, 1957, 1965). And finally, the empirical movement championed by Watson in psychology in the early 1900s and Bloomfield (1933) in linguistics devalued diary studies because they presumably lacked sufficient rigor and objectivity.

The *empirical movement* attempted to establish information on language acquisition by providing norms. It was reasoned that distributional evidence in the form of norms would adequately characterize language learning processes. The result was a flurry of normative studies. Two of the most ambitious and widely known were by McCarthy (1954) and Templin (1957). Templin's study provided norms for various speech sound acquisitions, speech sound discrimination, verbalizations (length of response, complexity, sentence inaccuracies, parts of speech), vocabulary, and several interrelationships among language skills. This period was known as the taxonomic era because inventories of various categories of language were taken as evidence of language acquisition.

Frequency of occurrence was the guidepost for linguistic considerations about the nature of language and developmental considerations about language acquisition. Consequently, this became a period of inquiry about language performance with not much consideration for emergent capacities. Said another way, this was an era of the study of verbal *products* rather than *processes*.

The empirical movement dealt mainly with *products* rather than *processes*.

This taxonomic or product oriented era lasted about 50 years. It had a considerable impact on the popular view of language, specifically Standards of English, correctness of grammar, parts of speech, sentence types, and the like. Moreover, the clinical fields have, until recently, largely followed the empirical tradition, that is, normative tests (ITPA, TOLD, CELF, etc.), developmental profiles, a priori intervention programs, and so forth.

Indeed, norm-referenced assessment became the byword of so-called *objective* assessment, which in the last analysis is itself actually *subjective* (Prutting, 1983). A review of the problems inherent in developmental profiles appears below. Comments about other normative tests appear in the assessment chapter.

So-called "objective" assessment is, in the last analysis, subjective.

The empirical movement prevailed until the late 1950s, when two major events occurred. First, Roger Brown (1958b) ushered in the developmental psycholinguistic movement (e.g., the Original Word Game). This was followed by Jerome Bruner's (1964) Original Thinking Game, which was a modest rendition of Piaget's theories. In any case, the emerging psycholinguistic movement constituted a merging of cognitive psychology and linguistics. This merger, coupled with the additional merger of the philosophy of language in the early 1970s, constituted a heavy blow against raw empiricism.

Second, Noam Chomsky (1957) attacked the empirical movement in linguistics on the grounds that it was apsychological and atheoretical. Chomsky (1957), Searle (1972) and others held that the Bloomfieldian tradition of linguistics merely categorized and inventoried verbal behavior in regard to parts of speech, sentence types, standard English, etc. Chomsky argued that psychological capacities are at the heart of language; these enable the child to learn and use language. Chomsky posited a transformational generative theory (the ability to generate an infinite number of sentences of a language but not non-sentences) about such capacities, which placed language in the biological arena in much the same way that Piaget placed cognition in the biological realm. However, both language and cognition eventually became tied not only to biological-psychological issues but also to environmental-experiential issues, especially social commerce.

> The merger of cognitive psychology, linguistics, and the philosophy of language in the early 1970s constituted a heavy blow against raw empiricism.

The *psycholinguistic movement*, of the 1970s, has turned to comprehensive studies of single subjects as they function in dialogue. Such studies draw upon the methodological features of the early diary studies, which, despite their problems, had considerable value. Both the early diary studies and the contemporary dialogue studies have certain advantages for describing and explaining language acquisition. The primary advantage is that they enable one to study underlying *systems and processes* rather than merely to inventory verbal products. A second advantage is that they are capable of identifying *contextual influences and determinants*, thereby extending the study of language acquisition beyond the child as an active consumer of available information. A third advantage is that acquisition *sequences* can be identified. Finally, the *role of others*, notably parents, peers, and even clinicians, in assisting language learning can be identified. In short, there were compelling reasons for turning away from the norm-referenced, taxonomic *product-oriented* approaches that had prevailed for about 50 years and toward the psycholinguistic *process-oriented* approaches. The latter has much more to offer for description, explanation, and applications.

Chomskian Revolution

Although Bloomfield and Chomsky had much in common, Chomsky's (1957, 1965) views moved the study of language away from a Bloomfieldian tradition (Palermo, 1971). Both theorists agreed that descriptive accounts of language acquisition define *what* is taking place. They differed, however, in their explanations of the generative capacities to comprehend and produce novel utterances. As Gleitman and Wanner (1982, p. 4) observed, "Bloomfield's learner came into the world scantily endowed ... Bloomfield's learning device could also draw inductive generalizations from the distributional properties of the grammatical classes ... For Bloomfield ... a grammar is a description of the analogies that hold for a language, and learning is the set of discovery procedures ... by which the child forms these analogies."

Similarly, Chomsky contended that language learning is an inductive process derived from fleeting, piecemeal contacts with language. In contrast to Bloomfield, however, Chomsky held that the learner is well endowed with predispositions that in effect guide and govern the language learning process. This is what he called the Language Acquisition Device (LAD). It was considered to be very powerful. Indeed, it was too powerful because it left virtually no room for descriptive, and certainly not explanatory, accounts of language acquisition.

> Bloomfield's learner was scantily endowed whereas Chomsky's learner was well endowed with a powerful language acquisition device (LAD).

Thus, both Bloomfield and Chomsky posited some kind of inductive generalization as the child has contact with language. There is, after all, no other recourse, because the acquisition process must make provision for the particular language a given child will learn. Bloomfield relied on generalizations from distributional properties of a language. This became a search for the distributional properties of linguistic categories under the faulty assumption that children's distributional knowledge of their contacts with language would endemically reflect the distributional properties of the language per se. Distributional properties of language refers to the relative frequency of occurrence of a structure in language use. The contemporary "motherese" studies (Gleitman, Newport, & Gleitman, 1984) show that such correspondences do not exist. Schlesinger (1977) held, nevertheless, that the child's linguistic input is a primary means for getting access to the grammatical system. Hence the normative approaches from the empirical tradition became rather pale in accounting for language acquisition. Furthermore, Bloomfield's notion of analogy was less attractive than the contemporary notions of grammatical rule (Chomsky, 1957), prototype (Bowerman, 1982; Nelson, 1974), deep and local homology (Bates, 1979), and even tuple (Harris, 1965). A grammatical rule is a prescribed operation for encoding or decoding aspects of a message. A prototype refers to skeletal categories constructed from original mental representations. Deep homology means that a single cognitive substrata is a precursor of early language acquisition, whereas local homology means that this substrate is composed of more than one cognitive skill. Tuple refers to the mental units involved in encoding and decoding messages, especially dealing with co-occurring units and transformation or changes of units.

Chomsky avoided the problem of induction governed by distributional evidence. He merely asserted that induction follows the biologically inherent structure of language. Thus, there was presumably no need to make any further claims. This resulted in the assertion by McNeill (1966b, 1970) that language learning is a process of generic learning that begins with the most general and pervasive notions and progressively continues through more and more specific dimensions.

Gold (1967), Gleitman and Wanner (1982) and others raised a troublesome demand for the very powerful inductive LAD; they called for more than the mere claim that LAD works. They asked, how does LAD keep unerrantly on track in the face of ambiguous and even negative information? Gleitman and Wanner (1982, p. 7) said, "Children are good, all too good, at forming inductive generalizations." Among the fleeting, piecemeal contacts children have with their language, some are highly ambiguous or even wrong, yet the active learning process is sufficiently robust not only to survive but to thrive. Evidently, ambiguous and negative information assist language learning just as positive information. *Positive* information may generate and confirm rules; *ambiguous* information may provide clues for extracting needed information concerning rule induction; *negative* information may be useful for determining the domain of a rule (Muma, 1978a, p. 158; Wexler, 1982). Thus, any information is potentially useful for induction depending to some extent upon the language learner's existing repertoire of verbal capacities (Schlesinger, 1977). Moreover, *intention* directs the use of language, and thus it is the single consolidating factor in this enterprise.

Positive, negative, and ambiguous information are potentially useful within the restriction of an adequate repertoire and intentional context.

Although Chomsky's innatist position was a decisive factor in the downfall of empiricism, its strong claim that LAD simply works was too radical. Also, Chomsky's theory emphasized the formal rules of grammar (syntax) too much. Parenthetically, he has been erroneously accused of ignoring semantics and, by implication, pragmatics. It should be remembered that even from the start Chomsky specified contextual (semantic, referential) constraints for the utilization of formal rules of grammar. Nevertheless, he did not posit the cognitive bases for abstracting formal rules of grammar. For Chomsky, such rules were given as predispositional products of LAD.

LAD was insufficient in dealing with details of language acquisition.

However, merely to accept semantic knowledge as "given" was simply too big of a pill to swallow. It was not palatable for those seeking to understand more fully the cognitive bases of language acquisition. Consequently, the *generative semantic* movement was launched to more fully define the semantic dimension to which Chomsky had seemingly given only short shrift.

The generative semantic movement divided the study of early language acquisition into two cognitive arenas: general cognitive precursors and substantive dimensions about the explicit content or propositionality of a message. The search for general cognitive precursors focused primarily on Piagetian skills. The search for the child's semantic knowledge or propositionality became a study of emergent semantic functions and relations. Leonard (1976) reviewed the literature on the progressive acquisition of semantic distinctions. Greenfield and Smith (1976) provide a good review of the literature and acquisition sequence for the emergence of semantic knowledge. However, this approach was largely inferential and thus vulnerable to misrepresentation. It was not long before two major questions were raised: What and how many semantic categories are psychologically real for the child? What criteria are needed to legitimatize inferences about semantic categories?

> The generative semantic movement resulted in a search for the cognitive bases of early language learning.

It soon became apparent that explicit semantic categories of a message function *informatively* against a background of implicit or presumed information. Therefore, interpretative semantics replaced generative semantics. Indeed, interpretative semantics was part of the pragmatic, or functionalist, movement. Fillmore (1972) pointed out that generative semantics is naked unless the presuppositional context is considered. Interpretative semantics is generative semantics clothed in presuppositional considerations. This, then, broadened the notion of a cognitive basis for language to extend to knowledge of the world (Bruner, 1981) or theory of the world (Palermo, 1982) from which semantic knowledge is derived (Bowerman, 1976). Moreover, this placed pragmatic *context* well beyond situational context. As Ochs (1979) pointed out, context is, potentially at least, an infinitely extendable notion. To reiterate, Fillmore (1981) appealed to internal and external contextualization to define functionalism within pragmatics. He said that contextualization refers to a text analysis of what "producers and interpreters of discourse are doing and what they are mentally experiencing" (p. 14). *Internal contextualization* is "the set of worlds in which the discourse could play a role" (p. 14) and *external contextualization* is "possible worlds compatible with the message content of the discourse" (p. 14).

> Interpretative semantics extended cognitive considerations to presupposition and worldly knowledge.

In short, these theoretical shifts (empiricism, psycholinguistics-syntax, semantics, pragmatics or functionalism) have changed the direction of inquiries into language acquisition. With these changes in direction, methodological procedures have changed as well.

> *Context* is both internal and external.

Methodologically, the concerns have shifted away from taxonomic inquiries about language products, toward cognitive-linguistic-communicative *processes* as they *function* in social commerce. Increased credence is given to theoretical propositions; and, empirical evidence is sought to support or refute theory rather than to generate norms per se. The scope of these interests and methods brings home a fuller appreciation of Brown's (1956, p. 247) comment that language acquisition is "a process of cognitive socialization."

> Language acquisition is a process of cognitive socialization.

Developmental Profiles

Perhaps the most widely used method for appraising the child language acquisition is the use of developmental profiles. Such profiles seem to be useful in ascertaining the child's developmental age level for language acquisition. The contemporary psycholinguistic literature, however, raises some serious questions about the *validity* of developmental profiles in assessing language acquisition. In short, the use of such profiles runs a decided risk of misrepresenting the child's verbal skills (Muma, 1981a). Table 4.1 summarizes these drawbacks.

The following 10 reasons show why developmental profiles may be of questionable value:

1. Brown (1973a) pointed out that language acquisition can be characterized by spurts of learning of unknown duration. But, developmental profiles are based upon steady increments of learning, such as, 1-month, 3-month, 6-month increments. Moreover, such profiles specify which verbal products should be obtained within certain prescribed increments of time.

2. Brown (1973a) indicated that rate of learning is notoriously varied but sequence is highly stable. He was especially interested in sequences *within* systems as contrasted to those *between* systems, nominal system, inflectional system, and so forth. Developmental profiles are, in a sense, backwards because they are predicated on the notion that rate of learning is stable and sequence is varied. Stability of rate is evidenced by the constant increments of time (age) on the profiles; varied sequence is evidenced by the fact that the entries from one increment to the next vary from one system to another. For example, one such profile (the Santa Cruz Special Education Management System—SEMS, 1973) had the following consecutive entries in its monthly increments:

   10 months: Uses 1-word verb in present tense, that is, *go, run.*
   11 months: Uses pronouns, that is, *me, my, mine.*
   12 months: Uses adjectives, that is, *good, big.*

Other entries in this profile appear to give sequences within systems, but these topological sequences reveal a callous disregard for the psycholinguistic literature. For example, this same profile gave the following entries:

   13 months: Uses noun with article
   14 months: Uses noun with possessive
   15 months: Uses noun with quantifier
   16 months: Uses noun with adjective
   17 months: Uses noun with locator
   18 months: Uses noun with demonstrator

The literature (Bloom, 1970, 1973; Bowerman, 1973; Brown, 1973a, 1973b; Greenfield & Smith, 1976) does not support this sequence. "Demonstrative

Table 4.1. Developmental Profiles' Ten Shortcomings

1. Language learning occurs in spurts of unknown duration.
2. Rate of learning is notoriously varied but sequence *within* systems is remarkably stable.
3. Processes are more important than products.
4. Systems function in co-occurrence with other systems.
5. There are grammatical equivalences.
6. Context is crucial.
7. Function, rather than structure, is at the core of language.
8. Language learning increments are not precise.
9. A posteriori assessment is more valid than a priori assessment.
10. Individual differences between children are commonplace.

with noun," for example, is one of the earliest relational constructions. Unfortunately, errors of this kind are common with many developmental profiles.

Within-system sequences are stable but *between-system* sequences lack stability. Yet, many development profiles use *between-system* sequences. An example of a *within-system* sequence is the following for the negation system:

	Structure	Example
Stage 1	Negation plus sentence	*I go. No.*
Stage 2	Negation included but not integrated	*I no go.*
Stage 3	Negation integrated	*I won't go.*

Bloom (1973) proposed that Stage 1 may be an anaphoric "no" rather than a true stage in this sequence. An anaphoric "no" is when the previous message is cancelled. Functionally, the sequence for negation appears to be: nonexistence, rejection, and denial (Bloom, 1973).

3. These profiles deal with *products* rather than *processes*. Consequently, it is questionable as to what can be appropriately inferred about verbal capacities. A telling problem with these profiles is that they rarely address the crucial question of *productivity* of verbal behavior. This issue is discussed below.

4. These profiles do not establish patterns for substantiating how various systems function in co-occurrence with other systems. Bloom (1973), Bloom and Lahey (1978), Bloom, Lifter, and Hafitz (1980), Brown (1973a, 1973b), Brown, Cazden, and Bellugi-Klima (1969), Harris (1965), Muma (1973a, 1978a, 1981a) and others have shown that co-occurrence is an important issue in early grammatical skills.

5. These profiles do not seem to be aware of equivalences of grammatical functions. That is, *he, the boy, Jim*, are equivalent in a formal grammatical sense but they have different degrees of explicitness that can be optionally used in social commerce.

6. These profiles inventory behavior but do not attend to contextual influences and determinants. Bruner (1981, p. 172) emphasized the importance of context and thus pragmatics by saying, "Context is all." Context can be viewed in regard to referential, linguistic, and intentional contexts (Muma, 1978a, 1981a). These are discussed below.

Context is all.

---

7. These profiles typically address *structure* but rarely, if ever, address *functions*. Yet the functions of language, especially *content* (both implicit and explicit) and *intent*, comprise the core of language. It is obvious that if assessment misses the core of language, conclusions cannot be drawn about language capacities.

The core of language is content and intent.

---

8. The developmental profiles typically have *false precision*. They claim to measure language learning in 1-year, 6-month, and even 1-month increments, but normal language learning cannot be measured as precisely as that. Brown (1973a, 1973b) showed that variances as large as 18 months are normal. Consequently, Brown and others have turned to sequence.

9. These profiles are a priori in nature. The categories are established before the child is assessed. Inquiries are made as to whether the child evidences behaviors in each of the categories. The child's natural spontaneous behaviors are ignored in favor of the behaviors on the profiles. In this manner, the child's behaviors become subordinated to those on the profile. Thus, the assessment imposes behavior on the child and ignores spontaneous behavior. Ironically, the use of such profiles has been thought to constitute an *individualized* assessment. A test administered to one child at a time, the reasoning goes, constitutes an individualized assessment. However, the extent to which the child's spontaneous behavior is abrogated is the extent to which individualized assessment has been jeopardized. A posteriori assessment does not impose foreign criteria as a priori assessment does. And, a posteriori assessment provides a means for true individualized assessment because it describes what the child is actually doing with language.

> Individualized assessment does not mean administering one test to one child; it means a posteriori assessment of the child's own behavior.

10. These profiles are based on the unwarranted assumption that all children learn alike. The literature (Bloom & Lahey, 1978; Muma, 1978a, 1978b) has shown again and again, however, that *individual differences* are outstanding and that children have alternative strategies for language learning.

In short, developmental profiles have serious problems. Developmental profiles carry a high risk of distorting and misrepresenting the child's language. Said another way, such profiles may yield *data* but it is highly questionable as to whether they yield *evidence* about the child's language acquisition.

> Developmental profiles lack validity which is the touchstone of assessment.

Language Sampling

Assumptions underlying various aspects of language sampling should be examined. Muma (1973b) examined quantitative and descriptive approaches, knowledge and use, structure and function, formal and informal approaches, language sampling, data handling, and validity. His discussion of language sampling centered on the issue of *representativeness*:

> The goal of language sampling is to obtain a sufficiently representative sample to display one's typical performance so that any conclusions drawn from this performance will be valid. (Muma, 1973b, p. 334)

Gallagher (1983, p. 3) argued that "the goal of language sampling also has remained essentially the same, to obtain a 'representative' sample."

> The goal of language sampling is to obtain a representative sample.

She went on to consider three different views of representativeness: comprehensive, idealized, and typical behavior. *Comprehensiveness* entails a representative sample that is "large enough to be interpretable and reliable but of a reasonable length to be efficient" (Gallagher, 1983, p. 3). She pointed out that to some researchers this has become operationalized as 50, 100, 200, or more utterances or 30-minute time samples. Muma (1973b, 1978a, 1981) held that it is inappropriate to set such criteria a priori; he emphasized the importance of *stability* of sampling.

Stabilization refers to a sampling procedure in which samples are obtained until the behavior of interest stabilizes. That is to say, the degree of variability remains relatively stable with subsequent samples. The assumption is that when performance stabilizes, a sufficient range of performance is obtained to practically exhaust the capacity of one's grammatical system. Variations within this range would reflect situational differences, whereas overall performance would reflect one's grammatical knowledge. Unfortunately, there are two major problems with this assumption. First, there is the problem of what stabilizes . . . Moreover, *stabilization is transient in verbal behavior.* When one dimension of grammar is relatively stable, other dimensions vary (although not in free variation). Menyuk (1963, 1964a, 1964b) reported a dampened oscillatory function in the reduction of errors in children's utterances. This function apparently pertains to the concept of stability and variation in co-occurring structures. Presumably, fewer errors occur when children constrain their verbal behavior to those structures within their repertoire, but more errors occur when new structures are used. This raises the second problem of the stabilization strategy—namely, *it is incompatible with language acquisition.* Language learning occurs in spurts associated with frequent rapid developments. Stabilizations are typically brief with significant variations in co-occurring structures and alternative functions. The stabilization procedure may be nothing more than a convenient ploy superimposed on a dynamic system. (Muma, 1973b)

Stabilization of sampling is more appropriate than an a priori sample size of 50, 100, or more utterances.

Gallagher (1983) discussed *idealized* performance as a way of dealing with representativeness. She cited McLean and Snyder-McLean (1978, p. 127), who indicated that sampling should be designed to "optimize the child's performance and to evoke the best possible sample of his abilities." This is essentially a theoretical goal rather than an operational statement. An idealized performance would presumably yield the child's best performance.

Gallagher (1983, p. 3) considered *typical* performance as one that adequately reflects usual, habitual, most frequent, or daily performance, cautioning that "even collecting more than one sample does not insure that either idealized or typical performance will be obtained."

While repeated samples may not insure representativeness, a single sample simply will not obtain a representative sample. The literature is abundantly clear that language use varies with contexts. Thus, it is simply inappropriate to rely on a single sample as representative of one's actual capacities. Consider how difficult it would be to package a representative sample of verbal capacities in a single sample. This would be an extraordinarily difficult task, even in the early stages of acquisition. Yet, assumptions have been made that single samples are sufficiently representative of verbal capacities. It is generally recommended to sample language in several contexts in which the child carries out a variety of roles in social commerce (Bloom & Lahey, 1978; Gallagher, 1983; Gallagher & Craig, 1984; McLean & Snyder-McLean, 1978; Muma, 1978a, 1981b).

> It would be extraordinarily difficult to package a representative sample of language in a single sample.

Additional criteria should be used to give some degree of assurance of representative language sampling. The following criteria are useful: spontaneity, buildups, and hesitation phenomena. *Spontaneity* is important because it is the product of intentionality, which is a primary dimension of language. Various elicitation tasks such as a priori sentence imitation tasks and even the picture description tasks should be questioned because they strip away intentionality. Slobin and Welch (1971) defined an important exception, the use of a posteriori elicitation tasks whereby the child's own best spontaneous utterances are removed from context (intentional, referential) then used in a sentence imitation task.

> Intentional utterances, buildups, and hesitation phenomena are useful indices of spontaneous speech.

Buildups and hesitation phenomena are good indices of spontaneous speech. Moreover, they are useful in ascertaining loci of learning within co-occurring systems (Clark & Clark, 1977; Muma, 1978a, 1981a, 1983a; Weir, 1962). Unfortunately, these dimensions may either get shorn off in transcription and segmentation or simply overlooked.

One further note concerns the use of "standard conditions" for language sampling. Presumably, these conditions afford one subject comparable conditions from which behavior changes might be observed, or they afford an opportunity to compare subjects. For these expectations to work, it is necessary to make certain assumptions about verbal behavior that "fall away" in a pragmatic or functionalist perspective. The primary assumption is that external context is the decisive purveyor of verbal performance. Even then, this notion of external context refers to the situational layout as opposed to the operative psychological notion of external contexts espoused by Fillmore (1981). Yet, constructionism in cognition points out that even early on the child is operating not on stimulation per se but beyond the information given (Bruner, 1957; Piaget, 1952). And, verbal behavior in social commerce constitutes the epitome of social constructionism, whereby one is operating from a presuppositional base in the realization of intentions. Thus, in order for the so-called "standard condition" to work it would be necessary for its architects to standardize the presuppositional conditions brought to bear on the external context. Even then, there is no assurance that performance will hold still—constrain generative capacities—to afford the desired outcomes. The standard condition notion seems to be another legacy from empiricism or behaviorism.

> The standard condition is tangential to the operative internal and external contexts of social commerce.

Productivity

Methodological issues extend to the question of when can you credit the child for productive verbal capacities. This is a complex issue, raising corollary issues about criteria for productivity. The Piagetian (1951) guidelines for the emergence of a system are useful. There are three levels of emergence: preparation, attainment, and consolidation. In *preparation,* a skill is evidenced infrequently and incidentally. Moreover, it is usually context bound. *Attainment,* which refers to the point at which a skill is evidenced frequently and is not context bound follows preparation. At *consolidation,* a skill is sufficiently integrated so that it can be combined with other skills. It occurs in free variation constrained only by language itself.

Some illustrations may clarify these points. In preparation, the child would say "Mommy" only incidentally and under certain conditions. Indeed, it would be difficult to elicit the word; thus, it is very strongly governed by the child's intention to say it rather than someone else's desire to elicit it. And, at this stage the utterance occurs infrequently. In attainment, "Mommy" is said many times in many contexts. It is easily elicited. In consolidation, "Mommy" functions in a variety of ways and combinations. Thus, "Mommy" could be indicative, agent, object, possessor, vocative, and so forth. Bloom (1970, 1973) showed, for example, that "Mommy sock" had five different interpretations. And in grammatical structure it evidences free variation: "Mommy came," "Mommy go," "Mommy eat," "Hi, Mommy," "No, Mommy," and so forth. Thus, it is useful to ascertain if a particular performance is in a preparation, attainment, or consolidation stage of productivity.

> Preparation, attainment, and consolidation are issues of productivity.

Brown (1973b) raised the issue of productivity as one of three criteria that might be considered in ascertaining distinguishable semantic categories: (a) an operational definition, (b) productivity, and (c) independence of vocabulary. *Productivity* was used in two ways: relative frequency (or its cousin, percentage) and combination. Indeed, they appear to be linked. "Frequency as such is not a very useful variable. But frequency generally goes with diversity of type . . . for only if closely related variants occur is it likely that performance of a certain construction represents full grammatical understandings. And diversity is generally associated with high frequency" (Brown, 1973b, p. 276). Combinatorially, constructions that vary are said to be productive. For example *my* is combinatorially productive as follows: *my hat, my shoes, my mommy, my juice,* and so forth.

> In deducing productivity, frequency or its cousin percentage are not useful alone; such measures should be considered in conjunction with combinatorial evidence.

Greenfield and Smith (1976, p. 68) outlined some problems in measuring productivity of semantic functions. In asking how do you know exactly when a child "has" a given semantic function, they cautioned against "tight" criteria. One problem is that you do not know what capacities were available to the child before the first assessment. It is conceivable that some capacities that were available earlier have been *replaced* by subsequent capacities (Bates, 1979). "A second problem is that frequency of occurrence, one aspect of productivity, is very much affected by situational structure, and some semantic functions are used only in relatively rare situations. Thus, measured productivity is a function of the context and, therefore, does not directly measure children's linguistic abilities" (Greenfield & Smith, 1976, p. 69). They said that productivity can be measured by variety and frequency of use. Variety includes combinatorial productivity as well as variations in manifest forms of a particular structure. Operationally, Greenfield and Smith (1976, p. 72) gave the following definition: "If we define the achievement of productivity by a function as the occurrence of three nonrepetitive instances during a single session . . . " They continued with, "The productivity of child language can perhaps be appreciated better by considering how a given word can be used in a variety of situations while the semantic function remains constant" (p. 73).

> In deducing productivity, how utterances function in a variety of situations is more useful than frequency.

Summary

The methodologies used to study language acquisition have varied considerably over the years. The diary studies in the early 1900s were detailed descriptions of individual children as they learned language. These were replaced by the normative studies because the earlier diary studies presumably lacked objectivity. However, the empirical movement in general, and the normative studies in particular, were found to have an unforgiveable flaw in that they did not explain *how* language is acquired. These studies dealt with verbal *products,* not *processes.*

The psycholinguistic movement inquired into the mental and social processes in language acquisition. This meant that rigorous and disciplined *inference* could play a legitimate role in defining certain data as evidence in understanding language acquisition. The Chomskian revolution was important in this regard because it placed the study of language on theoretical, psychological, and rational (philosophical) grounds.

Developmental profiles have been a widely used method for presumably ascertaining the child's *level* of language acquisition, but these profiles lack validity, the touchstone of assessment.

Language sampling is a primary methodological concern. An overriding goal for language sampling is *representativeness.* Issues of sample size might be redressed from the perspective of stability of sampling. It is essential that language samples be obtained from several contexts. It was suggested that the criteria for a representative sample would include spontaneity, buildups, and hesitation phenomena. The so-called "standard condition" for language sampling is not viable simply because the most important dimension (internal context) cannot be adequately standardized.

Productivity is a major recurrent methodological issue. Combinatorial evidence is a good way to address productivity. Varied contexts are useful also, better than frequency or percentage. Moreover, the Piagetian notions of preparation, attainment, and consolidation are useful.

5

METHODOLOGIES: "INSIDE"

The "Inside" perspective refers to the child's methodologies in striving to acquire language. These are primarily conjecture concerning *how* the child operates in the active attempts to acquire language. Such conjecture comes from a theoretical perspective but is supported to some extent by empirical evidence. Kessen (1979, p. 2) suggested, "Development can be understood only as a continuous interplay of principles and conditions, the dance of ontogenetic adaptation." The "Inside" methodologies of the child are movements in such a dance.

> Development might be thought of as an ontogenetic dance.

Active Versus Passive Learning

For years, behaviorism was the prevailing theoretical view. This view held that the child was essentially a *passive* learner waiting to be taught. Consequently, language acquisition was viewed in terms of how the child was or was not *stimulated*. In intervention, notions such as the following were raised: stimulation, reinforcement (schedules, types), individual/group, and "carry over." Moreover, issues of content, sequencing, pacing, and motivation were thought not to be "Inside" but vested in the instructor, teacher, or clinician. Such approaches essentially ignored children's active learning efforts and made them conform to the views imposed upon him by the teacher. This is what has come to be known as the a priori approach.

In contrast, mentalism holds that the child is essentially an *active* learner who is opportunistic about learning. Closely related to the notion of active learning is *readiness* to learn. Children are ready to learn something not because a teacher or clinician deems them ready but because they have had previous relevant learning that enables them to deal with new aspects. This notion of *psychological readiness* has been espoused by Piaget (1954, 1958) and Bruner (1957) and it has been substantiated by the research on *discrepancy learning* (Kagan, 1969, 1970, 1971; Kagan & Lewis, 1965; Lewis, 1967; Lewis & Goldberg, 1969; Lewis, Kagan & Kalafat, 1966; McCall & Kagan, 1967a, 1967b, 1969). Kessen (1979, p. 2) referred to active learning, readiness to learn, and opportunities for learning as follows, "Each developmental moment is a moment of creation, and an ever-recurring exchange between what the child's mind is and what his experience asks of him."

Readiness to learn coupled with active learning means that issues of content, sequencing, pacing, and motivation or reinforcement are essentially vested in the child rather than in the teacher or clinician. Children actively seek and avail themselves of relevant opportunities for language learning. Thus, the parent, teacher, or clinician's role is not to teach or instruct but to *facilitate* the child's own active learning (Bloom & Lahey, 1978; Bruner, 1981 ; Leonard, 1981; McLean & Snyder-McLean, 1978; Muma, 1978a). This approach is what might be regarded as the a posteriori approach, as opposed to the a priori approach.

The functionalist position is predicated on active learning.

LAD and LAS

Language Acquisition Device (LAD) and Language Assistance Device (LAS) are two theoretical perspectives about the child's language learning. The former is about an innate disposition governing the learning process. The latter is about environmental influences that direct the nature and course of language acquisition. Bruner (1981) proposed that LAD and LAS are complementary.

Even though Chomsky's LAD was too meager in its claims of what is going on in language acquisition and too strong about induction, it set the stage for the study of language acquisition as an active, dynamic psychological-experiential process. Bruner (1981) proposed that inasmuch as parents are active partners in assisting spontaneous language learning, perhaps LAD should be coupled with LAS (Language Acquisition System). To this end, Bruner detailed some activities that parents do to assist language learning, for example, formatting, highlighting and looming, joint action and attention, given/new information, rising/falling intonations, raising the ante, and so on. In these ways, the child's contacts with language are selectively subordinated to *intentions* in a functional context.

In Chapter 3, *informativeness* (Greenfield, 1980; Greenfield & Smith, 1976) was viewed as the key and *intent* was viewed as the lock for entering the front door of language learning—pragmatics. Thus, the inductive processes are actually shunted to pragmatic issues which will eventually become redefined for semantic, syntactic, and phonological realizations. This, of course, means that language acquisition is very much a matter of *socialization*. Moreover, these realizations are themselves cognitive in nature. In short, cognitive-socialization is the cornerstone of language acquisition (Brown, 1956). Much of language learning is social in nature, for example, conventionalization, formalization, and scripting.

Pragmatic realizations of social interaction comprise the substrata of linguistic realizations.

Indeed, cognitive growth itself is strongly tied to social issues. Schaffer (1979) gave three reasons for the importance of people to cognitive growth. Mandler summarized these reasons as follows:

> People are salient sources of stimulation, they control the parts of the environment to which the infant is exposed, and perhaps most importantly, they continually adjust the type of stimulation the infant receives during their interactions. The last characteristic embodies still another source of cognitive change: Adults tend to be the first objects the child, even if in primitive ways, can control. Objects in the hand or in the visual field may mysteriously disappear and do not come back upon command, but crying or fussing can and frequently does make mother reappear. Thus, a sense of mastery and causality seems to have its beginnings in the social sphere, as Piaget and others have pointed out. Schaffer emphasizes the social roots of cognitive growth. (1979, pp. 375–376)

This perspective of social cognition raises questions about the child's awareness of causality and agency (Bates, 1979) and what has come to be known as the *allative bias* (Freeman, Sinha & Stedmon, 1981; Wales, 1979). This bias is "that which moves has direction towards" (Wales, 1979, p. 260; Weist, 1982). This bias pertains to ego. In learning deictic terms, children typically learn those terms concerning movement toward themselves before learning terms about movement away from themselves. Thus, children learn *come* before *go* and *bring* before *take* (Clark & Garnica, 1974). This pertains to the animate/inanimate distinction (Schlesinger, 1974) so it is not fully social.

Socialization and cognition are keystones to language acquisition.

The Child's Task: Hypothesis Testing

Brown and Bellugi (1964) defined induction of latent structure in language acquisition as hypothesis testing. Hirsh-Pasek, Treiman and Schneiderman (1984) suggested that environmental cues help narrow down the child's hypotheses about language and that parental repetition of the child's utterances is one such cue. Schlesinger (1977) suggested that the child uses linguistic input as a guide for resolving *both* the interpretation problem (worldly knowledge) and the categorization problem (language knowledge).

Muma (1978a) detailed overt and covert ways in which hypothesis testing might be carried out, delineating four principles of language learning attendant to hypothesis testing. Figure 5.1 portrays overt and covert hypothesis testing in language learning.

Overtly, hypothesis testing can be done either by spontaneous imitation or by generative production. Bloom, Hood and Lightbown (1974) showed that some children spontaneously imitate frequently while others do so less frequently, that there are lexical and grammatical differences between imitative and generative speech, that imitated words eventually become spontaneously available, and that imitation is highly *selective.* The last point is especially relevant to overt hypothesis testing. Children selectively imitate utterances or parts of utterances that contain aspects of language they are in the process of learning. For example, children learning possessives are likely to spontaneously imitate an utterance like "Give me *my* hat," but not "Give me the hat." It is not known what learning function is served by such spontaneous imitations; possibly, they represent a kind of overt rehearsal, but this still does not answer the question of what learning function is served.

Regarding overt rehearsals, there is a correspondence between spontaneous imitation and spontaneous overt rehearsals. Weir (1962) and Bloom (1970, 1973) have reported that when children successfully attempt a new dimension or locus of learning, they sometimes follow an utterance containing such a dimension with an overt rehearsal of it. Conceivably, covert rehearsals occur as well. The point is that both spontaneous imitations and spontaneous rehearsals seem to index new loci of learning and their grammatical-referential contexts.

> Spontaneous imitations and spontaneous rehearsals are useful in identifying new loci of learning and their grammatical-referential contexts.

In overt generative production, children generate utterances in accordance with their hypotheses about language. Suppose one such hypothesis is that English pluralizes nouns by adding a phonological marker as follows :

/__s/ for words ending with:
voiceless stops, /f/, /o/

Figure 5.1. Induction of latent structure-operational hypothesis testing.

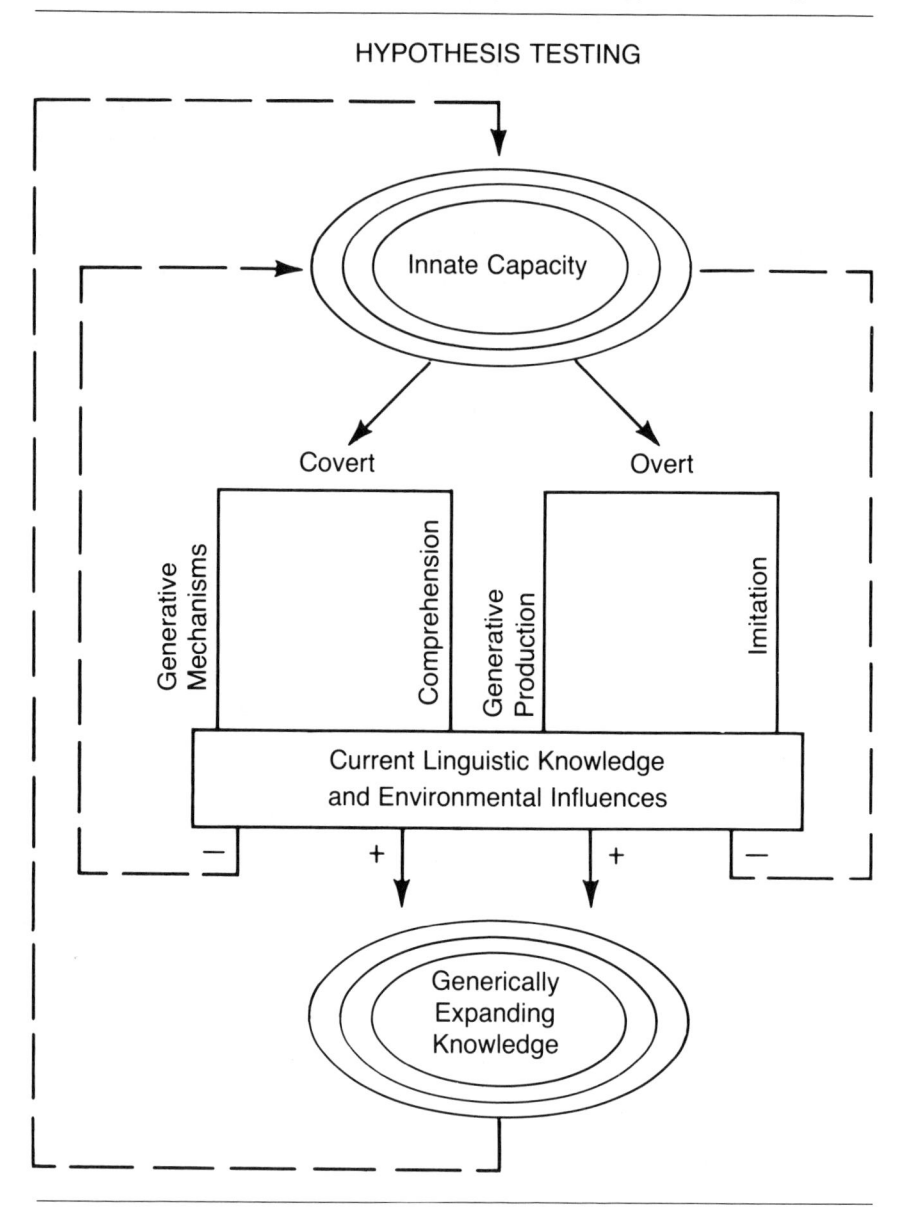

From *Language handbook: Concepts, assessment, intervention* (p. 156) by J. Muma, 1978a, Englewood Cliffs, N. J.: Prentice-Hall. Reprinted by permission.

/__z/ for words ending with:
voiced stops, /v/, /f/, nasals, vowels, liquids, glides
/__z/ for words ending with:
other voiced and unvoiced fricatives and affricates

Aside from the details of the phonological variations and their restrictions, the child simply hypothesizes that nouns are pluralized by adding a phonological marker. Then, the child generates words like *boats, cats, dogs, mans,* and *deers.* Needless to say, such performance will lead to environmental feedback that confirms some but not other products. The child is then left to sort out which hypotheses are on target and which need to be adjusted in accordance with environmental feedback.

Presumably, much of the same kind of hypothesis testing occurs *covertly* in comprehension and figuring out "permissible" hypotheses. In comprehension, children hear someone say something relevant to their hypotheses. The extent to which they understand the utterance in context is the extent to which they may be able to resolve relevant hypotheses. For example, children who expect to pluralize *man* by adding /s/ but hear someone say "men" instead are likely to adjust their hypothesis to note that *man-men* is an exception to the rule. The notion of figuring out or *discovering* (Bever, 1982) permissible hypotheses is difficult to explain. Indirect evidence indicates that given a nucleus of information (albeit ambiguous, positive, and negative) and a sufficient verbal repertoire (Schlesinger, 1977), children will spontaneously reconcile some latent hypotheses. Children do indeed generate derived morphemes without ever encountering them beforehand. For example, the child can say "unkind," "nonconforming," or "relatively" without ever having heard these words before, deriving them from previous encounters with *kind, conform,* and *relative,* respectively.

Language learning occurs both overtly and covertly in concert with environmental feedback.

Attendant Principles

Hypothesis testing is an *active learning process* by virtue of the child's intentions to inquire about language and to take these inquiries into communicative context for resolution. Muma (1978a) delineated four principles of language learning consistent with active hypothesis testing or discovery. These were contextual learning, partial learning, varied loci of learning, and switching loci of learning. Briefly, natural language learning is always context oriented. *Contextual learning* might be outlined in terms of referential context, grammatical context, and intentional context.

Macnamara (1972) contended that the child's knowledge of (a) an ongoing event, (b) its objects, and (c) their relationships provides the meanings for utterances used about these events, objects, and relationships. This is the *referential context*. Bloom (1970, 1973) said that young children use language in the "here-and-now." Their referential context is about *actual* referents. Olson (1970) showed that variations of actual reference are determinants of what is said. As children attain the cognitive capacity to deal with removed reference, representation, or symbolization, they attain the ability to deal with *presumed reference,* or more technically, presupposition and implicature. The shift from actual reference to presumed reference is what Marshall and Newcombe (1973), Muma (1978a), Sigel and Cocking (1977) and others have called *cognitive distancing.* In referring to Piagetian theory, Sameroff and Harris commented on cognitive distancing:

The referential context is a determinant of what is said.

The direction of cognitive development in Piaget's theory is from here-and-now interaction with the real world to successively removed levels of abstraction. When formal operations are used, the world has lost all its reality and concreteness and is manipulated only in terms of abstract symbols that gain their meaning entirely from the relations between themselves and other abstract symbols. The highest level of abstraction achieved determines the cognitive *stage* at which an individual is capable of functioning. (1979, p. 348)

A shift from actual to presumed reference constitutes a shift in cognitive distancing.

Grammatical context refers to co-occurring structures in utterances. Children learn from linguistic context. They not only learn something about each constituent as it relates to other constituents in linguistic context, but also about the inherent organization of the utterance itself (Greenfield, 1980; Schlesinger, 1977). In the latter instance, children gain information about the formal regularities of language, whereas in the former instance, children gain lexical information in the realization of semantic relations. The basic point is simply that grammatical context is a major means of language learning and cognition in general. As Schlesinger (1977, p. 167) said, "Cognitive development and linguistic input may thus be mutually supportive." He suggested that linguistic input may trigger both language learning and cognitive learning.

Grammatical context is a major means of language learning.

Muma and Zwycewicz-Emory (1979, p. 301) showed that there is a priority for linguistic context. "Apparently the first priority is to create a linguistic context when none is given; once a linguistic context is realized, semantic-syntactic equivalences have priority, followed by differentiation and integration."

Intentional context refers to the fact that intention plays a decisive role in language learning. Intentionality is the essence of active learning, for example, mentalism, constructionism, functionalism. When children intentionally strive to do something with language, they are ready to learn. On the other hand, children who are told or instructed to learn (or behavior is elicited in assessment) may lack intentional support for learning.

Intentional context is the essence of active learning.

In summary, contextual learning includes referential context (actual and presumed), grammatical context, and intentional context. These are all major issues in language acquisition.

Normal language learning is characteristically *partial learning*. That is to say, children follow sequences in the acquisition of verbal systems (Brown, 1973a, 1973b; Prutting, 1979). The phonetic inventory and simplification rules in child phonology attest to partial learning. The sequence for the inflectional rules—vocabulary stage, followed by the overgeneralization stage, and then the appropriate generalization stage—illustrates partial learning. Over- and underextensions and unmarked terms exemplify partial learning of words. Tag questions and inflected questions are other examples. If contextual learning is occurring, then partial learning is occurring, because children simply cannot encounter enough contextual information at one time to encapsulate a complete system.

If contextual learning is occurring, then partial learning is occurring as well.

Varied loci of learning means that the child learns several different aspects of language at once. The child does not learn cognitive skills, then pragmatic, then semantic, then syntactic, then phonological skills. Rather, the child acquires various aspects of all of these domains simultaneously once a minimal cognitive-pragmatic repertoire is in place.

Spontaneous buildups in child speech (Weir, 1962) provide evidence of varied loci of learning. The following is a buildup from a preschool-aged boy frequently cited by Muma (1983a):

I walk by myself.
I can walk by myself when get home.

I can walk by my _____?_____,
I could do it.
I could walk all by myself _____?_____ at home.

Each in this series of five utterances is built successively on the preceding utterance. The second utterance evidences two new loci of learning, *can,* and *when get home.* The third utterance is a spontaneous rehearsal. The fourth shows still another new locus with the tense change resulting in *could.* The predicate was glossed by the pronominals *do it.* And finally, the child went for the whole structure while incorporating two other new loci *all* and *at.* Clearly, he was attempting to deal with several aspects of syntax at the same time.

Muma (1983a) summarized several loci of learning from the psycholinguistic literature; these are discussed in the course of the book.

Individual children determine their loci of learning.

Switching loci of learning refers to the fact that learning occurs in spurts of unknown duration (Brown, 1973a). Children switch from one locus of learning to another according to their particular readiness to learn and appropriate opportunities. Children may be aware that they know a little about possessiveness. Then, they have an opportunity to learn about possessiveness by virtue of its use in a given context, so they may hold in abeyance some other aspect and switch to possessives. This in turn will be held in abeyance in favor of some other loci of learning. Eventually, children will return again to some more aspects of possessiveness. Such is the ambling opportunistic course of language learning.

Language learning occurs in spurts of unknown duration in accord with the child's readiness to learn and appropriate opportunities.

Varied loci, switching, partial learning, and contextual learning all illustrate why *individual differences* are considerable in language learning (Craig, 1983; Fey & Leonard, 1983; Furrow & Nelson, 1984; Muma, 1983b; Prutting & Kirchner, 1983; Rescorla, 1981; Stoel-Gammon & Cooper, 1984). Such differences undermine the value of normative age-referenced measures of language learning, such as, developmental profiles and normative tests. These measures may provide *data* but not necessarily *evidence* of the child's language learning (Muma, Lubinski & Pierce, 1982).

K. E. (Keith) Nelson (1981, pp. 229–232) outlined assumptions concerning the parent-child relationship in language acquisition. These assumptions are themselves predicated on the assumption that the child is actively hypothesizing about or discovering (Bever, 1982) the nature of language and utilizing available opportunities to discover relevant information. A shortened version of these assumptions follows:

Assumption 1: To fully master syntactically governed language, the child must engage in active communication in appropriate contexts with partners who are fluent in the language and who display . . . a full range of grammatical structures.

Assumption 2: Adults and older children do not directly teach young children to use syntactically well-constructed sentences; they do not know how to do such teaching, and they produce sentences that for the most part, play no essential role in the child's learning of syntax, although the sentences may be vital to acquisition of discourse and other skills (Shatz, 1982). Nevertheless, at certain points in development, the particular kinds of adult replies to the child are crucial for the child's syntactic progress.

Assumption 3: At any point in syntax development, the child must find relevant examples within an input set of sentences that are predominantly irrelevant . . .

Assumption 4: When a cognitive comparison occurs between a new sentence structure, for example, *the boy will run,* and a current sentence structure, for example, *the boy ran,* three outcomes are possible: (1) there is no discrepancy between the structures, and the child codes this as confirmation of the usefulness of the current structure, (2) a discrepancy exists, but the child cannot code the nature of the discrepancy, or (3) a codable discrepancy is noted. Only in the third case does the child's language system gain information from explicit differences between current structures and sentence structures in the input set.

Assumption 5: Codable differences are rarely noted by the child. This is because there are limitations of memory, attention, and motivation, and because most of the highly specific kinds of new sentences children require for comparison at each stage do not occur very frequently in input. A complete absence of such required forms for a period will lead to a plateau in syntax acquisition; conversely, a relatively high incidence of such forms will tend to accelerate the child's progress (an assumption directly tested in several of the studies presented below).

Assumption 6: The particular new sentence examples or replies required for syntactic advances in the child's system shift as one moves from one area of syntax to another, or from one stage to the next.

Assumption 7: The number of codable discrepancy comparisons that are required before a child revises his or her system to incorporate the new form may vary from child to child and from form to form, but research to date suggests that this number can be surprisingly low and may decline as development proceeds. Of course, some advances in language may be gradually realized after the child considers thousands of examples. However, the child more often makes a specific change in syntax after considering and coding only a small number (speculatively, 1 to 60) of discrepancies between his or her own sentence structure and that of adults.

Again, only those rare discrepancies that are actually noticed and coded could be useful to the child.

Assumption 8: The probability that the child will actually code potentially useful input exemplars will vary with the broader temporal and conversational patterns in which exemplars—and exemplar-displaying devices such as recasts—are embedded. This assumption carries many corollaries, two of which deserve note. One is that different rules of syntax may require (or "prefer") different complex patterns for ready processing and acquisition by the child. For example, the conversational patterns that may best display informative questions to the child could prove to be very unlike patterns that best display sentences with essential subject-verb agreement data. A second corollary is that although the child's speed in acquiring a rule is likely to be correlated roughly with the frequency of relevant and timely rule exemplars in input, this correlation should break down for certain forms to the extent that mothers (and other input sources) tend to use these forms with declining conversational appropriateness as their frequencies of using the forms increase.

Assumption 9: To understand how the child moves from no mastery of a form to complete mastery, it is necessary to consider four partially overlapping phases: (1) preparation, in which encounters with the form and related forms do not lead to analysis deployed in the next phase; (2) analysis, in which the child attends to and tries to code the input forms in relation to the system that has been established to that point; (3) assessment of new form analyses, involving attempts to use newly analyzed forms in production and analyses until some analysis of the form proves adequate; and (4) consolidation of the new acquisition in the system, ensuring that it will not become unstable or be forgotten. A complete account of a form's acquisition would specify for each of these stages the required input and the way in which the child processes and retains elements of the input...

Assumption 10: Many kinds of discourse sequences are useful in displaying the syntactic information the child must analyze in order to acquire a new form. (Elaboration on this topic is provided by Nelson, 1978, 1982.) Some of these may involve discourse sequences in which the child is merely an adjunct to, rather than a direct participant, in the conversation. However, among the most useful discourse exchanges are "recast comparisons" in which the following sequence occurs: the child produces a sentence, for example, *The unicorn yawned,* that is immediately given a reply such as *The unicorn stretched and yawned, didn't he?* that retains the basic meaning of the child's sentence but displays it in a new sentence structure, thereby allowing a short-term comparison with the child's own, related sentence. (For additional discussions of discourse sequences potentially useful to the child, see Brown, 1968; Moerk, 1972; Snow & Ferguson, 1977.).

Nelson (1981, p. 231; see also Nelson, 1977, 1978, 1982) said that the *rare-event cognitive comparison theory* was based upon the first seven of these assumptions:

> The (typically) rare events absolutely necessary to the child's advances in syntax are the successful comparisons between input constructions and closely related constructions already in the child's syntactic system. A few infrequent events in the midst of a vast amount of language interchange, and a small amount of the right kind of input information that the child closely attends to and analyzes comprise the core of developmental change in syntax, according to the theory. Thus, the nature of syntactic development reflects the nature of cognitive development generally. Research on phonological development, semantic development, and sensorimotor development also demonstrates that the child will ignore extensive input yet will show rapid learning when appropriate rare events are noticed and coded.

Impelled Learning

Children are seemingly striving to learn more about their language than they know even though what they know seems to be working; with a circumscribed environment, an intriguing question in the study of language acquisition is: What impels children to learn more about their language even when their verbal skills seem to be working?

McNeill said that

> a driving force behind language development is the rapidly growing variety of semantic interpretations for which the child must find some means of differentiation and expression... To say that a need for precision and cognitive economy motivates the developmental sequence is not to explain how a child is able to meet these needs or why he chooses the particular manner of meeting them that he does. For this we can only appeal to the child's innate *faculte de language*. (1966b, pp. 64–65)

Brown indicated that early utterances work well within a circumscribed environment.

> It is important to realize that the speech of the Stage I and Stage II child *works* very well within the range of situations he normally encounters in spite of its oscillating, apparently lawless optionality. He is normally talking about present or clearly impending circumstances or about desires he has which may be inferred from cues other than his speech. (1973b, pp. 241–242)

It may be that children seek to extend their range of experiences beyond a circumscribed environment. This alone could induce further learning.

Given that certain gestures such as the communicative point work as intended and that single words and simple word combinations work as intended, the question arises, what keeps the learning process going after such accomplishments? It could be that such communicative efforts work but not as they were *fully* intended. The child discovers that increased explicitness achieves a fuller realization of what was intended. Consequently, the child may strive to become more fully explicit.

Lock (1978, p. 7) implied that increased implicitness precipitates further learning. "Crying on its own leaves too much of the message 'unsaid,' too much to be supposed by the hearer. Apparently in response to this problem the developing infant begins to modify his crying, each with its separate developmental history."

> Impelled learning may actually be progressively fuller realizations of intentions.

Yet, explicitness alone is not the answer, because a message could be too explicit, thereby jeopardizing the felicity condition of excessive wordiness. Moreover, it is sometimes more propitious to be less explicit. When topics and reference are largely "known" by the participants in communication, a "restricted code" (Bernstein, 1970) is most useful in social commerce. A restricted code is when so much information is presumed that the code need not be fully explicit. For example, the comment "you know" presupposes that the listener knows the balance of the pertinent information so the message is not fully coded. Perhaps the impelling force is simply *power* or *utility* (Brown, 1958a; Brown & Gilman, 1960). As children achieve increased communicative skills, they come to realize more options, and consequently, more power or utility, in rendering appropriate messages. Such skills include the ability to adjust or revise messages in the course of playing the communication game (Gallagher, 1977, 1981; Gallagher & Darnton, 1978; Garvey, 1975, 1977; Muma, 1975a). These notions of impelling forces are placed at the footstep of *intention*.

Another way of viewing impelling forces is from a biological perspective as a consequence of the progressive development of innate faculties. Piagetian psychology attributed impelling forces to the progressive resolution of disequilibrium. As new knowledge is acquired, it provides a means for perceiving nuances that previously were unperceivable. These nuances then lead to a state of disequilibrium between existing knowledge and novel experiences. Thus, disequilibrium then resolved by assimilation or accommodation, only to be set ajar again by new experiences.

Mandler was concerned that this so-called *conflict* theory is probably no more fruitful than a goal directed or functional theory.

How should we account for the increasing sophistication of the young child in using tags such as "Isn't it?" or "Did she?" since these are patently unnecessary for communicative effectiveness? Certainly conflict will not help us, but neither is it clear that coordination will do so, although the possibility of using such grammatical devices for coordinating interpersonal and ideational messages is intriguing. Sometimes, conflict *can* account for progress, as in the example of miscommunication that Sameroff and Harris discuss, although even here it is not obvious that an analysis in terms of conflict will be more fruitful than some concept of goal-corrected search. (1979, p. 381)

It is possible that a combination of LAD (Chomsky, 1957) and LAS (Bruner, 1981) can account for impelling mechanisms in language acquisition. Certainly the language learning process is remarkably targeted and robust which implicates innateness or predisposition, but the process is also responsive to experience, which implicates environmental influences. The robustness and single-mindedness in staying the course in the face of considerable odds against it brings to mind a gyro. Perhaps LAD-LAS combinations might be called the "gyro hypothesis."

Natural language learning is remarkably targeted and robust.

The *discovery* capacities of the *learnability* theory also smack of a gyro function. In a sense, learnability theory, while strongly grounded on innate capacity, is a contemporary version of LAD and LAS because it acknowledges that discovery processes operate on contacts with language in natural communicative functions and contexts.

The innatist position accounts for impelled learning as a continuation of a biologically determined unfolding of verbal capacities. The achievement of subject-verb-object (SVO) constructions is viewed as a major stage in this process. In a sense, the coupling of LAD (Chomsky, 1957) and LAS (Bruner, 1981) establishes a momentum by virtue of progressive repertoires that impel further learning. This account simply asserts that language learning begets language learning.

Language learning begets language learning.

The literature on *metalinguistic* activities in language learning supports this view, indicating that the child advances in language acquisition through reflecting upon and playing with language (Cazden, 1975; Hakes, 1980; Kretschmer, 1984; Winner, 1979). Perhaps metalinguistic activities as well as social commerce activities will play increasingly important roles in language intervention in the future.

Metalinguistic activities are powerful in language learning.

McNeill (1966b) suggested that a release from limited mental capacities motivates advanced learning. That is, as children become mentally able to process more information via the use of linguistic rules and structure, they become increasingly more able to deal with complexity.

Other researchers, such as Bloom (1970, 1973), Brown (1973b), Bowerman (1973, 1976), Greenfield and Smith (1976) and Macnamara (1972), maintain that initially children learn to handle a relatively small set of information realized as raw vocabulary, but they are eventually forced into rule-governed behavior and possibly a reorganization of rules in order to manage large amounts of information. This is seen in the acquisition of morphological abilities (Cazden, 1968), syntactic abilities (Menyuk, 1963, 1964a, 1964b), and phonological abilities (Ingram, 1976; Vihman, 1981). The point is that early language learning is constrained by limited mental abilities. As these abilities extend, the potential for advanced learning is released. Bowerman (1982) has suggested that the child is attempting to reduce clutter in an otherwise well-organized, fluid information processing system.

Early on, children operate from a very limited mental capacity.

The releasing of potential for advanced learning as a function of increased mental abilities appears to be mostly a matter of memory processing capacity early on. But there appears to be a qualitative change in mental capacities related to the acquisition of formal grammatical processes beyond subject-verb-object (SVO). In particular, it is the acquisition of rudimentary logic as a cognitive base for extending SVO. This makes us cogently aware that SVO attainment occurs after sensorimotor achievements; that is, after sensorimotor achievements have been reorganized in the realization of preoperational skills that lead to categorization and rule governed behavior. Similarly, Bruner (1964) and Bruner, Olver, and Greenfield (1966) detailed a shift from iconic thinking or imagery to functional thinking or representation. In short, there appear to be stages of learning. Each stage means a reorganization of previous achievements; consequently, the child is a different learner at each stage. Gleitman and Wanner summarized these stages of learning as a metamorphosis or tadpole-to-frog hypothesis.

> It could be that there are relevant neurological changes in the learner that cause him to reinterpret linguistic evidence. Putting the same thing another way, it could be that there are a succession of learners, each of whom organizes the linguistic data as befits his mental state. This is a kind of metamorphosis, or tadpole-to-frog, hypothesis.

Whatever the causes of change, both discontinuous theories of language development assert that the surface-meaning mappings of an earlier semantics-based system are dropped, and learning begins anew with fairly trivial residue (including, perhaps, the lexical items and the guess about canonical order). The two theories differ, though, to the extent that the data-driven reorganizational hypothesis might claim there is a necessary movement through stages, while the metamorphosis theory says there is not. (1982, pp. 30–31)

Bowerman (1982) posited a data-driven reorganization theory. She was concerned about the role of errors in language acquisition. Early on, the child is relatively free from errors. This is known as the "vocabulary stage." Later, errors appear. Gleitman and Wanner summarized Bowerman's position in this way:

> As Bowerman argues, through internal analysis of these late-appearing error types, the novel usages imply that the learner has seen through to a new organization that relates the items learned separately and allows the child to project beyond the heard instance in various ways (some of them wrong).
>
> The question arises: What causes the child to reorganize his grammar—especially to reorganize it in a way that increases the abstractness of the relations between forms and meanings? Bowerman takes no stand on this matter. But it is possible to imagine that reorganization is motivated by a data-driven process, an aversion to "clutter" in the original data organization. Bowerman remarks that individuals, both children and adults, might differ in the extent to which they are inclined to tolerate first organizations, or to carry out these deep reanalyses. (1982, p. 30)

The functionalist views of impelling forces for greater complexity hinges on the notion of effective, and possibly efficient, social commerce. Intention and context are central issues. That is, as children experience failure or awkwardness in the effective realization of intentions, they have perceived the need to improve their capabilities. A primary means of achieving more effective realizations of communicative intentions is through an increased command of grammatical machinery.

Effective social commerce requires the realization of intention in context.

Notice that the functionalist view is compatible with the Piagetian (innatist) notion of disequilibrium, although Piaget's notion of disequilibrium was a biological state, whereas the functionalist view implicates disequilibrium of intentions as a matter of realized intentions in particular contexts. The point is that the functionalist view is not incompatible or far removed from the "weak form" of the innatist view. Indeed, in Bates's (1979) accounts of socio-emotional aspects of development as they relate to language acquisition, she used the term "harmony" which is compatible with the equilibrium principle.

Another functionalist view of impelling motivations for greater complexity in language learning is *cognitive distancing* (Sigel, 1971; Sigel & Cocking, 1977), which posits a continuum of cognitive difficulty from direct experience to experience removed in time and space. The communicative correlate is that messages increase in complexity as a function of displacement from direct experience. One version of such displacement is reflected in the continuum of difficulty from actual objects to representational objects to pictorials to words. Another version is Bruner's (1966) three stages in the course of cognitive growth: enactive or motoric processing, perceptual processing or imagery, and representational thought.

> The child's need to overcome problems in cognitive distancing may be an impelling force for language acquisition.

Finally, tentative indirect evidence supports both innatist and functionalist positions. This evidence pertains to spontaneous rehearsals, spontaneous imitations, spontaneous sentence repetitions, and "show-off" behaviors. Children actively engaged in language learning exhibit all these behaviors. Why do children show off their language achievements? Furth (1984) called this a "celebration of learning." Why do children spontaneously rehearse, spontaneously imitate, or spontaneously repeat full sentences containing new verbal achievements? Obviously, children do not engage in such behaviors "in order to" promote more effective communication—at least not at the moment of the behavior. The learning process involves an intrinsic, innate element which may be endemically related to impelling forces that precipitates such behaviors.

> Show-off behavior, spontaneous rehearsals, spontaneous imitations and spontaneous sentence repetitions involve an intrinsic aspect.

In summary, there are only tentative answers to the question: What impels language learning? The innatist speculation is that biological determinants are at work in the form of a progressive unfolding of increasingly complex capacities. Language learning begets language learning, but mental constraints limit learning.

The functionalist speculation hinges on effective communication and disequilibrium in the realization of intentions in social commerce. Both replacement (earlier skills are replaced by subsequent skills) and expansion (the child's repertoire of skills expands) are important aspects of functionalism; moreover, they are both compatible with nativism and functionalism. This deals with the first question about impelling forces in language learning. The second question is: What keeps the child rigidly focused in language learning in the face of many sources of error? A related question is, what are the true meanings of messages young children use?

Competing Influences But Narrowly Focused Learning

Potentially, at least, children are faced with many competing kinds of information. Yet, they are somehow narrowly focused. Eventually they emerge with the essential understandings of their world (cognitive categories), and language (semantic categories, and grammatical categories), so they are potentially capable of effective, and even efficient, social commerce.

Bowerman acknowledged the complexity of such a task as follows:

> Getting a word hooked up to exactly the right set of contextual properties is an extremely complicated matter. Every setting in which a child hears a word is composed of a complex configuration of discriminable components. Some of these components have to do with directly observable phenomena (e.g., objects, actions, and their properties), others with the speaker's feelings, reactions, beliefs about the feelings of others, and intention or purpose in speaking (e.g., to command, register a reaction "phew!", interrogate, etc.). The child learning language is faced with the task of trying to discover which of the innumerable aspects of the contexts in which he hears words used are the relevant ones. It is hard to imagine how he ever arrives at the right solutions, and correspondingly easy to see how he might pick out components or combinations of components that are salient to him but incomplete or irrelevant from the adult's point of view. (1976, p. 30)

Freedle (1972) acknowledged that the kind of learning that takes place in discourse is very complex, exceeding the scope of issues of contemporary learning theory and simple notions of memory and processing. The ability to stay on track and extract only needed information in the course of social commerce is so complex that it is laden with many sources of potential error. To the extent that the chances for error are high, and they are indeed high, it is all the more remarkable that a language learner stays the course but is nonetheless fallible. Freedle outlined this *fallibility* as follows:

> The conditions that must be met for the more complex type of learning to take place after exposure to discourse cannot be handled by such limited conceptions as short- and long-term memory, nor by such concepts as multiple copies of memory traces versus single traces, nor by a variable strength idea for traces, etc. Instead what is needed is some evaluative

apparatus that makes decisions concerning semantic believability and pragmatic importance and that *matches* the results of these decisions against the hierarchical system of knowledge that existed prior to exposure to the discourse. In addition, one needs some apparatus which will select those parts of the old knowledge system which need alteration (substitution, addition, or subtraction of semantic relations) in the light of the semantic and pragmatic decisions and which will also carry out the necessary changes. To do less than this is do a disservice to the complexity of our knowledge and the complexity of the internal representations of that knowledge. I readily admit, though, that the adequate modeling of such a complex mechanism is a forbiddingly difficult enterprise. To do a thorough job of the modeling one would also have to consider the fallibility of the subject and somehow represent the sources of error at each step of the decision process. (1972, p. 205)

Fallibility and errors are natural consequences of language learning.

In the face of such obstacles, errors would seem to be rampant, but in fact there are relatively few errors and these are restricted to a small set of loci, again implicating some kind of predisposition for keeping the child narrowly focused. Moreover, the errors that do occur are remarkably recoverable.

The Other Side of the Moon

What is on the other side of the moon? Is it something like the side facing the earth. That is craters, dormant volcanoes, and such? Is it a nifty Oz-like kingdom? Is it a chunk of cheese (which after all we had been led to believe when we were younger but such beliefs have long since been dashed)? Or, some more earthy matters might be: What is love? Do trees hurt? Or, what does it mean to say, "ball?" From *ball* to other cheesy questions such as the other side of the moon, infants and children are disarmingly adept in responding by laughing or smiling. Occasionally they may say *ball* and even accompany the utterance with a referential point or referential display. Aside from whether or not the child is asked what he or she "knows" about a referent and the labels for it, what the child actually *does* mean is an intriguing question.

What about the meanings of messages young children use? These messages are observable verbal events (inquiries, referents and their labels) but a most important issue in language acquisition is what is going on inside (mentally, emotionally). Knowing what *ball* refers to when it is used in context is a complex task for children. Macnamara (1972), Rosch et al. (1976), and Wells (1974) pointed out that the child's understanding of an event and its referents provides meanings for the words used in that context. The traditional view was just the opposite; asserting that the words used in a context gave meaning to what was named. Macnamara and Well's positions are more likely to hold. However, there is a major problem: How does the child *know* what *ball* refers to in a given context? Here again, early pragmatic capacities, especially intention, may be the key to how the child discerns that *ball* pertains to the referent object rather than to some other possibilities.

A simple but inadequate response is that children draw upon their knowledge of the world and an event to give meaning to utterances—the Macnamara (1972) proposal. On one level this is surely true. And, it gives reason for inquiring into various *cognitive underpinnings* that have (a) a general relationship to language (cognitive tempo, iconic/symbolic thinking, analytic/synthetic thinking, rule- or non-rule-governed learning, perceptual salience, Piagetian skills, etc.), (b) a *substantive* relationship to language (proposition or content, intent, etc.), and (c) a *processing* relationship in formulating messages (comprehension—construction and utilization; production—planning and execution). Finally, this proposal points to the need to consider available references.

On the other hand, this response is inadequate because it leaves out a truly remarkable facility that keeps the child *narrowly focused* while inducing the nature of language. Children must be narrowly focused because there are simply too many alternatives which could lead them astray. But, somehow they are remarkably directed to stay the course, even though relevant information may be fleeting, limited, entwined in ambiguity, and even negative or incorrect. Given such obstacles and the fact that normal language learning entails very complex issues that are obtained in relatively short order, there is reason to assume that some sort of innate capacity or predisposition is at work. And furthermore, it is evident that this predisposition is open-ended and focused upon environmental influences. Bruner (1981) suggested that LAD and LAS are complementary realizations of innate capacity and environmental influences in language learning.

Some researchers have been concerned that an innatist view would delimit language learning (Greenberg, 1963; Slobin, 1973). Such concerns, though, do not address the question of how children become so narrowly focused in their learning of language. An example of infant behavior illustrates this focusing process: The mother uses the word *ball* intentionally to label the blue ball with white stars that her infant held, patted, dropped, recovered, and inspected. How does the infant come to know that *ball* means this spherical object? It would seem that the infant could just as easily come to think *ball* means: 'hold,' 'pat,' 'drop,' 'recover,' or 'inspect.' *Ball* could mean 'blue,' 'stars,' 'blue' and 'stars,' or 'round.' Indeed, *ball* could logically be taken to mean something quite different such as 'speaker,' 'mother,' 'person looking at me,' and so on. These undoubtedly are the kinds of classifications available to the infant in this circumstance. To say merely the child relies on awareness of an event to give words meaning is not saying much about the rather remarkable skill involved in acquiring the knowledge of the appropriate referent in the face of many other potential interpretations.

> The child displays a remarkable propensity for discerning the intended referent and referential relations in the face of many other potential interpretations.

The child's theory of the world (Palermo, 1982), possible worlds (Stalnaker, 1972), or working knowledge of the world (Bruner, 1981) must be inherently organized to enable the child to sort out information and distinguish the relevant from the irrelevant. The figure/ground theory (Witkin, Dyk, Faterson, Goodenough, & Karp, 1962), which posits that the child becomes progressively able to discern relevant information by distinguishing figure from background, however, is insufficient, because it leaves the infant with many possible referents for *ball*. It appears that *intention* is the force that guides the child away from the many possible referents for a label and toward the designated referent. Coupled with intention are the social contracts, or more technically, felicity conditions, under which the participants should be honest, forthright, and helpful. Indeed, infants seem to be virtually unaware of violations of such social contracts.

> Intention seems to be the force that guides the child away from the many possible referents for a label and toward the particular designated referent.

Parents strive to deduce their children's intentions. Then, these deductions provide the guiding force for what can be said within a particular referential context. Children themselves act (verbally and/or nonverbally) with intent. The point is that while we do not know what a given label such as *ball* means to the child the probability is good that its meaning will be deduced from the child's intention, available referents, and the social contract. These, in turn, are tied to the child's theory of the world (cognitive, social, and emotional). And, in instances of early word learning, intentions are essentially extensions of the child's actions. As Greenfield and Smith (1976) put it, early words are extended actions.

> LAS is focused on intention.

Individual Differences and Strategies

Throughout the contemporary language acquisition literature individual differences stand out. Given the complexity of language and varied opportunities for learning, variability or *heterogeneity* in rate of learning is to be expected. It should be noted, however, that this variability is strongly evident in rate of learning but remarkably absent in acquisition sequences (Brown, 1973a, 1973b).

Needless to say, individual differences are even greater in clinical populations such as language disorders, aphasia, mental retardation, and hearing impairment. Given the wide range of evidence on individual differences of language learning in normal or clinical populations (e. g., Craig, 1983; Fey & Leonard, 1983; Furrow & Nelson, 1984; Muma, 1973b, 1978a, 1978b, 1981a, 1983a, 1983b; Nelson, 1981b; Prutting & Kirchner, 1983; Rescorla, 1981; Stoel-Gammon & Cooper, 1984; etc.), it is remarkable that viable language learning principles (i.e., sequence, the four big issues, informativeness, etc.) have emerged.

In addition to individual differences in rate of learning, the literature reports variation in *strategies* of language learning. It must be noted that strategies are quite different from stages. Stages are developmental steps and are relatively fixed; strategies are means for achieving language. These means, or "roads," are optional. Strategies are options for achieving certain capacities but the roads to achievement are presumably optional.

Nelson (1973b) suggested that two common strategies are "nominal" and "expressive," and that children often switch between these strategies. Nominal learners seem to be oriented toward the principle that one word has many referents and one referent has many words. Expressive learners seem to be oriented on the principle that new forms come in with old functions and new functions come in with old forms.

Ramer (1976b) reported two distinct styles of syntactic acquisition, rapid and slow. The *rapid* learners reached the syntactic criterion in 4-1/2 months whereas the *slow* learners took 6-1/2 months. The syntactic acquisition was from single-word utterances to the syntactic criterion which was when 20% of the child's syntactic utterances evidenced a subject-verb-complement (SVC) construction. This seems to be the same as an SVO construction.

Bloom, Hood, and Lightbown (1974) found that some children imitate available linguistic models much more than other children. Thus, some children are imitators and some are not. A convenient criterion for identifying an imitative strategy is if more than 15% of the language sample is imitation. Bloom, Lightbown, and Hood (1975) reported two strategies concerning the acquisition of nominalizations. Some children begin learning nominalizations as simple nominals (first proper nouns, then simple determiners such as *the, a, that* plus a noun). Other children begin learning nominals as pronominal forms. Thus, there appears to be the nominal and pronominal strategies. When the children reach a mean length of utterance (MLU) of 2.0 they seem to switch strategies. Cromer (1974) reported that most children prefer learning adjectival constructions in object noun phrases first, but some prefer doing this in subject noun phrases first.

Vihman (1981) suggested that some children strive to learn phonemic contrasts to overcome homonymy, but other children may actually seek homonymy. Regarding the latter strategy, Vihman said, "They may resort to such processes in order to merge two or more adult words in a single sound pattern. In short, instead of demonstrating a desire to achieve efficiency in performance, the child's goal in such cases almost seems to be the production of a maximum number of lexical items with a minimum repertoire of sound shapes" (p. 241).

Dore (1974, p. 350) identified two kinds of learner: code oriented and message oriented. The code oriented child used language "primarily to declare things about her environment" whereas the message oriented child strived "mainly to manipulate other people." The code-oriented child used more words and these words were to label, repeat, and practice. The message oriented child used fewer words but seemed to control a larger repertoire of prosodic features (intonation patterns). Perhaps, the code-oriented child is operating primarily on SVO or the Three Bears, whereas the message-oriented child may be operating primarily on the prosodic envelope. In a sense, then, there may be different "yellow brick roads" to the kingdom of social commerce via grammatical knowledge.

Some reported strategies appear to be true strategies, whereas others may be transitional devices. Surely further research will clarify the notion of strategy (and *stage* for that matter) and give fuller accounts of how they contribute to language learning.

Summary

The contemporary literature shows that the child is not a passive learner, but he is actively engaged in the learning process. Apparently, LAD and LAS are complementary accounts of this active learning process.

Children seem to achieve language learning through hypothesis testing. This can be accomplished both overtly and covertly. Four attendant principles to hypothesis testing are contextual learning (referential: actual/presumed; grammatical, intentional), partial learning, varied loci of learning, and switching loci of learning. The assumptions about parent-child interaction in language learning reflect the hypothesis testing process.

An interesting question in language learning is: What impels the child to learn an increasingly complex system, especially when earlier communication efforts work as intended? There are several speculations. One that seems to be most plausible is that increasingly fuller realizations of *intentions* constitute the key impelling motivation. In a sense, language learning begets language learning.

There are many competing influences in language learning yet the child is somehow narrowly focused, staying the course against considerable odds. The child is fallible, of course, but relatively few errors occur, and even then they are easily recoverable.

Much of what goes on in language learning is underground and thus is inaccessible to direct observation, control, or management. It is therefore all the more remarkable that children actually do grapple with the particular aspects that are most beneficial to them. In this regard, *intention* is somehow critical.

Individual differences among language learners are commonplace but the sequences in which language is learned are remarkably stable. Further, children use a variety of strategies and quasi-strategies for acquisition.

Finally, you might wonder why a chapter on methodologies has been devoted largely to inductive processes of language learning: Inductive processes have forced the study of language into the realm of inference. In order to make inferences about the child's verbal capacities, it is necessary to obtain contextually related information. It is simply inadequate to inventory the child's verbal behavior as evidence of language learning. Such information must be supported by relevant contextual information such as intention and actual and presumed reference. Evidence on productivity provides a license for inference.

Part 2

Chronological Perspectives of Language Acquisition

6

EMERGENCE OF SYMBOLIC CAPACITIES

The notion of cognitive precursors was raised in Chapter 2; here, this notion is expanded considerably. Cognitive precursors extend across the full gamut of capacities that afford the child entry into the acquisition of conventional and, eventually, formal grammatical mechanisms. Moreover, these new capacities provide opportunities for reflections about speech acts themselves, a metalinguistic capacity even during early one-word utterances that function as similes and metaphors. The capacities that allow entry into language acquisition include emergent perceptual capacities, actions or enactive processing, gestures and symbolization, and early phonological behavior. These capacities are used to realize early intentions in social commerce.

Camera, Action

Infants are operating from their rather primitive knowledge of the world (Bruner, 1981), which is basically perceptual and motoric or enactive in nature. Perceptual information pertains to how the infant perceives space, time, and relationships. Motoric information is derived from the infant's actions on his world. Kopp (1979, p. 30) suggested that motoric behavior in infancy is a primary means of entering cognitive, social, and emotional arenas. "Motor functions should be examined as a channel to social, cognitive, and emotional growth ..." As Bloom, Lightbown, and Hood said,

As the child acts on his environment and observes others acting on his environment in similar and different ways, he begins to organize his experiences. He develops schemata to represent mentally such relations among objects as persons acting on objects, persons habitually associated with objects... Such cognitive schemata are general and nonspecific to particular persons and objects... With each schema the child has induced a regularity... (1975, p. 30)

> **Motoric functions may be channels to social, cognitive, and emotional growth.**

Bornstein suggested that world knowledge is rooted in sensation and perception:

Perceptual features organize the world. They partition dimensions of sensation into stable units and provide critical information about those dimensions. Perceptual features are encoded, processed, and recognized with facility. Moreover, they provide a key basis for elementary learning. (1979, p. 74)

Regarding perception of faces, infants from 5 to 7 months old were operating from an abstraction rather than the stimuli themselves (Fagan, 1979). Bruner's (1957) notion of going beyond the information given (see also Anglin, 1973), Piaget's (1954) constructionism (see also Lewis & Brooks, 1975), and the previously cited literature on discrepancy learning all indicate that perception itself is an *active* learning process grounded on previous constructs brought to bear on new experience. As Garner (1966) indicated, in order to perceive, one must know. Thus, one can perceive something if equipped with concepts for that particular perception. Auto mechanics, for example, can perceive problems with an engine because they have established concepts for doing so, but customers without such concepts cannot perceive the same problems. This does not mean that the mechanic's knowledge is complete; existing knowledge only needs to be skeletal to render active learning from prototypical knowledge (Nelson, 1973a, 1974).

> **To perceive is to know.**

Pick, Yonas and Rieser (1979, p. 116) suggested that infants' perception changes as a function of their motoric skills, which allow them to perceive the world "upright" as compared to "horizontal." Initially, children have an egocentric and idiosyncratic view of the world. However, as they gain motor control, which enables them to change and adjust positions, their previous views of the world change. From relatively stable upright and forward-moving positions, the infant discovers up-down and layout frames of reference, respectively.

> Infant perceptions of the world change as a function of vertical postural positions and movement.

Pick, Yonas, and Reiser (1979) distinguished between perceptual and motoric representations of experience, and this is the reason for calling this section "Camera, Action." *Camera* pertains to perceptual imagery, and *action* pertains to representations issuing from enactive or motoric processing. Both seem to play important roles in the sensorimotor stage and early word learning.

> *Camera* pertains to perceptual imagery; *action* pertains to representations of motoric processing.

Pick et al. (1979) also distinguished cognitive advances that are achieved perceptually from those that are achieved motorically. Moreover, Pick et al. maintained that one may be held relatively constant as a referential base while the other is being explored. It appears, then, that both perceptual and motor functions operate in a parallel fashion affording the child different kinds of representations.

Sensorimotor Achievements

Roughly, the period during which sensorimotor achievements are attained is during the first 18 months of life. Some children go through this period relatively quickly whereas it may be protracted for others. The overriding significance of sensorimotor learning is that it affords infants access to the world initially through action-based or enactive processing (Bruner, 1964), which eventually becomes symbolized or representationalized. As cognitive skills shift from action-based or enactive learning to representational learning, thinking skills become increasingly *freed from direct stimulation* and increasingly *reliant upon representation* to deal with new events. The reliance on representation is what Piaget (1954) meant by *constructionism* and what Bruner (1957) meant by *going beyond the information given* (see also Anglin, 1973).

> Early on, the child becomes progressively freed from direct stimulation and increasingly reliant upon representation or symbolization.

The sensorimotor skills provide evidence that the child achieves cognitive capacities for becoming released from direct stimulation. *Object permanence* is a thinking skill that enables children to be aware that something exists conceptually even though it is not present. Clearly, this skill frees children from direct stimulation. For example, the baby stays at the edge of her crib, crying and reaching for her rattle even though she cannot see it. This shows that through previous experience with the rattle she stored some prototypic information, derived primarily through her actions toward the rattle. It is such prototypic information that keeps her occupied with absent or conceptual objects (Nelson, 1973a, 1974; Nelson, Rescola, Gruendel, & Benedict, 1978).

Presumably, the cognitive skill of object permanence is a necessary precursor for word learning (Bloom, 1973; Brown, 1973b; Corrigan, 1978; Golinkoff, 1980). The research is not clear about this matter, however. As children attain Stage 6 (Uzgiris & Hunt, 1975) in the formal tasks of object permanence, word learning may take a decided shift into high gear for rapid vocabulary acquisition. The perplexing part is that other children may make similar vocabulary spurts without evidencing Stage 6 of object permanence. This is a complex problem (Edwards, 1973; Ingram, 1978; Moerk, 1975; Morehead & Morehead, 1974; Sinclair, 1970).

One issue may be how object permanence is measured. The formal Uzgiris and Hunt (1975) tasks are evidently more conservative than free-field human sense tasks (Donaldson, 1978). A related issue is what level of acquisition is used to credit the infant for a skill: preparation, attainment, or consolidation. (These levels are discussed in Chapter 4.) Evidently, Ingram (1978) employed attainment: "The determination of a general stage is not established by isolated behaviors but rather by a cluster of behaviors at the same time" (p. 264).

Furthermore, the neo-Piagetian accounts (Bower, 1974; Gopnik, 1981, 1982, 1984; Gopnik & Meltzoff, 1984; Gratch, 1976; McCune-Nicolich, 1981; Moore & Meltzoff, 1978) raise a different concern about stages *within* the acquisition of object permanence.

> Basically, this account claims that during infancy the child accumulates specific rules which allow him to predict the reappearance of objects that have disappeared. At around 18 months these specific rules are replaced by a more general theory. According to this theory, all disappearances are the result of changes in the spatial relationships between the objects and the child. (Gopnik, 1984, p. 275)

Deferred imitation evidences a release from direct stimulation. Infants see or hear something happen; after an interval of time they imitate it. The interval means that information had to be stored; this performance shows that infants can recover the information from memory and reconstruct the event in sufficient detail to give it a likeness to the original event. Thus, deferred imitation evidences a reliance upon stored or represented information.

Anticipation is another sensorimotor skill that evidences a release from direct stimulation. Infants who have stored information about a previous class of experiences will use this stored information to anticipate another instance. For example, infants have many experiences in which their mothers approach then pick them up. Infants store information about these previous experiences, so when she approaches again they turn to her, raise their arms, and smile at her in anticipation of being picked up.

Causality is a sensorimotor skill whereby children realize cause-and-effect relationships. Such knowledge is presumably related to the animate/inanimate and ego/nonego distinctions (Golinkoff & Harding, 1980; Schlesinger, 1974). That is, infants realize that animate objects may be causative agents. Conceivably, knowledge of causal relations underlies the children's ability to code topic/comment relations. This is merely conjecture, and needs to be substantiated.

Bowerman (1973) indicated that the distinction between animate and inanimate nouns was evidenced early. She said this distinction was manifested as animate subjects and inanimate objects (see also Bloom, 1973; Greenfield and Smith, 1976). Moreover, this is also compatible with Schlesinger's (1974) proposal that very early semantic distinctions are animate/inanimate and ego/nonego. On the other hand, Bates (1979) showed that causality was an underlying sensorimotor skill for early language learning, likening the notion of word use to the broad notion of tool use.

Tools

It may be useful to draw a parallel between tool use and language use. This parallel underscores the centrality of language *functions* in social commerce, particularly instrumental intention. Elkind (1979, p. 234) referred to Bruner's (1975a) perspective in this way, "Cognitive processes are thought of as tools that extend man's adaptive capacities. From this perspective, language extends the possibilities of human thought much as shovels, hoes, and tractors extend the possibilities of human agriculture." Dale and Ingram also drew a parallel between tool use and language use:

> Many previous works have suggested that the role of gestures in the initial development of language is important. Bates (1976) proposed an explanation for the role of gesture. One of the most highly evolved human specializations is for tool-use, and this specialization is centered on the hands. Language, and communication more generally, can be seen as a tool, by means of which children can gain another person's attention, or cause another person to aid obtaining a desired object or state of affairs. Thus, the hands are most likely to be used for this function . . . gestures clearly are not supplanted by verbal language, but that during a child's third year, the two modalities supplement each other. (1981, p. 132)

Bates (1979, pp. 37–38) indicated that Piagetian psychology predicts a parallel between social and nonsocial developments at Stage 5 (Uzgiris & Hunt, 1975). Bates amplified this point by saying that their earlier work (Bates, Camaioni, & Volterra, 1975) indicated that there is a parallel in a child's capacity for social instrumentality and nonsocial instrumentality. Social instrumentality is using humans as agents to obtain objects or using objects to obtain adult attention. Nonsocial instrumentality is using an object to obtain another object.

By around 9 months, the child engages in what Piaget (1952, 1954) called "tertiary circular reactions" and "novel means to familiar ends." These are evidenced both socially and nonsocially as outlined below:

Nonsocial Tool Use: Object-to-object means-end sequences
Social Tool Use: Person-to-object sequences (Protoimperative)
Social Tool Use: Object-to-person sequences (Protodeclarative)

Bates (1979, p. 326) asserted further that tool use may be regarded as a type of symbolic activity. This is a particularly important point because it is apparent that early pragmatic skills begin with symbolization. Both Bates (1979) and Bruner (1981) defined the onset of verbal skills in terms of emerging symbolic capacities either in general (sensorimotor skills) or in particular symbolizations.

There is a common denominator for nonsocial and social tool use; and furthermore, tool use is a type of symbolic activity.

On the other hand, parallels between tool use and language use may distort the notion of the centrality of intention (Bloom, 1985). The notion that language is a tool regards language as essentially instrumental. However, intentionality of language is considerably more than an instrumental function. For example, intentionality extends to other functions such as interactional, imaginative, regulatory, and representational. Bloom (1985) showed, for example, that the relationships between the emergence of specific-imposed-constructions in play and early word learning are more compatible with the theory that language is intention than the theory that language is a tool.

Sensorimotor Achievements: Rekindling the Fire

Pointing a critical finger at cloudy attempts to show that sensorimotor achievements, of one kind or another, are precursors to early language achievements, Mandler (1979, p. 374) commented, "The promissory note of sensorimotor development as the key to language acquisition has remained largely unpaid. We know that the connections must be there, but how are we to dig below this surface knowledge?" Early on, there was reason to believe that a close relationship between the acquisition of object permanance and indicative or labeling would be found, but the ensuing research has been disappointing.

Bates (1979) hypothesized that certain sensorimotor skills comprised a "Cognitive Complex": object permanance, spatial relations, imitation, and means-ends. Additionally, she considered combinatorial play and symbolic play. Acquisition of these skills was compared to various achievements in what she called the "Gestural Complex" and the "Language Complex."

Bates (1979) pointed out that some neo-Piagetian theorists had proposed a distinction between "deep" and "local" homology. The deep homology notion asserts that there is a single unified cognitive substrata from which various communicative capacities are derived. The local homology notion, on the other hand, propose that there is more than one underlying scheme that presumably yields particular communicative capacities.

Bates indicated that her findings in general supported local homology. This was evident within cognition and between cognition and communication. She found that object permanence and spatial relations were poor predictors of gestural and verbal development, but means-ends, imitation, and some aspects of play were good predictors of both language and gesture. In regard to play, combinational and symbolic play were good predictors.

Tomasello and Farrar (1984, p. 490) raised serious doubt about the viability of local homology even during the sensorimotor stage, because "language in the sensory-motor period has a special relationship to cognition." Needless to say, local or deep homology needs further study.

One point should be made regarding the methodology in Bates' (1979) study. The Uzgiris and Hunt (1975) scale, which was used to measure sensorimotor achievements, may have biased the results in favor of local homology. The subscales on this measure have relatively low intercorrelations. Thus, the cognitive inquiry dealt with some relatively independent domains. About the only way deep homology could be revealed is to have several language measures correlate highly with one sensorimotor skill. Causality and means-ends might be good candidates. It would be well worth the effort to attempt such a study using different dependent measures for the language complex.

Bates (1979) raised two principles of learning that would be predicted by deep or local homology, the replacement and expansion principles (Bates, 1979). The *replacement principle* is that later developments replace earlier developments. For example, early communicative points become replaced by words. The *expansion principle* is that repertoire expands so children can do new things in new ways while retaining previous capabilities. For example, children may both point and label a referent. The two well known principles (new forms come in with old functions, new functions come in with old forms; one word-many referents, one referent-many words) reflect the expanded repertoire principle. It is evident that both principles are working, but how might they index motivation or impelling forces for language learning? We do not know. Both replacement and expansion are compatible with the nativist and functionalist views.

> Language learning may be evidenced by replacement of one skill by another and/or by an expansion of the repertoire of skills.

The study of early non-nominal terms has opened the door for a new perspective on the relationship of sensorimotor skills to language learning. Gopnik and Meltzoff (1984, p. 495) did a fine-grained appraisal of the acquisition of specific sensorimotor skills and words that code such acquisitions. They said, "These results suggest that there are strong and specific links between the acquisition of particular types of meanings and particular cognitive achievements." Specifically, Gopnik and Meltzoff reported the following:

> The results suggest that children acquire the word *gone* after they solve simple invisible displacement tasks but before they solve serial invisible displacement tasks. They also show that children acquire success/failure words after they use insight to solve the problem of the string but before they use insight to solve more difficult means-ends problems. These sequences cannot be explained in terms of age, general cognitive development or general linguistic development. It is argued that *gone* encodes a concept related to the concepts that underlie success on invisible displacement tasks, and that success/failure words encode concepts related to the concepts that underlie the development of insight. Children seem to acquire words that encode concepts they have just developed or are in the process of developing. (1984, p. 495)

McCune-Nicolich (1981) has shown that relational terms appear when children are in the late sensorimotor period. This suggests that such terms reflect cognitive organization achieved at this time. Tomasello and Farrar (1984) did a follow-up study that corroborated the early study. The findings were that relational terms appear in close relationship to Stage 6 (Uzgiris & Hunt, 1975) of object permanence development. More specifically, Tomasello and Farrar (1984, p. 477) reported, "Relational words requiring the conceptualization of the visible displacement of objects should emerge during Stage 5, those involving invisible displacements during Stage 6, and those referring to more complex spatial displacements only later during the pre-operational period."

Based upon the research of McCune-Nicolich (1981), Gopnik and Meltzoff (1984) and Tomasello and Farrar (1984, p. 490) there is reason to believe that, as the latter said, "Language in the sensory-motor period has a special relationship to cognition." Thus, they contended that the homology model espoused by Bates (1979) is inappropriate:

In all, it is difficult to imagine a child who talks about absent objects and comments on their disappearance, but cannot look for them when they are hidden. Our position is that, because overt sensory-motor activity is the means by which the child's knowledge at this stage is constructed—one might even say the sensory-motor performance *is* the cognition—it is a more direct expression of that knowledge than expression by means of a symbol. The sensory-motor scheme is prior to its symbolization, both logically and psychologically. (Tomasello & Farrar, 1984, p. 490)

Viewing these developments in stages, Tomasello and Farrar conceded that the homology model may have some value *after* the sensorimotor period when the child is operating cognitively from a representational base and communicatively from a symbolic base:

At later stages of development, after the child has constructed a representational model of the world, it may well be that various means of expressing this underlying knowledge, motorically and linguistically for example, are perfectly homologous. At the sensory-motor stage, however, the difference between overt activities directed toward objects and the process of linguistic symbolization is crucial. (1984, p. 490)

Their position is reminiscent of Gleitman and Wanner's (1982, p. 31) comment, "It could be that there are a succession of learners each of whom organizes the linguistic data as befits his mental stage. This is a kind of metamorphosis, or tadpole-to-frog, hypothesis."

Cognitive Distancing

Cognitive distancing refers to the ability to be removed in time and space but still be actively engaged with referents. Needless to say, *symbolization* affords such capacities. This is not an either/or capacity. There are degrees of displacement, or cognitive distancing. The notion of cognitive displacement derives from Piaget (1952); and it has been studied by Sigel (1970, 1971) and Sigel and Cocking (1977). The later defined cognitive distancing or the capacity to "create temporal and/or spatial and/or psychological distance between self and object. '*Distancing*' is proposed as the concept to denote behaviors or events that separate the child cognitively from the immediate behavioral environment" (Sigel, 1970, pp. 111–112).

Moerk (1977) also dealt with cognitive distancing, but it was from a different perspective. He was concerned with the infant's shift from enactive processing (finger, touch, mouth, pat) to iconic processing (see and hear), and in this regard Moerk echoes Bruner's theory for the course of cognitive growth, specifically the shift from enactive to iconic to symbolic thinking:

A gradual process of "distancing" or increasing "symbolization" seems to be built into the play activities of the child and the objects he uses. This distancing progresses systematically until it attains the level of real language. It begins with the child's encounter with shapes, colors, and sounds ... explored as merely sensory impressions; then it advances to toys ... only one step removed from the real object ... ; it reaches a higher level in pictures ... already symbols for the real objects; and it attains the final degree of remoteness in stories, which represent real or even imaginary objects through the signs of language only. (Moerk, 1977, p. 50)

Children's ability to move in their environment affords them an interesting cognitive skill; they can convert spatially distal stimuli into proximal stimuli. In this way, they attain some degree of control over the amount of distal stimuli they may have to cope with in a particular circumstance. Presumably, as children become increasingly able to deal with cognitively distant referents, there is a reduced need to convert spatial stimuli.

Bruner (1964, p. 4) indicated that language is a means to become freed from the immediate environment. "Once language becomes a medium for translation of experience there is a progressive release from immediacy." Similarly, Dale (1972, p. 203) commented that language is a liberating force, freeing the mind from dependence on the immediate environment. Likewise, Piaget said that infants are initially fused to their environment but eventually become cognitively released from it.

In the applied arena, Muma (1978a, 1981a), Burger and Muma (1980), Marshall and Newcombe (1973), and Beckwith and Thompson (1976) have shown that cognitive distancing is a viable construct. Put simply, a word-oriented assessment or intervention activity may be too difficult; when the same activity is converted into pictorial form or better still to object form, it may be easy enough for someone to handle. Words draw upon representations; pictorials upon prototypic knowledge; objects allow for enactive processing. It should be noted, however, that play objects themselves may be representational.

Cognitive distancing constitutes a continuum of difficulty from object to picture to word.

The emergence of symbolic play comprises another dimension in the precursors of language. However, before discussing symbolic play, it is useful to consider the role of gestures in the dawning of symbolic behavior.

Gestures: Protosymbolic Behavior

Bates (1979) said that the "Gestural Complex" contains giving, showing, communicative pointing, and ritual requests, and that this complex was the most highly correlated to the language measures. She noted a particular exception, the noncommunicative point. Citing Werner and Kaplan (1963), she indicated that the noncommunicative point was an act of "pointing for self" in the acquisition of reference; it designates "objects of contemplation." Thus, gestures are useful in realizing communication and reference.

Evidently, gestural communication has an initial short-term priority over verbal communication, as if gestures provide an entry into more elaborate symbolic systems. Indeed, Benedict (1979) and Greenfield and Smith (1976) regarded early words as extended actions. Snow (1981) was impressed with the relative ease of learning communicative gestures. She said, "It is not clear why gestural communicative systems are so ubiquitous, so precocious, and so much easier to learn than spoken language" (p. 205). She stated further that communicative gestures for the young child pertains to the value of game playing in working out communicative capacities.

> Given the naturalness of action and gestures as means of communication for the young child, it becomes clearer how extensive experience with game playing could contribute to communicative development. Games and other social routines involve practicing precisely those skills that enable the child to communicate: (1) taking his turn in a social interaction, (2) following the rules for how his turn should be filled in, and (3) within the limits prescribed by the rules of the game, varying the exact content of the turn. One would expect, then, that extensive early experience with games and other social routines would contribute to the early communicative use of gestures, and subsequently, perhaps to the early use of words. (Snow, 1981, pp. 205-206)

In general, gestures develop first; these are *replaced* by verbalizations; and then both gestures and verbalizations may be used in combination. Carter (1978, p. 342) showed a developmental relationship of this sort over the first 2 years of life. Carter's scheme appears in Figure 6.1.

Gestures basically work as intended in social commerce. Eventually, words and combinations of words work as intended also. But, gestural capacities are not language.

> Functionally there is little difference between the child crying and pointing at an object—gestural use, and later saying the name of that object with a whining intonation while pointing at it—language use. What difference there is would seem to be enshrined in the concept of symbolism... I

116 *Language Acquisition*

Figure 6.1. Chronological developments in the attention to object (AO) schema gesture-vocalization relationship.

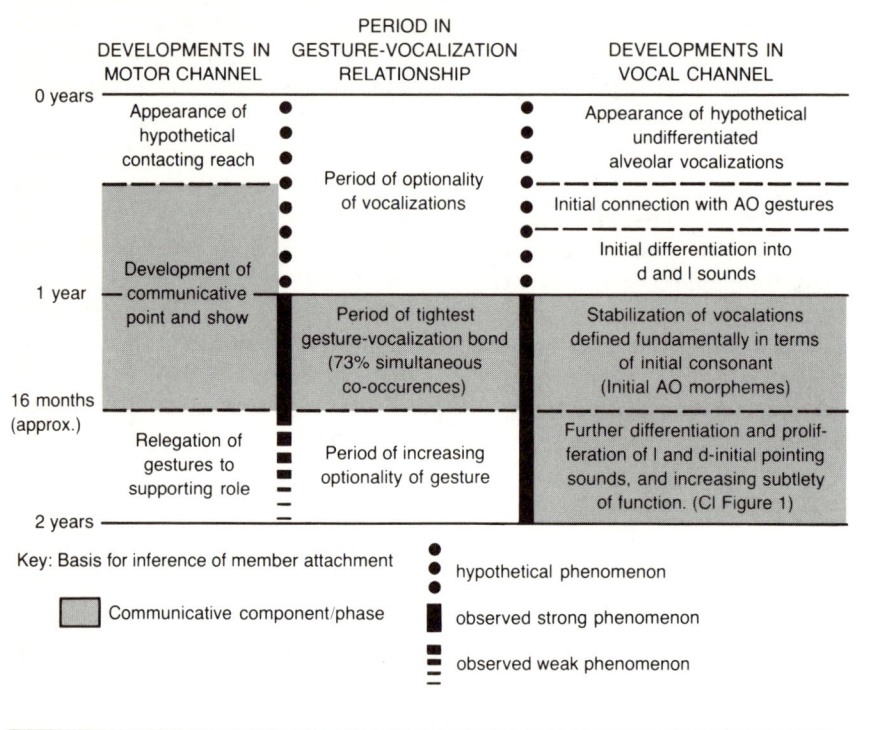

	DEVELOPMENTS IN MOTOR CHANNEL	PERIOD IN GESTURE-VOCALIZATION RELATIONSHIP	DEVELOPMENTS IN VOCAL CHANNEL
0 years	Appearance of hypothetical contacting reach	Period of optionality of vocalizations	Appearance of hypothetical undifferentiated alveolar vocalizations
			Initial connection with AO gestures
			Initial differentiation into d and l sounds
1 year	Development of communicative point and show		
		Period of tightest gesture-vocalization bond (73% simultaneous co-occurences)	Stabilization of vocalizations defined fundamentally in terms of initial consonant (Initial AO morphemes)
16 months (approx.)			
	Relegation of gestures to supporting role	Period of increasing optionality of gesture	Further differentiation and proliferation of l and d-initial pointing sounds, and increasing subtlety of function. (Cl Figure 1)
2 years			

Key: Basis for inference of member attachment
• hypothetical phenomenon
▮ observed strong phenomenon
▤ observed weak phenomenon
▢ Communicative component/phase

From *Action, gesture and symbol* (p. 342) by A. Lock, 1978, New York: Academic Press. Reprinted by permission.

would suggest that at this stage in his development the child has *mastered* the fundamentals of language: but I would not wish to go as far as saying he now *possesses* language. Whilst he can communicate his intentions in an unambiguous and structured manner, the messages he conveys are not objective in nature, nor are they propositional, and neither are they capable of being judged true or false. Language is still only implicit in his activities, and will remain so until he becomes able to name objects. (Lock, 1978, p. 8)

Onset of Symbolization

Symbolization is an extremely important skill for both cognition and communication. Symbolization provides a means of mental representation which, once achieved, greatly advances one's cognitive capacities (Piaget, 1954). Communicatively, symbolization opens the door of reference indexing and eventually convention and formalization. The primary accomplishment in early symbolization, from a communicative perspective, was succinctly stated by Bruner (1981, pp. 165–166), "The principle achievement during this active phase is that the child now becomes a giver of signals."

The stages of symbolic play extend over a considerable period of time, perhaps 2 or 3 years. What is the evidence of the onset of symbolic behavior? The first stage is symbolic play having to do with the recognition of appropriate use of objects. By virtue of prior contacts, the infant comes to know the functions of objects and "applies" this knowledge to them through appropriate actions. The young infant without previously represented or stored knowledge does not know the function of new objects so he will usually finger, touch, mouth, and pat the object until discovering its typical function. Thus, one way of approaching the onset of symbolization is the extent to which the child has begun to "package" (Bowerman, 1982) knowledge of objects, actions, and relationships in his world. Evidence of such knowledge is primarily through the emergence of symbolic play.

Another way of understanding the onset of symbolism is in what Bruner (1975a) called the "regulation of joint reference and attention," in what Bates (1979, p. 33) called two critical moments in the dawn of language. The first is the onset of communicative intentions via conventional means. The second is the emergence of symbolic behavior, in particular, labeling or indicative behavior. More is said about early communicative intentions below; at this juncture, it is necessary only to note early evidence of intention and symbolization. Such evidence is in the communicative point which appears at around 9 months of age.

Intention is evidenced much earlier. Six-month-old infants, for example, show intention as they reach or grab. Moreover, accompanying fussing or crying seems to be related to "the availability of the goal itself" (Bates, 1979, p. 35). However, communicative intention is evidenced about 9 months of age when the infant not only points to an intended referent, but breaks eye contact with the referent, then uses eye contact to address the other participant in the dialogue. Occasionally, the infant will accompany the communicative point with a protodemonstrative /um, um/. Thus, both the communicative point and the protodemonstrative are conventional ways of indicating an intention and its referent. Such behavior serves to regulate joint action and attention (Bruner, 1975a, 1981). Bates indicated that as children become assured that their listener does indeed attend to their communicative point, the accompanying visual check to be sure the other dialogue participant is attendant wanes. It is suggested below that such behaviors as these "intersubjectivity checks" are at the forefront of social contracts, felicity conditions, or cooperative principles. Indeed, a similar behavior appears in play episodes. At the end of a play episode, children frequently turn their eyes away from the task to other participants as if to say "See what I did." Eventually, these communicative points become streamlined, reduced to an incidental point or even a nod of the head in the general direction of the referent. A point will also be replaced by a word. Thereafter, a point and a word may be used jointly.

> Early regulation of joint reference and attention is achieved by a communicative point; additionally, intersubjectivity checks are at the forefront of the cooperative principle.

Bruner (1981) said that infants use their parents' "line-of-regard" to find a referent in space. That is, infants hear a vocative (attention marker) or a label with accompanying rising intonation. Infants are more attentive to rising intonation than falling intonation. The vocative or rising in tonation serves to regulate infants' attention and action. So, they stop what they are doing, turn to their mother, and fix on her eyes. They use her line of regard and point to direct their search for the intended referent. The mother, in turn, "reads" their line-of-regard to deduce if they found the referent. Upon finding it, they engage in a repetitive format of labeling, touching or holding the referent, and so on. But, what do infants do if they cannot find the referent or are uncertain of its identity? They look back to pick up the mother's line-of-regard again to resume their search. Mothers may make some adjustments such as taking infants to it or moving the referent closer to them. In this manner, the communicative point constitutes the beginning of communicative intention and symbolization.

The communicative point is a symbolic effort because infants are beginning to not use the referent itself as they do in some sensorimotor action. Now, they are using something in place of the referent, thereby entering the arena of symbolization. A point is not a symbol; it merely indexes a referent. A word, on the other hand, is a symbol. Before children label or indicate, they point or display a referent. Thus, the beginning of symbolization is a communicative point or referential display. In *referential display,* children hold up the intended referent as if to say, "See, this is what I'm talking about."

> A communicative point is early evidence of emergent symbolization.

Protopragmatics

What kinds of behaviors evidence the onset of pragmatic skills? Certainly, the communicative point, the referential display, and the intersubjectivity checks evidence early pragmatic skills. These are grounded in joint reference and attention in interaction.

Intersubjectivity checks pertain to the child's gradual awareness of felicity conditions in the realization of pragmatic skills. Austin (1962) posited that speech acts operate within the context of felicity conditions. Grice (1967) called these conditions the cooperative principle. In pragmatic cooperation, "Speakers try to be informative, truthful, relevant, and clear, and listeners interpret what they say on the assumption that they are trying to live up to these ideals. As Grice put it, speakers and listeners adhere to the *cooperative principle"* (Clark & Clark, 1977, p. 122). Young children are essentially naive about violations of the cooperative principle; they act as if cooperative principles are given but they seem to need some kind of check of assurance that their intended communicative efforts are perceived by someone else—the addressee. Consequently, these children will frequently check to be sure their addressee is attending to their words and actions, sometimes even interrupting their play to forcefully display a referent, tug on the arm of the addressee, whine, and use other behaviors aimed at restoring the communicative contract when they perceive that it is threatened. To be sure, such behaviors—intersubjectivity checks—are not about informativeness, truthfulness, relevance, and clarity per se, so they are only tangential to felicity conditions. However, to the extent that children perceive the need to "look up" at the addressee, deploy reference, and the like, they perceive a threat to the cooperative principle—not so much a substantive threat but a tactical threat to the realization of their intentions. This is what Wells called *intersubjectivity*.

> For the communication to be successful, therefore, it is necessary (a) that the receiver should come to attend to the situation as intended by the sender; (b) that the sender should know that the receiver is so doing; and (c) that the receiver should know that the sender knows that this is the case. (1981, p. 47)

Intersubjectivity checks are tactics young children use to ensure that the negotiable interaction between encoder and decoder is at least operable, even though they do not have the pragmatic wherewithal to fully play the communication game to negotiate messages-of-best-fit.

Even though Wells (1981) was discussing topic construction with attendant issues of the semantic interface between personal experience and the organization of meaning, his lucid statement is relevant to intersubjectivity checks, intersubjectivity, and early pragmatic activity. Wells (1981, p. 50) said, "Learning to manage this interface thus represents a major part of what is involved in language acquisition." Interface here refers to the relationship between intentions and their communicative realizations (vocally, gesturally) and the effects on the listener; this is also called "regulating joint action and attention" (Bruner, 1975a).

Schaffer (1979) maintained that the on-off nature of early sensorimotor behavior foreshadows turntaking in dialogue. Moreover, this on-off nature depicts the first stage in the acquisition of attention, with the second everlasting stage being discrepancy learning (Kagan, 1969, 1970, 1971; Kagan & Lewis, 1965; McCall & Kagan, 1967a, 1967b, 1969). Infants who are enthralled with repeated readings of their favorite story are operating from a *format* (Bruner, 1981), or prescribed set of expectations. Occasionally, they test these expectations. After several "readings," they have memorized the story but they still want it "read" so they can engage in various aspects of dialogue. Early on, their participation is in terms of smiling, reaching, pointing, and babbling, all of which essentially indicate referents. Eventually they substitute words or labels for these performative acts. Clearly, such behaviors allow infants to be socially engaged in the activity well before they learn language. Upon learning the words, they may tire of the story and go on to another. Infant story reading is a desirable language learning activity (Snow & Goldfield, 1983). Formats are antecedents of scripts in adult speech. They are discussed again somewhat later.

Even early on, children are using pragmatic devices to convey messages, albeit somewhat crudely. Retherford, Schwartz, and Chapman (1981) identified some early "conversational devices" of 1- and 2-year-old children. These are shown in Table 6.1.

Bruner (1981) has stressed that such devices provide a pragmatic scaffold for learning semantic-syntactic-phonological dimensions. These pragmatic devices make mothers strive to deduce their children's intentions and to use information about the ongoing event to discern meaning.

Humor and Symbolic Play

At the end of the sensorimotor stage, symbolic play and humor begin. Smiles to discrepancy, however, appear as early as 3 months of age (Kagan, 1971). Kopp (1979, p. 30) noted that infants enjoy motoric accomplishments. "Moreover, it is impressive to see the sheer delight children manifest by having at their disposal self-directed manipulation and locomotion; probably this, too, has ramifications for the development of other behaviors." Indeed, Kagan (1971) showed that smiles are important indices of information processing in both social and nonsocial domains. A thorough review of the literature on the ontogenesis of smiling and laughter appear in Bower (1977), Trevarthen (1979), and Sroufe and Waters (1976).

Horgan gave a succinct presentation of the initial interrelationships between symbolic play and humor:

> Towards the end of the sensorimotor period children begin symbolic play. According to Schultz (1976), humor and symbolic play are closely related in the beginning, but become more differentiated as the child develops. In symbolic play, a child reproduces a motor schema outside of its normal context. That is, a child begins to be able to pretend. Children at this age

Table 6.1. Examples of Seven Categories Coded as Conversational Devices in Mother and Child Speech

Category	Utterance	Context
Attention	Mother: *Abigail!*	M calling C who is climbing on couch.
	Child: *Mama!*	M dressing C while talking to another adult.
Affirmation	Mother: *Okay.*	C requests M assistance in putting puzzle together.
	Child: *Yeah.*	In response to M's offer of assistance.
Positive evaluation	Mother: *Right.*	C manipulating puzzle fits piece in correctly.
	Child: *Good.*	M places block on top of stack and C responds.
Interjection	Mother: *Oh.*	Following C's affirmative response to M question of activity of fishes.
	Child: *Um.*	C looking at M who has just queried C about doll's name.
Polite form	Mother: *Oh, thank you.*	C pouring M imaginary cup of coffee.
	Child: *Please mommie.*	M offers imaginary plate of cookies to C.
Repetition request	Mother: *What?*	C describing toy people's activities.
	Child: *Huh?*	M and C playing with toy farm: M asks question.
Accompaniment	Mother: *There you go.*	C attempting to wrap herself in blanket finally succeeds.
	Child: *There.*	C rearranging doll in bed.

From Semantic roles and residual grammatical categories in mother and child speech: Who tunes into whom? by K. Retherford, B. Schwartz, and R. Chapman, 1981, *Journal of Child Language, 8,* p. 592. Reprinted by permission.

pretend to be reading, sleeping, eating, putting on make-up, etc. Symbolic play can be viewed as self-constructed incongruity. Support for the relationship between symbolic play and humor comes from the fact that symbolic play is almost always accompanied by laughter: the child thinks it is funny to pretend to sleep, eat, put on make-up. McGhee (1979) describes what happens after the development of make-believe play. McGhee's stages are reflections of cognitive development and correspond to Piaget's descriptions of cognitive acquisitions. Stage 1 consists of incongruous actions towards objects, such as Piaget's child pretending a leaf was a telephone. Stage 2 consists of incongruous labelling of objects and events, such as calling a hand a foot. The absence of action towards the object characterizes the increase in cognitive ability. Stage 1 and 2 jokes are seen mostly during the pre-school years. Stage 3 may start around 3 years. This stage involves conceptual incongruity, which entails violating one or more aspects of a concept. McGhee describes examples of word play during this stage. Children's humor first approaches adult humor in Stage 4 with an appreciation of ambiguity. This begins around age 7 with attainment of concrete operations, and is the stage most systematically studied. Children now can understand riddles. (1981, p. 217)

In recent years, there has been a renewed interest in play as a means of acquiring cognitive, symbolic, and verbal capacities. Nicholich (1975, 1981) has defined and substantiated five stages in the emergence of symbolic play. In Stage 1, the children recognize the functions of objects in play (e.g., a horn is blown, a ball is rolled, thrown, etc.; a doll is hugged, kissed, etc.). In Stage 2, children demonstrate an ability to pretend action toward themselves. For example, children pretend to comb their hair, eat apples, dress, etc. Stage 3 has two parts, both of which are oriented to someone else. In one part, children address actions to other (i.e., sibling, peer, parent, and even a pet). These actions include pretending to feed, dress, or groom the addressee. In the other part, children may adopt a behavior of someone else (proto-imitation). For instance, children see someone dressing so they dress; or they hear someone sing so they sing, and so forth. Stage 4 has two parts also. One part is one action with several objects and the other part is one object with several actions. The former is evidenced when children pretend to feed several dolls the same "food." The latter is seen when the child pretends to feed one doll several different "foods." Stage 5 is the use of substitute objects as representations of actual objects. A stick could be a fork, a knife, a gun, and so forth. These stages are summarized as follows:

1. Recognition of function
2. Pretend actions toward self
3. Pretend oriented to others
    a. Actions toward self are now directed to others
    b. Actions of others are adopted by the child.

4. Multiple means-ends relations
   a. One action with several objects
   b. One object with several actions
5. Use of substitute objects

Bates (1979) attempted to replicate these stages; she found that Stages 4 and 5 should be reversed. However, Nicholich's data are equally impressive so it may be that the last two stages co-occur.

> Symbolic play emerges in stages: object recognition, autosymbolic awareness, address and inclusion of others, multiple actions, and substitute objects.

Dale, Cook and Goldstein (1981) devised a more detailed outline of stages in the emergence of symbolic play (see Table 6.2). This outline was derived from levels of symbolic play (Fenson, Kagan, Kearsley, & Zelazo, Nicholich, n.d., 1976; Piaget, 1951, 1962). Piaget's (1962) stages are as follows:

1. Pre-symbolic play: Child pretends at own routines (e.g., pretending to eat).
2. Stage 1 symbolic play: Child pretends at adult's routines (e.g., driving a car).
3. Stage 2 symbolic play: Child substitutes one item for another (e.g., child uses a block as a toy car).
4. Stage 3 symbolic play: Planned combinations (e.g., play consisting of sequences of actions resembling real scenes).

Dale, Cook, and Goldstein (1981) pointed out that Nicholich added two levels of play between Piaget's Stage 1 and 2, but they added that Nicholich's data did not fully support these seven levels, "In sum, only four levels of play can be distinguished: relational/single symbolic/sequential symbolic (no apparent planning or search)/planned symbolic sequences." Nicholich's (n.d.) seven stages follow:

1. Relational: Child puts cup on saucer.
2. Symbolic schema: Child pretends at own routines (Piaget's pre-symbolic).
3. Single symbolic games: Child pretends at adult routines (Piaget's Stage 1).
4. Single schema combinations: Child plays at only one action, but extends it to many objects (e.g., pretends to drink, then has doll drink).
5. Multi-schema combinations: Child plays at many actions with many objects, but without realistic sequencing (e.g., pretends to eat, then to drink, then to stir).
6. Planned single schema game: Involves some sort of search behavior, but only one action (some similarity to Piaget's Stage 2).

7. Planned multi-schema game: Tends toward realistic scene, some overall plan, search involved (Piaget's Stage 3).

Fenson, et al. (1976) suggested the following sequence for presymbolic play:
1. Pre-relational: Play with one toy at a time.
2. Nonappropriate relational: Child puts spoon to bottle.
3. Appropriate relational: Child puts cup on saucer.
4. Sequential relational: Child puts cup on saucer, then spoon in cup.
5. Symbolic acts: Child pretends to drink or makes the doll drink (Piaget's presymbolic plus Stage 1).
6. Sequential symbolic acts: Child pretends to stir, then to drink.

The results of the Dale, Cook and Goldstein (1981) study supported the stages outlined by Piaget and Nicolich (see Table 6.2).

As far as the relationship between the emergence of symbolic play and language is concerned, the findings are somewhat mixed, although generally the results show that the emergence of symbolic play and early language learning do not seem to be not closely tied. As Dale, Cook, and Goldstein (1981, p. 170) said, "It can only be concluded that early language development is not closely tied to symbolic play, and that it may or may not be related to other aspects of cognitive development."

As Terrell, Schwartz, Prelock, and Messick commented,

> Assessment of play has generally involved the observation of children's actions on replicas of real objects. This may not require the same type of symbol manipulation as that required in language. Play with objects that requires the use of double knowledge (e.g., using a coffee can as a truck) may be more related to the type of symbols involved in the expression of linguistic skills. (1984, p. 428)

In any case, a considerable amount of research on symbolic play and metalinguistic activities is anticipated in the near future. While the evidence is now only fragmentary (Lowe, 1975; Ungerer et al., 1981) and not very supportive, it appears to me—based upon clinical observation—that these two areas will eventually play an increasingly active role in cognitive intervention and language intervention. DeMaio (1984) has made a similar proposal.

A further note should be made about the viability of play as a means of learning. Kuczaj (1981, p. 131) showed that children from 3 to 6 years of age "more often responded correctly to future hypothetical questions than to past hypothetical questions and to hypothetical questions involving fantasy characters than to hypothetical questions involving the children's parents." Thus, it appears that they are more tuned to the potentialities of play. Bruner, Jolly, and Sylva (1976) made a similar observation in noting that play is child's work.

Table 6.2. A Coding System for the Emergence of Play

Initial Coding Level	Revised Coding Level
1. Pre-relational Play 　　One object at a time 　　Banging	Pre-relational
2. Relational Play 　　Giving object to mother 　　Nonfunctional relational 　　Functional relational 　　Grouping 　　Approximation to pretend play 　　Repeated relational actions 　　Sequential relational actions	Single relational Sequential relational
3. Symbolic Play 　　Known routines 　　　involving inanimate objects only 　　　self-directed 　　　directed to mother 　　　directed to doll 　　Repeated symbolic actions 　　Sequential symbolic actions 　　Planned symbolic actions	Single symbolic Sequential symbolic Planned symbolic
4. Symbolic Substitution 　　Known routines with some symbolic substitution 　　　involving inanimate objects only 　　　self-directed 　　　directed to mother 　　　directed to doll 　　Repeated actions involving symbolic substitutions 　　Sequential actions involving symbolic substitution 　　Planned actions involving symbolic substitutions	Single symbolic substitution Sequential symbolic Planned symbolic substitution

From *Child language: An international perspective* (p. 160) by P. Dale and D. Ingram (Eds.), 1981, Austin, TX: PRO-ED. Reprinted by permission.

Snow (1981) maintained that game play could contribute to communicative development because of the naturalness of action and gesture. But, Snow (1981, p. 207) said, "There is no experimental evidence that experience with game playing contributes to the acquisition of skill in turn-taking, slot filling, or the use of social words and expressions." She said that some evidence suggests such learning:

> Somewhat more direct evidence of the efficacy of game playing in teaching communication comes from scattered reports of infants who have learned specific communicative behaviors in the context of games, for example, signals to the mother to continue with the action in bouncing games (Bruner, 1975b), *please* and *thank you* in give-and-take games (Bruner, 1977), hiding one's face as a request to initiate peekaboo (Bruner & Sherwood, 1976; Ratner & Bruner, 1978), or hand-clapping as a request to initiate patty-cake (Snow, 1979). Clearly, in these individual cases, experience with specific games and routines led to specific learning, and created a situation in which the child was engaging in more complex or more precocious communication than he would have been capable of without the game playing experience. (Snow, 1981, p. 207)

In summary, the stages in symbolic play, game playing, and humor seem to be related in some way to the emergence of symbolization in language acquisition. Unfortunately, however, the relationships between symbolic play, game playing, and humor, on the one hand, and language acquisition, on the other, are not now well understood. Bates (1979) showed that play measures do correlate significantly with other aspects of cognitive development. Furthermore, she indicated that the strongest predictors of both gesture and language acquisition were the various play measures. Bates drew somewhat of a parallel between sequences in the emergence of symbolic play and early language acquisition:

	Symbolic Play		*Language Acquisition*
a.	Objects use is differentiated.	a.	An utterance is used as an appropriate part of a routine or format.
b.	The child pretends to do something outside of its usual context.	b.	An utterance is used in anticipation of a routine or format.
c.	The child pretends to do something that others do (i.e., role reversal).	c.	An utterance codes agent-action-object relations in part or whole.
d.	The child pretends with substitute objects.	d.	An utterance codes new information.

The essence of this parallel is the issue of decontextualization. In both symbolic play and early language acquisition, the child becomes progressively released from early circumscribed routines and formats. Bates (1979) indicated that with these structural parallels in early symbolic play and early language acquisition, it is likely that developments in language acquisition and symbolic play would be yoked in the second year of life.

Early Phonology

It takes several years for infants to acquire phonological systems and processes, which suggests a maturational function (Salus & Salus, 1974). Infants acquire increased control of the vocal mechanism in the first 6 months. "Cry and noncry vocalizations become stabilized during this period, and the sudden changes in pitch and amplitude . . . no longer occur" (Menyuk, 1974, p. 214). She stated further that infants are able to produce vocal stops and a variety of other consonantal functions as the result of babbling. Nakazima (1962) reported that infants of 8 or 9 months can imitate intonational patterns produced by their mothers but not words, syllables, or phonemes. During the babbling period, utterances increase in frequency and length, and their segmental and syllabic content changes. Referring to Nakazima, Menyuk (1974, p. 217) said, "At 9 months, however, there is a decrease in repetitive babbling and a reorganization of babbling . . . simpler sequences are produced and sounds are used as evocation and response to voice stimuli."

Kaplan and Kaplan (1970) and Turnure (1971) reported that at 2 to 4 months infants respond differentially to angry and friendly, familiar and unfamiliar, and male and female voices. Crowder (1972) said that such infants can only analyze and store auditory aspects concerning pitch, voice quality, location and loudness. Morse (1974), Eimas, Sigueland, Jusczyk, and Vigorito (1971), and Eisenberg (1970) reported that young infants are unusually responsive to phonemic sound patterns. They suggested that a speech receptor mechanism is activated as early as 4 months and possibly even 1 month. Reviewing this literature, Morse (see also Eisenberg, 1970) contended that early speech perception is not merely discrimination but categorization; moreover, the perceptual context is essential for categorization:

> Depending upon context the *same* acoustic cue will be perceived as different and *different* acoustic events will be perceived the same. This invariance problem is the basis of the whole issue of complex linguistic perception. It makes speech special and apparently requires the postulation of some specific decoder. (1974, p. 42)

Ingram (1984) raised a new issue concerning early speech perception, suggesting that at first the perceptual system is wide open but as children become increasingly familiar with the sound system of their language, their perceptual system narrows down and becomes somewhat debased. Under this process, children become increasingly tolerant of phonemic variation. Ingram contended that by 1 year of age children have become sufficiently familiar with the sound patterns of their language so this perceptual narrowing is clearly evident.

> It is possible that infant perception is wide open at first; then, with experience, it narrows down.

Ferguson (1978) identified an early speech-like unintelligible behavior that he called *vocables*. Vocables clearly have intention and meaning. Moreover, vocables are addressed to others under the assumption that others will understand. Dore (1975) made a similar observation regarding phonetically consistent forms (PCF) (see also Bruner, 1981). Infants reliably produce labels that are distinctive, yet these labels do not conform to known words of a language. This is a blatant instance of an attempt to use language in an unconventional way. Needless to say, such efforts are loaded with problems. Children would do well to avoid such problems by trying to acquire the phonological system of their language, thereby converting vocables or PCFs into the coin-of-the-realm for efficient social commerce. These are only preliminary comments about early phonology. A fuller discussion appears in Chapter 8.

> Vocables and PCF are blatant instances of attempts to use language in an unconventional way.

Summary

In summary, sensorimotor achievements occur roughly during the first 18 months of age and comprise important cognitive underpinnings for language learning. The specific relationship of these achievements to language learning is unclear. An overriding capability achieved by these skills is a release from direct stimulation and an increasing reliance of representation. Representational skills are at the heart of symbolization.

Infants begin to acquire symbolization and protopragmatic skills during the first year. These provide a foundation or scaffold for the acquisition of semantic-syntactic-phonological capacities. The communicative point, a referential display, and intersubjectivity checks comprise evidence of protopragmatic skills. The emergence of symbolic play is another significant skill that begins in the first year and extends over 2 or 3 years but its relationship to language acquisition is somewhat unclear.

7

CONVENTIONALIZATION: INDICATIVE

Bruner (1975a, p. 2) commented that "language is a specialized and conventionalized extension of co-operative action." Early cooperative actions are the communicative point, the communicative display, reaching and grabbing, and other performatives in the gestural complex. These may be "commissioned" or authorized by such things as "intersubjectivity checks." The gestural complex itself can evolve into conventionalized gestures such as those for 'bye-bye,' 'yes and no,' 'I don't know,' etc. In the conventionalization process, the child adopts customary means of indexing messsages. Early on, conventionalization is about gestures and word acquisition. Subsequently, conventionalization elaborates into *formal* grammatical mechanisms—syntax and phonology. This chapter deals with categories as they become conventionally realized as words—word acquisition and utilized as indicatives or labels.

Identification, Predication, Attribution

Greenfield and Smith (1976) and Olson (1970) credited Werner and Kaplan (1963) with formulating a general developmental sequence for grammatical capacities originating in the one-word stage. The sequence defines three major landmarks in the acquisition of conventional grammatical mechanisms. First is identification, then predication, and finally attribution. These are defined as follows:

Identification: joint reference via communicative points and performatives followed by naming or labelling objects.

Predication: prosodic envelopes for base constructions such as subject-verb-object (SVO) constructions with attendant predicate/argument propositions.

Attribution: qualification of predication; complement, particle, and adverbial modifications of predicates and determiner and adjectival modifications of arguments.

This model, proposed by Werner and Kaplan (1963), has empirical support from Greenfield and Smith (1976).

The three basic grammatical landmarks are identification, predication, and attribution.

The *identification stage* is intimately tied to the following: emergence of attention (Kagan & Lewis, 1965; Lewis & Goldberg, 1969; McCall & Kagan, 1967a, 1967b, 1969) especially discrepancy learning; concept formation (Flavell, 1977) in regard to natural prototypical categories evidenced as focal/peripheral exemplars (Rosch & Mervis, 1975; Anglin, 1977); differentiation and reorganization (Saltz, Soller & Sigel, 1972; Witkin et al., 1962); distinctive features (Gibson, 1969); learned equivalence and learned distinctiveness (Werner & Kaplan, 1963); alternative strategies (Bruner, Goodnow & Austin, 1956); and the determination of salience (Nelson, 1974; Werner & Kaplan, 1963) such as the allative bias (Wales, 1979), perceptual salience (Odom & Corbin, 1973; Odom & Guzman, 1972), and dynamic attributes (Nelson, 1973a, 1974). This stage comprises one of the two great intentions according to Bruner (1981). It is the *indicative* intention which is the designation of a referent by virtue of naming or labeling it.

Early in language acquisition, the *predication stage* deals with predicating both the basic intentions, indicative and requests (Bruner, 1981). The predication of *indicatives* yields a declarative message; these are assertions. Thus, indicatives have an acquisition sequence: communicative point, vocal performative, phonetically constant form (PCF) or vocable, conventional label, base assertion, and then modified assertion. These are discussed below. At this point, however, it should be pointed out that the base assertion may be only a skeletal prosodic envelope in which morphemes may, or may not, be inserted to realize the full base (Bruner, 1975a). Furthermore, it should be understood that the progressive realization of base constructions in English has a sequence: protolocatives, intransitives (SV), transitives (SVO), and states (Greenfield & Smith, 1976). And, even these syntactic mechanisms are foreshadowed by presyntactic devices (Dore et al., 1976).

The predication of requests yields *yes/no* questions, *why* questions, requests for action, and negation. Again, the acquisition sequence is the same as that for indicative. This suggests that the propositional or content dimension of a message has an acquisition process somewhat, but not fully, independent of its intention.

Predication has two functional components, the predicate component and the argument component. The *predicate component* is the verb with its auxiliary. The *argument component* is composed of the attendant nominal functions to realize particular predications. Some verbal and nominal component functions are illustrated as follows:

Argument	Predicate	Argument	Argument
He	ran		
He	opened	the door	
He	hit	the ball	with the bat

Thus, it is evident that verbs can be categorized as one, two, three and possibly even four argument verbs (Perfetti, 1972). Indeed, the acquisition sequence of predicates reported by Greenfield and Smith (1976) gives explanatory support for characterizing verbs in this way. Moreover, the differential acquisition of inflections (Bloom, Lifter, & Hafitz, 1980) gives further credence to this characterization.

> **Predication can be characterized in terms of one, two or three arguments.**

As for a common base underlying assertions and requests, there appears to be a strategy, of sorts, whereby children first try to lay down the base construction subject-verb-object (SVO) for realizing assertions and requests, but they are constrained by processing capacity. The prosodic envelope affords entry into such constructions even though children may not be able to lexicalize it fully. It would seem, then, that the strategy is to turn to the prosodic envelope as a temporary means of dealing with partial realizations of formal constructions. This sets the stage for a discussion of base structure (SVO), the prosodic envelope, and a related theory called "The Three Bears," all of which are related to early predication. These are the topics of Chapter 8.

In the *attribution stage,* predication and its arguments are qualified. Predication can be qualified by verb complements, particles, and adverbials. Arguments are nominals required by predicates. They are qualified by a variety of adjectivals, usually adjectives and relative clauses.

In the advanced stage of attribution, children learn several complex mechanisms. That is, the basic nominal structures are such things as:

Proper Noun: *Bill, Ann, . . .*
Personal Pronoun: *he, she, . . .*

Indefinite Pronoun: *someone, nobody,* . . .
Determiner plus Noun:
  Indefinite article   *A boy*
  Definite article   *The boy*
  Possessive   *My boy*
  Demonstrative   *That boy*
  Cardinal number   *One boy*
  Ordinal number   *First boy*

The use of such structures enables children to be relatively successful in social commerce. However, they will eventually learn many other complex nominals (Lees, 1965) and complementations (Rosenbaum, 1967). Following are some complex nominals that are usually acquired after 4 years of age:

To V: *To run is silly.*
Ving: *Running is silly.*
That + s: *That he runs is silly.*
For/to: *For him to run is silly.*

The progression from identification or indicative to predication or relational construction to attribution or modification provides children *increased explicitness* in realizing intended propositions. It is not that they should become more explicit to be more effective in social commerce, but various degrees of explicitness provide more options. It is the increased *options* that allow children to become more adept in realizing *informativeness* for social commerce. Adeptness (fully skilled in the use of language) is the topic of Chapter 11. First things first, this chapter deals with the first stage in the sequence, identification, indicative, or labeling.

Explicitness provides more options; increased options allows for increased adeptness in social commerce.

Categorization

Rescorla (1981) suggested that young children and infants have a working grasp of cognitive categories, or as Bruner (1981, p. 157) put it, "a working knowledge of the world." Rescorla said,

> It is also clear that young children have a working grasp of categorical relations and a wide knowledge of basic categories . . . Even the toddler

who is learning single words appears to have some rudimentary grasp of basic categories, some perception of kinship or similarity between different members of a common category. (1981, p. 225)

Bornstein (1979, p. 74) suggested that categorization has "its roots in infant sensation and perception... these earliest categorizations are nonarbitrary, and... they serve several variegated functions."

Bower (1977, p. 1) defined perception as "any process by which we gain immediate awareness of what is happening outside ourselves." This means that not only auditory and visual processes provide perception but also actions. Bower outlined four dimensions in perceptual development: growth, stimulation, habituation, and organization. *Growth* refers to maturational factors that provide a functioning nervous system with increased capacities. *Stimulation* refers to experience and environmental input. *Habituation* refers to a psychological state whereby "known" information is, in a sense, held in abeyance so that "unknown or discrepant" information can be acted on via perception. *Organization* refers to the manner in which information is placed in memory.

Perception is any process of immediate awareness of our world.

Categorization of the world provides a cognitive substrata for language acquisition. Several citations concerning categorization as a cognitive base of language acquisition were given previously; they are reiterated here.

Categorization provides a cognitive substrata for language acquisition.

"Categorization of sound patterns and of objects and events in the real world is basic to learning a language" (Nelson, 1973a, p. 21). "The abstractness underlying meanings in general... may best be understood by considering concept-formation the primary cognitive process, and naming (as well as acquiring a name) the secondary cognitive process" (Lenneberg, 1967, pp. 332–333). When Brown (1956, p. 247) defined first language learning as "a process of cognitive socialization," he also implicated categorization as a primary issue, maintaining that language learning involves "the coordination of speech categories with categories of the nonlinguistic world" (p. 247). And finally, Bowerman (1976, pp. 105–106) said that categorization is a central issue in cognition:

> According to Bruner, Goodnow and Austin, for example, "virtually all cognitive activity involves and is dependent on the process of categorizing" (1956, p. 246). The grouping of discriminably different stimuli into categories on the basis of shared features is an adaptive way of dealing with what would otherwise be an overwhelming array of unique experiences. As

Tyler puts it, "... life in a world where nothing was the same would be intolerable. It is through... classification that the whole rich world of infinite variability shrinks to manipulable size." (1969, p. 7)

Given this consensus on the importance of categorization, it is necessary to consider different theoretical perspectives of categorization and then to relate these to word learning and language acquisition.

The process of cognitive socialization entails shared categories.

Schlesinger (1977) pointed out that a working knowledge of the world should be distinguished from categorization in language. While it is tempting to presume that working knowledge of the world is essentially the same as categorization in language, this is unlikely. Schlesinger discussed the differences as the *interpretation problem* and the *categorization problem*:

> To function effectively, the child must attain certain cognitive skills which enable him to interpret what is going on in his environment. This interpretation problem can be solved without the aid of language; in fact its solution is itself a prerequisite for learning language. But language learning depends in addition on a categorization of objects and events, which is needed solely for the purpose of speaking and understanding speech. It will be argued below that the categorization problem cannot be dealt with independently of language: its solution is part and parcel of the language learning process. (1977, p. 155)

Furthermore, he cited Edwards (1973) in claiming that language concepts are almost invariably much more inclusive than the concepts of knowledge of the world. Then, Schlesinger held that the primary way in which categorization for language is achieved is by linguistic input. "The linguistic input, then, imposes order on the many unique occurrences of objects, events and relations" (Schlesinger, 1977, p. 159). In referring to two semantic distinctions for possessiveness, Schlesinger (1977, p. 160) commented, "There is nothing in nature or in the structure of the human mind which decrees that these two belong together; in fact there are languages which distinguish between the two. It is the linguistic input which shows the child whether or not to collapse these cognitively distinguishable relations into one." He held that interacting in the environment and observing others interacting in the environment provides information for constructing theory of the world (Palermo, 1982) or working knowledge of the world. As children attain linguistic categories, language facilitates learning about the world and conversely.

Above it was proposed that the function of linguistic input is to deal with the categorization problem: after he has constructed a map of the world through his extralinguistic experience, the child utilizes linguistic input to draw in the borders between adjoining categories. Now we suggest that linguistic input may also be responsible for constructing certain parts of the map itself. (Schlesinger, 1977, p. 161)

However, a repertoire of skills is needed for such reciprocal benefits. That is, the child apparently cannot do both from the beginning.

A modicum of cognitive development must precede any learning of language, because language remains meaningless unless referring to some already interpreted aspect of the environment. However, once some structuring of the environment has occurred and some primitive utterances can be understood in accordance with this structure, there is room for an influence of the form of these utterances on the child's cognitive development: they may direct him towards further interpreting events and states referred to. (Schlesinger, 1977, p. 166)

First, it is important to realize that the Piagetian sensorimotor skills such as object permanence do not in themselves constitute a theory of categorization. The Piagetian skills are a means for categorizing, but they are not categories themselves. Second, there are contrasting theories of categorization. Third, theory of the world (Palermo, 1982) via categorizations is not directly related to perceptions, even though categorizations govern what can be perceived (Garner, 1966). These are indirect relationships. Fourth, the relationship between underlying categories of the world and the words used are very complex. Fifth, and most importantly, the four big issues in language acquisition (see Chapter 2) center on different notions of categorization. Cognitive categories comprise the substrata for semantic categories, which in turn comprise the substrata for grammatical categories. All of these categories operate within pragmatic activity.

Given these complexities, it is nevertheless useful to attempt to define the state of the art in understanding *cognitive* categorization and its possible relationships to word learning. Gibson (1969) proposed a distinctive feature theory of concept acquisition. Maccoby and Bee (1965) made a similar proposal. They held that categorization is based upon a set of features that become organized into categories, and these features may become reorganized. Initial categories are *idiosyncratic;* they are limited to only one person's perspective. Moreover, there is reason to believe that the initial concepts are holistic rather than decomposable (Carey, 1982). As a concept takes on more features (or attributes), it is thought to increase in *status;* as the feature structure or organizaton conforms with that of others, it is thought to increase in *validity;* with increased status and validity, concepts become increasingly *accessible* for use (Flavell, 1970; Mussen, Conger & Kagan, 1969, pp. 429–430).

Saltz, Soller, and Sigel (1972) and Saltz (1971) argued differently, asserting that cognitive categorization is a process of progressive differentiation and subsequent reorganization. Witkin et al. (1962) also contended that cognitive categorization is achieved by differentiation.

Vygotsky (1962) said that there is a bidirectional relationship between concepts and labels in acquisition. If so, both a distinctive feature theory and a differentiation theory may have credence. In *spontaneous learning,* children spontaneously deduce features or attributes of concepts; the label serves to consolidate spontaneously deduced features. For example, the child's interactions with his or her dog may lead to an understanding of 'dog' according to certain attributes. Then, the word *dog* may serve to consolidate the child's previous knowledge about dogs. Spontaneous concepts are "saturated with experience from the very beginning" (Cazden, 1972, p. 230). In *scientific learning,* the child is given the label and then goes about hypothesis testing to discover alternative meanings for it. Bruner (1981) regarded this word assignment as the "initial dubbing ceremony," which itself may be flawed (Kripke, 1972) because of its reliance on the original informant, who is necessarily forced to make certain presumptions of the child's capacities that will eventually need to be augmented. "Spontaneous concepts and scientific concepts thus develop in different directions, the former 'upward' from concrete experience and the latter 'downward' from a verbal definition" (Cazden, 1972, p. 230).

Spontaneous concepts are consolidated by labels whereas "scientific" concepts are launched by labels.

As noted above, it is difficult to know what a word means either in terms of perceiving an actual referent or in terms of how it may fit into presuppositional structure. As Lyons (1968, p. 426), Nelson (1973a, 1974) and Bowerman (1976, p. 114) suggested, the actual psychological meaning for a word is unknown to an observer.

Nelson (1974) outlined three levels in the concept formation process: concepts, instances, and attributes. The process proceeds from whole to part. From a single instance, children can *synthesize a concept.* Over many and varied experiences they *perceive new instances* of the concept. Upon identifying these, they deduce attributes to establish a *functional core* or *prototypic concept* with hierarchically arranged focal, peripheral, or optional attributes. A prototype is very powerful because it allows children to deal with innumerable exemplars, whereas a specific set of exemplars is too restricted to deal with discrepancies. *Concept generation* pertains to the first level. *Concept identification* pertains to the second and third levels. Attaching a name to something experienced is a matter of knowing the label for a prototype and recognizing instances of it.

The actual meaning of a word is unknown to an observer.

Nelson held that the function of concepts is to produce fewer wholes from the complexity of available experience. *Concepts* are cognitive organizations of information about objects and events encountered in the world. Notice that concepts are internal and psychological in nature. The child's concepts are essentially beyond the parent's, teacher's, or clinician's abilities to perceive and deduce; they may only be inferred. Indeed, only one of the three levels (instances) of concept formation outlined by Nelson can be perceptually witnessed by someone else. Even then, it is witnessed as a perceptual whole; there is no way other than inference to suppose what is *salient* to the child in concept learning. The issue of salience is a complex one that was discussed in "The Other Side of the Moon" section of Chapter 5. Parenthetically, *salience* may be an issue in word learning or lexical selection (Braine, 1974), but this should be distinguished from the encoder-decoder notion of *informativeness* in message formulation (Greenfield, 1980; Pea, 1979).

In the early 1970s, a new proposal was made for understanding cognitive categorization. Heider (1971), Rosch (1973a, 1973b) and Anglin (1977) suggested that natural categories are organized in terms of prototypes. Evidence of the prototypes is based upon how the child utilizes focal/peripheral exemplars. Focal exemplars are conceptually central to a concept; they are clear examples of a concept. For example, an apple is a focal exemplar for the concept 'fruitness.' On the other hand, peripheral exemplars are on the periphery of a concept; they are possible but questionable exemplars. Thus, a nut is a peripheral exemplar of 'fruitness.' The importance of these distinctions is that focal exemplars may be used to define prototypic knowledge of a concept whereas peripheral exemplars provide evidence that a concept extends to the periphery. Thus, these distinctions provide a means of ascertaining whether a child has prototypic and extended knowledge of a concept. The children who have a reliable pattern of grouping focal exemplars evidence prototypic knowledge; if they also include peripheral exemplars, they evidence extended knowledge.

Focal exemplars provide evidence of prototypic knowledge and peripheral exemplars give evidence of extended knowledge.

There is something intrinsic about *action* that begets categorization. Piaget (1952) held that early schema or concept development are derived from actions. The theory of attention cast in the form of discrepancy learning owes much to action-based learning which provides information about dynamic changes in a referent. In infancy, such changes are the products of the child's own actions. Young children simply attend to and talk about things that change or vary but they are remarkably oblivious of things that remain constant. "Children in the early stages of talking do often comment on changes in the state of objects (e.g., 'open,' 'hurt,' 'broken,' 'all gone') but not on their invariant attributes" (Nelson, 1974, p. 281). Greenfield and Smith (1976) indicated that early words were extended actions. As Bowerman pointed out:

> Studies of children's first words have revealed that children tend to ignore names for items that are "just there" and do not do anything, like furniture,

trees, and rooms, in favor of names for objects that act or which they can act on, like pets and other animals, cars, shoes, foods, and toys (Nelson, 1973b, 1974; Anglin, 1975). For example, Huttenlocher (1974) discusses a boy who, despite his emerging ability to understand other words, apparently did not learn the referents of 'kitchen' and 'refrigerator' even after extensive and persistent maternal modeling and demonstration. It seems, then, that children's attention is drawn to objects with potentials for acting or being acted on, and they will tend to learn names for such objects earlier than names for more static objects. (1976, pp. 126–127)

> **Inasmuch as early concepts are action based, the children attend to and talk about things that change. And, the primary source of change is their own actions.**

Three relatively independent areas of study in cognition seem to be intimately related to action as an early means of categorization: discrepancy learning, animateness, and the allative bias. Indeed, the latter two may be why "agent" emerges early as a primary semantic relation (Bloom, 1970, 1973; Bowerman, 1973; Brown, 1973b; Greenfield & Smith, 1976; Schlesinger, 1971).

Discrepancy learning has been mentioned above, so it is only necessary to point out that children attend to known things. Moreover, the variations that are most potent in this regard are slight changes or discrepancies of known things. In infancy, discrepancy learning appears to be closely tied to actions. That is, as infants finger, touch, mouth, or in various ways manipulate objects (including self and others), they generate discrepancies that provide information to them. Moreover, as they move through their environment, they create visual discrepancies. In this way, the children's actions on objects and environment provide a means of cognitive categorization.

> **Children's actions on objects provide them with slight variations of information from which they learn about these objects.**

Through their own actions on objects, they come to learn about animate and inanimate objects and about movable and nonmovable objects. *Animate objects* are those that can initiate and respond to actions toward them. If these initiated or response behaviors are sufficiently close in nature to the child's, they have a potential of becoming socialized. Reciprocal events, such as imitation, between two animate participants constitute such a social nucleus. Schaffer (1979) pointed out that the on-off nature of early sensorimotor activities constitutes social nuclei for turntaking.

The *allative bias* (Wales, 1979, p. 260) is "that which moves has direction towards." This means that the child tends to do things with or toward things that move or are capable of movement. This is a somewhat different categorization than animate/inanimate. A ball, for example, is not animate but it is movable. The child is inclined to act towards the ball, particularly when it moves, but not towards a wall.

Freeman, Sinha, and Stedmon (1981) studied whether this bias is either attributable to or modulated by a natural response tendency, presence or absence of cues for directionality of movement, and task naturalness. Three-year-olds acted according to requests to move one object *to* or *from* another and they were to identify the source, path, and goal of these actions. These researchers found that "to" actions were easier than "from" actions. As they put it, "The main finding was a stubborn bias in favor of allative over ablative responding" (p. 292). These children encoded *path* contours but they were bad at inferring *source* from *path*. Yet, they could infer *goal* from *path*. And, when both *source* and *path* were contextually cued, the allative bias was not evidenced.

The onset of word learning, then, seems to be related to prior categorizations of the world. Gopnik and Meltzoff (1984, p. 495) attributed word acquisition to recently learned concepts or concepts in the process of acquisition. "Children seem to acquire words that encode concepts they have just developed or are in the process of developing. These results suggest that there are strong and specific links between the acquisition of particular types of meanings and particular cognitive achievements."

Word Functions: Two Main Views

Evidently words, even early words, function in two main ways: cognitively or communicatively. Research by Gopnik (1981), Gopnik and Meltzoff (1984), Golinkoff (1981), McCune-Nicolich (1981), and others on early relational or non-nominal words suggests that such words may assist in problem solving and in deducing relationships. Communicatively, early words, particularly nominal expressions, seem to designate reference as a means of regulating joint attention.

Words or labels can facilitate the acquisition of cognitive categories. Brown (1956, p. 278) indicated that a word is a "lure to cognition." Gagne and Smith (1962, p. 378) made a similar comment, "It would appear that requiring verbalization somehow 'forced the Ss to think'." This is known as a *mediation* process. Everyone can probably recollect experiencing new insights or a clearer grasp of something when they have talked about it. Clinicians frequently say, "I learned more in clinic (or on the job) than I did in the classroom." Part of the reason for this is that one brings to the clinic (or job) various constructs that become operational (often by verbalization). The act of converting theoretical issues into applied issues often entails some form of mediation.

> **Words are lures to cognition.**

Returning to words and labels as facilitators, Cazden (1972, p. 229) suggested that a word draws attention to another instance of a concept (see also Nelson, 1974). Apparently, Dollard and Miller's (1950) notions of learned equivalence and learned distinctiveness underlie the later speculations of the uses of words in cognition. *Learned equivalence* is when a word denotes similarity for referents that have been regarded as dissimilar. For example, the word *glass* could denote that a tall brown ice-tea glass is similar to a small clear juice glass. *Learned distinctiveness,* on the other hand, is when a word denotes differences between two referents that may otherwise be regarded as similar. For example, the word *my* in the utterance "my glass" could distinguish a particular glass from other similar glasses.

Regarding early word learning, Gopnik showed that the early non-nominal words serve cognitive functions.

> Many early words encode aspects of plans, that is, actions performed in order to bring about events. *Gone* and *down* encode the fact that an action is intended to bring about a certain type of event. *There* and *oh dear* encode the success or failure of plans, *no* encodes the rejection of a plan. *More* encodes the repetition of a plan. It is argued that the concepts encoded by *gone* and *down* are like the concepts that underlie trial-and-error problem-solving and are developed after 12 months. The more abstract concepts encoded by *there, oh dear, no* and *more* are associated with the development of insight after 18 months. These early words are acquired because they are relevant to the child's cognitive problems. (1982, p. 303)

Such words are inherently cognitive as opposed to grammatical. Yet, other early words, although not strictly grammatical, comprise the nucleus for grammatical learning. These are labels of entities that will eventually become realized as particular semantic categories—the relational notions of agent and object. These are words that serve a communicative function as contrasted to a cognitive function.

Other issues pertaining to semantic categories are animateness, the allative bias, and what might be called an "ego bias." As Schlesinger (1974) pointed out, "At first it is only the child himself which functions as agent" (p. 138). However, agent—as ego—need not be expressed; it can be implicated by context. The ego bias (referring to self) appears in the discussion of deictic reference in Chapter 8. Figure 7.1 gives Schlesinger's model for semantic categories, in particular agent, action, and object. He proposed that these basic semantic categories are interrelated in acquisition. He said,

> There is a progressive extension of the agent concept. At first it is only the child himself which functions as agent. Then other animate beings can be

agents, and at last actions are ascribed also to inanimate agents. As mentioned, the agent is at first only given in the situation and left verbally unexpressed. When the agent is first expressed, it is typically animate. As for the action concept, demands are expressed before other actions (referred to by "acts" in the table). However, there seems to be no comparable development of the object concept, since inanimate objects seem to appear very shortly after animate objects in the earliest stages of one-word speech.

The gradual widening of the child's concepts may be graphically represented by means of concentric half-circles. The child moves from the center of the circle outward, and just as each larger half-circle includes each smaller one, so each stage of conceptual development adds to the preceding one and includes it. For instance, at the time the child talks about inanimate agents, he can also talk about animate ones. (Schlesinger, 1974, pp. 138–139)

Figure 7.1. Schematic representation of the development of agent, action and object concepts.

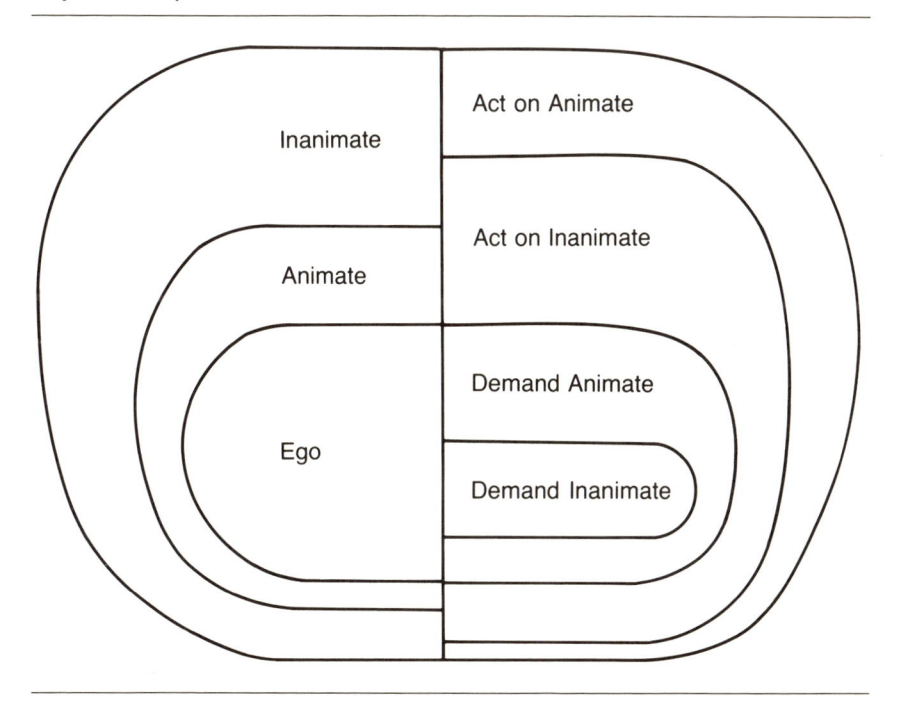

From *Language perspectives: Acquisition, retardation, and intervention* (p. 140) by R. Schiefelbusch and L. Lloyd, 1974, Austin, TX: PRO-ED. Reprinted by permission.

These and other early cognitive achievements provide the child with:

considerable knowledge about basic categories by the time they are 2 years old. While it can be assumed . . . that toddlers do not yet have an understanding of the structural properties of hierarchical systems, they seem to have a working grasp of categorical relations . . . Thus, this research supports the notion that as children progress through the single-word period their mastery of basic categories becomes more highly differentiated and more internally structured, while their verbal labels become more circumscribed in application with increases in vocabulary. (Rescorla, 1981, p. 237)

Word Learning: The First Word?

Greenfield and Smith (1976, p. 52) credited Werner and Kaplan (1963) for viewing *naming* "as the fundamental cognitive activity that makes possible all later types of linguistic predication." Early word learning demarks an early conventional dimension of language acquisition. It means that the child has opted to label objects, actions, and relationships the way that others do. Such shared labels are the building blocks of verbal convention.

Mutual labels are the building blocks of verbal convention.

The literature of word learning has some special problems. That is, what is the evidence of word learning? What are the relations between underlying categories and word acquisition? When is the first word learned? Even though it is commonly thought that the first word appears at about 12 months of age, no one really knows. It is very difficult to know when the first word is learned for several reasons. "We do not know in fact when the child ceases to babble and produces 'real' language" (Menyuk, 1969, p. 29). First, it is conceivable that the child comprehends at least in some rudimentary way certain words well before producing them. As a crude yardstick, Ingram (1984) suggested that production may lag behind comprehension by about 3 months in early learning. Second, what criteria need to be used to credit the child for producing the first word? This is a very difficult problem. Just because the child produces a word is itself insufficient evidence. Early words are context bound and some are strongly coached, for example, *mommy, daddy.* Even so, does the child know that "mommy" is a particular female? Is the word productive in the sense of being context free and free to enter into new word combinations? Has the word been evidenced many times spontaneously so the child can be credited with a productive pattern of use? Is the word relatively free from over- or underextensions? Needless to say, when the child first says "mommy" or "daddy" there are many questions as to whether he or she has said the first word; but, there is no doubt that it deserves a commencement ceremony with parental accolades, for surely someone is entering a social career richly vested in symbolization and convention.

It is virtually impossible to know when the first word appears.

Word Learning: Overextension

An *overextension* is a word in which its meaning extends beyond the normal adult use. The child points to a cow but calls it "doggy" shows an overextension. An *underextension* is a word in which its meaning is too narrow compared to normal adult use. The child who does not allow someone to call a new dog "Doggy" because his dog is called "Doggy" shows an underextension. Bloom (1973) used the terms over- and underinclusion to indicate that such problems may not be with the words per se, rather, the underlying concepts may be insufficiently established.

Word over- and underextensions are complex matters. Indeed, overextensions apparently serve communicative or heuristic functions whereas underextensions serve an hypothesis-testing function (Kamhi, 1982). Such behavior may provide new insights into language learning that not only pertains to word learning but also other aspects of language acquisition, that is, insufficient categorization, mental processing capacity, phonological avoidance, and even early metalinguistic capacities (metaphor, simile).

When overextensions were first reported by E. Clark (1973a, 1973b), their explanation seemed to be at hand. She posited the semantic feature hypothesis that predicted that overextensions occur because the underlying concepts for certain words lack particular semantic features. Reich (1976) and Barrett (1978) suggested, instead, that early word meanings are narrow initially and may become overextended later. And, there have been several viable alternative explanations since, some of which conflict and some of which draw upon possible acquisition processes not necessarily specific to word learning per se.

The notions of over- and underextension may imply that early words are unstable. That is, sometimes a particular word is used appropriately whereas other times it may be overextended. Donaldson and McGarrigle (1974) held that early words are essentially stable but are subject to three loosely coordinated rules: lexical rules, syntactic rules, and local rules. *Lexical rules* "are not finely specified." Thus, word use evidences first an unmarked and then a marked stage. For example, children may say "big" when they mean 'big' and also when they mean 'little.' This is followed by contrastive terms whereby they will say "big" only when they mean 'big' and "little" only when they mean 'little.' Donaldson and McGarrigle (1974, p. 193) said, "... there are assuredly SYNTACTIC RULES." Schlesinger (1977) agreed, asserting that these rules, as manifested by linguistic input, render semantic-syntactic categories visible to the child. The LOCAL RULES pertain to the organization of an event (or topic). Such rules specify what is informative and what can reside in presupposition.

The notion of unstable underlying meanings for words was supported by Bernstein (1983, p. 381). He said, "A different, less stable typicality structure was found in the children's category." "Typicality structure" seems to be comparable to Nelson's (1974) and Bowerman's (1978) notions of prototype. Unstable underlying meanings of words might reflect unset 'natural glue' whereby the inherent correlational structure of entities is not yet adequately perceived (Rosch, Mervis, Gray, Johnson, & Boyes-Braem, 1976). Some critical issues need to be kept in mind, however. Performances for words in isolation and dealing with elicited as opposed to intentional meaning are substantively different from performances with words in referential, linguistic, and intentional contexts. So, it is not surprising to find seemingly conflicting results in this and some other studies.

Perceptual or Functional Attributes

Anglin (1977), E. Clark (1973a, 1973b), Bloom (1973), Rescorla (1980, 1981), and others suggested that overextensions reflect underdevelopment of conceptual and lexical knowledge. They focused on perceptual knowledge, but Nelson (1973a, 1974) focused on functional knowledge. Bates (1979, pp. 142-153) has summarized some of these arguments. Based upon a review of the literature on production errors, E. Clark (1973b) concluded that early categorization is based upon *perceptual attributes*. She indicated that early semantic features are oriented to shape, then size, sound, movement, and material, with color somewhat later. Nelson (1973a), on the other hand, held that early categories are based upon *functional attributes* rather than perceptual attributes.

> Although it has frequently been reported that children tend to overextend words on the basis of perceptual similarity (e.g., Anglin, 1977, Bowerman, 1978, Clark, 1973), when children were asked to extend the possible functions of objects they demonstrated an appreciation of functional characteristics which took precedence over perceptual features. (Hudson & Nelson, 1984, p. 345)

Functional attributes are *dynamic* features, whereas perceptual attributes are *static* features. Thus, a ball has functional or dynamic properties such that it can be: carried, thrown, hit, rolled, bounced, and so on. Its perceptual properties are its color, size, and shape. Nelson (1974) suggested that children first establish a prototypic concept based upon varied actions (functional attributes); they then learn perceptual attributes and possibly a label.

> Functional attributes seem to be learned before perceptual attributes for ostensive terms.

Bowerman (1976, 1978) suggested that the perceptual argument may hold for the acquisition of relational terms, whereas the functional argument may hold for ostensive terms. However, she provided for perceptual learning for both. *Relational* terms are those that indicate a relationship of some sort, for example, object to space—locative, object to known information—*the* book, object to immediate context— *allgone* ball, existence and contrastiveness of attributes—*big* ball. 'Big' is only big when compared to something smaller. *Ostensive* terms are the names of objects (animate or inanimate), actions and relations that are manifestly demonstrative. That is, they are available via direct experience such as actions.

> Labeling mistakes such as over- and underextensions provide clues to loci of learning even though they are not fully understood.

Mental Processing Capacity

Thomson and Chapman (1977) gave another interpretation of over- and underextensions, contending that such behaviors reveal a breakdown in production recall. That is, the child may have an underlying concept but cannot recall the label for the particular concept. This sounds very much like the production deficiency problem in recall reported by Corsini, Pick, and Flavell (1968), Moely, Olsen, Halwes, and Flavell (1969), etc. Rescorla (1981) observed that overextended words occur with highly frequent words and easily acquired words. This casts doubt on the Thomson and Chapman interpretation.

Ingram (1984) suggested that if overextensions are perceptually and functionally based, then there should be overextensions in comprehension as well as production. Some evidence suggests that this is so, but Ingram questioned whether there was sufficient evidence to solidify these positions. He turned to Bloom's (1973) conjecture that overextensions (overinclusions) occur because of a limited lexicon, which would predict overextended object knowledge. Then, he turned to Thomson and Chapman (1977), who suggested that overextensions reflect a retrieval error whereby the child has the word in receptive vocabulary but cannot call it up for production. This sounds like the child's version of the tip-of-the-tongue problem (Bolinger, 1961; Brown & McNeill, 1966; Clark & Clark, 1977; Nooteboom, 1967; Rubin, 1975).

Phonological Avoidance

A study by Schwartz and Leonard (1982) showed that young children behave differently toward nonsense words that are phonologically *within* their capacities as compared to nonsense words *outside* their capacities. Words outside phonological capacities were seemingly avoided. Such words might get overextended. Thus, if the child cannot say "orange," he or she simply avoids the word and says "ball," resulting in an overextension. Based on this study, Schwartz and Leonard (1982) said the child may have two receptive vocabularies. Words "inside" the phonological system may be understood and produced, whereas those "outside" the system may be understood but not produced.

> Ferguson (1978) posited an inverse relationship between phonetic accuracy and vocabulary growth, noting that some children acquired vocabulary slowly and tended to produce their words quite accurately while others evidenced rapid vocabulary growth associated with a higher rate of mispronunciation. Menn (1979) also observed this 'trade-off' between phonetic accuracy and rate of lexical acquisition in two children she studied. (Stoel-Gammon & Cooper, 1984, pp. 248–249)

Rescorla (1980, 1981) pointed out that overextensions occur most often with words acquired earliest and used most frequently. This weakens the argument that overextensions are due to inadequate underlying concepts and strengthens the phonological avoidance hypothesis.

Early Metalinguistic Capacities

A more recent view has challenged the phonological avoidance position and others. It is the view that overextensions are analogies (metaphor, simile). This view challenges the phonological avoidance position because the studies in this area showed that the children were overextending for words already in their vocabularies. These studies (Hudson & Nelson, 1984; Nelson, 1975, 1976, 1979; Winner, 1979; Winner, Engel, & Gardner, 1980; Winner, McCarthey, Kleinman, & Gardner, 1979; Winner, Rosenthiel, & Gardner, 1976) showed that overextensions appear as renaming behavior in play of children (1;8–2;4). Usually such renaming occurred for ambiguous objects. Moreover, at the preschool level, analogic overextensions were common (72%–91% of the overextensions).

There is some confusion as to whether these analogic overextensions are metaphor or simile. The confusion concerns the definition of analogic extensions. Hudson and Nelson provided the following definition:

We define analogic extensions as extensions of words to unconventional referents for the purpose of making a comparison between the conventional and unconventional referents. This definition encompasses both literal and figurative comparisons. Literal comparisons are direct statements of similarity such as similes (X is like Y, X looks like Y) while figurative comparisons are made in metaphors (Juliet is the sun). Although these forms are distinguishable in mature speech, they cannot be differentiated in children's early overextensions. (1984, p. 338)

Hudson and Nelson outlined a developmental shift whereby early analogic extensions seemed to be about metaphors and similes whereas later similes are used for literal comparisons, but word substitutions are for metaphoric comparisons. They put it this way:

In general, children produce more overextensions during the earlier stages of language acquisition. This could, in part, result from the fact that children initially use overextensions for both literal and figurative comparisons. At later ages, children are able to use the simile form to make literal comparisons while word substitutions are used for metaphoric comparisons. Thus children's use of overextensions as communicative devices may change as children acquire more sophisticated forms to make their meanings clear. (Hudson & Nelson, 1984, p. 339)

The various views of *overextensions* are summarized as follows:

A. Insufficient categorization: perceptual, functional
B. Inadequate mental processing capacity: retrieval problem
C. Phonological avoidance
D. Early metalinguistic capacities: metaphor, simile

Possibly *invented* words are related to overextensions. Word mortality is when invented words drop out and become replaced by conventional words. If it is so that invented words occur because the underlying concept is insufficiently established, the child needs to learn the concepts for invented words. If it is a production recall problem, the child needs to have experience using a given label for a variety of referents. Such behavior may foreshadow a production deficiency problem later on. If it is a phonological insufficiency, there should be a strong correspondence between phonetic inventory and the phonetic structure of invented words.

The nature of invented words may help sort out the controversies surrounding the explanations of overextensions.

Early Phonology Revisited

Another major issue in conventionalization is phonology. That is, as children strive to produce words and utterances that conform more or less to the phonological structure of language, they evidence conventionalization.

This acquisition process extends over several years. In the preceding chapter some early phonological behaviors in the first year were mentioned, for example, evidence of a speech receptor mechanism, initiation of maturational control of the vocal mechanism, acquisition of some prosodic patterns. Here, the emphasis is on the initial stages in the acquisition of phonology.

Early on, there seems to be an intimate relationship between word acquisition and phonological acquisition (Ferguson, 1977b, 1978; Ingram, 1976; Leonard, Fey, & Newhoff, 1981; Menn, 1980; Moskowitz, 1970, 1973a, 1973b; Waterson, 1971, 1981, 1984). In short, this literature suggests that the child's entry into phonology is not in terms of phonemes or distinctive features, as had been previously believed; rather, it is in terms of syllable and word acquisition. These syllable and word acquisitions appear to be as skeletal spectra of phonemic word structure (Waterson, 1984) that enable the child to produce remarkably good phonetic patterns for a brief period.

This is before the child has organized phonological capacities into a syntax of sounds. Ingram (1976, p. 19) discussed early phonological acquisition and early word acquisition in this way, "The child is not simply acquiring a system of sounds, but also a set of lexical items. The acquisition of specific patterns and sounds may be greatly influenced by the words in which they occur." Moskowitz (1970), Waterson (1971, 1981, 1984), and Ferguson (1977a, 1977b, 1978) made similar observations. Ferguson (1977a) suggested that early on the child has a small active vocabulary (lexicon) that is usually evidenced as CV or CVCV (reduplication) structures. Regarding reduplication, Ferguson (1977a, p. 11) said, "They most commonly exhibit full reduplication or syllable harmony (same consonants) or vowel harmony (same vowels)." Furthermore, he said that a word may fluctuate considerably in its production.

In early word learning, children are surprisingly adept at relatively clear articulation even for some complex phonological structures. This remarkable behavior is evidenced for the first set of words, roughly 50 words (Ferguson, 1977a, 1977b; Ingram, 1976; Menn, 1980; Moskowitz, 1973a, 1973b, 1970; Waterson, 1971, 1981, 1984). Then, children's phonological systems begin to organize into rules, presumably because they are faced with a memory overload problem. They simply cannot maintain an increasingly large vocabulary storage, so they begin working out phonological rules that enable them to handle thousands of words. Overtly, children's shift to rule-governed behavior is somewhat deceptive because it appears as if they are losing some phonological skill. That is, they now make mistakes on words that they had previously been able to produce well.

Waterson (1984) suggested that this literature on early phonology challenges the notion of phonemic theory with its attendant principle of phonemic contrasts. The latter, proposed by Jakobson (1941/1968), has become known as the phoneme or segmental view of phonology. Indeed, Jakobson had proposed that segments could be viewed as clusters of distinctive features. The more recent view, however, asserts that word or lexical acquisitions provide a working matrix from which phonological rules may be "discovered." This working matrix model is especially attractive because it provides children with a small but useful set of words that permits them to engage in social commerce.

Waterson (1984) contended that early phonological acquisition is not by phonemic contrasts but by pattern recognition. This means that it may be more appropriate to have a small vocabulary of high utility words that provides children with skeletal spectra from which they may discover a phonological system.

During this period, it is useful to ascertain children's *phonetic inventory, homonymy,* and to deduce *simplification processes* which they may have (Ingram, 1976, 1981). A *phonetic inventory* is the set of initial consonants, vowels, and final consonants acquired roughly during the acquisition of the first 50 words (Ingram, 1976). Ingram reported that the early initial consonants in English are $b, p, t, d, k, g, f, s, m, n, h,$ and $w,$ and the early final consonants in English are $p, t, k, f, s, m,$ and $n.$ The early vowels evidence major distinctions between front, back, and low (Stampe, 1973). Ingram (1976) showed that /i/, /u/, and /a/ were early vowel contrasts. "Vowels, then, are not acquired during the first 50 words, although at least the basic triangle is probably established in this period" (Ingram, 1976, p. 19). Ingram pointed out that early phonetic inventories vary as a function of the language that is being acquired. This observation implicates rule learning and suggests that phonological systems are likely to be local rather than universal.

The phonetic inventory is evidence of early phonological rules.

Basically, phonological acquisition is an effort to overcome *homonymy* (Drachman, 1973, p. 150). That is, as children attain increased phonological contrasts, they become increasingly able to express words with these contrasts. This enables them to make words that had seemed similar, in sound production, distinctive if the intent is to be distinctive (Priestly, 1980). It should be noted, however, that some children may actually strive to retain homonymy (Vihman, 1981). Early on, homonymy is evidenced simply because the child has only a few sounds. However, as the child continues to acquire more sounds and make more phonological contrasts, homonymy becomes reduced. In this sense, phonological acquisition is an attempt to overcome homonymy.

> Phonological acquisition is an attempt to overcome homonymy.

Priestly (1980) defined various possible conditions of homonymy. Table 7.1 outlines six instances of presumed homonymy as they compare to "pure homonymy" and articulatory "contrast." The point is that what may be regarded as homonymy may actually be any one of the following conditions: subconscious half-contrast, detectable but unnoticed, detectable and noticed, attributed to intention, proprioceptive secret, and hearer's error. Thus, it is important to establish criteria for making conclusions about homonymy. One kind of criteria that would be useful is relativity—patterns of phonological behavior including children's judgments of *their* own phonetic contrasts. Aungst and Frick (1964) showed that it was important for children to judge their own expressions rather than those of someone else.

Locke (1979) and Vihman (1981) argued that homonymy is a strategy. Vihman said,

> Instead of avoiding homonyms, some children seem to collect them; instead of resorting to unnatural or apparently unmotivated processes in order to maintain a surface contrast, they may resort to such processes in order to merge two or more adult words in a single sound pattern. In short, instead of demonstrating a desire to achieve clarity in their speech they demonstrate a desire to achieve efficiency in performance. The child's goal in such cases almost seems to be the production of a maximum number of lexical items with a minimum repertoire of sound shapes. (1981, p. 241)

Simplification processes are mechanisms that serve to reduce or simplify otherwise complex processes. The adult phonological system is too complex for children; they have means whereby they can employ simplified versions of the adult system. Then, these simplified versions can be progressively elaborated until an adult system is attained. However, it may be presumptive to use the term "simplification" (Locke, 1983) in order to not credit the children for competences that would enable them to simplify adult systems. It is more conservative simply to refer to early phonological processes (Ingram, 1976; Laila Khan, 1982; Leonard, 1985). Some early phonological processes are outlined as follows:

a. *Vowel nucleus:* Consonantal factors are not present, only vowel nuclei are evidenced.
b. *Open syllable:* Syllabic structure is either vowel nuclei or consonant-vowel (open syllable). Thus, other syllable structures are not evidenced. Indeed, a child will convert other structures into these thereby simplifying the system.

Table 7.1. Six Instances of Presumed Homonymy Compared to "Pure Homonymy" and Articulatory "Contrast"

Articulatorily the same?	Acoustically the same?	Same for the speaker?	Same for the hearer?	
Homonymy				
yes	yes	yes	yes	Pure homonymy
no	yes	yes	yes	Subconscious half-contrast
no	no	yes	yes	Detectable, unnoticed
Half-contrast				
no	no	yes	no	Detectable and noticed
Pseudohomonymy				
yes	yes	no	yes	Attention on intention
no	yes	no	yes	Proprioceptive secret
no	no	no	yes	Hearer's error
Contrast				
no	no	no	no	Contrast achieved

From "Homonymy in child phonology" by T. Priestly, 1980, *Journal of Child Language, 7,* p. 416. Reprinted by permission.

c. *Reduplication:* Two open syllables are duplicated. Thus, the child may show an awareness of a bisyllabic word by reduplication but the phonemic structure has been reduced to a simple reduplication. As the child becomes ready to release from reduplication he or she may show differentiatd stress or vowels on the two syllables.
d. *Voicing:* In adult speech voicing is organized phonemically in regard to voiced and voiceless cognates. However, in early child speech voicing seems to have syllabic significance because the child adopts the simplification rule of voicing the initial consonant and unvoicing the final consonant of a syllable.
e. *Fronting:* Some articulatory movements are placed more forward in the vocal mechanism than they would otherwise be. Thus, the child may make /k/ and /g/ as /t/ and /d/ respectively.

f. *Weak syllable deletion:* The young child who does not yet have a full command of differential syllable stress may simply delete unstressed syllables thereby avoiding this problem.
g. *Cluster reduction:* The young child who cannot yet handle combinations of consonants as a single consonantal factor in syllabic release or arrest may simply reduce the cluster. Thus, the child may say /top/ for /stop/ and /tet/ for /stret/.
h. *Coarticulation:* Daniloff and Hammarberg (1973) indicated that phonetic features influence each other such that *feature spreading* occurs in natural speech. "The locus of the influence is the segment, and the element of influence is the articulatory feature" (p. 242). The study of these influences is the study of coarticulation. Daniloff and Hammarberg defined coarticulation "as the influence of one speech segment upon another; that is, the influence of a phonetic context upon a given segment. Phonetic context is most varied within connected conversational speech. Thus, coarticulation or carryover coarticulation is most extensive in running speech" (p. 239). Forward coarticulation or carryover coarticulation is when one sound influences another sound that follows it. Thus, the child might say /sos/ for 'soap.' Backward coarticulation or anticipatory coarticulation is when one sound influences another sound that precedes it. Thus, the child might say /pop/ for 'soap.'

The child may simplify a complex adult phonological system.

Not considering the vowel nucleus, the open syllable or CV seems to be a primitive syllable. It has attracted a considerable amount of attention (Ferguson & Farwell, 1975; Ingram, 1976; Panagos, 1974; Panagos & Hoffman, 1971; Renfrew, 1966). Although most of the attention has been on the consonant in CV structures, as Stoel-Gammon (1983) pointed out, the consonants in CV structures seem to be constrained by the vowel. Jakobson (1941/1968) concluded that many children simply cannot produce a labial sound before a front vowel. Labials did not occur before front vowels but alveolar consonants had no such restriction. Fudge (1969) made a similar observation. Stoel-Gammon suggested that CV syllables in early phonology should be studied in terms of vowel constraints that seemingly govern, at least early on, permissible consonants. This implies that the vowel is the nucleus of the syllable.

Research in recent years has explored the relationship of phonological capacities to other aspects of language, notably word acquisition and morphophonology (MacWhinney, 1978). Indeed, research that shows the child with a phonological impairment may have a general language impairment (Panagos, 1974).

Stoel-Gammon and Cooper (1984, pp. 269-270) reviewed the research on phonological acquisition and word learning and summarized this research in terms of the following claims:

1. The order of acquisition of phonemes and phonemic contrasts is rather stable across children (Jakobson, 1941/1968).
2. The initial consonantal position in syllables is "the most stable environment" for consonant production and is a "testing ground" where consonants are first acquired (Branigan, 1976; Panagos, 1974; Renfrew, 1966).
3. The CV syllable is the 'primary syllabic unit' in early word production (Branigan, 1976; Panagos, 1974; Renfrew, 1966).
4. "Lexical selectivity operates on the first phone to determine whether the child will attempt the word or not" (Shibamoto & Olmsted, 1978, p. 454).
5. The early lexicon "typically consists of a dozen or so vocables of which only one or two are clearly based on adult words" (Ferguson, 1978, p. 280).

However, Stoel-Gammon and Cooper (1984, p. 270) found that *individual differences* were so extensive that it was difficult to support these claims. As they said, "While a number of these statements hold true for some (or even most) children, none is accurate for our small sample of three subjects." Furthermore, they said, "The three subjects differed significantly in their early lexical and phonological development. Their vocal productions were most similar in the late babbling—very first word stage, and from then on they proceeded to become more and more divergent" (p. 269).

Summary

Once children begin word learning, they enter the conventional dimension. Word learning must be considered in terms of categorization and communication. The relationship between categorization and words is unclear, especially in regard to semantic categorization and grammatical categorization. Early vocables and PCFs are unconventional labels, whereas true words are conventional. There are some unanswered questions about the occurrence of the child's first word. Word learning and communication raise the point that the "well known" traditional anchor point of 12 months for the first word is of dubious value. This was followed by a consideration of over- and underextensions and invented words.

Early phonology is intimately tied to early word learning. This finding has essentially debased the traditional phoneme or segmental notions in phonological acquisition. Early phonological acquisition is now considered from the following perspectives: phonetic inventory, homonymy, and simplification processes.

8

CONVENTIONALIZATION: PREDICATION AND EARLY FORMALIZATION

The stage following identification or indicative in the Werner and Kaplan (1963) language acquisition model is predication. Inasmuch as predication entails grammatical relations, this constitutes the early acquisition of formal grammatical relations.

Budding Grammatical Relations

When do grammatical relations begin? This question refers to the big issue of grammatical categories. There is a controversy in psycholinguistics over the question as to when grammatical categories or relations begin and what form they take. In the early 1970s, the various semantic functions and relations of one- and two-word utterances were presumed to be the genesis of early grammatical relations. See Leonard (1976) for a good review and Greenfield and Smith (1976) for a comprehensive study.

By the end of the 1970s, however, a number of questions had been raised about the credibility of the various accounts of semantic functions and relations. On the philosophical front, Fillmore (1972) held that generative semantics was inadequate without considering presupposition. He proposed interpretative semantics which is generative semantics clothed in presupposition. On the psycholinguistic front, the lingering question as to what semantic functions or relationships could legitimately be credited to the child came to a head

(Beckwith, Rispoli, & Bloom, 1984; Bloom, Capatides, & Tackeff, 1981; Duchan & Lund, 1979; Golinkoff, 1975, 1981; Howe, 1976, 1981; Macrae, 1979; Rodgon, 1977). This problem was anticipated by Brown who said,

> Chomsky (1969) and Katz (1967) have argued that many of the semantically based linguistic theories are merely "notational variants" of the standard theory and, from the linguistic point of view, I think they are right. From the psychological and developmental point of view, however, the new theories pose real empirical questions about the kinds of constructs that are, in fact, functional. (1973b, p. 146)

Brown (1973b) had presaged not only this controversy about the psychological reality of presumed semantic categories, but also the attendant issue of providing empirical evidence for resolving the controversy. Brown said,

> The relations or roles are abstract taxonomies applied to child utterances. That it is not known how finely the abstractions should be sliced and that no proof exists that the semantic levels hit on by any theorist, whether Bloom, Schlesinger, Fillmore, or whomever, are psychologically functional. Nor is this a nonsense question. It is an empirical question awaiting a technique of investigation. (1973b, p. 146)

Similarly, Bloom, Capatides and Tackeff (1981, p. 407) commented, "The ultimate problem for IA (interpretative analysis) is the problem of determining the extent of confidence in one or another set of results."

Semantic functions and relations attributed to a child may not be psychologically real but may be mere observational artifacts.

Brown (1973b, p. 169) pointed out that Chafe (1970), Fillmore (1968), Bloom (1970), Schlesinger (1971) and Bowerman (1973) seemed to converge on essentially the same set of compositional meanings, and that the set is not a large one. Brown (1973b) gave the following list of two-term relations:

1. Agent and action
2. Action and object
3. Agent and object
4. Action and locative
5. Entity and locative
6. Possessor and possession
7. Entity and attributive
8. Demonstrative and entity

Thus, it appears that the semantic functions and relations identified by these researchers would have psychological validity. As a composite, it appears that the child with such utterances has the rudiments of an "agent-action-dative-object-locative" construction (Brown, 1973b, p. 205). However, these are compositional constructions rather than true grammatical constructions. The claim is a grammatical one.

> The fact that various studies converge on essentially the same small set of basic categories lends some credence to the psychological reality of "observed" semantic categories.

Howe (1976), Rodgon (1977), Macrae (1979), and Duchan and Lund (1979) suggested that the various notions of semantic relations should be collapsed into a set of categories even smaller than the studies just mentioned would suggest. Howe (1976), in particular, suggested that the following three categories are useful: action of concrete objects; state of concrete object (attributive, locative, possession); and name of concrete object. However, Golinkoff (1981) held that Howe's reductionistic solution is not a good one. She pointed out three other ways of dealing with the issue of crediting psychological reality for a given semantic category. One way is to *predict* from context when the child uses one or another semantic case. A second way is to demonstrate its existence in *comprehension*. A third way is to establish *nonlinguistic parallels* for these concepts.

There is no denying that they are compositional, not because they are two-term utterances, and even three-term utterances, but because the constraints of grammatical order are not evident. Early on, these compositional utterances are somewhat order free (Braine, 1976). Moreover, as the child makes two-, three-, and even four-term utterances, the early efforts appear to be nothing more than concatenations or overlays with redundant elements deleted. Thus, "Mommy eat" and "Eat cookie" could be concatenated to yield "Mommy eat cookie." This concatenation looks something like this:

Mommy eat
    eat cookie
―――――――――
Mommy eat cookie

Brown, (1973b, p. 177) indicated that such relations are defined semantically rather than grammatically because they do not necessarily imply a serial order. But, order soon enters the picture. As Bowerman (1973, p. 213) contended, "Children launch their syntactic careers by learning simple order rules for combining words which perform semantic functions."

> Early word combinations are compositional rather than grammatical constructions.

Brown (1973b) also anticipated some problems in operationally defining semantic categories for observational purposes. This is an exceedingly difficult task because actual semantic categories are internal psychological notions rather than external "observables." Thus, inferential safeguards are needed to establish some degree of confidence that a semantic category actually exists.

Greenfield and Smith (1976, p. 50) agreed and instituted their criteria for inferring the existence of semantic categories (see Chapter 3). They were concerned that semantic relations may be ascribed to children but such relations may not be actually operative in their utterance. Howe (1976, 1981), Rodgon (1977), Duchan and Lund (1979), and Macrae (1979) gave reason to be conservative in attributing specific semantic relations to early word combinations. However, Bloom, Capatides, and Tackeff (1981) and Golinkoff (1975, 1981) held that as much specification as can be legitimately attributed is needed and that their criteria allow for more specification than Howe and others have done. Howe (1981, p. 446) replied, "Rather than criticizing interpretive analysis as a general technique, I am advocating greater selectivity in its use." She said it was necessary to spell out potential meanings of an utterance and to specify nonverbal information that would resolve ambiguities. She indicated that if such information is not available interpretive analysis should not be used for the utterance. These criteria are reasonable to the extent that information of this kind is needed to support interpretive analysis, but these particular criteria may constrain analyses so much that they could undermine legitimate a posteriori interpretations. Leonard (1983) detailed some problems in operationally discerning the psychological reality of semantic functions and relations. Problems such as these have resulted in a somewhat conservative interpretation.

> Operationally, there are problems in crediting semantic categories to the child.

Transition: Early Semantic Categories to Grammatical Categories. In addition to the controversy about the psychological reality of the characterizations of semantic categories, there is also a dispute concerning the relationships between early semantic categories and later grammatical categories. The former establishes a link between theory of the world and basic ideas for coding messages. The latter provides a generative basis for formal codification. Gleitman and Wanner (1982) maintained that the question is not whether the child makes a transition from semantic categories to formal grammatical categories, but how such a transition is accomplished. They pointed out that various explanations center on the degree to which the relationship between semantic and grammatical categories are considered to be simple and direct or complex and indirect.

> The child makes a transition from semantic to grammatical categories.

Gleitman and Wanner (1982) summarized arguments along these continua (simple to complex; direct to indirect). They began by indicating that Fillmore's (1968) "psychologically real" semantic categories required an interpretive device, which he himself admitted (Fillmore, 1972). Moreover, Fillmore never argued that these semantic relations would be simple, immediate, or direct. Furthermore, there have been recurring questions about the descriptive adequacy of various generative semantic categories as either psychologically real or grammatically valid (Brown, 1973b). Bowerman (1973, 1976), Howe (1976), Macrae (1979), Duchan and Lund (1979), and Leonard (1983) raised similar concerns.

In a sense, then, the generative semantic movement had much to say about possible relationships between theory of the world and the use of ideas in coding early "quasi-grammatical" utterances or compositions. However, as children enter the arena of formal grammatical systems, they must somehow convert semantic knowledge into grammatical knowledge. Referring to Bowerman (1982), Gleitman and Wanner (1982, p. 14) said, "The learner must eventually transcend his initial semantic-categorial organization of language to acquire certain grammatical categories and functions."

Those theories that argue for a direct or continuous relationship between initial semantic categories and subsequent grammatical categories run into a roadblock. Braine and Hardy (1982), for example, suggested that grammatical categories are mapped directly onto underlying semantic categories. They delineated five principles of simplicity and efficiency that presumably afford such direct mapping. Gleitman and Wanner (1982) dubbed this "direct mapping" and characterized the five principles of simplicity and efficiency as directions to a good God or a sane creator. However, they did not think that Braine and Hardy's accounts fit reality. "We have just argued that the real deity has not been so benevolent . . ." (p. 29).

The following three quotes from Gleitman and Wanner (1982) indicate that the semantic-based syntax is a false step in understanding language acquisition which appears to be discontinuous in transition from semantic to grammatical categories. "If learning is taken to be continuous—that is, if the earliest learned properties are a proper part of the full learning to follow—the semantics-based syntax is a false step" (p. 30). " Whatever the causes of change, both discontinuous theories of language development assert that the surface-meaning mappings of an earlier semantics-based system are dropped, and learning begins anew with fairly trivial residue (including, perhaps, the lexical items and the guess about canonical order)" (p. 31). The two discontinuous theories were the "clutter reduction" theory by Bowerman (1982) and the "metamorphosis" theory by Gleitman (1981). These are discussed below. Another quote regarding this discontinuous relationship is: "But this claim for an initial 'conceptual language' commits one to a discontinuous claim about language learning, just because the final knowledge state partly dissociates semantic and grammatical categories" (Gleitman & Wanner, 1982, p. 30).

> There is a discontinuous relationship between early semantic categories and subsequent formal grammatical categories.

Bowerman (1982) used error patterns over time as evidence that a reorganization process is at work as the child enters a formal grammatical system. She pointed out that some early utterances are errorless yet well formed. These are regarded as highly rehearsed, even repetitive, in early dialogues. Bruner (1981) regarded such behavior as formats that effectively released the learner from learning the formal mechanisms of language, thereby allowing opportunities to attend to pragmatic issues as a scaffold for learning subsequent semantic–syntactic–phonological dimensions. The "two-person sentence" reported by Greenfield and Smith (1976) seems to afford the child similar opportunities. Then, Bowerman noted that errors suddenly appear. She suggested that these errors are evidence that the child has entered a period of reorganization. This proposal has been offered elsewhere as well (Menyuk, 1963, 1964a, 1964b). Reorganization presumably indexes stage or discontinuous learning. Bloom (1984, p. 220) put the notion of reorganization in language learning as follows,

> But children do not simply add (or subtract) sounds and structures; development is not additive. Rather, children continually restructure their knowledge of language on the basis of their exposure to and their perceptions of increasingly complex aspects of language, for expressing increasingly complex ideas, in more and more complex social contexts.

Moreover, there is other evidence (besides verbal) that prior learning becomes reorganized. Piaget's theory of stages of cognition is a prime example, (see also White, 1965). It appears that the central nervous system is "hard-wired" such that a *repertoire* of certain capacities comprises a key to unlock subsequent capacities (Schlesinger, 1977). In the instance of semantic capacities, it may not be a padlock but a combination lock. That is, it is only after children attain a variety of semantic categories and *combinations* of them that they become ready to learn the formal mechanisms of language. This certainly appears to be a stage process that is not unlike Piagetian stages in principle. Consistent with the notion of acquisition stages, Dore et al. (1976) delineated transitional phenomena antecedent to syntax.

> Early semantic achievements constitute a formula for unlocking the entrance to formal grammatical systems.

Greenfield and Smith posited that semantic categories themselves evidence stages of learning. They said,

> As was pointed out repeatedly, the use of almost every semantic function passes through a number of stages before it is first used in two-word utterances. Most functions appeared in isolated one-word form. From this point, there are two directions of development. One is the use of single words in relation to verbal, as opposed to nonverbal, context. The other is the use of single words in sequences, as opposed to in isolation. Conversational sequence might be considered a combination of these two developments. The exceptions to this order of development are relatively few. (1976, p. 166)

Other evidence of reorganization is seen in phonology and in morphology. In phonology, children may do surprisingly well in producing a few early words (Ferguson, 1978; Moskowitz, 1973a, 1973b). But as the vocabulary process reaches a mental limit, they are forced into deducing phonological rules. Theoretically, such rules can yield an unlimited phonological skill; yet, how do childen intuitively know that? Why don't they grudgingly persist with their previously successful behavior? They actually could do so but it would leave them with stultified verbal skills that would be inadequate for social commerce. Their recourse is to reorganize and proceed.

Similarly in morphology, children begin using words they hear but they do not realize their structural significance. So, early on, they will say "eat," "open," "man," "ball," and even "ate," "opened," "men," and "balls." Upon deducing relevant inflectional rules, they will overgeneralize to produce "eated" and "mans"; and then eventually the rule becomes sorted out for appropriate generalization. The point is that initially the child was right, then errors occurred as the result of an induced rule (reorganization of prior learning), and finally correct production was re-established by virtue of appropriate applications or restrictions on the rule (Cazden, 1968; deVilliers & deVilliers, 1978; Palermo & Eberhart, 1968). In phonology, for example, Kiparsky and Menn (1977) suggested that progressive and regressive idioms afford the child realizations of phonological rules. *Phonological idioms* are closer approximations of adult forms. *Regressive idioms* are performances that diverge from the adult model.

Reorganization is evident in early language learning.

Gleitman (1981) and Gleitman and Wanner (1982) offered a sister proposal to the reorganization proposal within successive mental limitations: "There are relevant neurological changes in the learner that cause him to reinterpret linguistic evidence" (Gleitman & Wanner, 1982, p. 30). Said differently, "It could be that there are a succession of learners, each of whom organizes the linguistic data as befits his mental state. This is a kind of metamorphosis, or tadpole-to-frog, hypothesis" (p. 31). To the extent that reorganization is actually an integral part of language learning, it is no wonder that traditional learning theory (behaviorism) has not accounted adequately for language acquisition.

> Stages of learning may mean that there is a succession of learners each prepared to do something different than he or she could do before.

Whatever the case, children still must learn the formal grammatical system of language in order to use it in social commerce. On this point, too, there are major theoretical conflicts. Maratsos (1982) suggested that grammatical learning is largely independent of semantic acquisition. In referring to Maratsos (1982), Gleitman and Wanner (1982, p. 32) said, "It follows that such categories must be acquired on some basis that is at least partly independent of semantics, a fact that is something of a conundrum for any theory of acquisition run exclusively on semantic machinery." Maratsos proposed the "distributional analyzer," which is "basically an inductive scheme capable in principle, of classifying words together on the basis of shared contexts" (Gleitman & Wanner, 1982, p. 33). This is credible inasmuch as children are remarkably responsive to *stress,* which signifies open-class words, and to *order,* which gives a preliminary structure. Moreover, this seems to rely on the co-occurrence of categories (Harris, 1965). And, it is somewhat close to an earlier proposal by Braine (1976) that itself had antecedents in co-occurring categories—contextual generalizaton (Braine, 1963a, 1963b, 1965).

Co-occurrence. Proposals about co-occurrence presuppose the analysis of grammatical morphemes. This is problematic because to a certain extent it explains how grammatical morphemes are learned, yet it presupposes such learning. That is, the early distributional or co-occurrence behaviors of two- and three-word utterances are merely compositions lacking the vernacular structure of formal rules. However, once the child enters the arena of formal structure, co-occurrence may play a significant role in early acquisition.

Bloom, Lifter, and Hafitz (1980) showed that the co-occurrences for certain semantic distinctions of verbs were determining factors in which inflections would be learned. The semantic distinctions for action verbs were durative/nondurative and completive/noncompletive. These distinctions, coupled with the respective inflectional acquisitions, yielded the following:

Action Verbs	Inflection	Example
Durative noncompletive	-ing	We're playing
Durative completive	-s	It fits
Nondurative completive	-ed	I drank it

(The *-ed* inflection could be either the regular or irregular form.) They also noted that "all-purpose" verbs usually had more than one inflection. These so-called "all-purpose" verbs are evidently *glossed* forms (See Chapter 10). They made a similar observation about the acquisition of inflections for *state* verbs. However, these acquisitions seemed to operate on a different set of semantic distinctions:

State Verbs	Inflection	Example
Internal	(none)	*She want some candy*
Observable	(inflected)	*She sleeps*

These observations pertained to newly acquired verbs. Bloom et al. (1980) said that these findings underscored the importance of co-occurrence in grammatical acquisition. Moreover, these particular findings suggest that the motivation for acquiring inflections issues from *informativeness* about the organization of an event being encoded (durative/nondurative, completive/noncompletive, internal/observable) rather than the tense marking about when a message itself is made.

Weist (1982) showed that semantic co-occurrence operates in the acquisition of intransitive and transitive verbs. Young children distinguish intransitive verbs according to animacy but not action role. Three-year-olds had animate subjects for words like *run* but not for process verbs like *hit*. But for transitive verbs, action role was critical rather than animacy. Thus, words like *open* and *break* were treated differently.

> Co-occurrence may play a useful role in acquiring early formal structure.

In any case, the child learns formal grammatical rules after attaining a repertoire of semantic categories, but the relationship of the formal grammatical rules to the earlier semantic categories appears to be complex, indirect, and discontinuous. Such a prospect requires a rule-governed orientation. Several proposals have been made, mostly derived from innately driven transformational possibilities. These constitute what might be called the neo-transformational movement.

Prospects of grammatical rule learning. Wexler (1982) contended that grammatical rule learning is merely inaugurated via semantic categories, but it is only true rule learning in the acquisition of formal grammatical rules. Moreover, formal rule learning seems to be innately driven but responsive to environmental influences. Children turn to formal rules not because they are told to do so or because they know in advance this is *the* way to go in achieving proficiency.

Indeed, their early efforts often result in reduced proficiency. Yet, children stay the course.

Wexler (1982) addressed the concept of *learnability*, major new theoretical development in language acquisition. As Gleitman and Wanner (1982, p. 37) put it, "Wexler's study of learnability is an important move in developmental psycholinguistics." Learnability means, in effect, that the child is predisposed to acquire a formal grammatical system. The child's innate predisposition defines the most likely alternatives in the grammatical maze; yet the child's performance remains volitional, allowing for errors. However, the errors are relatively easily recoverable. And, the nature of language is such that universal features make the basic system learnable.

> In theory, such schemata contain empty slots that the child needs only to fill in to learn his own language. Under this idealization, which is often called "parameter setting" to distinguish it from the hypothesis-testing framework, the child might come pre-armed with schema for core grammar rules informing him that (say) a noun phrase is composed of a head noun plus specifier, but leaving open the problems of determining which order these elements appear in, how specification is marked in this language, and so on. (Gleitman & Wanner, 1982, p. 38)

Learnability keeps the child on course in language acquisition.

Given this predisposition and the related prospect that the relationship between performance and knowledge is indirect, Gleitman and Wanner (1982, p. 38) suggested that an excessive reliance on description could actually hinder or distort explanations of language acquisition. Further, they challenged the widely held view that "motherese" (mother's baby talk to her baby) may assist in language acquisition.

Learnability theory involves *discovery processes* and uses a posteriori methodology, both of which constitute new ways of viewing language acquisition. Briefly, discovery theory attributes to the child the ability to extract useful information from a complex maze of otherwise conflicting, ambiguous, and even negative information (Bever, 1982; Wexler, 1982). An a posteriori methodology derives information about acquisition after the data are in, enabling the researcher to "discover strategies and nascent structures that make it possible to decide upon a target structure, *a posteriori*" (Beckwith, Rispoli, & Bloom, 1984, p. 686).

Learnability theory involves with it two other major issues: discovery processes and uses an a posteriori methodology.

Nelson (1979, pp. 332-333) sketched the budding of grammatical relations as a coordination of social and object relations embedded in a linguistic form, albeit at first a raw composition that eventually takes on grammatical character. Like Slobin (1973), Nelson (1979) maintained that the initial indicatives (performatives, communicative point, referential display, labels) refer to only one relevant dimension—presumably the most informative from the encoder's perspective—whereas other relevant dimensions must be inferred from context. The child is not yet ready to coordinate both an informational dimension and its context. It is enough for the child to discern what may be informational and act on that.

Nelson (1979) held that primitive coordination at the one-word stage derives from the social dialogue structure of the communicative participants (see also Greenfield & Smith, 1976). Greenfield and Smith said that the child first expresses an entity that is related to another entity in the world. Thus, communicative context provides the intended meaning for single word expressions. This is comparable to Wittgenstein's (1953; see also Bar-Hillel, 1954; Montague, 1972) notion of indexical expression. Early words are context bound, with the word denoting one feature of the underlying concept and the context carrying its referential significance.

Nelson (1979) said that two-word spontaneous expressions constitute a major milestone because such expressions permit the child to coordinate relations symbolically with or without contextual support. With such constructions, children can encode *both* the informative aspect and the relevant context. Functionally, they become able to encode both frame (symbolic context) and insert (information) on given (context) and new (informativeness) information. Whereas previously they were only able to identify entities in context, they can now express symbolically entities and their relationships, both interpersonal and ideational. Interpersonal information concerns social relationships; ideational information is children's views of the world (i.e., perceptions, thoughts, actions, etc.). "The full intercoordination of social and object, interpersonal and ideational, requires a system of grammatical rules, which at this point, and only at this point, the child begins to learn" (Nelson, 1979, pp. 332-333). She also said that early on, grammar is not needed for purely interactive expressions. Figure 8.1 summarizes Nelson's views.

> The proposed line of development is shown in schematic form in Figure 8.1, where development is seen to proceed from an undifferentiated cognitive system in the first 6 months through differentiated social and object schemes in the second half of the first year. From 13 to 18 months these schemes are coordinated, and single words are used to refer to one aspect of them. Finally, at 19 to 24 months the child makes the coordination explicit on a symbolic level and begins to develop rules for the uses of sentences and dialogue. (Nelson, 1979, p. 333)

Figure 8.1. Hypothesized course of differentiation and integration of social and object domains during first 2 years.

0–6 months		Undifferentiated cognitive schemes	
7–12 months	Social schemes		Object schemes
13–16 months		Social-object co-ordinated schemes -------------	WORDS (used for one aspect only)
19–24 months	Interpersonal Ideational	----------------	SENTENCES (symbolic relation made explicit)

From *Psychological development from infancy* (p. 333) by M. Bornstein and W. Kessen (Eds.), 1979, Hillsdale, N.J.: Erlbaum. Reprinted by permission.

Greenfield and Smith (1976) posited a similar model. However, they held that single-word utterances have combinatorial relationships to an event. This is what Nelson regarded as "primitive coordination." But, Greenfield and Smith (1976, p. 43) said that the structure of dialogue is derived from semantic structure. "Dialogue in general is treated as a semantic structure created by two people together." They maintained that the use of word-action relationships such as those discussed by Nelson are achieved early on in dialogue via the two-person sentence." All of the two-word utterances that had antecedents in sequences also had antecedents in earlier dialogue" (p. 182). "In dialogue, the presupposition is given in the verbal context whereas in spontaneous utterances it is given in the nonverbal context" (p. 196). "The two-person sentence also suggested the possibility of a structural role of dialogue in the language acquisition process" (p. 30).

In our view, the developmental achievement of dialogue is structural rather than functional: For the first time word is combined with word. In early questions-answer dialogue, the child contributes but a single word, but his word is related semantically to the adult's question. Later he, in a sense, internalizes the role of the adult questioner, forming word combinations by himself. Dialogue is thus the two-person model for the child's earliest grammar. (Greenfield & Smith, 1976, p. 209)

Dialogue is a joint semantic structure.

Grammatical Functions: Core Structures

Armed with cognitive categories via knowledge of the world (Bruner, 1981), which provides the bases of semantic knowledge or semantic categories, the child is on the threshold of grammatical knowledge. Bloom (1973, p. 31) stated:

> The important distinction for the child's learning language is more likely between LINGUISTIC categories—categories that are dependent on semantic and syntactic specification of relationship—on the one hand, and COGNITIVE categories on the other hand, which are dependent on the mental representation of experience. If the child learns language as a linguistic coding of certain cognitive representations of his experience as it is proposed here, then it is necessary to question the use of the notion of a "sentence" as "input" for the child's learning grammar. It will be argued, in the discussion that follows, that the emergence of grammar towards the end of the second year derives from and depends upon an underlying COGNITIVE basis. In short, children using single-word utterances know little if anything about sentences, but they have begun to know considerably more about the world of objects, events, and relations.

How does the child enter the grammatical arena? It is not clear, but several scholars have suggested possible explanations. Bloom (1973), for example, observed that early one-word and two-word utterances constitute two basic kinds of semantic categories: functional relations and grammatical relations. Similarly, Schlesinger (1971) identified operations and relations; and Brown (1973b) identified operators of reference and semantic relations. These categories are summarized in Table 8.1.

Early semantic categories are of two types: functional and grammatical.

Bloom defined *basic grammatical relations* and *functional relations* as follows:

Table 8.1. Three Perspectives on Early Semantic Categories

Bloom (1970, 1973)	Schlesinger (1971)	Brown (1973)
Functional Relations	*Operations*	*Operators of Reference*
Existence	Negation	Nomination
Nonexistence	Ostension	Recurrence
Recurrence		Nonexistence
Grammatical Relations	*Relations*	*Semantic Relations*
Agent, Action, Object	Agent, Action, Object	Agent, Action, Object
Possessive	Modifier and Head	Affected Person, State, Object
Attributive	(includes attributive and possessive)	Locative
Locative	Locative	Possessive and Attributive
	Dative	Demonstrative
	(one instance)	Dative

From *One word at a time* (p. 26) by L. Bloom, 1973, The Hague: Mouton. Reprinted by permission.

Thus, in addition to sentences in which conceptual relations between persons, objects, and events were coded by the BASIC GRAMMATICAL RELATIONS subject-object, verb-object, subject-verb, there were other sentences in which different conceptual notions—existence, nonexistence, and recurrence—were coded by the FUNCTIONAL RELATIONS between words. The meaning of such sentences derived from the inherently relational meaning of the function forms, for example, "more," "no," and "this." It is important to point out that the distinction between the two kinds of semantic relations—grammatical relations and functional relations—in these early sentences was not based on distributional evidence. (1973, p. 23)

It should be emphasized that these early basic grammatical relations are not truly grammatical. They are merely compositional (Brown, 1973b), incapable of yielding truly rule-governed constructions. Yet, it is precisely these basic grammatical relations that comprise a semantic base; or, as Bloom (1973, p. 26) said, "semantic primitives" that together constitute a subjective-verb-object (SVO) grammatical core for the emergence of syntax. This semantic base is agent-action-object.

The core grammatical functions are SVO.

Drawing upon Schlesinger (1971), Bloom gave a succinct statement about "semantic primitives" as a grammatical core.

> If grammar is viewed as a semantically based construct, then the underlying conceptual relations can be seen as providing the semantic input to the syntactic component of the grammar. In this view, the notions that have been described—the relation between the AGENT of an action and the OBJECT of that action, for example—are "semantic primitives" which are encoded by syntax. This was essentially the model for early child grammar proposed by Schlesinger: that children learn notions of agent, action, object as concepts which are realized or mapped onto the early syntactic utterances. Thus, the syntactic component of a grammar for child language would function to provide the means whereby such semantic information is realized in sentences. (1973, p. 26)

The semantic categories provide the basis for learning and using syntax; therefore, Bloom and Lahey (1978) used the term semantic-syntactic structure. Bloom underscored the notion of an SVO core in her comment about early grammatical relations:

> That is, there were certain recurring structural meanings that (1) occurred with different words and (2) derived from the transitive relationship between the words (as, for example, between actor and action, action and goal, agent and object). Particular words, for example, "Mommy" or "sock," occurred with specific function (that is, agent or object) only relative to each other (or to other words). Such meaning relationships are coded in English by the BASIC GRAMMATICAL RELATIONS (subject-verb-object) of sentences. (1973, p. 21)

Bowerman (1973) and Greenfield and Smith (1976) have made similar observations of the early grammatical relations. Bowerman (1973) compared the early syntactic development of five children as they acquired a different language and observed that all children in the early stages of structure were dealing with subject-verb-object (SVO) constructions but not necessarily the whole structure at once. Early two-word combinations were subject-verb (SV) and verb-object (VO) with some subject-object (SO). And indeed, they eventually produced a few SVO constructions. This is similar to Bloom's (1970) notion of *reductionism*, which asserts that early two-word combinations were mostly reduced versions of SVO constructions. Presumably, the child has rudimentary knowledge of SVO as a basic construction, but memory constraints are such that the most salient dimensions survive (Braine, 1976). Greenfield (1980) contended that *informationality* rather than *salience* determines the code. Slobin (1973) commented that the two-word stage is evident across languages and that these combinations are used to code larger, underlying—presumably nuclear—constituents, but mental capacity precludes full realizations. He meant that two-word utterances show that the system is constrained. Apparently, young children operate with a rather limited programming capacity for utterances.

SVO seems to be a core underlying structure that is realized only as two units early on because of a fixed programming capacity.

SVO seems to be the earliest realization of true grammatical relations even though it may be manifest as only two- and possibly even one-word utterances, notwithstanding non-nominal expressions. Yet, the earliest of these constructions are likely to be only compositions lacking true grammatical character. These early compositions eventually become grammatical as they evidence productivity for SVO constructions. The verb seems to be the pivotal component (Bloom, Tackeff, & Lahey, 1984). Bloom et al. (1984, p. 405) said, "The subcategorization of verbs exerts a major influence on the acquisition of increasingly complex structures."

The centrality of the verb in SVO constructions is only speculation. There seems to be an early stage of verbs in which a few verbs are all-purpose verbs or glosses (Bloom, Lifter, & Hafitz, 1980). Brown (1973b, p. 150) referred to such verbs as "unmarked generic verbs." He (Brown, 1973b, p. 150) commented that parents, using situational cues, interpret such verbs in only four ways:

1. As expressing the occurrence, contemporaneous with the utterance, of some action or process of temporary duration; in short present progressive aspect.
2. As expressing the occurrence in the immediate temporal past of some process or action; in short past tense, limited to the immediate past.
3. As expressing the child's current intention or wish; the meanings carried by such semi-auxiliaries as *wanna, gonna, hafta*.
4. As imperatives.

Moreover, he pointed out that it is just these semantic distinctions—derived from parental interpretations—that comprise the basis from which the child inflects verbs and modifies auxiliaries.

The verb may be the pivotal component of SVO.

The relational or grammatical relations categories for SVO are innate in the sense that they are "part and parcel of our way of viewing the world" (Schlesinger, 1971, p. 98). The SVO seems to be, in a sense, the core of relationships for expressing the child's view of the world. However, the cognitive categories are apparently not mapped directly into semantic categories and these, in turn, are not mapped directly into grammatical categories (Wanner & Gleitman, 1982).

> The SVO seems to be the core of grammatical relationships, but it is not compatible with either cognitive categories or semantic categories.

Greenfield and Smith (1976) posited that the child is operating from perceptions of context—situational cues. These cues are basically *entities* and *relations*. An entity is any "point-at-able object and ... a relation is any action, operation, or state that an entity may undergo" (p. 61). They contended that the *base structure* of language acquisition is the perception of entities and relations. "If the base structure is a perceptual-cognitive structure of ongoing events, then the base will not be *linguistically* more complex than the surface, although it may be *cognitively* more complex. The verbal realization of the base may, of course, affect the nonverbal framework by endowing its different components with greater articulation" (pp. 63–64). "This formulation is identical in spirit with that proposed by Schlesinger (1971)" (p. 64).

Recognizing that the full underlying semantic base need not be coded in early utterances, Greenfield and Smith (1976, p. 64) characterized language acquisition as follows. "Within this framework, it is possible to think of the development of utterance length as an *accretion* process whereby progressively more of the base structure is given verbal realization."

> Language acquisition might be regarded as an accretion process whereby progressively more of the base structure is given verbal realization.

According to Greenfield and Smith (1976), mental constraints (processing capacity) force the child to *select* part of the base structure for social commerce. The choice of which entities and relations to code is essentially a cognitive rather than a linguistic problem. The child chooses the *most informative* aspects for coding. "The child encodes that aspect of an event where he sees alternatives, where there is uncertainty in terms of the situational structure ... in terms of presupposition: The child will not express verbally the presupposed element in the situation" (Greenfield & Smith, 1976, p. 64). Brown (1958a), Brown and Gilman (1960) and Pea (1979) suggested that children use the communicative codes (gestures, words, sentences) that have the most *utility*. The most informative aspects of an event or referent have the most potential for "point-making" (Bates & MacWhinney, 1979; Greenfield & Smith, 1976), or utility (Brown, 1958a). Accordingly, it is likely that children will encode the most informative aspects of a message, especially when faced with a limited processing capacity which forces them to be selective.

> The child chooses the most informative to talk about.

In short, even with one- and two-word utterances, early grammatical relations of the sort reported by Bloom (1970, 1973), Schlesinger (1971), Brown (1973b), Bowerman (1973) and Greenfield and Smith (1976) implicate a core structure, not necessarily ordered, which is the SVO structure. Early on, children seem to adopt a "groping" strategy (Braine, 1976) that allows them to settle on the particular order for their language. Also, early on, children operate from a limited processing capacity that does not allow the full realization of the SVO core. The above researchers suggest that this is the case.

Bloom (1970) proposed that less than full realizations of SVO structure result from *reductionism*. Reductionism indicates that the child may be making SVO constructions in rudimentary ways. But, the SVO constructions are reduced to only two of the three SVO components, with the third implicated by context. So, the child may say the following two-word utterances that together reveal knowledge of SVO constructions:

S	V	O
Mommy	*eat*	
	Eat	*cookie*
Mommy		*cookie*

Limited processing capacity results in reduced versions of SVO.

Thus, reductionism or other accounts of constraints of limited processing capacity are predicated on the assumption of a structural base something like SVO. Three other pieces of the puzzle support the contention of an SVO core structure; these are buildups, transitivity, and "natural unit." *Buildups* are successive utterances built upon each other (see Chapter 10). At this point, it should be noted that Bloom (1970) discussed buildups as behaviors predicated on a larger underlying propositional base. If this were not so, children would simply use their initial construction within a fluent segment of discourse; but, with buildups, they intentionally disrupt fluency, for the moment, to work out a fuller realization of the underlying proposition.

While buildups may index a larger propositional base than the utterance itself, buildups do not necessarily support the contention of an SVO core structure. Specifically, buildups are used by children who have surpassed SVO constructions; and, such buildup constructions reveal a propositional base that is an elaboration of SVO. To the extent that the propositional base is an elaboration of SVO, this may not be a serious problem. Brown (1973b, p. 206) suggested that early two- and three-word constructions seemed to be leading to agent-action-dative-object-location constructions, but he was not proposing this as a grammatical core. As he said, "It is not, of course, the case that every sentence the child produces could ... contain all five constituents" (p. 206).

> Buildups might index a hitherto unrealized underlying preposition.

In the emergence of *transitivity,* evidence suggests that children are progressively realizing predication until they achieve transitive relationships, SVO. Then, the acquisition process seems to shift whereby the child learns various *formal* mechanisms (e.g., modulation meaning, sentence types, modification—verbial and nominal, coordination, embeddedness, and derivation). Ingram (1971) has posited the emergence of transitivity. Greenfield and Smith (1976) have provided developmental evidence for it. However, before looking at their evidence, some observations by Bowerman (1973) are relevant.

Bowerman (1973) observed that the early grammatical compositions were simple, lacking modulations, modifications, pronominalizations, etc. "Almost all constructions were simple and could not be broken down into more elementary components" (p. 118). Inflections were rarely evident. "The vast majority of the children's utterances consisted of no more than two morphemes" (p. 118). Early on, three morpheme utterances were infrequent, but by the end of the early stage these utterances were very frequent. It was as though the child needed to fill the SVO slots before striving for other accomplishments.

> Slot filling processes for SVO appear to be an early goal.

Once SVO constructions have become productive, the child seems to strive for qualitative changes within sentences. Bowerman (1973) reported that SVO, three-morpheme utterances abound. They contain predicate constructions of two main types even though the verb itself may not be evidenced. The verbal constructions are copular *(BE)* or main verbs. She reported the following kinds of copular constructions:

demonstrative-noun:	*(this* + noun)
noun-noun (locative):	*(airplane garage)*
noun-adjective:	*(duck big)*

"Main verb constructions consisted of two, three, or ... four constituents selected from an underlying pattern which had the following form for most of the children: subject-verb-modifier-object-indirect object-locative" (Bowerman, 1973, p. 170).

Greenfield and Smith (1976) offered developmental evidence of the emergence of transitivity. In short, they showed that verbial constructions begin with a pseudolocative, then evidence the following sequence: intransitive (SV), transitive (SVO), and state verbs. Further indirect support of this sequence, and at least of the notion that intransitives, transitives, and state verbs are processed somewhat differently, came from Bloom, Lifter, and Hafitz (1980), who showed that the acquisition of inflections varies as a function of these distinctions. Weist (1982) showed that children distinguish among intransitive verbs according to animacy, but not action role. However, action role, not animacy, is used to make distinctions among transitive verbs. Evidently, the distinction between one argument and several argument verbs (Perfetti, 1972) is psychologically real. This supports, to some extent, Harris's (1965) delineation of basic sentence types.

> The emergence of transitivity is compatible with the SVO grammatical core.

Kuno (1973) suggested that there is a universal tendency for keeping the verb and object together, irrespective of order. He called verb and object a "natural unit." The reason that order need not be specified is because languages seem to have a core predicate structure for different orders of constituents. In English, this structure is SVO but in Japanese it is SOV (Kuno, 1973).

Similarly, McNeill (1975, 1982) suggested "semiotic extension" which posits that "two thoughts are needed to make a meaningful action" (McNeill, 1982, p. 523). Regarding the SVO structure, the two relations would be *agent* and *action-object;* such thoughts are better appreciated as subject/predicate, topic/comment, predicate/argument, and given/new information. These latter models are functional in nature (Bates & MacWhinney, 1979).

Functionalism

Although the notion of an SVO grammatical core structure in English is appealing, the evidence is not concrete. Further, SVO relies on the "hard-wired" notion that SVO is the grammatical core of language. Bates and MacWhinney (1979) hold that grammar is a secondary or derived system. They contend that the acquisition of grammar is not guided by abstract categories such as those which might lead to an SVO grammatical core. The functionalistic view is that such grammatical knowledge becomes realized from the child's cognitive-social awareness of discourse within social commerce subject to various constraints of the speech channel. They summarized their functional views as "point making":

1. Point making operates at different levels in codification, i.e., presupposition-proposition, topic-comment, and so on.
2. Point making may be motivated for several reasons, i.e., new contrasted to old information, salience, topic shift and so on.
3. Point making may be recursive thereby resulting in nested comments. Thus, points can be made within other points.

4. Point making can be accomplished in a variety of ways in the service of the above issues.

Rather than grammatical learning per se, the child may simply be following pragmatic options in point making.

These issues about point making are remarkably similar in principle to those of Greenfield (1980), Greenfield and Smith (1976), and Pea's (1979) considerations of informativeness. And furthermore, they seem to be derived from Brown's (1958) notion of utility of word use. Bloom (1973) holds the view that early syntax maps underlying cognition, *informativeness*. Her view hints of functionalism, especially when she points out that children, faced with limited processing capacities, are forced to be *selective* in what they choose to talk about—the most informative.

Dore et al. (1976) identified some *presyntactic devices* (PSD), forms that were evidenced before the child could be credited with syntactic constructions. They held that prosodic features are useful in distinguishing successive-single-word utterances from those that have "a true combinatorial output." They said that early word combinations were regarded as syntactic if they met the following two criteria: "two or more words which are produced forming one intonational pattern AND in which the relation among the words is one of the factors determining the meaning of the utterance" (Dore et al., 1976, p. 21).

Using these criteria, Dore et al. (1976) identified the following presyntactic devices:

a. *Dummy element productions:* These are productions containing one phonetic element which does not have meaning. It is a "conventional word preceded by a single phonetically unstable unit." For example, the child said, "[I] ball."

b. *Dummy form productions:* These productions are similar to dummy element productions but the preceding element is clearly syllabic. They reported a child who said "bottle" several times each of which was accompanied (preceded) by various meaningless syllables: [dæ] bottle, [mv] bottle, [te] bottle, [wɔ] bottle.

c. *Reduplication productions:* These are single words produced successively usually two or three times within a single intonation contour. For example, they reported a child who said, "car, car" when he saw a car passing by.

d. *Empty form productions:* These are phonetically stable units linked to a conventional word. The phonetically stable unit lacks an identifiable reference; it acts like a handle for the conventional word. It is what Bloom (1973) regarded as an "archetypal pivot."

e. *Rote productions:* These are two conventional words combined together. While they may occur as one, they do not evidence other combinations. They reported that for the rote production "no more" both "no" and "more" occurred as single word elements but structures like 'no house,' 'no car,' 'more ball,' and 'more juice' were not evidenced.

In addition to these, Bloom (1973) reported "successive single-word utterances," which foretold early syntax. Moreover, she indicated that the prosodic pattern for such words was unmistakable. Yet, these prosodic patterns were NOT sentential intonation contours; rather, the single words in succession had a terminal falling pitch, relatively equal stress, and a distinct pause.

Cognitive Functions: Operators of Reference

In short, SVO appears to be the grammatical core or base from which grammatical categories or knowledge are launched. The primary evidence for this issues from the study of early one-, two-, and three-word utterances expressing compositional or proto-grammatical relations. This is only part of the story, only one side-of-the-coin as it were, because there is another set of expressions called "functional relations" (Bloom, 1970, 1973), operations (Schlesinger, 1971), or operators of reference (Brown, 1973b) that provide semantic categories of a different sort. These seem to function *cognitively* rather than *grammatically* (see also Chapter 6.) Bloom (1973) said that functional relations were relatively more frequent than grammatical relations in expression of early two-word compositions; for example, *no* and *more* were among the words used most frequently by the young children. "Relational *function* forms occurred earlier, persisted, and were used more often (in the first half of the second year) than the *substantive* form, which came to predominate in the last half of the second year" (Bloom, 1973, p. 139). Greenfield and Smith (1976, p. 210) contested Bloom's view that such expressions were more frequent than substantive forms. In any case, the primary concern is not their frequency but their *function*.

Functional relations or operators of reference seem to function cognitively rather than grammatically.

Gopnik (1981) and McCune-Nicolich (1981) provided intriguing insights into early structure in this regard, showing that *non-nominal expressions* occur during the one-word period (e.g., *that, gone, no, more, there*). Even though they are one-word expressions, they constitute the beginning of structure because they are *relational*. But, the primary function of this structure seems not to be grammatical per se; it seems to be cognitive.

Gopnik (1981) detailed the following properties of these non-nominal expressions. They do *not* refer to specific types of objects, relationships between objects, or particular actions or types of actions. Moreover, they do not appear to be social, conversational, or expressive devices. Such expressions have "a certain egocentric quality," especially early on. They seem to be used "to mark relationships between themselves and objects, or between themselves, their actions, and objects" (Gopnik, 1981, p. 101). In these ways, they seem to illustrate problem solving and other cognitive activities.

Gopnik (1981, p. 102) stated further, "The expressions did not seem to encode actions or intentions as such; instead, the expressions were used when the child predicted that a certain consequence would ensue if he acted in a particular way, or if other actions occurred ." Finally, she said, "The concepts encoded by these expressions seem to be both egocentric and abstract" (p. 103). Such expressions seem to reflect raw cognitive achievements about reference. Even as two-word expressions appear, these non-nominal expressions persist. The second word in such compositions identifies the intended referent. Gopnik (1981, p. 103) held that such expressions "play an important role in the cognitive development of 1-2-year-olds."

Relational expressions seem to express raw cognitive achievements about reference.

Gopnik suggested that such expressions may actually assist the child in solving certain cognitive problems. These problems are not identifying simply referents, but relationships to referents. Thus, children use non-nominal expressions to spontaneously encode newly realized cognitive relationships early in development. As one-word utterances, they have "combinatorial meaning" (Greenfield & Smith, 1976) whereby the event or context of use defines the intended relationship. Two-word expressions of this kind may simply specify one referent of the relationship; three-word expressions may specify two referents and their relationships.

Assume that Bloom's (1970, 1973) distinctions between utterances expressing grammatical relations and those expressing functional relations are psychologically real. And furthermore, assume, for the moment, that such early grammatical relations yield a structural core or base for learning grammatical systems for "point making" and that functional relations provide a means of problem solving. Under these assumptions, it appears that Bloom's distinction between grammatical relations and functional relations are vestiges of what Halliday (1975) regarded as the *pragmatic* and *mathetic* functions of language, respectively.

The Three Bears

We do not know the particular ways in which categories (cognitive, semantic, grammatical) and words are related nor do we have clear evidence as to how words are learned (Miller, 1974). Even so, there are some proposals about early word learning and how such learning fits into a larger scheme of language and cognitive learning.

In the mid-1960s, there was considerable interest in single-word utterances; such utterances were thought to be sentence-like holophrases. However, the holophrastic notion did not hold up, mainly because the child might be credited with too much knowledge. So other explanations were sought for single-word utterances.

Drawing upon Slobin (1973), Gleitman and Wanner (1982, p. 11) claimed that "the child conceives the word as the natural domain of simple concepts." Carey (1982) demonstrated that early words are acquired holistically and they are situationally bound. Such words are neither labels of complex concepts nor are they decomposable into semantic features. This contradicts some feature theories of early word learning. Bowerman (1982) also held that early words are holistic or "unopened packages"; as Gleitman and Wanner (1982, p. 12) put it, "Each early word is an unopened package; only much later does productive lexical analysis begin to appear."

Gleitman and Wanner (1982, p. 12) also describe the functions of words in early sentences in terms of "The Three Bears" proposal. *"Each word must code exactly one of the arguments of a predicate, the predicate itself, or a logical word* (such as *and* or *not*) . . . To the extent a received word codes more than one of the countenanced functions, it is too big; less than one, it is too small; exactly one, and it is just right" (Gleitman & Wanner, 1982, p. 12).

"The Three Bears" proposal states that each word codes one aspect and only one of a grammatical base.

The particular countenanced functions are the following components of a proposition: an argument of a predicate, the predicate itself, or a logical word. An argument is a noun phrase intrinsic to predication. Perfetti (1972) suggested that there are one-, two-, three-, and possibly four-argument verbs. These are illustrated as follows:

Argument	Predicate	Example
One	Intransitive	*He walks*
Two	Transitive	*He opened the door*
Three	Transitive (expanded)	*He hit the nail with the hammer*

Notice that this scheme compares favorably with the sequence of acquisition of predicates reported by Greenfield and Smith (1976).

The Envelope Please

Bloom (1973) observed that before syntax, children made successive single-word utterances. She held that these successive single-word utterances were related because they reflected a continuity between the topics and context of an event, usually a child-centered action event. She suggested that such behavior might be regarded as *relational* behavior because these utterances express relationships between the coded referents and contexts. These are not grammatical relations, but their antecedents. "Successive single-word utterances presented evidence of awareness of the intersection of different aspects of a situation" (p. 53). She indicated that inasmuch as most successive single-word utterances seem to have a primitive discourse relationship, the naming behavior interpretaton is not supported. And, the topic-comment account of this structure did not hold either. Apparently, these utterances, although related, were not sufficiently related to be given full-fledged grammatical or discourse status. "The reason why sentences did not occur—and the reason why their single-word utterances cannot accurately be characterized as 'sentences'—is that children did not as yet know the LINGUISTIC CODE for mapping conceptual notions onto semantic-syntactic relations in sentences" (Bloom, 1973, p. 55).

Bloom (1973) described two kinds of successive single-word utterances: chained and holistic, "There appeared to be a developmental progression from predominantly chained successive single-word utterances in the period from 16 to 21 months" (p. 47). Chained successive one-word utterances occurred with successive movements. "Chained successive single-word utterances appeared to accompany performance of schemas . . ." (p. 51). Holistic successive one-word utterances were comments about the entire situation rather than particular actions or shifts in context.

> The HOLISTIC successive single-word utterances appeared to occur with a mental representation of the complete schema from the outset, and movements and utterances were directed towards the anticipated schema. Developments towards this holistic structure coincided with the development of what Piaget has called the interiorization of actions as the child becomes capable of a mental representation of actions prior to (or instead of) their performance in this same period of time (p. 52). Allison's single-word utterances were apparently mapped onto successive movements first, and then, subsequently, successive single-word utterances were mapped onto mental representations of a whole event (object or relation) in experience. (Bloom, 1973, p. 52)

It is important to note that it was the *prosodic* pattern that distinguished these successive single-word utterances.

> The prosodic pattern that distinguished such words as these said in succession, as single-word utterances, was unmistakable. Each word occurred with terminal falling pitch contour, and relatively equal stress, and there was a variable but distinct pause between them, so that utterance boundaries were clearly marked. (Bloom, 1973, p. 41)

It appears that a prosodic format is operating as an early structural form. Indeed, prosodic capacities may have a kind of priority early on. Nakazima (1962) reported that 8- and 9-month-old infants can imitate intonational patterns produced by their mothers but not words, syllables, or phonemes.

The prosodic envelope notion as a means of identifying the place for grammatical morphemes is somewhat difficult to support, even though it is attractive. One of two positions must hold for the prosodic envelope to work, continuity of prosodic skills *or* prosodic awareness as an immediate outcome of SVO awareness. Both are tenuous, but possible.

Continuity of prosodic skills refers to the notion that prosodic behavior before syntax—one word utterances—would be somewhat continuous with that after syntax or at least in the early stages of syntax. If prosodic continuity exists, the argument could be made that prosodic capacities usher in syntax. The data on this question are mixed and incomplete. Lahey (1972) reported that the intonations at 16 months were not evidenced at 20-22 months when the child was learning syntax. Yet, at 28 months the child showed sentential intonation patterns. Greenfield and Smith (1976) had data that conflicted with those of Lahey. While Greenfield and Smith did not have data concerning intonation contours for questions, they did have such data for the acquisition of early syntax from one-word utterances. As they (1976, p. 215) said, "They show clear prosodic continuity between one-word and later speech in the distinct expression of statements and demands." Bloom (1973) claimed, based upon the Lahey study, that sentence prosody is learned after syntax. Greenfield and Smith (1976, p. 215) agreed that syntax is not learned from prosody.

Prosody as an immediate outcome of early syntax is possible. As Greenfield and Smith pointed out, prosody could temporarily drop out only to reappear in service of a fuller fruition of SVO. Certainly there is other evidence that early verbal behaviors drop out and may or may not reappear—perhaps *replacement* is more accurate because the subsequent skills are qualitatively different. Such behavior occurs with inflections, with vocabulary items in phonology, and with invented words (word mortality).

In order for prosody to serve as a guide for grammatical acquisitions, two conditions need to be met. First, prosody should be operative early on, at least immediately upon realizing SVO. Second, prosody should have a faithful continuity to sentential intonational contours. These conditions seem to hold in early syntax (Lahey, 1972), so it may be that the prosodic envelope notion is a consequence of SVO.

Prosody may be a means of entering formal structure.

Bruner (1975) suggested that the child locks onto prosodic patterns as a way of entering the formal grammatical structure of language. He posited the role of prosodic patterns as follows: "It consists of the child learning phonological patterns almost as place-holders, imitatively. They constitute, even preverbally, a kind of prosodic envelope or matrix into which the child 'knows' that morphemes go—an interrogative and vocative/demand contour, and possibly an indicative" (p. 10). This is compatible with Chomsky's (1980) more recent innatist proposal for rich knowledge of grammatical rules. Gleitman and Wanner put it this way:

> In theory, such schemata contain empty slots that the child needs only to fill in to learn his own language. Under this idealization, which is often called 'parameter setting' to distinguish it from the hypothesis-testing framework, the child might come pre-armed with schema for core grammar rules informing him that (say) a noun phrase is composed of a head noun plus specifier, but leaving open the problems of determining which order these elements appear in, how specification is marked in this language, and so on. (1982, p. 38)

Perhaps the "hardwired" prosodic envelope is the means of deducing morphemic slots. Moreover, it may be just such a process that keeps the child narrowly focused—slots of the envelope. Possibly prosodic features may provide an entry into the verbal systems of some hearing-impaired children (Weiss, Carney, & Leonard, 1985) and maybe other language-impaired children also.

The prosodic envelope may keep the child narrowly focused in language acquisition.

The Three Bears proposal is predicated on the notion of linguistic slots as well. However, these slots pertain to components of propositions rather than the assignment of possible morphemes. In this regard, the Three Bears proposal seems to be a deeper notion of slots (arguments of a predicate, the predicate itself, a logical word) than the prosodic envelope.

Read and Schreiber (1982) said that phrase boundaries are largely a matter of intonational contours for 7-year-olds. Another note on the potency of intonation is the responsivity to rising intonation as opposed to falling intonation for label requests. Bruner (1981) pointed out that parents use rising intonation to denote new information whereas falling intonation means the mother expects her child to know the appropriate word. And, Furrow (1984) showed that young toddlers used prosodic elements for communicative purposes.

These early utterances appear to be "slot fillers" in the sense of SVO, the Three Bears, and the prosodic envelope. Thus, they are becoming true formalizations by virtue of the fact that they are abiding by the constraints of language itself (prosody, SVO, propositional components) and are single-mindedly (or blindly) directed even while suppressed by mental constraints.

A note of caution should be made about the methodological problems associated with speculations and research on prosodic aspects of language. Crystal (1978) said that prosodic features were measured poorly in several studies (e.g., attributing meaning to rising or falling intonation when other variables could have been implicated, and attributing intention on the basis of prosodic cues).

The Formal Grammatical Arena

After the child achieves a *repertoire* of SVO constructions (pragmatic, semantic, syntactic) he or she utilizes formal grammatical mechanisms in message construction. There are obvious questions about this shift toward increased grammatical complexity once basic or core structure has been achieved. What *impels* the child to enter domains of increased complexity? What further achievements are realized by employing more complex constructions?

Only speculation is possible on both questions. The speculations about impelling motivations are more spindly than those about what is achieved by increased complexity. The speculations about impelling motivations derive from both innatist and functionalist positions (see Chapter 5). The issue of further achievements via increased complexity is addressed from a functionalist perspective—increased options for *informativeness* in social commerce (see Chapters 3, 9 and 10).

As children continue, their word combinations become increasingly fuller realizations of sentences. At first they are merely rudimentary sentences, concatenations (Bowerman, 1973), reductionistic (Bloom, 1970, 1973) and telegraphic (Smith & Miller, 1966). Eventually, they become simple sentences and then elaborate sentences. As children grasp grammatical mechanisms for sentence construction, they enter the domain of *formal* rules, which are those rules that are shared by others for organizing messages.

In a sense, vocabulary and the attendant contentive and intentional functions, coupled with limited phonological structure, arm the children with ammunition for formulating sentences. But, they have to learn the formal mechanisms for doing so. These formal mechanisms are the semantic-syntactic systems with their accompanying morpho-phonological realizations.

Before discussing early grammatical acquisitions, it is useful to reiterate the anatomy of a speech act as it may be expressed in basic SVO grammatical relations. The following portrays the anatomy of the utterance "He opened the door."

Intention: Intent: Assertion—Informational
Proposition: Explicit Content: Semantic Categories: Agent-Action-Definite-Object
Presupposition: Implicit Content: Knowledge of the world sufficient to give this expression meaning
Informatives: Explication of uncertainty within the context of presumed "known"
Pragmatics: Negotiated message-of-best-fit
Formal Structure: Grammatical Structure: Subject-Tense-Action-Determiner-Inanimate Object
Locution or Utterance: Phonological realization of "He opened the door."
Perlocution: Effects on the listener: Comprehend: Construction and utilization of information

From the functional view, grammatical structure is a surface manifestation of more substantial issues of language. The formal grammatical structure is subordinate to its functions in social commerce. And, to reiterate and emphasize, the coin-of-the-realm is not grammar per se but the functional use of grammar in becoming selectively informative.

The coin-of-the-realm of social commerce is informativeness.

Brown's Five Stages

Brown (1973a, 1973b) proposed a five-stage model for early language acquisition. Stage 1 dealt with the acquisition of semantic functions and relations. These are basic notions coded in an utterance. Stage 2 pertained to modulations of meaning centered essentially on inflectional morphemes. Modulations of meaning are accomplished by pluralization, tense marking, and so on. Stage 3 was about modalities of sentence types. These modalities pertained to *yes/no* questions, *wh-* questions, and negations. Stage 4 dealt with sentence embedding which is placing one sentence within another. An example is the relative clause *(The boy who sat here is my brother)*. Finally, Stage 5 was about sentence coordination, or the use of various conjunctions. Moreover, mean length of utterance (MLU) was used as a crude gauge for demarking each stage.

These five stages and their associated MLU values have been widely referenced.

Brown (1977) regarded these stages as hypothetical. In Stage 1, there is a need to place semantic categories within presupposition (Fillmore, 1972). And, the relatively recent research on non-nominal expressions needs to be incorporated. In Stage 2, the notion of the 14 morphemes and the sequence of acquisition have been questioned (Block & Kessel, 1980; Moerk, 1980, 1981) and partially reaffirmed (Pinker, 1981). Stage 3 might be redressed as intentions. Finally, Stages 4 and 5 need fuller explanation. In general, though, they seem to hold. The major problem with these stages is that they emphasize structure. The contemporary literature emphasizes the centrality of function. Consequently, the stages approach is undergoing revision.

> Brown's five stages with the attendant MLUs are undergoing revision.

The use of MLU as a gauge for language acquisition is questionable basically because it has a very narrow range of value. That is, MLU from roughly 1.5 to 3.50 is an index of language acquisition. Below this range it is virtually meaningless; above this range it becomes a *performance* index rather than a *developmental* index (Bloom, 1970, p. 2; Cazden, 1968; Cowan, Weber, Hoddinott, & Klein, 1967; Shriner, 1969). Brown (1973a, 1973b) recognized that an MLU over 4.0 is not a viable index of language acquisition (see also Dale, 1980). Brown (1973b, p. 54) said,

> By the time the child reaches Stage V, however, he is able to make constructions of such great variety that what he happens to say and the MLU of a sample begin to depend more on the character of the interaction than on what the child knows, and so the index loses its value as an indicator of grammatical knowledge.

> MLU has a very narrow range of use as an index of language acquisition: 1.5–3.5.

Fourteen Morphemes

As for marking, Brown (1973a, 1973b) showed that in the early structures children begin to *modulate meanings* by incorporating various inflections. Indeed, Brown identified an acquisition sequence for the emergence of 14 inflectional morphemes. It should be noted that the acquisition of these morphemes begins early, but full acquisition is protracted over several years. Furthermore, they are

Table 8.2. The 14 Morphemes that Appear in Early Grammatical Structure

Morpheme	Example
Progressive *(-ing)*	Tata going
Locative *(in)*	Ball in box
Locative *(on)*	Ball on hat
Regular Plural *(-s)*	Doggies here
Irregular Past	Ate cookie
Possessive *('s)*	Tata's candy
Uncontractible Copula	Daddy is here
Articles	The doggy ate a bone
Regular Past *(ed)*	He opened the door
Regular Third Person *(-s)*	It runs
Irregular Third Person	He does it
Uncontractible Auxiliary	He is sleeping
Contractible Copula	He's big
Contractible Auxiliary	He's sleeping

Derived from Brown (1973b)

unstressed aspects. Thus, the contribution of the prosodic envelope for launching grammatical acquisition seems to have fallen away or been reorganized for other considerations—namely contrastive intonation.

Table 8.2 shows the 14 morphemes. They are: *-ing, in, on,* regular plural, irregular past, possessive *'s,* uncontractible copula, articles, regular past, regular third person *-s,* irregular third person, uncontractible auxiliary, contractible copula, and contractible auxiliary.

The *present progressive* has two disjointed aspects: *be* and *-ing*. It is incorporated in such a way that the tense marker accompanying the *be* and the *-ing* is connected to the main verb. For the sentence, "I opened the box," the *be* + *-ing* are incorporated thus:

I past+ *be open* + *ing the box.*
I was opening the box.

In learning such disjointed systems, the child goes through three stages. The *-ing* alone is connected to the main verb. Then, the *be* and *-ing* are connected with or without tense marking. It looks like this:

I walk
I walking
I (be) walking
I am walking

The progessive structure is applicable only to action verbs, not state verbs. Thus, the child not only has to learn this mechanism but also make appropriate semantic distinctions between verb types (Bloom, Lifter, & Hafitz, 1980).

The prepositions *in* and *on* are two other early morphemes. These identify location. However, it should be noted that some early prepositions are actually protopredicates (Greenfield & Smith, 1976). Therefore, one needs to be cautious about crediting the child with true locatives.

Full acquisition of the 14 morphemes identified by Brown (1973a, 1973b) extends over several years.

The marking of *regular plural* is a way to modulate the meaning of a noun. Brown (1973b), Palermo and Eberhart (1968), Cazden (1968), and Kuczaj (1981) identified three stages in the acquisition of plural, possessive, and tense. First is a *vocabulary stage,* in which children learn words holistically (Carey, 1982). Children do not realize that words have a stem and possible inflectional (indeed, derivational) markers. Accordingly, at the vocabulary stage children will say "boys," "man," "men," and so forth. The second stage is called the *overgeneralization stage,* when children discern regular inflectional rules but generalize these rules to all instances, irregular as well as regular. This is when children say "boys," "mans," "mens," and so forth. The third stage is *appropriate generalization,* in which children use the rule appropriately and learn the irregular exceptions. Then they return to saying "boys," "man," and "men." Thus, it *appears* as if children had skill, lost it, then acquired it again; but actually their prior capacity became reorganized into rule-governed behavior. Incidentally, some mothers who notice this "false loss" become concerned that their child is losing language.

The child goes through three stages in acquiring inflectional rules: vocabulary, overgeneralization, and appropriate generalization.

The *irregular past* tense is relatively frequent in English. Inasmuch as early word learning is rote learning as opposed to rule-governed, it is not surprising that children learn irregular past tense marked verbs early. However, this early learning does not necessarily mean that they understand irregular past tense marking. Children puzzle out this kind of knowledge during the three stages; in the case of irregular past tense, this may take several years.

It is not clear exactly when the *possessive* or genitive inflection emerges. Bowerman (1973) and Cazden (1968) asserted that possessives appear relatively early. Brown (1973b) put them in the middle of the 14 morphemes whereas Greenfield and Smith (1976) held that they come in somewhat late. It should be noted that possessives can be marked in other ways as well, such as a prepositional phrase *(the sleeve of the shirt)*. Thus, inflectional tags comprise only part of the story of possessives.

The *uncontractible copula* means that the *BE* verb is not joined or contracted to the preceding noun phrase. In English, there is an auxiliary *be* and a copular *BE*. There are three kinds of copular *BE* verbs, which are respectively defined by subsequent constituents, specifically: noun phrase, adjectival, adverbial of place. The following illustrates these different kinds:

Auxiliary *be* + *-ing*	*I am walking*
Copular *BE* + NP	*I am a student*
Copular *BE* + Adj	*I am big*
Copular *BE* + Adv-p	*I am here*

When the copular forms are first acquired, the child may not yet realize that it can be optionally joined as a contraction *(I'm a student)*. Moreover, "the uncontracted forms are, in general, *phonologically* simpler than the contracted in that they involve fewer phonological rules" (Brown, 1973b, p. 305). Thus, the early appearance of the copula is in an uncontracted form.

Moreover, it should be acknowledged that the acquisition of the various forms of auxiliary and copula *(am, was, is, are, were, be)* is protracted much like the acquisition of various pronominal forms.

The *articles the* and *a* are part of a larger determiner system that is most frequently evidenced by the definite article *(the)*, indefinite articles *(a, some)*, demonstratives *(this, that, these, those)*, possessives *(my, your, our)* and numbers *(first, second, two, three)*. These appear before nouns or modified nouns to determine or distinguish a particular noun. Joined to a modified or unmodified noun, they establish a noun phrase.

The and *a* appear somewhat early in the child's formal structure because they function pragmatically to differentially denote *given* and *new* information, respectively. It should be recalled that Bruner (1981) suggested a *scaffolding process* in language acquisition whereby pragmatic capacities provide a scaffold for learning semantic and syntactic capacities. The acquisition of *the* and *a* constitutes a cogent example because these words provide a means of formal explicitness of a pragmatic awareness of given and new information.

Emslie and Stevenson (1981) reviewed research on the acquisition of definite and indefinite articles and found that it centers on the distinctions between *nominative* (definite articles) and *identifying* (indefinite articles) uses of articles. There are adverbial counterparts to these distinctions in adult language, *naming* and *specifying*, respectively. *Nominative* is a naming function whereas *identifying* is a specifying function. The nominative function is used to lock onto a particular instance of a category. The nominative function comes in first because naming is simpler than specifying a uniqueness of a referent. Maratsos (1976) affirmed the simplicity of nominative as compared to specification. Both Brown (1973b) and Maratsos (1976) reported that at approximately 3 to 4 years of age the child is able to distinguish the use of indefinite (name) from definite (specify) articles. Warden (1976) found that while this might be so for a naming task it is not so for a describing task. "Warden concluded that children under 5 fail to take into account their audience's knowledge of a referent (their referring expressions are predominantly definite), that there is referential language only from 9 onwards" (Emslie & Stevenson, 1981, p. 315). This raises another issue in the acquisition of articles, egocentricism. The definite article is used deictically (to separate speaker-listener perspectives). Egocentrically oriented children may use definite articles excessively because they assume that what they know others know also.

Another part of the determiner system is also evidenced before the articles. The demonstrative or at least a proto-demonstrative /um/ appears very early in conjunction with the early referential point (Bruner, 1981). Moreover, Ramer (1976, p. 705) reported a demonstrative pronominal "that one" as explicit deixis with two-word utterances.

The *regular past* is the use of *-ed* to mark a past tense. This marker may appear as an overgeneralized form attached to irregular verbs: *goed, wented, hitted*. Eventually, children sort out these and use the regular past tense marker only for regular verbs. Overgeneralization rarely occurs with modals, yet modals carry tense markers.

The *third person singular* is a device in English to show concordance or agreement between the plurality of the third person case of the subject noun phrase and its verb. This is shown as follows:

Third person singular:	*He works hard.*
Third person plural:	*The boys work hard.*
First person singular:	*I work hard.*

The full acquisition of the third person singular marker may be protracted. Indeed, the acquisition of the 14 morphemes may be protracted.

The *uncontractible auxiliary* refers to the first component of the two components in the progressive and the perfect. It refers to the modals (sometimes called helping verbs: *can, will, shall, may, must*). These are optionally contracted in adult speech but in child speech they are first learned in an uncontracted form. The following illustrate the point:

Auxiliary	Uncontracted	Contracted
Progressive		
Present:	*I am singing*	*I'm singing*
Past:	*I was singing*	(awkward)
Perfect		
Present:	*I have sung*	*I've sung*
Past:	*I had sung*	*I'd sung*

Modals
  Present: I will sing   I'll sing
  Past: I would sing   I'd sing

The *contractible copula* is the contraction of the *BE* verb with its subject. The contracted form is learned well after the noncontracted form. The *contractible auxiliary,* shown above, is learned after the noncontractible counterpart.

There has been a debate about these 14 morphemes. Brown (1973b) proposed that they appear in a stable sequence, the order of which is independent of the frequency of language input to the child (see also de Villiers & de Villiers, 1973). Moerk (1980, 1981) and Block and Kessel (1980) raised some questions about the order of the 14 morphemes, but Pinker (1981) examined these problems and concluded that Brown's position should be upheld. Moerk (1981) reiterated some problems concerning the generalizability of these 14 morphemes. Briefly, he was concerned that Brown's original sample may not be sufficiently *representative* to allow for normative conclusions. Nevertheless, it should be remembered that the full acquisition of these morphemes extends over several years.

Modulations of meanings begin early on in the formalization of language learning but extend over a considerable length of time.

Summary

The predication stage in the emergence of grammaticality pertains to the complex question of how and when children convert their semantic categories into grammatical categories. The literature points to a stage or discontinuous relationship between semantic and grammatical knowledge. Moreover, there is a considerable debate concerning the psychological reality of characterizations of semantic categories. In a nutshell, it appears that the "clutter reduction" theory (Bowerman, 1982) and the "metamorphosis" theory (Gleitman, 1981) most adequately address these issues.

Reorganization, co-occurrence, rule learning based upon positive, negative, and ambiguous information, and learnability seem to play roles in the acquisition process, but these roles are not yet well understood.

Early structures seem to reveal two *functions,* cognitive and communicative. The SVO construction emerges as a grammatical base in early predication. Reduced versions of SVO may be evidenced because of limited processing capacity. The presyntactic devices show that the child is aware of structure but lacks knowledge of formal mechanisms.

The Three Bears proposal and the prosodic envelope proposal appear to be compatible with the notion of the SVO grammatical core. Brown's five stages are undergoing revision because they overemphasized structure. Brown's 14 morphemes provide various ways to modulate meanings in becoming informative.

9

ASSISTANCE

Does a child get assistance in language learning? If so, what is the nature of this assistance? And, is the acquisition process hearty (strongly, unfailing) or fragile (frail, easily altered) such that assistance may foster or hinder learning? These are important questions throughout language learning but they are especially important in the early stages and when a major undertaking is launched such as a shift from semantic to formal grammatical categories.

In a sense, this chapter is inserted in an otherwise continuous discussion of the acquisition of formal grammatical systems which itself may be discontinuous in the sense that it progresses in stages. It is logical to insert a discussion of assistance between the predication and attribution stages of language acquisition because much of the literature on assistance deals with the acquisition of the early stages of language learning: symbolization, conventionalization, and early formalization.

LAS Revisited

Bruner (1981) proposed the Language Assistance System (LAS) (see Chapter 5). To reiterate, Bruner proposed that the mother has an active partnership role in assisting (not directing) her child's active language learning. LAS is considered complementary to LAD. At this juncture, it is useful to describe some mechanisms of LAS as delineated by Bruner. These are mother-child interactions focused on communication. They include: highlighting and looming, regulating joint action and attention, given/new informational intonations, tuning, raising the ante, and formatting all of which are discussed below.

In the development of referential meaning, the mother may *highlight* and *loom* the referent. Such behavior serves to identify unquestionably the topical referent. *Highlighting,* or forefronting, is to place the object directly in front of the child. Mothers do this in two ways. Mothers constantly monitor their child's line of regard so the mother can tell when to move the object to keep it forefronted (Collis & Schaffer, 1975). Another way to highlight is to show different angles or functions of the object as it is forefronted. For example, the mother places the jack-in-the-box in front of her son. The mother checks her child's line of regard to see if he sees it. Then, she points to it and names it. If he shifts his line of regard away from the referent, she will move it to fall into his line of regard again; then she will point and name it again. Once she is sure he sees it, she may move it slightly thereby giving him a new perspective or a discrepancy, elicits and maintains attention and schema development. Then, she may proceed to demonstrate its function.

Looming is a form of highlighting in which the referent, once placed in a line of regard, is moved toward and away from the child. The child then tends spontaneously to reach for, and grasp, or point to the referent. Highlighting and looming often result in the infant engaging in enactive or motoric processing of the referent and possibly indexing by virtue of pointing, a referential display, or a performative. "Maternal gestures have more of a role in maintaining attention and the flow of interaction for young childen than they do in providing specific cues to the grammars the child is acquiring" (Schnur & Shatz, 1984, p. 29).

In *regulated joint action and attention,* a communicative point, some other performative, or a label serves to regulate the actions and attention of both mother and child. For example, the mother may point to a referent and say, "Oh, ball." Any or all of these three maternal behaviors (point, vocative "Oh," label "ball") may serve to regulate joint action and attention. Thus, the baby ceases doing what he or she was doing motorically and visually turning to her to pick up her line of regard and using it to locate the referent. Meanwhile the mother assists by highlighting and looming the referent. Thus, the actions and attention of both are jointly fixed.

Given and new information inflections or intonations are mechanisms that the mother uses to assist her child in locating and comprehending referents. If the mother thinks her child knows the name of the particular referent, she will use a *falling intonation*. This is a "matter-of-fact" statement about known or previously given information. It is now used in restricted social commerce—mother-child formats. However, if the mother thinks her child may not know the name of the particular referent, she will use a *rising intonation* (Sullivan & Horowitz, 1983) and the label. Indeed, she may use an *attentional vocative* ("Look!") as well. Thus, the mother assists her child by an attentional vocative and rising or falling intonation to attend to the referent as it is being labeled.

Bruner (1981) called the initial labeling process a *dubbing ceremony* whereby the child is told the name of something. In effect, the child has to take the label or leave it. The child has an insufficient conceptualization to question the appropriateness of the label. Actually, the appropriateness of some early labels might be questioned in some instances because they will eventually need to be revised to conform to the adult world. Here, some early dubbing ceremonies may yield some "tin metals," whereas others are everlastingly bronze, although somewhat tarnished by wear.

Tuning and *raising the ante* refer to the mother's skill to be sufficiently cognizant of her child's repertoire of verbal capacities to direct her choices of what to say in a given circumstance. Parents and even older siblings tailor their speech for young children (Brown & Hanlon, 1970; Cross, 1977; Newport, 1977; Gleitman, Newport, & Gleitman, 1984; Snow & Ferguson, 1977; Sullivan & Horowitz, 1983). It seems that older speakers tune their utterances to be comparable to (or slightly more advanced than) those of the language learner. This tuning seems to assist the child not only by "speaking his or her language," but also by introducing potential achievements within the child's range. Tuning does not refer to the mother's saying two- or three-word utterances because her child does so. Rather, tuning refers to the finely honed skill of making *particular* semantic–syntactic–phonological mechanisms available to the child.

Raising the ante is a maternal behavior that shows fine tuning and presumably assists language learning. Bruner discussed raising the ante:

> The first crucial point about the mother's role is that she drastically tailors her output at the start to the nature of the task and to the child's apparent competence. She changes with a steady regularity from the eleventh to the eighteenth month as she observes her child's changing competence. There are four constituents that make up her side of the dialogue, four key utterances types that appear in a strikingly fixed order: ATTENTIONAL VOCATIVE, *Look;* a QUERY with a distinctive rising contour, *What's that?;* a LABEL, *It's an X.* Finally, there is a FEEDBACK UTTERANCE, *Yes.* For each of the types, a single token accounts for from nearly half to more than 90% of the instances. The mother's utterances, moreover, are organized almost exclusively in the order stated and far in excess of what might have been predicted by chance, and the successive deployment of its four constituents is highly linked to what the child says or does. Mothers interacting with infants in communicative exchanges are very steady, and when they vary it is with good reason. If a child responds, the mother responds to him, and if he initiates a cycle by pointing or vocalizing, she responds even more often. Her "fine tuning" is fine indeed—for example, if the child succeeds in labelling after her QUERY, she will virtually always skip the label and jump to feedback. (1981, pp. 166–167)

To assure that two minds are indeed focused on a common topic, the mother develops a technique for bypassing the Wittgensteinian dilemma of how to know what feature a label refers to: 90% of her labels refer to whole objects, and since half of the remainder are made up of proper nominals which also stand for the whole, she seems to create few difficulties of this order. They seem to be together on the referent. This supposes that the child responds to whole objects as well—a point most recently urged by Quine (1973, pp. 52-53) and by Schlesinger (1978) and referred to as "body-mindedness." It seems highly unlikely that body-mindedness solves all of the Wittgensteinian dilemma, but it certainly seems to help in this instance.

The mother's (often quite unconscious) approach is indeed exquisitely tuned. When the child responds to her attentional vocative by looking, she follows immediately with a query. However the child initially responds to the query, by gestures or smile, she will then supply a label. But as soon as the child shows he can vocalize at the query juncture (no matter how) she raises the ante: she will withhold the label and repeat the query until the child vocalizes, and then give the label (often, as Garnica, 1977, has shown, with heavy stress). Later still, when the child has learned to repond with shorter, morpheme-length vocalizations to the mother's query for a label, she will no longer accept an indifferent vocalization. When the child begins producing "phonologically constant forms" (PCFs, Dore, 1975), she holds out for them. Finally, the child produces appropriate words in the correct privilege of occurrence in the dialogue. Even then, the mother remains tuned to the developing pattern, helping the child recognize and further partition the labelling task. After a certain period, for example, two forms of intonation develop for the *What's that* query, one with a falling intonation contour inquires about those words for which, in the mother's estimate, the child already knows the label; one with a rising intonation is for those that are newly introduced. So that even in the simple labelling game, mother and child are well into making the distinction between the given and the new (see Clark & Clark, 1977; Chafe, 1970).

Retherford, Schwartz and Chapman (1981, p. 583), on the other hand, found evidence that may be against the fine-tuning hypothesis. "It was the children who changed to become more like their mothers, both in the semantic roles present and their relative frequency of use." However, their dependent measures of range of semantic categories and their relative frequency may have been misleading. As Bruner (1981) said, mothers "raise the ante" if they think their children can do more. Perhaps Retherford, Schwartz, and Chapman should have done a topic/comment, frame/insert, given/new kind of analysis, rather than relying upon frequency, to ascertain if the mothers were actually tuned but were 'raising the ante.' The 'raise the ante,' 'tuning' and other related notions are predicated on the assumption that the mother adjusts to her child. Furrow and

Nelson (1984) showed that mothers' references to objects and persons were related to children's style.

Many early pragmatic behaviors are placed in a special infant-parent context called *formats* (Bruner, 1981). These formats are highly rehearsed routinized behaviors. Ninio and Bruner (1978) indicated that, "Participating in a ritualized dialogue, rather than imitation, was found to be the major mechanism through which labelling was achieved." Both participants know in advance their particular roles. The infant or young child is free to vary his input but the adult partner is held to a narrowly prescribed set of behaviors. In this way, the child can rely on certain content and certain outcomes; he only has to carry out his end or make whatever alterations he chooses to test their effects.

> **Ritualized dialogues afford the child an early means of language learning, especially early pragmatic skills.**

Formats occur in many ways throughout the day. A common format is the respective roles taken in 'story reading' (Ninio & Bruner, 1978). Snow and Goldfield (1983) and Wheeler (1983) reported that 'story reading' is a useful way of facilitating language learning. Children like to hear the same story again and again. They listen for certain points to ensure that the story is on-schedule. Indeed, violations that are not theirs may make them laugh or fuss. It is interesting to watch children engage in dialogue while reading a favorite story. They are operating within a narrowly prescribed set of expectations. Occasionally, they will test these expectations. After several "readings," children have memorized the story but still want it "read" so they can engage in various aspects of dialogue. Early on, participation is in terms of smiling, reaching, pointing, and babbling, all of which indicate referents; eventually, they substitute words or labels for these performative acts. Clearly, such behaviors allow children to be socially engaged in the activity well before they learn language. Upon learning the words, children may tire of the story and go on to another. Formats are antecedents of cultural "scripts" in adult speech.

Formatting is a term devised by Bruner to refer to highly routinized mother-child dialogue. Bruner (1981) discussed formatting as follows:

> With respect to contexts in early communication, I think that the communicative life of the young child is circumscribed by a highly limited set of them. Another way of saying it is that young children don't do many different things. Or in Nelson's terms, the young learner of languages has a rather small library of scripts. I shall later call this limited set of scripts *formats,* and they are of crucial importance in the child's mastery of the arguments of action and of the "functional core" that he builds up. They provide steady frameworks in which he learns effectively and by dint of interpretable feedback how to make his communicative intentions plain.

And just as strikingly, these reliable and rather monotonous formats provide the mother as well with a basis for interpreting the child's communicative acts. These formats are, so to speak, the microculture of mother and child. They often have a game-like or playful quality along with a rule structure that develops within them. Mothers say the same things over and over with only a few variations. Even linguist mothers, listening to tapes of their interactions with their own children, are struck by this.

A format is a constrained and segregated transaction between child and adult with a goal, a mode of initiation, and a means-end structure that undergoes elaboration. A format provides a familiar locus and a familiar routine in which communicative intentions can be conventionalized and interpreted. As it becomes increasingly familiar and conventionalized it comes to serve as a matrix for organizing presuppositions about what is given and what is new. Above all, a format is what frames communication and locates it in a particular segment of reality where the child can cope well enough to steer his hearer. We shall meet several of them in detail in the second part of the paper . . .

But as soon as attending to indicated objects occurs consistently in the child's repertory, the mother frames them in formats that permit the child to recognize what signs lead to what consequences. She steadily if unconsciously conventionalizes her way of signalling change of referent until the child shows an uptake of her conventionalized form, and then she imbeds the newly-established and reliable routines into higher order routines. It is striking that each step in the progress she is establishing a place-holder for a higher order, more symbolic routine to be substituted later. Undifferentiated deictic markers and undiscriminating attentional vocatives like *da* and *umm,* once attained, are quickly replaced by pointing and then by PCFs and genuine morphemes. Undifferentiated babbles in Book Reading are first replaced by morpheme-length sound patterns, then by words. Or if we go up to the end of the second year when Richard has managed *dere* and *Nana* (the name of a familiar dog) each separately, he now handles them together as *dere Nana* in the same indicating context where each sufficed on its own. (The same for *bebe ouse* or *mummys gaggas* combined for indicating.) One has the sense in all this that when the infant has mastered the routine of the prior level there is now enough processing space for him to manage the next step. What permits the steadying to occur is the opportunity to try out the routines in mother-steadied formatted dialogue and to gain more real-world scripted knowledge about the situation in which the dialogue or action is occurring. If you should now ask what leads the child to take the step forward, why he does not stay at the level where he was, then I will speculate that you are back with LAD. That is to say, the performance condition necessary for the child to take a next step forward is not simply a natural context that allows him to recognize regularities in the mother's (or another adult's) speech. (pp. 162, 168–169)

Retherford, Schwartz, and Chapman (1981) reported the following routines—formats—in mother-child dialogues:

Animal. Mother: "The cow says 'moo'." Child: "Moo."
Story/song/poem. Reading "Green Eggs and Ham." Mother: "Would you like it on a train. Would you, could you in the _____." Child: "Rain."
Counting/alphabet. Counting child's fingers. Mother: "one, two, three, four, _____." Child: "five."
Greeting. Play telephone. Mother: "Hello. Who is this?" Child: "Hello, Taylor."
Say "X". Receiving a gift from another child. Mother: "Say 'thank you'." Child: "Thank you."
Sounds accompanying. Mother pushes car toward child. Mother: "R,r,r,r." Child: "R,r,r,r."
Naming. Naming toy doll. Mother: "What's your name?" Child: "Annie."

Maternal partnership in language learning includes highlighting and looming, regulating joint action and attention, given/new informational inflections, tuning, raising the ante, and formatting.

These maternal behaviors are subtle yet apparently effective in assisting both cognitive and linguistic advancements. A key to such assistance is the mother's awareness of the child's verbal capacities. This enables her to make reasonably good decisions about what kinds of assistance are facilitative at any given moment (Rocissano & Yatchmink, 1983). *Readiness* to learn is a crucial issue with such assistance. Readiness is experientially defined in regard to what has already been attained. Gopnik put it this way,

> The adult language provides a series of signposts that help the child find his way around uncharted cognitive territory. However, the child can only make use of the signposts that he is able to comprehend. As the child covers more cognitive ground, he can take advantage of new linguistic signposts. (1981, p. 104)

It should be abundantly clear that the mother is an active *partner* in facilitating rather than directing language learning. *Facilitation* entails the ability to be tuned and flexible (Bloom & Lahey, 1978; Muma, 1978a).

This parent-child partnership is itself complex. K. E. Nelson (1981, pp. 229–232) outlined some assumptions that must hold for such a partnership to work in the child's prehension of relevant rare events in natural language. These assumptions are compatible with hypothesis testing as outlined by Muma (1978a; see Chapter 5, this volume).

Some Possible Pitfalls

Even though it is clear that mothers take an active role in the language learning process, hopefully a facilitating role, it is not clear how beneficial maternal activities truly are. Gleitman, Newport, and Gleitman (1984, p. 43) suggested that the benefits of maternal assistance may be restricted to young learners. They said, "Most effects of the mother on the child's language growth are found to be restricted to a very young age group." Concerning the role of mothers as help or hindrance in language acquisition, Gleitman and Wanner (1982) said that there are both empirical and logical difficulties with the "motherese" hypothesis for assisting language acquisition. Motherese refers to the kind of talking mothers make to their young children. Logically, this hypothesis places weight on the mother for being appropriately *fine tuned* to the needs of her child. This is a considerable demand. The mother not only has to be sufficiently cognizant of what her child can do but also must draw upon intuitive knowledge of what kinds of facilitation are needed. Given the complexity of context and language, this is a very demanding role.

Gleitman and Wanner (1982, p. 39) were pessimistic about the evidence of maternal speech as a facilitator. "The evidence of maternal speech does not support the view that it would aid the acquisition of syntax." They pointed out that there is a considerable mismatch between maternal sentences used and the emerging structure of the child's language. The child strives to learn simple active declarative sentences, but input sentences are mostly imperatives and questions. They stated further that as the child becomes more competent the percentage of simple declaratives increases rather than decreases, and complex forms decrease. They presumed that the opposite should take place. However, if a *functionalistic* argument is invoked these empirical findings could be viewed as supporting the motherese hypothesis. That is, in social commerce imperatives and questions may provide a format for labels and simple predications. And, a reverse in pragmatic roles may occasion simpler maternal sentences over time so the child is given a format opening for elaboration.

The apparent structural mismatches between motherese and child performance may mean that mothers are providing pragmatic formats rather than syntactic assistance.

Gleitman and Wanner (1982) posited that maternal speech may be detrimental to language learning because it constrains language learning opportunities. Chomsky (1975), Cazden (1972), Wexler (1982), and others have been similarly concerned about possible detrimental effects on language learning if the opportunities for learning are externally controlled or contrived. As Muma put it,

> Chomsky and Cazden warned that what is done in intervention may be contradictory to what an individual needs. Chomsky felt that the learning situation should not be constrained by what an interventionist thinks it should be. The special needs of an individual's intellect are not yet explicitly known. (1978a, p. 229)

As Chomsky himself said (cited in Cazden, 1972, p. 28), "What little we know about human intelligence would at least suggest something quite different: that by diminishing the range and complexity of materials presented to the inquiring mind, by setting behavior in fixed patterns, these methods may harm and distort the normal development of creative abilities." Cazden (1972, p. 28) amplified this point, "Maybe the child is such a powerful consumer that the nature of the environment matters little as long as certain ingredients are present; maybe teaching specific primitive responses will even ultimately retard the development of more advanced processes." Gleitman and Wanner (1982, p. 40) summed up Wexler and Culicover's (1980) position, "The formal description of learning is materially *complicated* by the plausible assumption that mothers speak *simply* to their young offspring." Gleitman and Wanner indicated that they were baffled as to why developmental psycholinguists have had difficulty grasping the point that "learning should be more difficult from limited and biased . . . data than from rich and unbiased data" (p. 40).

"Simplifying" language may actually make language learning more difficult.

For these observers, thus, the study of motherese is not productive, and they do not understand why developmental psycholinguists continue this line of study. Gleitman and Wanner (1982) suggested that such research seeks to identify some subtle effects of motherese, and that Shatz (1982) delivered the *coup de grace* against the motherese research. Shatz found that "form-function relations are not materially simplified to young learners, and that children are quite insensitive to whatever gestural supports to comprehension these parents might be giving" (Gleitman & Wanner, 1982, p. 41). Gleitman and Wanner (p. 41) they said, "Her discussion secures that we will have to look primarily at children, not at their mothers, to understand language learning."

Child performance, not motherese, is the primary source of information about language acquisition.

While it is clear that Gleitman and Wanner do not accept the argument that motherese is very facilitative, they do not necessarily discount the motherese hypothesis entirely. "General social-interactive properties of the mother-child discourse will causally determine the actual form-meaning pairings the child learns" (Gleitman & Wanner, 1982, p. 41). This statement is exceedingly important because it draws upon contextually derived restrictions that presumably expedite ongoing social commerce. Such restrictions are quite different from a priori prepackaged language assessment and intervention programs of questionable value (e.g., Distar, Monterray, Goal, etc.). Such programs surely fall into the detrimental bin; the motherese hypothesis, squarely based in social commerce may not.

Gleitman, Newport, and Gleitman (1984) seemed to concede that while the onus for learning is essentially on the child, "motherese" may play a facilitating role. Possibly motherese might facilitate the child's resolution of general issues in the interpretation problem and the categorization problem (Schlesinger, 1977), Gleitman et al. (1984, p. 76) commented:

> The child is selective in WHAT he uses from the environment provided; he is selective about WHEN in the course of acquisition he chooses to use it; and he is selective in what he uses it FOR (i.e., what grammatical hypotheses he constructs from the data presented). We conclude that restrictive and non-obvious predispositions of the learner—both about information-handling and about language itself—rather than transparent inductions from the input corpus, bear most of the burden for language learning.

The functional nature of motherese in social commerce may define its significance in language acquisition. A priori structure in formats provides a context for verbal exploration.

Another point should be made about formats: Utterances within formats may not be finely tuned to a child's verbal capacities (Snow, Perlman, & Nathan, 1985). Indeed, rather elaborate utterances may appear. Consequently, it is necessary to distinguish between fine tuning in the normal course of social commerce, fine tuning within formats, and non-tuned utterances within formats. These elaborate utterances within formats may provide contexts for verbal exploration.

Saving Grace

Motherese in social commerce may be the *saving grace*. The various language assistance behaviors Bruner discussed also appear to facilitate language acquisition. At this juncture, it is useful to mention a few other mechanisms that give rather direct evidence of maternal assistance. These are expansions, two-person sentences, and expatiations. The generic term for these and others is "communicative payoff."

Communicative payoff (Muma, 1981a) means that when someone tries to use language (gestural, verbal) and it works as *intended,* the speech act is paid off. At first glance this appears to be reinforcement but upon careful review it clearly is not. First, it should be noted that reinforcement theory has not worked in language *acquisition* although it may have some relevance, albeit limited, in language *performance.* Bruner (1981) made this point (see Chapter 1, this volume). Indeed, behavior modification and its associated reinforcement theory were procedural rather than substantive, recent neobehaviorism notwithstanding.

Nelson (1973a, 1974) also asserted that most substantive learning is nonobservable in language and therefore beyond the purview of reinforcement theory. Moreover, stimulus-response (S-R) theorists agreed that such theories are inadequate in accounting for language learning. "In principle, such S-R analyses of language behavior can never adequately account for the acquisition and maintenance of language" (Palermo, 1971, p. 152). Deese (1970, p. 5) put it as follows:

> If we were to argue that a sentence is nothing more than a complicated kind of conditioned response (as has been suggested; see Mowrer, 1954, for example) or a set of associations, or some more complicated version of these via the principle of mediation (see Osgood, 1968), we would be asserting (1) that each element in a sentence is a reaction to some preceding stimulus, and (2) these reactions are always chained together in a string. There are several ways of showing that these two propositions are false (Chomsky, 1956).
>
> These operations—which constitute the result of generative theory—cannot be accounted for, derived from, or otherwise interpreted within the traditional psychological points of view about intellectual processes. They are particularly difficult for any theory that reduces cognition to associations between elements. (Deese, 1970, p. 42)

Traditional reinforcement theory held that reinforcement increases (positive reinforcement) or decreases (negative reinforcement) a target behavior. *Communicative payoff* is different because a behavior not only increases in use but, perhaps more importantly, variations occur. We have a videotape of a preschool-aged child who said, "Ladder," as a comment about his varied actions with a dump-truck which included a ramp that he called a ladder. He already knew the word *ladder.* However, no one responded to his comment; no one paid him off. Then, he attempted his comment a few more times without success. So, he stopped his play and sat watching the other two children and an adult interact for a few minutes. Then, with an attentional vocative and stress he said, "Hey,

LADDER," whereupon the adult responded by a comment about the ladder. This was communicative payoff. He immediately resumed his play with the truck and did some new actions and word variations as a consequence of being paid off. The key to communicative payoff is *intention*. Intention places communicative behavior in a paradigm that differs from that of the traditional notions of cause-and-effect (Bruner, 1978). As Brown (1977, p. 26) said, "If you concentrate on communicating, everything else will follow."

> When children's attempts to use language *as intended* are paid off, they will not only make more attempts, but they will also attempt variations of the original attempt.

Expansion is another kind of payoff. Brown and Bellugi (1964) identified maternal expansions, for example:

Child: *Doggy run.*
Mother: *Doggy run home.*

Thus, the mother expanded her child's utterance. It should be remembered that the child's utterance is intentional and has referential support. Moreover, it was issued from present linguistic capacities. Any new developments would legitimately be derived from the existing repertoire. Thus, the maternal expansion constitutes an elaboration presumably within reach. Brown and Bellugi (1964) said that on occasion the mother and child engage in cyclic exchanges—mother expanding, child reducing, mother expanding, child reducing, mother expanding, and so on. They noted that these playful exchanges may go for two or three rounds; then, it is not unusual for the child to adopt a new dimension from the maternal expansion. In this way, the child may get assistance in language learning. Notice that such learning is not instruction or direction, but active construction within intent, reference, and context. Here the context includes an alternative code derived from the child's repertoire. This is facilitation.

Greenfield and Smith (1976) reported a similar maternal behavior which they called the *two-person sentence*. For instance, a son comments, "Daddy" (as he watches his father leave). His mother comments, "Go" (as a predication). Thus, *Daddy/Go* comprises an Agent-Action relationship befitting the event of the father leaving the house. This seems to be related to Bloom's notion of successive single-word utterances. As Slobin (1973) pointed out, the child does not have enough processing capacity to code both words. Greenfield and Smith (1976) suggested that the two-person sentence achieves a release from mental processing limits. Indeed, it is not unusual for the child to respond to two-person sentences by a smile or laugh and even to engage in cyclic exchanges where both participants play with two-person sentences.

Cazden (1965) conducted a study of expansions in which she added two other conditions. One of these conditions was one in which preschool teachers were asked to respond to child utterances with simple sentences. Another condition was one in which no special instruction was given. The group that received simple sentence responses obtained greater gains than the group that received expansions. McNeill (1966b) observed that the simple sentences served the pragmatic functions of enlarging a child's topic. Therefore, he called this the *expatiation* condition, which means 'to enlarge upon.'

Cazden's expansion condition did not result in significant gains. At first glance, it would appear that expansions are not facilitative. Brown (1973a) expressed concern that expansions had been used excessively and therefore had been satiated. He suggested that if they had been used sparingly their potency might have been realized. Subsequent research (Scherer & Olswang, 1984) showed that expansions are facilitative.

Hearty or Fragile

The satiation of expansions raises the question of how hearty (strongly single minded; unerrant; robust) language acquisition is. On the one hand, language acquisition appears to be hearty. Evidence on heartiness comes from two main sources. First, it is remarkable that language acquisition occurs in a relatively short time in view of only piecemeal and fleeting input. The child has only fleeting and surface contact with language yet he or she is able to deduce complex underlying systems and processes. Second, language learning is robust because it thrives not only on positive or correct information but also on negative and ambiguous information.

Yet, satiation implicates some fragile (frail, easily altered) aspects as well. It should be noted that relatively small doses of expansions, on the order of 25% to 30%, may be more effective than larger doses. Bloom, Hood, and Lightbown (1975) made a similar observation about spontaneous imitation. Roughly, spontaneous imitation about 15% to 20% of the time may be effective. Again, these kinds of limits implicate the primacy of language functions. That is, too many expansions or imitations may undermine the communicative function of utterances and thereby reduce their effectiveness in language learning. Thus, assistance implicates a fragile system to the extent that assistance may undermine communicative functions.

Goldin-Meadow and Mylander (1984, p. 114) posited that there are resilient and fragile aspects of language acquisition. Resilient aspects are the so-called hard-wired or deep structures; thus, one is predisposed to learn as a consequence of maturation. The fragile aspects are the result of environmental contact with a naturally functioning language. They put it this way:

What does seem clear, from our data and from others', is that the process of acquiring fragile properties of language requires more environmental assistance than does the process of acquiring other, more resilient properties of language. A child appears to need the explicit guidance (such as it is) of a language model to acquire language properties that are fragile but can develop properties that are resilient without the helping hand of a conventional language model.

Language acquisition appears to be hearty and robust unless communicative functions become undermined.

Socio-Emotional Aspects

The *interpersonal* functions of language are means of achieving effective social commerce. These entail affective dimensions as well as cognitive, linguistic, and social ones. Thus, the functionalist approach is very much concerned about socio-emotional aspects of language. In general, the interpersonal functions of language can be conceived of as a single function—the communicative function. However, both the *communicative* and *expressive* functions of language are important for communication, while the *representational* and *mediational* functions of language advance cognition. Relatively little has been said about socio-emotional development as it relates to language acquisition.

Baby Talk

In discussing the baby talk (BT) register usually used by adults to address babies, Ferguson (1977b) suggested that BT has three major functions: simplification, clarification, and expression. *Simplification* refers to the various ways in which adult language is simplified for an infant. These have been summarized by Snow and Ferguson (1977). In short, "motherese" and BT are intuitively tuned to what an infant presumably can handle. *Tuning* is an active dynamic maternal process of simplification that continually adjusts to new accomplishments (Bruner, 1981). The underlying motivation for tuning is effective communication: "Communication is the most important single determinant of tuning" (Brown, 1977, p. 13). *Clarification* is the means by which special assistance is given to mark or to define informativeness for a message. Garnica (1977) cited the following six prosodic features used by parents to clarify a message for infants:

1. Elevated fundamental frequency

2. Increased pitch range
3. Rising terminal pitch on questions and imperatives
4. Occasional whispering
5. Protracted utterance of separable verbs (verbs plus particle: *look up, get in, take out,* etc.)
6. Two primary syllable stresses on words that usually have only one

Brown (1977, p. 16) suggested that clarification is used "in short, to guarantee communication."

Prosodic features of BT clarify messages.

The *expressive* function needs to be distinguished from the *communicative* function. While both are interpersonal functions, the former conveys *affect* whereas the latter conveys *content.* There has been very little study of affect and language acquisition. "As noted earlier, the great chasm to be bridged . . . is that between affective and referential communication" (Lock, 1978, p. 8).

In BT, the expressive function typically expresses joy, fun, acceptance, and affiliation. Thus, it appears that when mothers use BT they intuitively lay down an affective state from which social commerce can be conducted. It is as if mothers "know" that the socio-emotional condition of the infant should be within certain prescribed states for functional communication.

Mothers "know" a certain positive affect is needed to transact social commerce.

Some research on the socio-emotional state of infants as they learn language is pertinent. But first, it is necessary to consider the only theoretical model of assistance in language acquisition that explicitly provides for *affect* in the language learning equation. Brown (1977) suggested that from a co-occurrence standpoint the three functions of BT delineated by Ferguson (1977b) (simplification, clarification, expression) collapse into two. He indicated that both simplification and clarification are essentially *communicative* whereas *expression* is affective. Thus, he proposed that the BT register is a combination of two major components: communicative and expressive. It appears that adults use BT to communicate content and affect.

Adults place a heavy weight upon affect in the use of BT. Perhaps this emphasis on affect stems from the adult's appreciation of the socio-emotional achievements infants and young children deal with. These achievements are well documented in the literature on attachment, separation, and stranger anxiety (Ainsworth, 1973; Rutter, 1972, 1979; Sroufe & Waters, 1976).

Attachment

Bates (1979) and her colleagues turned to the literature on attachment in an attempt to document socio-emotional development as it may relate to language acquisition. They focused on a very narrow window (around 11 to 12 months of age) and only found a few suggestive relationships. The rationale of such studies is based on the assumption that the parent-infant relationship influences socio-emotional states which, in turn, influence language acquisition.

The primacy of affect in the BT register suggests, albeit intuitively, that the quality of the relationship between the infant and the adult has a major influence on the learning process. Bates (1979) pointed out that *affect* was regarded as an important issue: (a) in the emergence of symbolic behavior (Mead, 1934; Werner & Kaplan, 1963); (b) neo-Freudian speculations; (c) Piagetian notions of equilibrium; and (d) implicitly in the contemporary functionalist views (Lewis & Rosenblum, 1977; Schaffer, 1979). Bates (1979) asserted that attachment theory (Ainsworth, 1973; Bowlby, 1969, 1973; Rutter, 1972, 1979; Sroufe & Waters, 1976) provided both direct and indirect support for the notion that socio-emotional aspects are an important influence on language acquisition. *Directly,* harmonious mother-child relationships seem to contribute to the emergence of symbolic thought. *Indirectly,* such relationships afford the child opportunities to explore and discover the world on his or her own terms.

Affect seems to have a direct and indirect relationship to language acquisition.

In attachment theory, the parents, especially the mother, are viewed as a security base for social-emotional development. That is, the mother is viewed as a security base from which the infant operates. Under stress or anxiety, the infant shows attachment to the security base. However, as infants feel more secure, they release from the security base and explore their world.

Bates posited the attachment-exploration and the attachment-teaching hypotheses. Briefly, these respective hypotheses stated:

(a) When the infant has assurance that his mother is available and responsive, he will tend to explore his environment.
(b) When the infant has a harmonious and affective synchrony with his mother, he is in a position to acquire cognitive and communicative skills through interaction with her. (1979, p. 225)

Appropriate attachment facilitates exploration and motivation.

Bates and her colleagues conducted a study of socio-emotional development and language acquisition of 11- and 12-month-old infants. The study was based upon the two attachment hypotheses: exploration and teaching. They conjectured that the *exploration* of infants is a function of the dynamic infant-mother relationship. Mothers who are warm, accepting, and appropriately responsive (Cazden, 1966) or tuned (Bruner, 1981) are more likely to have babies who explore more than babies who do not receive such attention; the latter are more anxious and less inclined to explore. Spontaneous exploration is regarded as a potentially desirable activity for learning about the world and how to function in it via communication.

The *teaching* function of attachment was viewed from a motivational standpoint. Pleasurable social interactions lead to further and more varied social interactions. Bates and her colleagues suggested that mutually satisfying interactions were conducive to the acquisition of symbolic behavior, cognitive capacities, and communication. The games of infancy and childhood are important for socio-emotional development, thinking skills, and communication because they are joyful and contain content.

Bates and her colleagues used the research procedure known as "the strange situation" (Ainsworth & Wittig, 1969). This situation provides a means of observing natural mother-infant interaction during play with various opportunities for showing attachment. In the course of the session maternal separation from the infant is attempted and stranger stress is introduced and removed. Based upon this kind of situation three types of infants have been identified (Bates, 1979; Main, 1976). These were called Infant A, Infant B, and Infant C. They were distinguished in regard to exploratory behavior, reaction to the presence of a stranger, maternal separation, and maternal attachment following separation. Table 9.1 outlines these distinctions.

Infant B fares better than Infant A or Infant C.

Further, maternal caregiving behaviors varied by infant type. Studies by Bell and Ainsworth (1972), Ainsworth and Bell (1969), Blehar, Lieberman and Ainsworth (1977), Main (1976), and Ainsworth, Blehar, Waters, and Wall (1978) suggested that maternal caregiving shapes infants' behaviors. Basically, the maternal-infant interactions for Infant B are smoother and more harmonious than those for Infants A and C. The result is that the Infant B seems to be more competent in interactions with their mothers and in general mothers of both A and C infants were less responsive to their babies. Rejection of infant initiatives, especially physical contact, was evident with A mothers. C mothers had inconsistent response patterns.

Mothers of B infants are more appropriately responsive than those of A and C infants.

Table 9.1. Infant Behaviors in Various Socio-Emotional Conditions

	Infant A	Infant B	Infant C
Exploration	Explores in mother's presence	Explores in mother's presence	Explores little or not at all; is very passive; sticks close to mother
Stranger	Is not wary; is not distressed when left with stranger	Plays in constrained manner	Is wary
Separation	Is stressed; searched for mother	Cries	Cries
Attachment	Refuses to greet returning mother; snubs her return	Quickly, actively seeks maternal attachment; is easily soothed	Shows strong attachment; is hurt by separation

Derived from Bates, 1979 and Main, 1976.

Research on cognitive development or communicative development as they relate to A, B, and C infants is somewhat equivocal. In general, the predicted relationships for cognition and language to quality of socio-emotional attachment were not found. But, the evidence is only piecemeal and suggestive. What evidence there is indicates that B infants consistently fared best.

In short, B infants at about 20 months of age tended to have longer periods of exploration of a single toy, more enjoyment in play, more intense engagement in play, fewer frustrations while attempting to solve a task, more compliance to maternal suggestions, and larger vocabularies. While these differences suggest that B infants are better off than A or C infants, it must be remembered that the evidence is only suggestive and incomplete.

In the Bates (1979) study, the evidence gave a mixed picture about possible relationships between attachment, cognition, play, and language acquisition. Quality of attachment was related to means-end relations but not to object permanence, spatial relations, or imitation. It was related to symbolic play but not combinational play. Even more puzzling, quality of attachment was related to gestural level but not to language comprehension or production. Bates was also concerned about this mixed outcome. One way to reconcile the situation is to consider that different aspects of cognition and communication are differentially influenced by socio-emotional aspects. Of course, another view is to recognize that the ways of measuring these variables may not have been appropriate.

The distinction between *attachment* and *affiliative* behaviors may help clarify some aspects of socio-emotional development and cognitive and language development. *Attachment* behaviors are used in reference to a security base from which the infant may separate in order to explore the environment. *Affiliative* behaviors do not evidence contact, but show an awareness of others and at least a tentative acceptance of them. Lamb (1977) regarded the following behaviors of 2-year-old infants as attachment or affiliative behaviors, respectively:

Attachment	Affiliative
Seek proximity	Smiles
Seek touch	Vocalizes
Approaches	Looks
Seeks to be held	Laughs
Fusses	Proffers
Reaches	

It should be remembered that these behaviors had to be directed to a particular person.

> A distinction between attachment and affiliation may help clarify mixed results.

Further study of the mother's role as an active *partner* (Bruner, 1981) may clarify the question of the relationships between socio-emotional development, cognition, play, and language acquisition. At this juncture, it appears that affect plays an important role; however, the exact nature of that role is not clearly understood.

Bloom (1985) presented data on the onset of first words and spurts of early word learning as they relate to affect. Early on, most early words express affect, but after a spurt of word learning, only about one-third of the words express affect, with the balance expressing propositions. Two other findings were especially important. First, fluctuations in affect or expressivity predicted first words and possibly a vocabulary spurt. Second, long durations of neutral affect (studied or focused attention) predicted vocabulary spurts.

Peer Influences

What about peer or sibling influences as assistance in language learning? While it is clear that parents play a decidedly active role in assisting (not instructing or teaching) language acquisition, it is not yet clear as to the actual benefits from this assistance. As Bruner (1981) suggested, the parent is an active partner in facilitating learning. He delineated some kinds of facilitating activities that parents do. But we still do not know their effects on the language acquisition processes. The state of affairs regarding peer and sibling influences is similar.

Peer Interaction

It is clear that peers and siblings may take active roles that presumably assist language learning, but we do not know the effects of these roles. In this section, some studies on peer interaction are reviewed briefly; they show that peers actively interact with infants and young children, albeit sometimes vicariously. Beneficial effects are inferred from such interactions. After this, some issues about potentially different kinds of impacts on language learning between parental assistance and peer assistance are considered.

Infants and toddlers are seemingly awkward in peer interaction; even so, they participate, at first with reservation and later with increased interest in what peers may be doing. Mueller and Lucas (1975) suggested that toddlers' social interactions are in parallel play with common toys. Mueller and Brenner (1977, p. 854) concluded, "Parallel play, rather than merely reflecting an inadequacy of early peer relations, represents a natural facilitating context for such relations." They also reported a linear increase in the amount of peer interaction over time. Brenner and Mueller (1982) used the unusual tactic of identifying the content of peer interaction rather than making an inventory of behavioral consequences. Content was comprised of the *themes* of peer social interaction of toddlers. They identified 12 themes; the most frequent were motor copy, object exchange, and object possession struggle. They found that "longer interactions tend to contain shared meaning..." (Brenner & Mueller, 1982, p. 380).

> Thematic analysis of peer infant interactions is much more useful than an inventory of behaviors.

Eckerman and Whatley (1977) showed that the traditional view that infants are not socially aware of peers is basically false. Ten-month-old infants regarded their peers in the following ways: usually contacted each other, smiled and gestured to each other, and duplicated actions of the other. Moreover, they showed and exchanged toys and "spent more time synchronously manipulating similar play materials" (p. 1,645). It might be said, in a loose sense, that they were "social *hombres*."

> Contrary to popular belief, infants are "social *hombres*."

As for peer communication, toddlers usually do not respond verbally to peer messages, but their joint actions and imitations of actions of others suffice. That is to say, while they are not yet skillful with symbolic exchanges in conventional ways, they are nonetheless actively communicating through action and joint reference.

Brinton and Fujiki (1984) showed peer influences for some pragmatic skills in topic manipulation. They studied 5-year-olds' and 9-year-olds' pragmatic skills of topic introduction, reintroduction, maintenance, and shading (which incidentally appears to be what McNeill (1966b) called expatiation or topic enlargement). Older children had few topic introductions and reintroductions; they maintained more topics containing longer sequences of utterances; and, they had more topic shading or expatiation.

Stage and Reorganization

It is conceivable that peer influences are qualitatively different from parental influences in assisting language learning, even if the topographical behaviors of parents and peers appear to be the same (e.g., both parents and peers expand or expatiate child utterances). Peers and parents have different theories of the world because they are at different stages of development. Thus, parents and peers communicate differently. The adult who has passed through the different stages probably has a considerably different perspective on what the child may be dealing with in an earlier stage than the peer has. It is likely that the peer is at the same stage, has recently been at the same stage, or is preparing to be at the same stage. Given this developmental proximity, peers may, in a sense, be better able to assist language learning than parents. On the other hand, parents, by virtue of their more highly developed tuning skills, may be more sensitive than peers to some of the child's communicative needs. Thus, both parents and peers serve the child in qualitatively different ways as "significant others" in language assistance.

Peers and parents may assist the child in qualitatively different ways.

The notions of stages of learning and reorganization are not new, for example, Piagetian cognitive theory or Kohlberg's (1969) moral development theory. Stage theory has also been assumed or proposed in language acquisition (Bowerman, 1982; Brown, 1973b; Gleitman, 1981; Menyuk, 1963, 1964a, 1964b). Gleitman and Wanner (1982) suggested that there are two ways of viewing the stage of discontinuous theories of language acquisition. One is the reduction of "clutter" (Bowerman, 1982) and the other is the tadpole-to-frog or metamorphosis (Gleitman, 1981).

According to the former theory, the *reduction of clutter* is a data-driven process whereby children are faced with too much data, and their current ways of handling the data are awkward and inefficient. Under these conditions, children are forced to reorganize data into more efficient processing modes. McNeill (1966b) made a similar point in language learning. Ingram's (1976) vocabulary learning and early phonetic inventory with a shift to rule-governed learning is based upon a similar premise. The various accounts of the acquisition of inflectional rules (Cazden, 1968, 1972; de Villiers & de Villiers, 1973, 1978; Palermo & Eberhart, 1968) are based upon stages and reorganization in the reduction of clutter. And, the shifts from enactive processing to iconic processing to symbolic processing (Bruner, 1964) are also based on stages and reorganization.

Alternatively, there is the metamorphosis, or tadpole-to-frog, hypothesis (Gleitman, 1981). There is even indirect neurological support for stages in cognitive and language acquisition (Geschwind, 1965a, 1965b; Lenneberg, 1967). Such neurological changes presumably account for the relative ease of language learning of preschool children, or indeed, the ease of foreign language learning. Geschwind and Lenneberg provided justification for the "critical periods" of learning, but really this is only a loose idea. For example, there are developmental shifts in cognitive and language learning at about 7 years of age (White, 1965). The metamorphosis position is that as the child succeeds in attaining a given stage, prior accomplishments are no longer active. In this sense, acquisition means a succession of new learners. As Gleitman and Wanner (1982, p. 31) put it, "Learning begins anew with fairly trivial residue."

Acquisition may mean a succession of new learners. With each new stage, learning begins anew with fairly trivial residue.

To reiterate, peers are more closely matched to active stages of the child learning language than parents. But, parents are more likely to be more finely tuned and more motivated to facilitate communication. Both peers and parents seem to have different but important contributions to language acquisition.

Summary

Does the child get assistance in language learning? Yes. Parents and peers play active but different roles in assisting or facilitating language learning. Parents highlight, loom, regulate, differentially intone, referentially dub, tune, raise the ante, and format. Even though parents are active partners in the language learning process, it is unclear as to how these activities actually work in facilitating language learning. Simplifying language could be detrimental to language learning; yet, it could facilitate such learning.

If communicative efforts work as *intended* (payoff), language acquisition could be facilitated. Brown (1977, p. 26) made this point as follows: "Believe that your child can understand more than he or she can say, and seek, above all, to communicate."

Language acquisition appears to be hearty and robust unless communicative functions become undermined. It is hearty in the sense that it transpires with only piecemeal and fleeting surface opportunities, coupled with parent and peer assistance. And, it is robust because it is seemingly not compromised by false and ambiguous information. In fact, false and ambiguous information can advance language learning.

Brown's (1977) two-component theory of baby talk indicated that parents are oriented toward both communicative (content) and expressive (affect) dimensions of language. One major implication of the *affect* component of baby talk is that socio-emotional development needs to be considered.

The *attachment* literature provides a useful perspective on the affective aspects of language acquisition. This literature provides two hypotheses relevant to the socio-emotional support for language acquisition. The *exploration* hypothesis holds that as children feel more secure they will move away from the security base and explore the world. Such exploration may be conducive to cognitive and language acquisition. The *teaching* hypothesis posits that as children evidence harmony and enjoyment in their socio-emotional relations, they will be motivated to learn.

The attachment literature identified three kinds of infants with their associated maternal behaviors. Type A infants explored toys, were less wary of strangers, had little distress during maternal separation, searched for their mothers on separation, and snubbed their mothers upon reunion. Type B infants explored toys, constrained play with strangers present, cried on separation, quickly reaffirmed maternal attachment, and were soothed easily. Type C infants explore little, were passive, stuck close to their mothers, were wary of strangers, and showed strong attachment with fussing.

Maternal interactions with B infants were more harmonious; mothers and infants were both more self-assured. Both A and C mothers were less responsive than B mothers to infant initiations and bids for physical contact. These data, however, were not conclusive.

While it is clear that peers are actively engaged with each other, even in infancy, the nature of peer interaction in assisting language acquisition is unclear. The stage and reorganization theories suggest that peers and adults communicate with infants differently, not so much in terms of the topology of behavior, but in terms of their developmental proximity to the infant. Both peers and parents presumably assist language acquisition, but in different ways.

10

SUBSEQUENT FORMALIZATION: MODIFICATION

Language acquisition continues well beyond basic SVO constructions and simple modulations of meaning. Chapter 8 presented those issues of acquisition for attainment of predication and early formalization. Following the Werner and Kaplan (1963) model as a general framework for language acquisition, the third major accomplishment is *attribution* or *modification*. Functionally, the acquisition of various formal grammatical capacities for modifying messages affords increased options for explicitness of information. Presumably such options enable the child to become more adept in language use. *Adeptness* and reflection on the child's own verbal behavior—metalinguistics—are two major pragmatic skills that seem to accompany the acquisition of formal grammatical capacities for modification. *Metalinguistics* is discussed in Chapter 11.

Mean Length of Utterance (MLU)

Dale (1976, p. 112) said that the first complex constructions appear at an MLU of 3.5–4.0 and are usually object noun phrase complements (see also Brown, 1973a, 1973b; Limber, 1976). Further, Brown said that the object noun phrase is learned first and more elaborately than the subject noun phrase.

It is important to note that once the child has achieved a full-blown SVO construction, MLU loses its value as an index of language acquisition and becomes a performance index (Bloom, 1970; Cazden, 1968; Cowan et al., 1967; Shriner, 1969). Brown (1973b, p. 54) said that by the time the child has attained Stage 5 he or she is "able to make constructions of such great variety that *what* he happens to say and the MLU of a sample begin to depend more on the character of the interaction than on what the child knows, and so the index loses its value as an indicator of grammatical knowledge." Moreover, even within the 3.5-4.0 range, MLU is not a good indicator of pragmatic skills (Dale, 1980).

> MLU loses its value as a developmental index at about 4.0. It then becomes a performance index.

Thus, when MLU exceeds 4.0, knowledge of formal grammatical mechanisms can no longer be indexed by increments in MLU. Elaborate constructions jeopardize the linear notion of MLU in several ways. For example, some elaborate constructions lengthen sentences while others shorten sentences; other constructions alter the order of morphemes; and finally, some entail various combinations of operations that lengthen, shorten, and rearrange components.

Hunt (1964) used the T-unit (sentence plus transformations) index, which is similar to MLU. He showed that school-aged boys produced shorter sentences than girls, but these sentences were similar in complexity. Boys employed more deletions than girls, and girls employed more elaborations. O'Donnell, Griffin, and Norris (1967) reported similar findings. The old adage that girls are more advanced than boys in language learning was not supported by these findings.

Furthermore, Hunt (1964) showed that there were two periods of sudden change in linguistic performance, the kindergarten and first-grade period and the fifth to the seventh grade period. Both periods evidenced sudden increases in the use of new grammatical structures with associated high error rates on these constructions. Further, both periods evidenced increases in embedding transformations, complex nominals, adverbials, and coordinate constructions. In the earlier period, children showed increases in adjectives and prepositional phrases in the later period, they showed increases in coordinated nominals and predicates.

Palermo and Molfese (1972) concluded that there is a gradual *consolidation* of language structures from about 5 to 12 years of age with some associated abrupt shifts in performance.

> It may be that the child is acquiring rules for different syntactic structures at these ages and these rules affect and disrupt other structures which the child has previously dealt with in a competent manner. Language is an integrated system in which a change in one structure cannot help but affect other structures within the system. (Palermo & Molfese, 1972, p. 417)

Sequence

Brown (1973a, 1973b) showed that *sequence* is highly stable whereas *rate* of language learning is highly varied. Similarly, Greenfield and Smith observed,

> Sequence is much more important than age. Thus, we do not compare the ages of acquisition of a given function, but compare its position in the developmental sequences. Such emphasis on sequence and de-emphasis of chronological age is consistent with current thinking in developmental psychology (e.g., Piaget, 1966). (1976, p. 70)

Thus, acquisition follows a predictable and stable developmental sequence; the chronological rate at which the sequence unfolds, though, varies. Structurally, negation first appears outside of the sentence ("I go. No."); then, it appears inside the sentence but not integrated into the auxiliary system ("I no go."); and finally, it appears in adult form ("I won't go."). Functionally, negation first appears as *nonexistence*. For example, when a ball rolls under the table and out of sight, so the child might say, "No, ball." *Rejection* means to not want something. For example, the child might say, "No, juice" as the mother offers juice. *Denial* means to deny the truth of an assertion. For example, the child might say, "No, doggy," when the mother says, "Look at the pretty doggy," in reference to a dog that is different from the child's notion of 'dogginess.' For language intervention, thus, it would be much more useful to know where a child is in such an acquisition sequence than to attempt to put the child at a certain age level. This conceptualization of the acquisition process is a heavy blow to the traditional reliance on age norms. In sum, the study of language acquisition has become a search for acquisition sequences.

Sequence is highly stable but rate is highly varied in language learning.

Modulations of Meaning

Given the search for acquisition sequences, a logical question is, What developmental sequences ensue after the acquisition of SVO? A functional perspective is useful for inquiries of this kind: What new functions are realized as the child acquires new grammatical skills? In general, such skills afford the child new options for becoming informative.

First, the child modulates meanings *within* SVO constructions. This has three important implications for understanding language learning in *stages*. First, it is as if the attainment of SVO constructions constitute such a major accomplishment that it is encumbent upon the child to tinker around *within* SVO constructions to be sure they are fully realized before attempting something new.

Upon learning SVO constructions, the child turns to filling them out by modulating meanings.

Second, from the standpoint of reducing uncertainty, modulations of meanings tend to clear up and clarify ambiguity. Earlier on, when utterances were in the "here and now" raw SVO constructions sufficed. But as the child attempts to traffic information within covarying dimensions of reference, relations, space, and time, he or she needs formal mechanisms that tag intended meanings as referential anchors for designation. With the ability to modulate meanings, the child becomes ready to modify meanings. The cost of learning to modulate meanings is low, but the returns on the investment are high. Such extensions of SVO multiplies the child: communicative skills considerably. Third, this and subsequent accomplishments seem to center on SVO constructions; this points to the centrality of sentences in general and base constructions (such as SVO in SVO languages) in particular.

Modulations of meaning coupled with SVO provide a base from which modifications can be used.

Modulations of meaning refers to grammatical mechanisms—the inflectional system and the determiner system—that vary meanings slightly but retain basic grammatical relationships. The *inflectional* system does this through plurals, tense markers, noun-verb agreement, and so forth. The *determiner* system does this through demonstratives, articles, genitives, and numeral designators. The following are examples of the inflectional and determiner systems:

Inflections
    Plural: *book - - → books*
    Tense: *open - - → opened*
    Noun-verb agreement: *He walks*
                                           They walk

Determiners
    Demonstratives: *That boy*
    Articles:
        Indefinite: *A boy*
        Definite: *The boy*
    Genitive: *My boy*

Numeral:
   Cardinal: *One boy*
   Ordinal: *The second boy*

Note that the meanings of *book, open,* and *walk* remain essentially the same; their respective meanings have been modulated or modified only slightly. Similarly, the meanings of *boy* are modulated as a *function* of the various determiners employed.

From the perspective of informativeness, these syntactic devices function in several ways. *Pluralization* means to consider a class of referents rather than a single instance. *Tense* marking means to mark an event temporally. *Noun-verb agreement* means to reiterate the linking of two ideas—semiotic extension—and to locate their predicate-argument relationships in surface structure. *Demonstratives* are used to distinguish *deictic reference*. Deictic reference is the distinction between encoder and decoder perspectives. The word *that* means 'closer to the decoder than the encoder,' whereas *this* means the opposite.

Indefinite articles are used to refer to any member of a noun class, whereas *definite articles* refer to a particular member. *Genitives* (possessives) not only refer to particular members of a noun class but also specify a particular relationship. *Cardinal numbers* specify amount (i.e, 1, 2, 3, etc.) whereas *ordinal numbers* specify order (i.e., first, second, third, etc.). Use of cardinal and ordinal numbers emerges relatively late in acquisition.

To reiterate, the child's first major hurdle in the acquisition of formal grammatical capacities is the attainment of SVO constructions. Limited mental capacities result in reduced versions of SVO. Next, the child seems to be progressively released from these mental restrictions and works out substantive dimensions *within* SVO that permit more informativeness. These are the inflectional and determiner systems, which serve to modulate meanings. While these considerations are about the basic SVO construction, with its attendant structures *within,* it is appropriate to make a few points about language learning of basic syntactic structures. These points pertain to other aspects of syntax as well, but they are most easily seen in the acquisition of the basic SVO construction itself.

Loci of Learning

The more language learning advances, the more and more there is to learn. In a sense, children have many options for learning the rather complex grammatical machinery of language. Yet, they cannot exercise these options on a fully discretionary basis. They are, to a certain extent, at the mercy of what their previous learning allow them to learn, that is *readiness,* and their *opportunities* are, by and large, a matter of contacts with or accessibility to needed grammatical systems. Consequently, they may evidence a variety of language learning loci (specific aspects of the grammatical system) at any moment or in a relatively short period via spontaneous samples of language.

It is important that these loci of learning be detected because they are authentic indices of *active* learning processes. Moreover, in many instances it is possible to not only identify loci of learning but the *contexts* of such learning. Loci of learning constitute truly powerful information about the child's language learning; they easily surpass any formal a priori measure of language acquisition (developmental profile, normative tests, and so on) because they are produced with intention and have referential (actual, presumed) support (Fillmore, 1981), grammatical support (Schlesinger, 1977), and pragmatic support (Bruner, 1981). All of these issues are essentially beyond the purview of formal a priori measures.

The psycholinguistic literature has identified several ways of detecting loci of learning (Muma, 1983a):

Word Learning: overextensions/underextensions, invented words, word-referent relationships, ostensive/relational terms, production deficiency/mediation deficiency, unmarked/marked terms

Grammatical Learning: co-occurrence, false starts, revisions, buildups, glossing, selectivity of spontaneous imitation, spontaneous rehearsal, buttressing, developmental sequences, individual strategies of learning

Phonological Learning: phonetic inventory, reduced homonymy, simplification processes

The loci of interest in this chapter are those that index grammatical learning.

Co-occurrence. Compositely, co-occurrence is simply the linguistic context in which a given target structure occurs. Harris (1965) defined *co-occurring structure* as an issue in transformational operations. Klima and Bellugi-Klima (1969) showed that the acquisitions of questions and negation were related to co-occurring structures (see also Bloom, 1970, 1973; Bloom & Lahey, 1978). Bloom, Lifter, and Hafitz (1980) showed that the acquisition of the inflectional system is related in part to which verb structure is connected to a particular inflection; this exemplifies the influence of co-occurring structures in language learning. Bever (1970) considered co-occurrence an important issue in comprehension. That is, the linguistic context was a primary determinant as to whether a noun phrase was comprehended as a subject or object in passive and nonpassive sentences. Muma (1973a) reported that co-occurrence was a useful construct for identifying the syntactic context for the acquisition of new

Subsequent Formalization: Modification   219

structures. Similarly, Daniloff and Hammarberg (1973) showed that co-articulatory influences operate in attaining phonological structure.

> Co-occurrence defines the linguistic context of language learning.

Co-occurrence is usually defined syntactically, but it can be defined semantically, syntactically, pragmatically, and phonologically. This is important for language acquisition because the child seems to be somewhat *selective* when attempting new structures. This selectivity is not unlike the selectivity reported by Bloom, Hood and Lightbown (1974) for spontaneous imitations. The child is selective within the co-occurring context of relatively known structures. This can be easily seen in *buildups* and *revisions*. An example is given below.

Selectivity seems to be a joint venture between mother and child, although usually not at the same time. Recognizing *informativeness* as the-coin-of-the-realm of social commerce, linguistic input guides the child to select what can be said in a given circumstance (Greenfield, 1980; Schlesinger, 1977). Uses of *yes/no* questions and responses to *yes/no* questions (similarly *wh-* questions, negations, coordinations, pronominalizations, relativizations, modifications, topicalizations, and contingent queries) seem to highlight or forefront certain aspects of information against the backdrop of other aspects. Furthermore, such mechanisms show the child that particular information can be shifted from implicit content (presupposition) to explicit content (proposition) and vice versa in the service of *informativeness*. Thus, co-occurrence is multidimensional: it operates within and between utterances, and internal and external contexts (Fillmore, 1981). Figure 10.1 illustrates the multidimensional nature of co-occurrence.

Figure 10.1. The multidimensional nature of co-occurrence.

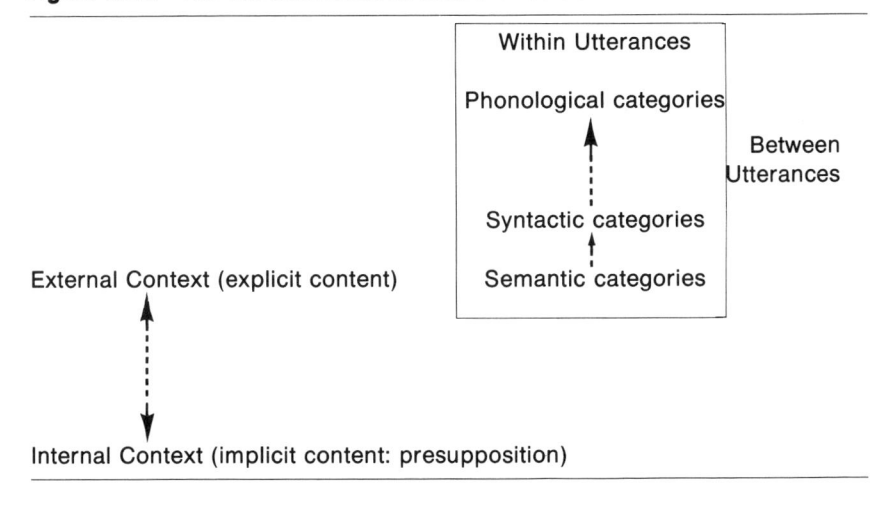

```
                          Within Utterances
                          Phonological categories
                                  ↑                    Between
                                  ⋮                    Utterances
                          Syntactic categories
                                  ↑
                          Semantic categories

External Context (explicit content)
        ↑
        ⋮
        ↓
Internal Context (implicit content: presupposition)
```

False Starts and Revisions. In a spontaneous *revision,* the child has a *false start* and then spontaneously revises his or her own message (see also Clark & Clark, 1977). Elicited revisions, on the other hand, are responses to contingent queries (these are discussed at the end of this chapter).

An example of a spontaneous revision follows: The child says, "I just tell you. I just *told* you." There was an accompanying stress on "told." This revision shows that the child is working out tense markers for the irregular transitive verb *tell.* The co-occurring structures with the tense are: subjective personal pronoun, intensifier, past tense, transitive verb, and objective personal pronoun. Thus, the child gives two kinds of information about his or her language learning. First, the child indicates that he or she is in the process of learning tense marking for this (and possibly other) irregular verbs. Second, he or she shows the linguistic context (co-occurrence) that supports this learning.

Buildups. *Buildups* are when successive sentences build upon the preceding sentences. They operate on co-occurrence, and they yield information about new loci of learning in linguistic context. Weir (1962) was the first to identify buildups in child speech, which are regarded as a primary index of spontaneity; they may be a "celebration of learning" (Furth, 1984) as well. Kulikowski (1981, p. 633) suggested that "buildups" reported by Weir were "the practice of a learned ability." Bloom (1970) said that buildups provide evidence of larger propositional structure underlying surface forms. Kulikowski (1981, p. 634) pointed out that buildups are "sensitive to acquisitional phenomena in phonology and syntax." Thus, spontaneous language samples that contain buildups, revisions, false starts, and so on, are likely to be more representative of the child's skill than elicited language samples.

An example of a buildup follows (Muma, 1981b):

Security base:	*I walk by myself.*
New structures:	*I can walk by myself when get home.*
Rehearsal:	*I can walk by my ____(unintelligible)____.*
New structure and glossing:	*I could do it.*
Fully developed sentence:	*I could walk all by myself ____(unintelligible)____ at home.*

Buildups reveal loci of learning and their linguistic context.

The buildup example above is a series of five uninterrupted sentences uttered by a young boy. The first would have put him in good stead pragmatically. That is, he could have continued his topic. However, he decided to build up the initial construction by adding two new loci of learning *(can, when get home)*. He rehearsed his new accomplishments. Then, he added a third new locus by changing the tense marker, thereby converting *can* to *could*. And, he opted to *gloss* the predicates by saying *do it* (explained below). Note that he had more than one locus at a time. This is typical.

Children typically do not attempt only one locus of learning at a time. That is, they do not tend to produce linguistic "songs" one note at a time. Rather, they choose to play a tune, albeit discordantly. They usually have several loci of learning at the same time (pragmatic, semantic, syntactic, prosodic, phonological). This is testimony to the fact that contextual learning is taking place. Indeed, there is reason to believe that if the learning contexts were reduced to single dimensions, which is often what the applied fields try to do in assessment and intervention, language learning would be excessively difficult (Cazden, 1972; Chomsky, 1972).

Active language learning entails several loci at the same time.

Glossing. Children realize it when excessive complexity gets them into mental processing difficulty, and they have several options for extricating themselves. One option is simply to stop talking, but this option means a forfeiture of intention, which is undesirable. A second option is to retreat via simplification by not attempting new loci or greater complexity. However, this too may be undesirable because it threatens the fluency of social commerce. Further, such an option only postpones an eventual striving; it may be better to risk pushing forward with new loci while the supporting context and intention are ripe. A third option is *glossing*, in which children use "all-purpose" pronominal forms to sidestep the difficulties of more explicit, detailed forms. In the example of the buildup shown above, for instance, the child converted the entire predicate into the glossed forms, *do it*. The glossed form relieved him of a processing capacity overload, which in turn allowed him to attempt a third new locus of learning. Then, he went for the full-blown structure.

Faced with recurrent threats of a processing capacity overload and the competing pressure to explicitly carry on communication, it is no wonder that children turn to the pronominal system somewhat early. Tanz (1977) found that 3-year-olds know the pronoun *I*. Noun phrases can be glossed by simple pronouns such as *it, one, some, you, they,* and so on.

Verb phrases are often glossed in child speech with *wanna, gonna, hafta,* and, of course, *do*. Bloom, Lifter, and Hafitz (1980) showed that children learn early verb forms such as *do, go,* and *make,* which can be used to gloss some verbial distinctions that will be acquired later. Brown (1973b, p. 150) commented that *wanna, gonna,* and *hafta* are semi-auxiliaries. The extent to which they may also be main verbs is the extent to which they may be used as glossed forms.

> *Glossing* refers to the use of all-purpose forms.

Spontaneous Imitation, Spontaneous Rehearsals, and Buttressing. Bloom, Hood, and Lightbown (1974) observed that *spontaneous imitation* is highly *selective*. Typically children do not imitate something they know or something they do not know. Rather, they spontaneously imitate something they are striving to learn about. For example, children striving to learn about relative clauses do *not* spontaneously imitate "The boy can swim." But, they are likely to spontaneously imitate "The boy who took his shirt off can swim." Thus, spontaneous imitations are likely to contain new loci of learning. These loci can be identified by comparing a particular spontaneous imitation to a recent language sample. New aspects in such a comparison are likely to be new loci of learning in the context of the remaining co-occurring structures.

> Spontaneous imitation is selective and therefore useful in identifying new loci of learning.

Spontaneous rehearsal, such as the one that appeared in the buildup above, is also *selective*. Once children achieve the goal of a message-of-best-fit, they often rehearse it spontaneously, especially if it contains a new locus of learning. This is what Furth (1984) called a "celebration of learning." Thus, like spontaneous imitations, spontaneous rehearsals can be useful for identifying loci of learning.

Muma (1981b) described the process of *buttressing*. MacWhinney (1981) described a similar process that he called "overmarking." And, Cotton (1978) used the phrase "noun-pronoun pleonasms" for this process. These are basically the same processes whereby children replace subjective pronominal forms with objective forms that were used subjectively and they add a second noun phrase to it. For example:

Old Forms:	*Him go. Daddy go.*
Old Form Buttressing New Form:	*Daddy he go.*
New Subjective Pronoun:	*He go.*

Aside from the verb inflection (third person singular), note that when the child first tried a new form *(he)* it was buttressed by an old form *(Daddy)*. Buttressing seems to be more descriptive of these events than "overmarking" or "double-marking." In any case, buttressing indicates new loci of learning. Schiff-Myers (1983) reported several categories of pronoun confusion in early acquisition. These confusions not only underscore the complexity of the pronominal system but also point to the possibilities of other acquisition processes in addition to buttressing.

> *Buttressing* refers to the use of an old (familiar) form to back up a new form.

Developmental sequence and individual strategies of language learning are useful in identifying *where* the child is in the course of acquiring a given system and *how* the child is going about language acquisition, respectively. That is, they are useful in ascertaining loci of learning. Individual strategies of learning are discussed in Chapter 5. Ironically, the grammatical loci of learning seem to be outside of the purview of a priori formal tests.

From another perspective, loci of learning can be viewed as aspects of what Bates (1979) called *decontextualization,* the process of achieving independence from here and now expressions. Sigel and Cocking's (1977) notion of cognitive distancing is similar. And, it should be remembered that only a few months prior to achieving SVO, the child achieved cognitive skills releasing him or her from a reliance on direct stimulation (sensorimotor capacities). All in all, the child is becoming decontextualized cognitively, verbally, and socially.

Specific Grammatical Systems

Questions and Negatives. Upon attaining a repertoire of SVO constructions carrying inflectional and determiner mechanisms, the child begins to make grammatical manipulations on SVO constructions. The early manipulations are simple efforts to make questions and negations. In the developmental sequence for questions, children first make them prosodically through inflected sentence contour. It should be noted that when parents know their child knows the name of a referent, they typically query with a falling intonation contour. However, when parents are unsure as to whether their child knows the name of a referent, or if they are certain the child does not know the name, they use a rising intonatonal contour to query or to signal new information, respectively. Given this use of rising intonation, it is not surprising that when children first attempt questioning, they employ a rising intonational contour for SVO constructions. The rising intonational contour may be on the SVO constructions themselves or they may be outside on a tag. Thus, the child might say,

"Daddy eat cookie." ↑
"Daddy eat cookie. Right."

Notice that the sentence is constructed with the interrogative superimposed as an intonation or externally marked as a tag. This again implicates the priority of SVO constructions.

Greenfield and Smith (1976) suggested that "dialogue and sequence are related functionally as transitional forms" (p. 182). They turned to the function of questions to illustrate the point. "The child can extract the role of the other as well as her own from a question-answer interchange: She can, in fact, process dialogue as a two-person sentence . . . All of the two-word utterances that had antecedents in sequences also had antecedents in earlier dialogue" (p. 182). Greenfield and Smith used adult-child dialogue at the single-word stage (Question: "What do you want?" Answer: "Shovel" [shovel]) to illustrate their point:

> Again, the answer supplies all the information the questioner was seeking ("new" information) and no more. What is presupposed from the question—"I want something"—is not expressed in the answer. Hence, single-word answers to questions follow the same principle as spontaneous single-word utterances: express the most informative element. The only difference is that, in dialogue, the presupposition is given in the verbal context whereas, in spontaneous utterances, it is given in the nonverbal context. When the child relates his single-word utterance to verbal context through dialogue, the distinction between "new" and "old" information does correspond to the distinction between more and less informative elements. In dialogue, the adult verbalization provides the "old" information which is presupposed by the child's reply. Adult comment or question thus takes the role of what the child had perceived as "given" or noninformative in the nonverbal situation. (1976, p. 196)

Thus, questions are not only useful as grammatical devices for making selective inquiries about particular aspects of informativeness. The child can also use questions as a two-person construction to reduce processing and referential loads yet slicing the information pie into palatable pieces.

It should be noted that these are *yes/no* questions. Eventually, the child deals with *wh-* questions. *Wh-* questions are about constituents in SVO constructions. It is useful to know that the first *wh-* questions deal with the two basic ideas entailed in SVO, that is, *who* and *what* questions. *Who* questions are about agents. *What* questions can be about either predications or objects. These are followed by *where, when, how, which,* and *why* (Brown, 1973b). Erreich (1984) found that the subject-auxiliary inversion in *yes/no* questions does not necessarily precede such inversions for *wh-* questions. And, she found that non-inversion errors are a characteristic of the acquisition of *wh-* questions *(When will he go?)*.

Consider the relevance of each *wh-* question in rendering information. Structurally, the *who* question is relatively easy to accomplish and its informational role is to denote "given" information. Accordingly, many early utterances do not contain topics, because they are presumed to be known by virtue of the immediate context (Bruner, 1975a, 1975b; Limber, 1976). In any case, the *who* question is achieved by merely replacing the subject (agent or topic) with *who* as shown below:

Mommy ate my apple.

Who ate my apple?

Thus, *who* is a query for clarification for the identification of the subject (agent or topic). This is one of the two main ideas in SVO.

The next *wh-* construction to be obtained deals with the second main idea in SVO; it is the verb-object (VO). Thus, the next interrogative acquisition is the *what* question. This is structurally more complex because it entails movement of the tense and any associated auxiliary with the assignment of *do*. The following examples illustrate these structural changes:

Mommy can swim.

What can Mommy do?

Daddy ate my apple.

What did Daddy eat?

It is clear from these examples that the auxiliary is in a deep structure sense distinguishable from the two basic ideas. That is, the auxiliary seems to be a device for tagging local dimensions (time, modal) on the two basic ideas of SVO.

The other *wh-* questions are mechanisms for clarification of particular aspects of *informativeness*. *Where* deals with a clarification of locative or location. *When* deals with a clarification of time, *how* a clarification of manner, *which* a clarification of reference, *whose* a clarification of ownership, and *why* a clarification of reason.

An encoder may err in formulating messages regarding *informativeness*. That is to say, an utterance may not be a message-of-best-fit (Muma, 1975a), taking into account intention, reference, topic, perspective of the listener, and so forth. Mechanisms such as *yes/no* questions and *wh-* questions function to rectify such problems while maintaining active dynamic social commerce.

Each question form provides a request for clarification of different aspects of *informativeness*.

Sentence *negations* are ways of indicating that a given proposition is false. There are other forms of negation as well (i.e., anaphoric and constituent). Anaphoric negation is when *no* is used to cancel the previous sentence, whereas the constituent *no* is used to negate the predicate. Sentence negations are acquired at about the same time as sentence questions (*yes/no* questions). Structurally, the acquisition sequence is as follows:

S + N   *I go, no.*
S (N)   *I no go.*
NS   *I won't go.*

Functionally, the acquisition sequence is nonexistence followed by either rejection or denial (Bloom, 1970, 1973; McNeill, 1970). *Nonexistence* is a statement that a referent is not present when the speaker expects it to be present. *Rejection* means to reject a referent as a willful option. *Denial* is logically more complex because the child must admit to the existence of what is being denied; if it does not exist (presuppositionally), then it cannot be denied.

In sum, the primacy for SVO constructions is clear. Once the child obtains these on a rudimentary level, the child turns to learning grammatical devices *within* SVO (modulations of meaning: inflectional and determiner systems) and then grammatical mechanisms for explicating informativeness. Further, it was noted that initial grammatical learning concerns the entire proposition and its two basic ideas. Subsequent acquisitions deal with components of SVO. This pattern of general to specific suggests that generic learning (McNeill, 1970) is occurring.

Pronominalization. Grammar has devices to route information explicitly (sometimes too explicitly and sometimes not explicitly enough). The pronominal system can be very powerful in routing information, but pronouns can also be a hazard leading to detours and blind alleys. The primary function of the pronominal system is *anaphoric reference,* the maintenance of a previously identifiable referent. The following illustrates anaphoric reference for pronouns:

Billy rode the bicycle.
He fell off it.

He refers to *Billy;* it refers to *the bicycle.* Thus, once certain information has been explicitly routed there is no need for further explication. Pronominals can be used to maintain reference.

There are, of course, some problems in anaphoric reference. One common problem is the *vacant* anaphoric reference, that is, when someone uses pronouns without establishing their referents. In such cases, confusion arises. An example of this is when someone says, "She didn't tell me," without identifying who *she* is.

Anaphoric reference and pronominal usage are complex and involve many potential pitfalls, for example, *competing* anaphoric reference:

Tom saw Bill at the store.
He swiped his hat.

Who is *he*? Whose hat was swiped? We do not know. A general rule is that a pronoun refers to the last mentioned reference that could fit it. According to this rule, *he* is Bill. If that is so, then Bill swiped Tom's hat. Yet, it is not unreasonable for the encoder to mean that *he* was Tom because both Tom and *he* are topics in a running topic. In short, Tom and Bill are competing anaphoric referents.

Another problem is *anaphoric loading*. That is, the first use of pronoun to maintain reference is likely to be understood, but subsequent uses involve increased risks that the original reference will be lost. The following illustrates the point:

Tom walked to town.
He went to the post office then to the drugstore.
He bought an ice cream cone but he dropped it.
He tried to clean the ice cream from his shirt but he made a bigger mess.

Here, *he* was used six times to refer to Tom. Adults do not find this difficult; but the child would find perhaps two or three uses of an anaphoric referent difficult to follow. The hearing-impaired child, particularly, would have difficulty with both anaphoric competition and loading.

In the anaphoric no, the encoder wants to cancel out a previous message and begin anew. For example, a child might say, "I like candy bars. No, ice cream cones best."

Returning to the pronominal system, it is complex not only anaphorically but structurally. There are pronominal variations for virtually every pronominal function (grammatical, spatial, quantitative, pragmatic). Indeed, these variations are justified because they mark the particular anaphoric status of intended referents. Tanz (1980) argued that the explicit marking of pronouns facilitates learning. This may be so, but another useful way of looking at pronouns is in regard to their functions. The explicit marking of pronouns may mean that their primary function is not only structural relations but also anaphoric relations.

The primary purpose of pronouns is anaphoric reference.

Thus, pronouns vary as functions of subjective and objective case, male, female and neuter; singular and plural; accusative; possessive; and reflexive. Table 10.1 illustrates these variations. Loveland (1984) showed that spatial awareness is prerequisite to understanding the speaker's point of view. This awareness governs the pragmatic distinction of I/you pronouns. It would, of course, be interesting to know how such awareness pertains to the *allative bias* (Freeman, Sinha, & Stedmon, 1981; Wales, 1979).

Pronominal difficulties with anaphoric reference include: vacant reference, competing reference, and loading.

Table 10.1. A Delineation of the Various Distinctions Demarked by the English Pronominal System

Subjective				Objective			
Singular		Plural		Singular		Plural	
Male	*I*	Male	*we*	Male	*him*	Male	*us*
Female	*she*	Female	*we*	Female	*her*	Female	*us*
Neuter	*it*	Neuter	*they*	Neuter	*it*	Neuter	*them*

Possession: my/mine, his, hers, our, your, their...

Reflexiveness: myself, himself, herself, themselves, ourselves...

Deictic reference: this/that, these/those

Nondefinite reference: no one, nobody, nothing, everyone, everybody, everything, anyone, anybody, some...

Bloom, Lightbown, and Hood (1975), Nelson (1973a), and others found that in learning noun phrases some children are nominal learners and some are pronominal learners. Eventually, both groups switch strategies in order to balance out their grammatical knowledge of nominals. Nelson (1975) called this the "nominal shift." Nominal learners go about learning noun phrases as proper nouns first, followed by simple determiner plus noun constructions. Moreover, they may show a preference for either animate or inanimate and/or ego or nonego constructions (Schlesinger, 1974). Pronominal learners, on the other hand, strive to learn noun phrases as pronouns. Inasmuch as both begin with rote learning (MacWhinney, 1978), both are initially successful. However, they will eventually be pushed to abandon rote learning; then, by necessity, they will turn to rule-governed learning. Here is where pronominal learners will run into considerable difficulty not because the pronominal system lacks rules (it surely does not lack rules), but because the rules are so much more complex.

> The pronominal strategy may run into trouble.

Pronominal learning provides some insight into the potency of recency learning. It is a common observation that objective pronouns are learned first. Indeed, both pronominals and nominals are learned first and more elaborately as object noun phrases (Brown, 1973a, 1973b)—verbal objects to be sure. Subsequently, the child may use objective pronouns as subjective. Thus, the child would say, "Him go," "Them here," etc.

Returning to buttressing, MacWhinney (1981) mentioned an interesting acquisition process he called "double marking" or marking something twice. For instance, the child might say,"*Daddy he* go." Muma (1981a) described such constructions as *buttressing* because the child buttresses a new form with an old form. This is illustrated as follows:

Old form:	*Daddy go.*
Old form:	*Him go.*
Old/new forms:	*Daddy he go.*

Buttressing seems to act as an intermediate step in learning appropriate pronominals.

Double marking or buttressing is consistent with Menyuk's (1964a) notion of redundancy. She defined an acquisition sequence whereby "errors" or restricted structures evidenced a pattern toward the acquisition of adult structures. Omission errors occur first; distortions and fragments replace omissions; redundancies replace distortions; and adult forms replace redundancies. The following illustrate these:

Omission:	*Daddy go; Go*
Distortion or fragment:	*Daddy going; Him go*
Redundancy:	*Daddy he going*
Adult form:	*He is going*

Modification. So far, the case was made for the primacy of SVO constructions. The child continues to acquire formal grammatical structure by first filling out basic SVO constructions with determiners and inflections. Then, basic operations on SVO itself are learned; these are *yes/no* and *wh-* questions and negations. Children then proceed to learn about modification.

There are two basic kinds of modifiers, noun phrase modifiers and verb phrase modifiers. Adjectivals and relative clauses are the main ways of achieving noun phrase modifiers. The function of noun phrase modification is to explicitly designate referents. Verb complements and adverbials are the main ways of achieving verb phrase modifications, the function of which is to achieve greater specificity of predication. This is discussed further in Chapter 11.

Coordination. It may be more propitious to conjoin topics or comments because they share certain presuppositional histories. Thus, it may be easier to traffic information by conjunction or to contrast information by disjunction than by embedding information. The conjunction of topics and comments is illustrated as follows:

Conjoined topics:	*Bill and Joe walked home*
Conjoined comments:	*Kathy skipped and jumped*
Disjoined topics:	*Bill or Joe slept late*
Disjoined comments:	*Kathy smiled or laughed*

Imperative, Ellipsis, Emphasis. Eventually, the child learns that it is more effective and efficient to delete the specification of a referent if it is already known within the topic or context. *Imperatives* are directives to do some course of action. Usually the addressee is known so there is no need to specify him or her. Thus, rather than saying, "You wash the dishes," a speaker would say, "Wash the dishes."

Elliptical constructions achieve a similar effect for comments. Comments are usually about unknown or ambiguous information pertaining to topics in topic-comment constructions. However, sometimes the comments are known but the speaker wants to amplify or stress some aspect. One way this can be achieved is through the use of elliptical constructions. The following illustrates such constructions:

He can swim.

He can. (Assumes the predication is known)

Another way of achieving this is to stress a particular aspect of a message. *Emphasis* affords the speaker a means of focusing on particular aspects of presupposition. The following are examples:

He can swim.   (Distinguishing who)
He can swim.   (Distinguishing volition)
He can swim.   (Distinguishing predication)

There are, of course, other formal grammatical mechanisms that can be learned. The point of this presentation is to stress the pragmatic function of these grammatical mechanisms. As children obtain increased knowledge of these syntactic devices, they become increasingly adept in using language in social commerce.

Another point needs to be made. Formal grammatical mechanisms provide ways of trafficking information. It should be understood that trafficking operations themselves can become unwieldy and disrupt a message. Menyuk (1969) identified a continuum of increasing difficulty when more than one transformational operation is used in one sentence. She pointed out that a sentence is easier to construct when more than one transformational operation is applied to separate constituents than if the operations appear in the same constituents.

Summary

The attribution or modification stage in grammatical acquisition begins with relatively simple modulations of meaning within the SVO base. Next to appear is sentential achievements, specifically *yes/no, wh-* questions, and negations. These are followed by major modifications of constituents; these are followed in turn by embedding and coordinations as rather complex modifications.

Mean length of utterance has a very narrow range of value (1.5-4.0 morphemes) as a language acquisition gauge. *Sequence* is a major characteristic of language acquisition. Loci of learning may be revealed in several different ways. Grammatical loci of learning may be revealed in co-occurrence, false starts, revisions, buildups, glossings, selectivity of spontaneous imitation, spontaneous rehearsal, buttressing, developmental sequences, and individual strategies of learning. These are all powerful not only because they may be used to identify new loci of learning for the child but also because they usually specify the grammatical *context* for such learning.

Pronominalization is a unique grammatical system that functions on anaphoric reference. This system might be viewed in regard to the following: vacant anaphoric reference, competing anaphoric reference, and psychological loading of anaphoric reference. Buttressing is a particular behavior that is often seen in the acquisition of the pronominal system, especially the shift from objective to subjective pronominal structures as grammatical subjects.

11

LATE FORMALIZATION AND METALINGUISTICS

Some aspects of formal grammatical knowledge emerge late in acquisition. Children are still learning complex grammatical constructions and subtleties in the late elementary school period. At this stage, children are learning to become more *adept* in language usage. And, their ability to *reflect* on verbal skills—*metalinguistics*—is increasing. Their emergent metalinguistic skills provide a means to effectively convert aspects of intuitive knowledge into explicit knowledge, thereby enabling them to achieve intermodality transfer of language knowledge, resulting finally in the acquisition of *reading* and *writing*.

Complex Grammatical Constructions and Subtleties

O'Donnell, Griffin, and Norris (1967) studied language acquisition in children from 5 to 14 years of age. They reported two periods of language acquisition, between 5 and 6 and between 10 and 14 years of age. These periods are marked by large increases in new grammatical constructions or sudden increases in use of previously infrequently used constructions. Both periods evidence increased sentence length and more frequent use of sentence embedding. Furthermore, both periods evidence an enlarged repertoire of nominal, adverbial, and coordinate constructions. During the first period, children achieve nominals containing adjectivals and prepositional phrases; in the second period, they show significant increases in the coordination of nominals and predicates.

> There appear to be two periods in which previously infrequent constructions evidence large increases in frequency, 5-6 years of age and 10-14 years of age.

Interestingly, O'Donnell et al. (1967) reported that 77% and 90% of the utterances during the first and second periods, respectively, conform to SV or SVO constructions. Passives are rare. This finding underscores the primacy of subject-predicate constructions. Presumably, children are "groping" to learn (Braine, 1976) such constructions, possibly as a base of operations for increasing variety of other constructions.

> In grade school, there seems to be a gradual consolidation of language learning but also two periods of abrupt shifts in verbal performance.

Dale (1976) delineated an acquisition sequence for the emergence of complex constructions. Complex object noun phrases are followed by *wh* clauses for subject, object, instrument, locative, and time. These are illustrated as follows:

Subject	*Whoever opens the door is foolish.*
Object	*She did what she thought was best.*
Instrument	*He hit the nail with what was a valued object.*
Locative	*They told him where to go.*
Time	*The movie will start when it gets dark.*

Dale also noted that clauses for location and time typically precede other *wh* clauses. This is also true for the emergence of *wh* questions. And, he noted that relative clauses are related to *wh* clauses. Relative clauses follow *wh* clauses in acquisition. Relative clauses with the relative clause marker are acquired first, then the optional deletion is learned. Thus, the child would learn the following two sentence constructions in this order:

The boy who is near the tree is Joe.
The boy near the tree is Joe.

> The acquisition sequence for complex constructions is: complex object noun phrases, *wh* clauses (subject, object, instrument, locative, time), and then relative clauses.

Gentner (1975) defined three levels of semantic complexity for the verbs *give, take, pay, trade, spend, buy* and *sell*. *Give* and *take* (Level 1) are the simplest. They both entail an agent and a recipient. They differ in their deictic reference. For *give* the agent is the possessor and the recipient is the nonpossessor whereas for *take* the agent is the nonpossessor and recipient.

Pay and *trade* (Level 2) are more complex than *give* and *take*. *Pay* and *trade* mean not only change of possession and causal action but also information of value for conducting the transaction. *Pay* means that the value is in terms of money whereas *trade* means that the value is in terms of goods.

In comparison, *buy, sell* and *spend* (Level 3) are even more complex. These entail causal action, change of possession, value of possession, and other relational considerations that culminate in a transaction beyond the exchange of pay. Such complexity is predicted by the "semantic feature hypothesis" (Clark, 1973b) which means that meanings of words are acquired through the accretion of semantic features.

C. Chomsky (1969) and Palermo and Molfese (1972) described several other subtle aspects of language that are learned after 4 years of age. One is the "Minimum Distance Principle" (MDP), which is a characteristic of English complements. The MDP states that the first noun phrase to the left of the complement is regarded as the subject of the complement. The following illustrates the point:

John told Diane to be late.

Diane is the first noun phrase to the left of the complement, *to be late* so *Diane* is the subject of the complement. She is the one *to be late*. However, there are a few exceptions to this rule in English, for example, *promise* and *ask*. The following sentence illustrates the exception:

John promised Diane to be late.

In this sentence it is *John*, not *Diane,* who will be late.

Children learn exceptions to the MDP rule after they learn the regular instances (C. Chomsky, 1969). In short, most 5-year-old children know the MDP, and some know that *promised* is an exception; however, some 10-year-olds have still not learned this exception. Similarly, *ask* has a wide range of acquisition. McNeill (1970) pointed out that the acquisition of *ask* is more complicated than that of *promise,* because at first children interpret *ask* as *tell*.

Kessel (1970) also studied the acquisition of *ask* and *tell*. He obtained results similar to those of C. Chomsky, but at somewhat earlier ages. Concerned about C. Chomsky's methodology, Cromer (1970) and Kessel (1970) used different procedures that were more ecologically real for the children (Donaldson, 1978). Cromer's (1970) study dealt with variations of adjectives that denoted different deep and surface structural relationships to the subjects. He used puppets to act out the sentences. Some sentences had adjectives that clearly required the noun to be the subject; some clearly required the noun to be the object; and some were ambiguous about these relationships. His results showed that children up to 5-7 years regarded all sentences as if the noun were the subject; children up to 6-6 years appeared to be in a transition stage, they correctly interpreted the first sentence type but have some correct and some incorrect interpretations of the second sentence type. By 6-8 years, they were interpreting both the first and second sentence types correctly.

Another subtle rule that children learn after 5 years is the "Nonidentity rule" for pronouns. When a pronoun is the subject and comes before the predicate noun phrase, then the pronoun and the predicate noun phrase cannot be about the same referent. The following illustrates the point:

He ate the apple Bill had kept.

The pronoun *he* is the subject and *Bill* is a predicate complement noun phrase. Thus, *he* cannot be *Bill*. C. Chomsky (1969) showed that all children older than 5-6 years knew this rule, but none younger knew it. This is an unusually sharp cut off. Most language acquisitions evidence a considerable range. Needless to say, more study needs to be done to substantiate this very sharp learning curve; it is peculiar.

In contrast, Palermo and Molfese (1972) reported that other investigators observed difficulties with pronominal acquisition at the junior high school. Loban (1963) found a marked increase of pronominal errors at the seventh grade; these errors subsided at about the ninth grade. Palermo and Molfese cited a study by Chai (1967) indicating that junior high school students had difficulty with pronominal referents in compared sentences.

Slobin (1966) showed that reversibility is a factor in the comprehension of passive sentences. A reversible passive is one in which the semantic constraints are open, allowing the subject to function as the object and vice versa. The following is a reversible passive:

The boy was chased by the dog. / The dog chased the boy.

A nonreversible passive contains semantic constraints that prohibit the possibility of the object becoming the subject:

The sandwich was eaten by the boy. / The boy ate the sandwich.

Sentences that are not reversible are learned earlier. Similarly, Turner and Rommetveit (1967a, 1976b) reported that about 9 years of age, children can handle the reversible passive. Turner and Rommetveit (1967b) attempted to elicit passive constructions in certain contexts. First grade children produced more than 50% passives but younger children did not produce any. Those who used passive forms tended to be more advanced linguistically.

Hayhurst (1967) showed that co-occurring structures were related to the acquisition of passives. When passive sentences are negated, difficulty increases;

but, when they are truncated, difficulty decreases. Truncated passive sentences are those in which the object is assumed therefore it need not be specified *(I ate lunch* could be truncated to *I ate).* Gaer (1969) reported by 6 years of age, children comprehended passives but continued to have difficulty producing passives. Embedded constructions were difficult for 5-year-olds especially for more than one embedding. Embedded constructions are those in which one sentence base is within another sentence base *(The boy who ran fast is in the blue shirt* contains the embedded sentence base *The boy ran fast*).

Returning to early syntax for a moment, Lust and Mervis (1980) reported that sentential coordinations appear before phrasal coordinations, and most early coordinations are accomplished by the use of *and.* deVilliers, Flusbery, and Hakuta (1977) did not find a primacy for early sentential coordinations, possibly because they used different criteria for determining sentential structures. Lust and Mervis (1980, p. 300) suggested that sentential coordination appears before phrasal coordination because the so-called length constraint may become independent of structural constraints. "It is obvious that the structural constraints above are independent of length." However, Ardery (1980) challenged this conclusion. Lust and Mervis suggested that there is a role for structural constraints. That is, they contended that knowledge of sentential coordination coupled with knowledge of phrasal coordination seems to open a door to a wide variety of possible phrasal coordinations that had not been envisioned before. They also found a parallel in *active construction* in the acquisition of connectives and the acquisition of phonology.

> These developmental findings, that children first evidence full-formed but infrequent coordination, and then go through a period allowing production of non-full-formed coordination, before reaching a final stage of essentially correct and productive coordination, are analogous to developmental facts in acquisition of phonology (cf. Kiparsky & Menn, 1977). They suggest a general constructive aspect of language development which holds for both syntax and phonology. (Lust & Mervis, 1980, p. 303)

Two studies (Bloom, Lahey, Hood, Lifter, & Fiess, 1980; Hood, Lahey, Lifter, & Bloom, 1978) found that the early connective forms most frequently used were *and, because, what, when* and *so;* the less frequently used connectives were *and then, but, if, that,* and *where.* As for sequence, Bloom et al. (1980, p. 235) gave the following portrayal of emergence for connectives:

> The first syntactic connective the children learned, *and,* was the most general: semantically, *and* was used to encode conjunction with all of the different conjunction meaning relations in the order Additive ⟨ Temporal ⟨ Causal ⟨ Adversative. Other connectives were semantically more specific, and were learned subsequently with different syntactic structures in the order Conjunction ⟨ Complementation ⟨ Relativization.

According to Katz and Brent (1968), the meanings of *because, then,* and *therefore* change between the first and sixth grade. At the first grade, all three words are used temporally to mean *then.* First graders did not seem to understand *but* and *although;* sixth graders had less difficulty but still had some trouble. Neimark (1970) showed that even high school children frequently do not discriminate between *or* and *and.* Olds (1968) reported that 9-year-old children did not comprehend *unless,* interpreting it to mean *if.*

Scholnick and Wing (1983) and Wing and Scholnick (1981) reported the following acquisition sequence for conjunctions concerning presuppositions of propositions: Belief *(because, although)* was easier to detect than uncertainty or disbelief *(if, unless).* Positive entailment *(because, if)* was easier than negative entailment *(unless, although).*

To reiterate, *co-occurrence* is important in language acquisition. The integrative nature of grammar is the essence of *co-occurrence.* Harris (1965) discussed the integrative nature of language and coined the term "co-occurrence." Brown et al. (1969) showed that children stay within a circumscribed set of known co-occurring structures when they first attempt a new structure such as *yes/no* questions (see also Bloom, 1970, 1973). Bloom et al. (1980) presented details about the role of co-occurrence in the acquisition of inflections. Muma (1973a, 1978a) and Bloom and Lahey (1978) elaborated on the role of co-occurrence in language learning. Hayhurst (1967) showed that co-occurrence is a significant factor in producing passive constructions between 5 and 9 years of age. Negated passives were more difficult than truncated passives. Gaer (1969) found that 5-year-old children had considerably more difficulty in both comprehension and production of embedded constructions when more than one embedded structure co-occurred in a sentence, especially in the same constituent (see also Menyuk, 1969).

Co-occurrence is evident in language acquisition.

Verbal Shift at 7 Years?

The *syntagmatic-paradigmatic shift* occurs at approximately 7 years of age (Brown & Berko, 1960; Emerson & Gekoski, 1976; Entwisle, 1966; Entwisle, Forsyth & Muuss, 1964; Ervin, 1961; Francis, 1972; McNeill, 1966a). Given a stimulus word, children under 7 typically give a syntagmatic response. For instance, the stimulus word is *cookie,* a young child might say "is good" or just "mm." However, older children and adults give another word from the same form class as the stimulus: For *Cookie,* they are likely to say "cake" or "candy." A syntagmatic response places the stimulus word in a syntactic context. A paradigmatic response gives another word in the same class (i.e., noun-noun, verb-verb, adjective-adjective). Unfortunately, the mechanisms that underlie the shift from syntagmatic to paradigmatic reponses are not well understood. Francis (1972) conjectured that some type of reorganization in the semantic domain accounts for the shift.

Muma and Zwycewicz-Emory (1979) developed a task intended to give new insight into the shift. It presented regular, single-syllable, pluralized high frequency nouns in systematically varying contexts. The contexts were as follows:

Noun (animate) _____

Noun (inanimate) _____

_____ noun (animate)

_____ noun (inanimate)

Noun (animate) _____ noun (animate)

Noun (animate) _____ noun (inanimate)

Noun (inanimate) _____ noun (animate)

Noun (inanimate) _____ noun (inanimate)

_____ noun (animate) _____

_____ noun (inanimate) _____

Subjects were asked to utter the stimulus word and anything they thought went into a given context. My wife conducted the study on children who were clearly younger than the age at which the shift occurs, as well as on children who were older. Her work led to refinements in the task and the development of the data reduction procedures. Muma and Zwycewicz-Emory (1979) used the task to study 5-year-olds, 9-year-olds, and adult subjects. Each context was repeated eight times, but in different sequences.

The responses to the various contexts were remarkably similar and strong. At the 5-year-old level listing behavior was strongly evident. Their responses were almost entirely nouns. At the 9-year-old level the responses were differentiated across the various contexts. At the adult level the responses were not only differentiated but well integrated. Nondifferentiated responses included listing behavior similar to that of the 5-year-olds as well as varied responses to each of the contexts over the eight replications. For example, adults merely said, "frogs, horses" or "cows and trees." Differentiated responses occurred as different types of responses for each context. For example, if the open slot appeared before a noun, the response was typically an adjective, but if it occurred after a noun, it was typically an intransitive verb.

Two levels of integration occurred. Nine-year-olds manifested first-level integrations. A given linguistic system appeared across the eight replications and the *same* exemplar was used. For example, 9-year-olds usually used the same word, such as *big* every time an adjective was needed. In second-level integrations, a given linguistic system occurred across the eight replications and *different* exemplars were used. Thus, rather than using the same word several times, 9-year-olds used a variey of exemplars *within* the same class, for example, several different adjectives when adjectives were needed.

What about the syntagmatic-paradigmatic shift? First and foremost, major changes in performance occurred after the age (7 years) at which the syntagmatic-paradigmatic shift presumably occurs. The paradigmatic responses of the 5-year-olds were quite unexpected. However, word association tasks are different. In such tasks, words are placed in isolation. In the context study, however, various linguistic contexts were provided. Apparently, young children need a context, and if it is not there, they will create it.

White (1965) reported several cognitive and linguistic changes that occur at about 7 years of age. Evidently, some kind of cognitive reorganization takes place at this time and it is manifested in different behaviors.

Evidently, some kind of cognitive reorganization takes place around 7 years of age.

Adeptness

It is one thing for a child to know the basic grammatical machinery of language but quite a different matter to be *adept* in its use. "What is crucial is not so much a better understanding of how language is structured, but a better understanding of how language is used, not so much what language is, as what language is for" (Hymes, 1972, p. xii). The distinction between knowledge and use was also made by Hammond and Summers (1972), who asserted that it is one thing to know something but another to use knowledge in adept ways.

For example, the child knows that conjunctions are used to connect or conjoin equivalent constituents, the largest of which is the sentence. So in the early stages in the use of conjunctions, the child will connect sentences with simple conjunctions, particularly *and* (Bloom et al., 1980; Hood et al., 1978). This happens in both speech and early writing. Both speech and writing are mentioned because such evidence shows that language processing is *not* modality specific.

Conjunctions between sentences appear to function for *topic maintenance* and *turn taking*. Conjunctions tell the listener or reader that the topic is continuing and they preserve the speaker's turn in talking. From the point of view of *informativeness,* conjunctions operate anaphorically to remind the decoder to keep the presuppositional set of the preceding sentence in mind for decoding the next sentence. Eventually, the child will learn to debase the conjunction between sentences with a filled pause, /um/, to indicate to the decoder that he or she is still processing relevant information and wishes to continue. Of course, short pauses evidence adeptness. The extended pause, on the other hand, invites a turn taking exchange.

> It is one thing to know something but another to use one's knowledge in adept ways.

Language learning continues throughout life in the semantic domain through differentiation and reorganization of concepts gleaned from experience (Nelson, 1973a, 1974). Important developments in cognition occur after the preschool period extending into adolescence, the concrete-operations stage and the formal-operations stage (Piaget, 1954, 1962, 1970). In adolescence, the acquisition of cognitive skills presumably entails dialectics (Riegel, 1975). While preschool children may have vestigial communicative skills, social cognition in general and pragmatics in particular evidence a considerable amount of growth until approximately age 10 or 12 (Flavell, 1968). During this time, children learn to be efficient in coding messages, develop the role-taking attitude that is used to perceive listener cues in communication, and develop selection rules for coding the best message for a perceived context. Thus, preschool children have learned a great deal, but they have a great deal more yet to learn.

Except for subtle nuances, preschool children know virtually all of the rules of adult language (Menyuk, 1963, 1964a, 1964b). Yet, there is a considerable difference between the language of preschool children and that of adults. Aside from vocabulary, the difference is facility or use of language. Preschool children are not as *adept* in language use as adults. They need to learn the rules of language use from two different perspectives: *efficiency* and *appropriateness*. They tend to string out a series of utterances in which small changes are made from one utterance to the next. The young child might say, "Mommy, I saw a kitty. The kitty was pretty. The kitty was soft. The kitty is Tom. Mommy, the kitty has tiny fingernails. The kitty has sharp fingernails." An adult would be much more efficient, saying, "I saw a pretty cat named Tom with soft fur and sharp claws." Of course, such an utterance would be addressed to another adult. This raises the issue of appropriateness.

> After acquiring basic grammatical knowledge, it is necessary to become efficient and appropriate in the use of this knowledge.

Appropriateness. Speakers have options concerning not only what they want to talk about but also how they can code a message in a particular context for a particular effect. They use *selection rules,* which pertain to the psychological dynamics of a situation. This is sociolinguistics or pragmatics. Children need to learn how to selectively produce the appropriate code for a particular context; they need to know the rules of language usage. This is very complex. Ervin-Tripp (1971, p. 37) referred to the complexity of language use in this way, "everything that can be said about linguistic rules can be said about sociolinguistic rules."

Everyone knows that children are sometimes startlingly frank. Such frankness is usually attributed to honesty, but it may be ignorance of appropriateness of language usage. Said differently, it is probably not honesty so much as it is the child's inability to select an alternative code that would be more propitious or appropriate for the particular circumstance.

Young children perceive and talk about the "here-and-now" (Bloom, 1970, 1973). Communicative repertoire is limited virtually to "talk to" behaviors, possibly accompanied by simple emotive displays for immediate need gratification. When faced with communicative obstacles, young children usually either repeat or abandon their efforts. This topic is discussed below in terms of contingent queries in playing the communication game. The egocentric speech of young children lacks the volitional and motivational character of adult speech.

By 8 years of age, most children have successfully played the "original word game" (Brown, 1958b), in which knowledge of the world or theory of the world (Palermo, 1982) becomes socialized in language; and, they have played the "original thinking game" (Bruner, 1964; Bruner et al., 1966), in which one is released from direct experience to rely on representational or symbolic experience. Thus, 8-year-olds have essentially acquired the grammatical and referential machinery of their linguistic community. Nonetheless, they are not yet communicatively competent, though some vestiges appear at preschool ages (Shatz & Gelman, 1973) and even in infancy as a pragmatic scaffold for language acquisition (Bruner, 1981). "They must still learn to play the communication game to ascertain the messages best suited to a particular situation and thereby realize effective and efficient communication" (Muma, 1975a).

The "original word game" and the "original thinking game" provide the grammatical and cognitive bases, respectively, for the communication game.

Role Taking. By 8 years of age, the dimensions of communication have changed in several important respects. Issues about the nature of language no longer pose significant obstacles. That is, these children have learned the major semantic-syntactic-phonological aspects of language. Topics are more adultlike. Communication is primarily, but not exclusively, representational. Most important, 8-year-olds have lost an exclusively egocentric orientation. They have become aware that effective communication can occur only if they consider the other participants in the process. They realize that the decoder is not merely to be talked to but a *partner* in finding the message best suited for a particular situation (Bruner, 1981). The awareness of the encoder-decoder partnership in communication provides a way of becoming fully adaptive in playing the communication game. Awareness of the encoder-decoder partnership in communication has been variously called role taking (Flavell et al., 1968; Miller, Kessel, & Flavell, 1969), role of the other (Mead, 1934), edited social speech (Glucksberg & Krauss, 1967), speaker sampling and comparison (Rosenberg & Cohen, 1966), social speech (Piaget, 1951, 1952, 1954, 1955), and communicative speech (Vygotsky, 1962). This literature has been reviewed by Glucksberg, Krauss, and Higgins (1975).

Both speaker and listener are active partners in communication.

Message-of-Best-Fit. Communicative competence is the capacity not only to conceive, formulate, construct, and issue messages but also to perceive the degree to which intended meanings are appropriately coded in a matrix of referential codes. Thus, communication is much more than issuing and receiving a message. *Interpersonal communication* is issuing messages in the most appropriate way(s) for conveying intended messages to a particular person for particular effects. It is more complicated than an active speaker talking to a passive listener. Both encoder and decoder are active participants in arriving at a message-of-best-fit. They are dealing not only with essential meanings (semantic categories), but also with the ways in which meanings can be effectively conveyed. Consideration must be given to the form or nature and type of code, reference or representation, and acceptability or communicative license. Moreover, the participants must be able to switch between producing or *dumping* intended messages of presumed best fit for a particular circumstance and *playing* the communication game to resolve obstacles (Muma, 1975a) such as contingent queries (Gallagher, 1977, 1981; Garvey, 1975, 1977). This means that the participants must frequently be able to interchange encoding and decoding roles or use "main moves" in communicative exchanges (Wells, 1981). Main moves are *initiations* (solicit, give) and *responses* (give, acknowledge).

Dumping denotes the product of underlying mental operations in which communicative intent is coded in a *message-of-best-fit* for a particular situation. Assuming that a message-of-best-fit is dumped or issued, the probabilities are high that only essential meaning rather than complete, accurate, or faithful meaning is conveyed. This is because encoding represents only selected aspects of an intent and decoding is naturally biased. Thus, some distortion is inevitable. No matter what level of agreement may result between encoder and decoder regarding form, reference, and acceptability, the message will be unwittingly distorted to some degree. Some distortions are merely incidental to a message, but others could seriously jeopardize it. Unintentional influences may overshadow the message: "It wasn't so much what he said but how he said it." Distortions are likely when a message differs significantly from the decoder's values, beliefs, or morals: "I can't believe what I hear." Conflicts between what the decoder knows and perceives in a message can result in a cognitive dissonance problem (Festinger, 1957). Perception alone can screen out information, thereby creating a distortion, since perception is to a great extent governed by what one knows (Garner, 1966). All in all, the probabilities of distortion are very high even though consensus may have been established as to form, reference, and acceptability.

The encoder strives to construct a message-of-best-fit, but, even then, the probabilities of distortion are very high.

Code Matrix. The message-of-best-fit is a complex matrix of referential codes. These are linguistic, nonlinguistic, paralinguistic, and, in resolving communicative obstacles, metareferential. *Linguistic* codes are obviously more complicated, versatile, and powerful than the others. The particular combination of coding devices employed in any particular situation is intimately tied to topic and context in addition to a host of sociological influences (Bernstein, 1970; Labov, 1972; Shuy, 1970) and available reference (Brown, 1958a; Olson, 1970). *Nonlinguistic* devices include postures, pointing, facial expressions, head nodding, eye contact, holding, touching, movement and proximity in space, and figure/ground orientation. *Paralinguistic* devices are typically superimposed upon a verbal utterance. These include pausing and other hesitation phenomena, intonations, inflections, rate variations, aspiration, and certain gestures. Kasl and Mahl (1965) identified psychological distinctions between "ah" and "non-ah" hesitation phenomena in spontaneous speech. "Ah" behaviors indicate information processing whereas "non-ah" behaviors indicate anxiety states. Several reviews of nonverbal communicative behaviors are available (Birdwhistell, 1970; Knapp, 1972). *Metareferential* devices signal communicative obstacles: "Tell it like it is." "Don't give me that jive." They are comments about the message itself.

A message is placed in a code matrix.

Encoding and Decoding. Communicative competence depends on the capacity to function as either encoder or decoder for a complex matrix of codes in communicative context. The *encoding function* involves the ability to perceive the communicative context in terms of actual and presumed reference, and through linguistic and other coding devices, produce a message appropriate to the encoder's communicative intent and the decoder's need for information. An encoder tries to produce the message-of-best-fit for his other perception of the situation, intent, and the listener's needs. Cognitively, an encoder attempts to take the role of decoder in determining the message-of-best-fit.

The *decoding function* entails the ability to decipher available codes (linguistic and otherwise) to discern intended meanings. Brown (1965) called the decoding function an ability to *"cash words into referents."* Clark and Clark (1977) defined construction (p. 45) and utilization (p. 90) processes in comprehension. These processes are closely tied to the propositional nature of a message and the theory of the world for deducing relevant presuppositions. The decoding function presupposes a perceptual-cognitive-linguistic system essentially similar in nature (presuppositional history) and use to that of the encoder. Decoders can ascertain meaning as if they were the encoder. The decoding function also involves the recognition and identification of communicative obstacles. The decoder can selectively apprise the encoder of these obstacles and their nature so the encoder can revise the code to produce a message-of-best-fit.

The identification and resolution of communicative obstacles is what Muma (1975a) called *playing* the communication game. The communication game has two major components: dump and play. "Dumping" a message refers to the perceptual-cognitive-linguistic operations of the encoder in producing a message of presumed best fit for a particular context (topic, referent, listener, intention, etc.). If the code is consistent with the encoder's communicative intent, deals with available referents (actual or presumed), and is in an appropriate form, the decoder may be able to discern the meaning of an intended message. However, if these requirements are not met, intended meaning may not be conveyed. If the decoder recognizes this and indicates it to the encoder, they may play the communication game to identify the nature of the problem and reconcile it. "I don't understand _____." "Huh, what did you say?" "Don't beat around the bush, tell me what you want to say." Figure 11.1 depicts such encoder-decoder relationships.

The encoder-decoder model has received considerable attention in recent years. The works of Flavell et al. (1968), Glucksberg, Krauss, and Higgins (1975), Longhurst and Siegel (1973), Longhurst and Berry (1975), Garmiza and Anisfeld (1976), Keller (1976), Maratsos (1973), Shantz and Wilson (1972), Clark and Delia (1976), and others have documented the dynamic nature of the encoder-decoder processes in communication.

The encoder-decoder processes should not be linked to or associated with the traditional notion of expressive and receptive language. This latter notion separated verbal processes that are inextricably related (Bloom, 1974). It led to arbitrary distinctions in the applied fields that have been detrimental to clinical assessment and intervention, because it emphasizes differences and de-empha-

Figure 11.1. The encoder-decoder relationship.

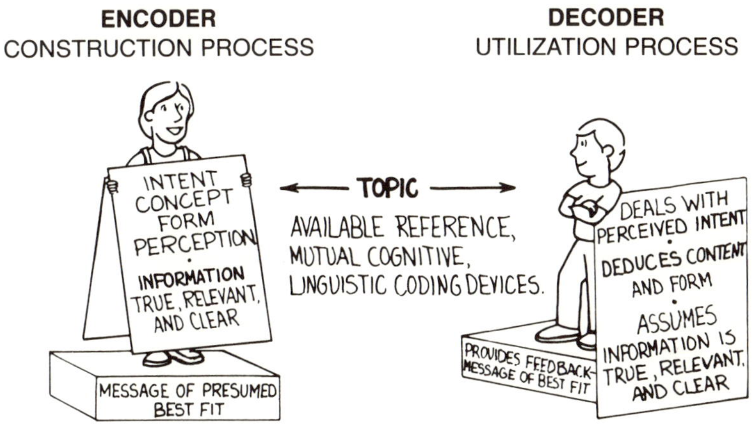

ENCODER
CONSTRUCTION PROCESS

INTENT
CONCEPT
FORM
PERCEPTION
INFORMATION
TRUE, RELEVANT, AND CLEAR

MESSAGE OF PRESUMED BEST FIT

⟵ TOPIC ⟶
AVAILABLE REFERENCE, MUTUAL COGNITIVE, LINGUISTIC CODING DEVICES.

PROVIDES FEEDBACK-MESSAGE OF BEST FIT

DECODER
UTILIZATION PROCESS

DEALS WITH PERCEIVED INTENT
DEDUCES CONTENT AND FORM
ASSUMES INFORMATION IS TRUE, RELEVANT, AND CLEAR

From *Language primer* (p. 37) by J. Muma, 1981, Austin, TX: PRO-ED. Reprinted by permission.

sizes similarities; this is the opposite of natural behavior. The same problem has occurred regarding modality differences and similarities. The clinical fields have tried to make much of modality differences when, in fact, similarities are more substantial—indeed, fundamental—to clinical assessment and intervention. Again, encoding and decoding in a communicative model should not be compared to the notions of expressive and receptive language. Such comparisons may only perpetuate misconceptions in the clinical fields.

> The expressive/receptive modality distinction is not as useful as the encoder-decoder process orientation.

The terms "message," "code," and "map" are used interchangeably. An encoder strives to make a message, code, or map that brings a decoder to think or behave in intended ways. "Map" means that it directs the decoder to think about an intended message in certain ways; underlying intended propositions become mapped onto surface forms.

Communication is the primary function of language (Brown, 1977). It is realized not only through verbal codes but also through a matrix of complexly integrated coding mechanisms in a communicative context. This context, actual and presumed, is the primary determinant of what, when, where, why, and how something is said and/or done. Communication is not unidirectional—a speaker talking to a listener. It involves the concerted needs and efforts of both encoder and decoder. Both functions are usually assumed by each participant.

Communication is the primary function of language.

The what, when, where, why, and how issues of communication are traceable to social systems and group dynamics (sociolinguistics) and to an individual's perogatives in communication (pragmatics). Since clinicians deal with individual problems, their primary concern is with pragmatics. It is helpful to place pragmatics in the context of a general model of communication and an overview of sociolinguistics. This is what *functionalism* is all about.

Thus, there are several aspects to increased adeptness. In communication, children become increasingly adept at coding a message-of-best-fit whereby they must consider intention, command of language, available reference (actual and presupposed), and their listener's perspective and presumed verbal capacities. Needless to say, it is a complex process of negotiating messages under such considerations.

Aside from these issues, the act of formally coding messages in linguistic structure evidences increased adeptness. In referring to the results of two studies by Loban (1963, 1966), Palermo and Molfese (1972, p. 416) said, "The results indicate that as children get older their speech performance improves as indicated by decreases in incomplete syntactic structures, increases in the variety of structural patterns used, and greater variation in the positions of phrases such as adverbial modifiers, nominalizations and so on."

Another view of adeptness is how children choose to use language in various situations. This is known as *scripting* (Nelson, 1981a). Early on, children participate in highly routinized social interactions, most often with their mother. Bruner (1981) called these routines *formats*. Children may explore many variations within the formats, but the basic structure remains constant. This can be seen in early child-mother story reading. Children have a favorite story they want read again and again. *Within* the context of the story, however, there are many opportunities for variation. Children are sensitive to any changes made. For example, if the adult attempts a shorthand version of the story, children are likely to object and rather soberly put the parent back on track because it is, after all, "their" story. "Their" intentions for learning from the story are indeed serious intentions and whatever variations that are allowed issue from "their" jurisdiction.

Adeptness might be considered from different perspectives, coding a message-of-best-fit, commanding of linguistic structure, and scripting messages for particular situations.

Upon engaging in a number of formats, the children learn rudimentary rules about turn taking, topic maintenance, adult-child roles, peer roles, and so forth. Armed with such pragmatic skills and with grammatical knowledge about how to formally code messages, children become increasingly *scripted* about how to perform in different situations.

Bates (1979) maintained that the language learning process unfolds in three stages: contextualized, decontextualized, and recontextualized (see also Halliday, 1975). In the *contextualized* stage, verbal behavior is context bound. This is early on when the child first learns words. In the *decontextualized* stage, verbal behavior is not context bound; it is productive. Such behavior enables the child to generate novel utterances. Zaporozhets and Elkonin (1971) suggested that decontextualization is the most significant achievement of language acquisition. The *recontextualization* is synonymous with scripting. Basically, in this stage the child learns how to tailor verbal capacities to particular contexts. Bloom and Lahey's (1978) notion of language *use* in the content-form-use model also refers to scripting.

Language learning unfolds in three stages related to context: context-bound learning, decontextualization, and recontextualization or scripting.

Contingent Query: A Structural Consequence

Increased grammatical skill enables participants in social commerce to invoke and respond to contingent queries. A contingent query is an inquiry about the speaker's previous utterance. For example, when the listener does not understand, the listener may say "What?" to the speaker. These function pragmatically as metalinguistic comments concerning how well social commerce is or is not working. Garvey (1975, 1977, 1979) posited that knowledge of the contingent query is not so much a "conversational refinement" as a structural one because contingent queries appear to emerge as a consequence of emerging grammatical skill. Yet, they do function in the management of social commerce.

Gallagher (1981) said that the contingent query sequence has four basic components: an original utterance, a contingent query, a response utterance, and resumption. Studies on the acquisition of contingent queries cast doubt on the so-called talk to attitude of young children. This is an attitude whereby a child delivers a message but does not attend to listener feedback. Gallagher (1977) showed that children responded appropriately to adult requests for clarification about 80% of the time. These young children had invested some of their communicative skills in the functions of utterances as opposed to raw structure. Gallagher identified three kinds of contingent queries:

REQUESTS FOR CONFIRMATION (RC), *yes-no* questions, were complete repetitions of the original utterance with rising intonation (e.g., C: *Build something.* R: *Build something?*); repetitions with elaboration (e.g., C: *More brick.* R: *Some more brick?*); or repetitions with reductions (e.g., C: *Puppy in it.* R: *Puppy?*).

NEUTRAL REQUESTS FOR REPETITION (N) were neutral queries with rising intonation such as *What?, Huh?, Pardon?* or a small set of declarative utterances such as *I don't understand you.*

REQUESTS FOR SPECIFIC CONSTITUENT REPETITION (SCR), *wh-* questions, were partial repetitions with a *wh-* element replacing a constituent in the original utterance (e.g., C: *After came a knock at the door.* R: *After came what?* (rising intonation) (1981, p. 54).

In Gallagher's (1981) study, the RC easily accounted for two-thirds of the queries. The N was infrequent and SCR varied considerably in frequency. These were queries of adults to children. Child-initiated queries were relatively infrequent with RC somewhat high, N quite high (for two children) and SCR virtually nonexistent. Such relative frequencies suggest that adults in adult-child discourse are the primary managers of statements about topics.

Conti-Ramsden and Friel-Patti (1983) found that mothers' discourse adjustments to language-impaired children were similar to those of non-language-impaired children, although the discourse performance for these two groups of children was not similar. And, Liles (1985) showed that normal and language-disordered children altered their use of cohesion; they were similar in some respects, but they differed in their manner of cohesive organization, cohesive adequacy, and comprehension of the story. Communicative cohesion refers to the use of some element that is dependent upon that of another. For example, in the sentence: *He opened the box* the pronoun *He* is dependent upon knowing who *he* refers to.

Indirect Speech Acts

It is one thing to learn to codify a message for direct decoding; indirect decoding requires a much different metalinguistic skill. It constitutes a relatively advanced level of formalization. *Indirect speech acts* rely to a great extent on context and possibly paralinguistic marking via prosodic devices. On the one hand, formal grammatical mechanisms function to traffic or direct pertinent presuppositions. On the other hand, indirect speech acts intentionally specify which presuppositions are secondary to intended messages. The listener is supposed to deduce the secondary status of these presuppositions from the context of the message and other coding devices in the code matrix of linguistic and paralinguistic codes. For example, a man says with a frown on his face, "That was a good movie." The linguistic code explicitly states that the movie was good, but the frown indicates that the speaker regards the movie as inferior. This speaker could have stressed the word *that* ("*That* was a good movie") to emphasize that it was truly a good movie. He could have stressed *that* but also superimposed an interrogative intonational contour, which would mean that it was questionable whether it was a good movie.

To reiterate, when children can handle indirect speech acts, they are well into formal grammatical mechanisms. Indirect speech acts are metalinguistic. The extent to which children can talk about and play with language, including indirect speech acts, is the extent to which they have attained metalinguistic capacities. Such capacities are very powerful for facilitating language learning.

Metalinguistics

Cazden (1975) held that emergent metalinguistic abilities (abilities to reflect upon and play with language itself) are the basis for learning to read and write.

> Our concern as educators with this particular kind of language performance comes from increasing arguments that it is at least very helpful—and maybe critically important—not so much in the primary processes of speaking and hearing as in what may be considered the derived or secondary processes of reading and writing.

Turning to Vygotsky, Cazden held that metalinguistic awareness is the basis of literacy. She pointed out that speaking and listening are based upon intuitive and tacit knowledge, but literacy (learning to write and read) entail a process of making tacit or unconscious knowledge of language explicit or conscious. The conversion of implicit to explicit knowledge is within the province of metalinguistics in language and metacognition in cognition. Muma (1977a, 1978a) used the term *intermodality transfer* to refer a method of teaching children how to make tacit knowledge of language explicit in learning to write and read.

The conversion of tacit knowledge to explicit knowledge is the essential province of both metalinguistics and metacognition.

Mattingly (1972) contended that reading relies critically upon the reader's awareness of the primary activities of speaking and listening.

> There appears to be considerable individual variation in linguistic awareness. Some speaker-hearers are not only very conscious of linguistic

patterns, but exploit their consciousness with obvious pleasure in verbal play, e.g., punning (and versifying, solving crossword puzzles, and talking Pig Latin) or verbal work (e.g., linguistic analysis). Others never seem to be aware of more than words ... this variation contrasts markedly with the relative consistency from person to person with which primary linguistic activity is performed. (Mattingly, 1972, p. 140)

Thus, verbal play and conscious verbal work are metalinguistic activities, the key to which is linguistic *awareness*. In the last analysis, language is only a tool or a vehicle for communication. As such, it is transparent. As Clark and Clark (1977, p. 49) said, raw speech and its phonological representation in "working memory" become purged once construction processes have worked out the propositions of a message in comprehension. What survives is the gist of the message; what is transparent and lost is the grammatical structure (Fillenbaum, 1966) .

Awareness of verbal behavior is metalinguistics.

Metalinguistic awareness refers to a shift from transparency (out of awareness) to opaqueness (in awareness) (Cazden, 1975; McNeill, 1973). McNeill suggested that this shift comprises a number of options about awareness of language (i.e., phonological, syntactic, semantic, intention, and so on).

> The processing of language can be stopped anywhere ... Hence rather than a dichotomy between opaque meaning and transparent syntax or phonology, there is a series of opaque-transparent oppositions, depending on how far linguistic processing had advanced before it is stopped. (McNeill, 1973)

Kretschmer defined metalinguistics as follows:

> Metalinguistics refers to those aspects of language functioning concerned with: 1) a person's knowledge about language and language operations; and 2) the planning, monitoring, and checking activities that an individual might undergo during language comprehension and production. (1984, p. 212)

Kretschmer viewed metacognition and metalinguistics as similar processes; except that the individual can "step back" and reflect upon the nature of the metalinguistic domain; metacognitive domain, by contrast, is more elusive and transparent. Kretschmer identified three major theoretical perspectives on metalinguistics, which vary as a function of how they characterize the relationship between thought and language: the cognitive dominant approach, the language dominant approach, and the communicative interactional approach.

According to the *cognitive dominant approach,* language serves to map out that which is already known. Language is thus an aspect of cognition. Furthermore, certain cognitive abilities are prerequisite for language acquisition. This approach can also be understood from the competing perspectives of local and deep homology (Bates, 1979). Deep homology posits that there is a common cognitive core for language acquisition whereas local homology posits that different cognitive capacities are antecedent to particular verbal capacities. Bates's (1979) research largely supported local homology.

> **The cognitive dominant view holds that verbal behavior maps out what is known.**

The *language dominant approach* asserts that language presumably determines thought. This conjures up the old Sapir-Whorf (Sapir, 1921; Whorf, 1956) hypothesis of linguistic determinism, which has not received much support. It also suggests that comprehension is a word-dominated process, but the contemporary view holds that comprehension is a process issuing from cognitive awareness of a context (Macnamara, 1972) that provides meaning for words and entails construction and utilization processes for deriving appropriate propositions for coded messages. The language dominant approach does not view language as a tool or vehicle for communication. Rather, this approach implies that language and a verbal code as ends unto themselves.

> **The language dominant view regards verbal codes not as tools for communication but as ends unto themselves.**

The *communication interactional approach* asserts that cognition and language are inextricably related in symbolic behavior (Bates, 1976, 1979; Bruner, 1981). Thus, cognition serves language as evidenced in pragmatic or communicative functions and language serves cognition as in mathetic functions (Halliday, 1975). Muma (1978a) termed these interpersonal communicative functions and intrapersonal functions (representation, mediation), respectively.

> **The communicative interactional approach holds that there is a complex interrelationship between cognition and language.**

From the cognitive dominant perspective, metalinguistic skills are seen as a subset of metacognition. From the language dominant perspective, metalinguistic activities "bring metacognitive awareness into full fruition" (Kretschmer, 1984, p. 212). The communicative interactional approach states that metalinguistic activities are "semi-autonomous, inextricably related and mutually reinforcing" (Kretscher, 1984, p. 212). The cognitive dominant and the communicative interactional views of metalinguistic activities seem to be compatible.

Kretschmer (1984, pp. 217-218) reviewed the literature on the acquisition of metalinguistic skills. In that review, he summarized Clark's (1978) taxonomy of metalinguistic skills, which parallels the Brown and DeLoach (1978) taxonomy for metacognitive skills:

1. Monitoring ongoing utterances—repairing a person's own speech spontaneously; practicing various speech and language units; and adjusting his or her speech to the age and status of the listener
2. Checking the results of an utterance—seeing whether or not communication has been affected and repairing the conversation when necessary; commenting on the utterances of others; and correcting the utterances of others
3. Testing for reality—making decisions as to whether or not a word or description will or will not work
4. Deliberately trying to learn language units, either by practicing them or role playing
5. Predicting the consequences of language units and rules, such as applying inflections to new words or nonsense words and making judgments of grammaticality
6. Reflecting on the product of an utterance—identifying linguistic units, providing definitions, and constructing puns and riddles

Kretschmer (1984) held that the Bloom and Lahey (1978) model of form-content-use fits with this hierarchy of metalinguistic skills. And, he suggested that the following metalinguistic abilities be added: (a) the ability to note synonyms, antonyms, hyponyms, entailments, and presuppositions; and (b) the ability to generate paraphrases.

deVilliers and deVilliers (1978) said that metalinguistic capacities enable individuals to reflect on language. Reflective linguistic behaviors are evidenced by comments on the ways language is used, for example, verbal play, joking, and the contrived use of language to deceive and lie. Horgan (1978) portrayed joke telling as a metalinguistic activity. Through metalinguistic skills, individuals become aware of speech sounds, words, grammatical rules and devices, ambiguity, and humor. Similarly, Slobin (1978b) maintained that metalinguistic capacities provide means for becoming aware of the need to (a) self-correct or restate, (b) comment on the speech of others, (c) make explicit inquiries about speech itself, (d) comment on speech and grammar, and (e) respond to direct questions about language. Indeed, Slobin contended that there may be a relationship between the emergence of metalinguistic capacities and the development of consciousness and self-consciousness.

While some taxonomies include humor, others do not. Perhaps the various taxonomies should be regarded as preliminary because the study of *humor* is sure to alter our views of metalinguistic abilities (McGhee, 1974, 1977; Shultz, 1976) especially the child's emergent awareness of metaphor and simile (Billow, 1975; Cometa & Eson, 1978; Gardner, 1974; Gardner, Kirchner, Winner, & Perkins, 1975; Gardner, Winner, Bechofer, & Wolf, 1978; Gentner, 1977; Winner, 1979). Hudson and Nelson (1984) showed that most of the so-called overextensions in early language acquisition were actually analogies (metaphor, simile). Thus, it appears that metalinguistic capacities are evident as early as 18-24 months. These concerns about humor, metaphor and simile can be traced back to Werner and Kaplan's (1963, p. 454) distancing notion. Here, distancing refers to the cognitive distance between sign and referent, and symbol and referent. Werner and Kaplan specified three levels of distancing: minimal distance, intermediate distance, and a more advanced distance that deals with "alluding metaphors." A communicative point has a minimal distance index-referent relationship depicting direct relationships between the knower and the known. "Alluding metaphors" fix a referent. Such concerns about distancing lead us to issues of icons-indices-symbols (Peirce, 1932) and degrees of arbitrariness of symbolization (Bates, 1979). That is, as the child can allude to a referent, he can deal with formal mechanisms of language such as words and grammatical devices. These are the kinds of skills that Peirce (1932) referred to in the indice-symbol notion and that Bates (1979) referred to as degrees of arbitrariness of symbols.

The domain of metalinguistics surely extends to an understanding of humor and metaphor. These in turn deal with issues of cognitive distancing.

The domains of *rhyme* and *music* also seem to be related to metalinguistic abilities. My daughter Taylor, for example, had developed an awareness of rhymes and singing by 2-2 years. This activity coincided with a large surge in language learning between the period of 2-2 years and 2-8 years. By "awareness of rhymes and singing" I am not referring to the highly formatted nursery rhymes and songs that were presented to her again and again just as her favorite stories were presented repeatedly. I am referring to the metalinguistic awareness that enabled her to discover and create *novel* rhymes and songs. One day, she spontaneously said, "Mommy, pilot and pirate sound the same." In her phonological system they were phonetically the same. This was not an isolated instance; she seemed to enjoy discovering rhyming words; she actively and spontaneously searched for words that rhyme.

Discovering and creating novel rhymes and songs should be added to the list of metalinguistic activities.

One of her favorite activities was to sing to the accompaniment of my trombone humming. These "songs" usually began as simple prolonged but varied intonations of no recognizable melody. After a few "verses," she frequently requested me to stop my humming or my vocal matching of her "singing," then she launched into her own novel songs. These were usually simple narrations of things she had done during the day. And, they usually contained long sentences. The point is that I'm quite sure these rhymes and songs are metalinguistic and that they have played a significant role in accelerating her language acquisition.

Just before the onset of this highly productive metalinguistic activity, Taylor had three very peculiar behaviors: (a) unusually complex sentences, (b) severe stuttering, and (c) excessive sentence repetition. Each of these behaviors lasted about two weeks with abrupt onset and termination. Shortly after her second birthday, she began uttering sentences averaging slightly more than eight words. After about two weeks of this, she began to stutter severely. It was like night and day. One day she was impressively verbal; the next, she struggled to say a word. As parents, we were concerned about Taylor's behavior, but since her father stutters it was not surprising. What surprised us was the severity and the sudden onset of this behavior, and in about two weeks it terminated rapidly. From then on, there has not been even a hint of stuttering, but she began to repeat sentences excessively; this also lasted about two weeks (although it still happens occasionally). That is, she would make a comment once, then again, whereupon her listener would respond appropriately (seemingly). In spite of the response, she repeated the sentence several times, perhaps five or six times, before she forged ahead with the topic or responded to the listener in some way. What motivated these repetitions, and what stopped them? Whatever was going on, metalingustic activities blossomed thereafter, and she has been making giant strides in language learning since: pragmatically, syntactically, and semantically with relatively limited progress in phonology.

At the same time, David Ingram was visiting Texas Tech University for a two-week conference, and he observed that the son of the clinic director, Joy Munson, acquired a morphological rule *before* syntax; through the use of a reduplicative pattern. This is quite unusual. Munson and Ingram (1985) conjectured that a circumscribed set of experiences triggered this learning and that it was facilitated by somewhat advanced phonological capabilities. Such development, they suggested, raises questions about the priority of syntactic acquisition over morphological acquisition. Given that such learning eventually has to be reorganized in the course of future learning, they suggested that *learnability* theory should allow for such events.

This brief detour from emerging metalinguistic abilities was not far afield, because these instances of maverick language learning seem to entail some measure of linguistic awareness—metalinguistics.

Table 11.1. Acquisition of Metalinguistic Skills

Age	Metalinguistic Skill	Source
2 years	Monitor comprehension (rudimentary)	Clark, 1978
	Judge grammaticality	
	Self-correct errors of pronunciation, word forms, word order	
	Comment on their own speech abilities	Limber, 1973
	Comment on superior speech of others	Smith, 1973
	Make judgments about their own speech	Weir, 1962
	Comment and play with different linguistic units, segment words into syllables and sounds, make puns and rhymes	
	Make simple judgments of grammaticality	Gleitman et al., 1972; deVilliers, 1972; Carr, 1979
	Query about the right meanings of words	Clark, 1978
	Restate when communication fails	Gallagher, 1972; Foppa, 1978
	Repeat and modify utterance when communication fails	Scollon, 1976
	Become narrowly adaptive	Brown, 1973
	Assume talk to attitude	Bloom, 1973
3–4 years	Inquire about pronunciation	Gleitman et al., 1972
	Correct speech and language of others	Maccoby & Bee, 1965
	Segment utterances into words and syllables	Fox & Routh, 1975
	Discriminate anomalous vs. true sentences based upon semantic constraints	Howe & Hillman, 1973
	Define words idiosyncratically	Anderson, 1975
	Equate "word" with the act of speaking; view number of words in sentence as *two* denoting 'topic' and 'comment'; equate "word length" to size of its referent	Berthoud-Papandropoulous, 1978
	Comment on what they cannot do	Markham, 1977
	Make judgments of politeness	Bates, 1976

256 *Language Acquisition*

Table 11.1. *continued*

Age	Metalinguistic Skill	Source
	Adjust speech to:	
	(a) Roles with family and other roles	Anderson, 1977
	(b) Age of the individual addressed	Sachs & Devin, 1976
	(c) Presumed knowledge of the individual addressed	Merig-Peterson, 1975
	(d) Presence or absence of perceptual supports	Maratsos, 1973
	Demonstrate rudimentary awareness of the effects of message length, noise age, and time constraints on communication	Yussen & Bird, 1979
5 years	Comment on how others speak, apply phono-morphological rules to unfamiliar words	Berko, 1958
	Shows sensitivity to puns and certain ambiguities	Hirsh-Pasek et al., 1978
	Express primitive metaphors	Gardner, 1974;
	Simple word definitions as group of letters	Gardner & Lohman, 1975
	Utter appropriate speech acts; simple sentences for younger children and more complex language for adults	Scholl & Ryan, 1975
6–7 years	Participate in school activities; demonstrate reading readiness; segment words, identify, learn sound/symbol association	Kavanagh & Mattingly, 1972
	Define words; identify salient properties	Berthoud-Papandropoulous, 1978
	Understand concept of word as parts of larger meaningful expressions (syntagmatic)	
	Begin to resolve lexical or semantic synonymy	Sack & Beilin, 1971
	Begin to resolve phonological and lexical ambiguity but not syntactic ambiguity	Shultz & Pilon, 1973
8 years	Equate definition of word with grammatical parts of speech (paradigmatic), define other words using both perceptual and functional features	Berthoud-Papandropoulous, 1978; Olver & Hornsby, 1966

Table 11.1. *continued*

Age	Metalinguistic Skill	Source
10–11 years	Resolve phonological and semantic ambiguity	Hirsh-Pasek et al., 1978
13–15 years	Resolve syntactic ambiguities; Monitor inconsistencies in reading text (with difficulty)	Shultz & Pilon, 1973 Markham, 1977
16 years	Participate in roletaking in communication	Flavell et al., 1968

Derived from *Developmental language intervention* by K. Ruder and M. Smith, 1984. Austin, TX: PRO-ED.

Metalinguistic activity seems to play a major role in large spurts of learning.

Returning to Kretschmer (1984) Table 11.1 presents an adapted version of his review of the literature on the acquisition of metalinguistic skills.

Summary

Even though children have acquired the basic knowledge of language by about 4 years of age, further learning occurs during the elementary school years. Indeed, lexical learning is a never-ending process. Children learn complex grammatical constructions and subtle nuances after the preschool period, and verbal shift is evident at about 7 years of age.

There appear to be two primary developments after the preschool period. Children become increasingly *adept* in the use of language, which is evidenced as they become more skilled in constructing elaborate sentences and indirect speech acts. As children become more adept, they become better able to deal with listener cues in constructing and revising messages. Finally, adeptness is evidenced when children use language in accordance with cultural scripts, and they tailor their language to specific social settings.

In the second primary development, children become increasingly aware of their verbal capacities: *metalinguistic* awareness. With this awareness, they can transform intuitive knowledge of language into explicit knowledge, which enables them the abilities to write and read. Seemingly, metalinguistic capacities catapult the language learner into considerable gains.

Part 3

Issues in Application

12

APPLICATIONS: ASSESSMENT

The previous chapters discussed substantive perspectives on language acquisition; these constitute the substantive base for the applied fields. This chapter presents timely issues concerning language assessment. The substantive perspectives of language acquisition compose the basis for assessment and intervention.

Construct Validity

Chief among the basic issues of assessment is *construct validity*. Construct validity might be thought of as theoretical relevance. That is, the extent to which an assessment is predicated and explained by theory, and evidences congruity with this theory, is the extent to which it has construct validity. Messick, one of the foremost experts in the field of measurement and evaluation, wrote a seminal paper on test validity and the ethics of assessment. Drawing upon Guion (1977a, 1977b, 1980), Messick (1980) warned that assessment often ignores the centrality of *construct validity* by dealing only with subordinate issues of validity or, even worse, by dodging issues of validity altogether. As Messick put it,

> One consequence of this simplism is that many test users focus on one or another of the *types* of validity as though any one would do . . . There is an implication that once evidence of one type of validity is forthcoming, one is relieved of responsibility for further inquiry. (1980, p. 1,014)

Messick (1980) and Guion (1980) stressed the importance of all three types of validity: criterion, content, and construct. Guion was concerned that these three types of validity are too often treated "as something of a Holy Trinity representing three different roads to psychometric salvation. If you can't demonstrate one kind of validity, you've got two more chances!" (Guion, 1980, p. 4). Messick (1980) acknowledged that there are different kinds of validity, but he emphasized that construct validity is the most important. Like Guion, Messick bewailed the tendency for mistaking types of validity for the basic issue of construct validity. "Worse still, any one of these so-called validities, or a small set of them, might be treated as the whole of validity" (p. 1,014).

> **Construct validity is a mandatory consideration of assessment adequacy.**

Consider why Messick placed *construct validity* as the central issue in assessment. First, he showed that other aspects of validity are derived from construct validity. After listing 17 kinds of validity within three generic categories (content validity, criterion validity, construct validity), Messick (1980, p. 1,015) argued that with the exception of the general notion of construct validity, "none of these concepts qualify for the accolade of validity, for at best they are only one facet of validity and at worst, as in the case of content coverage, they are not validity at all." As he said, a major theme of his writing over the years has been the centrality of construct validity: "*all measurement should be construct referenced*" (Messick, 1975, p. 957; 1980, p. 1,015). Guion (1977b, p. 410) came to a similar conclusion: "*All* validity is at its base some form of construct validity . . . It *is* the basic meaning of validity."

> **All measurement should be construct referenced.**

Second, Messick said that construct validity establishes the *evidential* (evidence) or *substantive* (evidence and theory) base of assessment; the applicability of particular assessment concepts to an individual's needs is tied to the ethical consequences of its use. Thus, there is a close relationship between construct validity and the ethics of assessment.

> **There is a close relationship between construct validity and the ethics of assessment.**

This close relationship between construct validity and the ethics of assessment is summarized in the distinction between *data* and *evidence* (Messick, 1980, p. 1,014; Muma, 1978a, 1978b, 1981a, 1981b, 1983b, 1983c, 1984, 1985; Muma, Lubinski & Pierce, 1982; Muma & Pierce, 1980). As Messick said,

"Another way to put this is to note that data are *not* information; information is that which results from the interpretation of data" (Mitroff & Sagasti, 1973, p. 123). Or as Kaplan (1964) states, "What serves as evidence is the result of a process of interpretation—facts do *not* speak for themselves; nevertheless, facts must be given a hearing, or the scientific point to the process of interpretation is lost" (p. 375). Facts and rationale thus blend in this view of evidence. (1980, p. 1,014)

Muma held that *evidence* is *data* that have demonstrated relevance to an individual's needs. In this way, Muma challenged the ethics of various a priori assessment and intervention procedures that are used in special education in general and with language impairments and learning disabilities in particular (Muma, 1984, 1985).

> The distinction between *data* and *evidence* challenges the ethics of a priori assessment.

In summary, *construct validity* and its ethical consequences are at the core or central issues of assessment. This has raised subordinate issues concerning *data* or *evidence* in assessment. It behooves clinicians to critically evaluate their language assessment approaches to ascertain construct validity (Muma, 1984, 1985).

Psychometric Versus Descriptive Approaches

Developments in psycholinguistics over the past two decades have brought a decided shift in language assessment away from a psychometric normative orientation toward a descriptive orientation (Muma, Pierce & Muma, 1983; Muma, Webb & Muma, 1979). Thus, the critical evaluation of language assessment falls logically into two basic approaches: *psychometric* and *descriptive*. In terms of clinical assessment, it is argued here and elsewhere (Muma, 1983b) that the descriptive approach is better than the psychometric approach in terms of its construct validity and ethical consequences.

Greenfield and Smith (1976, p. 16) argued for a descriptive approach:

> If we are to discover structure in, rather than to impose structure on, child language, it is useful to have a descriptive system which allows separate treatment of each element of the situation. In that way, we can trace the gradual development of a linguistic structure without assuming the presence of the total structure from the outset.

> Descriptive approaches are more adequate in dealing with the seven basic language assessment issues than psychometric normative approaches.

Table 12.1 summarizes this comparison across the seven basic assessment issues. Both approaches deal with the *clinical complaint* or statement of a problem by virtue of noting the referring source, obtaining identifying information, and writing verbatim comments about the problem from the perspective of an informant.

The *problem/no problem* issue is also addressed by both psychometric and descriptive approaches. In fact, this is the essential contribution of the psychometric approach to clinical assessment. Yet, there are drawbacks in terms of its adequacy and relevance. On a measure such as a developmental profile, a child's performance falls within or outside of test norms. If performance is within the "normal" region of the norms, no problem is thought to exist. But, a score below the normal range is interpreted to mean that a problem exists in the domain tested.

However, there is some question about the legitimacy of such conclusions. This kind of assessment may be inadequate for resolving the problem/no problem issue because of limited *power* and *precision*. Furthermore, it may not provide *relevant* data—evidence—because such instruments are a priori. These problems are largely, but not fully, overcome by descriptive approaches.

Assessment power, precision, and the a priori nature of psychometric approaches have serious limitations for dealing with the problem/no problem issue.

The *power* problem is that extreme scores lack evidence for the assessment variables. That is to say, the extent to which a score is at the extreme end of a

Table 12.1. Comparisons Between Descriptive and Psychometric Orientations in Dealing with Basic Theoretical Domains in Clinical Assessment

Theoretical Domains in Clinical Assessment	Psychometric	Descriptive
Clinical complaint	Yes	Yes
Problem/no problem	(Yes)	Yes
Nature of problem	No	Yes
Individual differences	No	Yes
Clinical Implications	No	Yes
Prognosis	?	?
Accountability	No	Yes
	Data	Evidence

From *Pragmatic assessment and intervention issues in language* (p. 199) by T. Gallagher and C. Prutting (Eds.), 1983, San Diego: College-Hill. Reprinted by permission.

distribution (norm) is the extent to which inferences about what is being assessed by the test may be unwarranted. Said differently, the probabilities are higher that extreme scores are a function of unknown extraneous variables rather than the domain being assessed. Thus, conclusions based on extreme scores should *not* be made about the child's skills.

The problem with *precision* is similar. Suppose that a test or developmental profile addressed only large pieces of the puzzle regarding verbal skills. For example, it measured the child's use of pronouns, but ignores many other issues concerning the pronominal system. The child's performance on such a test would be a hit-or-miss in terms of assessing skills.

To amplify how imprecise such assessments can be, consider for a moment some of the complexity of the pronominal system. This system functions primarily anaphorically. The anaphoric function for pronouns is to maintain the identity of previously identified referents. Thus, primary issues in assessing the pronominal system are:

Anaphoric loading: how many times a particular pronoun can be used before its referent is lost

Competing anaphoric reference: the extent to which one pronoun may disrupt the anaphoric function of another pronoun

Deictic reference: the ability to use pronouns to demark differentiated perspectives between encoder and decoder (*mine/yours, us/you,* etc.)

Grammatical marking: the ability to differentiate subject and object (*he/him, she/her,* etc.)

Number and gender marking: the ability to note number and gender (*I/we, him/they* and *he/she, his/hers*)

Needless to say, mere casual inquiries as to whether the child uses pronouns is hardly precise enough to make *any* conclusions regarding the child's knowledge of the pronominal system. Moreover, psychometric instruments are notoriously weak because they are not sensitive to *productive* abilities in terms of preparation, attainment (Prutting, 1979), or consolidation skills. *Consolidation skills* refer to the ability to combine domains. For example, pronouns can be used in a variety of linguistic contexts (*He runs, he goes, he and she, Will he go?,* etc.). Ingram (1979) and MacWhinney (1975, 1981) held that information about combinatorial skills is necessary in order to credit the child for productive grammatical skills.

Fortunately, the descriptive approach addresses these and other issues, notably contextual (grammatical, referential, intentional) influences. So, the descriptive model provides more precise and more powerful (allowing for legitimate inferences) information. The descriptive approach deals with the problem/no problem question from a functional perspective (Bloom & Lahey, 1978). If verbal behavior works as intended, there is no problem. If it does not, there is a problem.

As for *relevance,* the main problem with the psychometric approach is that it is a priori rather than a posteriori. A posteriori descriptive approaches do not impose systems and processes on the child (Beckwith et al., 1984; Greenfield & Smith, 1976). A priori approaches establish various substantive issues *before* seeing the child to be assessed. These issues include content, task, response, and scores. In such a priori assessments, children are asked to conform to the test; the test is not geared toward assessing the individual's repertoire of skills. A priori assessments run a decided risk against assessing a child's abilities simply because systems and processes are *imposed* on the child; thus these instruments do not describe the child's capacities.

The Peabody Picture Vocabulary Test (Dunn, 1965) (PPVT) is a case in point. Children are asked to respond to various words given to them to assess their vocabulary, but there is no attempt to inventory the words, word/referent relationships, or word learning processes of the children being assessed. Yet, ironically enough, the PPVT is *claimed* to be a vocabulary test. Similar statements can be made about many widely used psychometric tests and developmental profiles in language assessment.

> A priori approaches make the child conform to the assessment process, whereas a posteriori approaches conform to the child's capacities.

Psychometric approaches are inadequate for dealing with the following basic clinical assessment issues: nature of the problem, individual differences, intervention implications, prognosis, and accountability. Descriptive approaches, on the other hand, are *adequate* and *appropriate* for dealing with all of these issues except prognosis. Thus, psychometric approaches are considerably weaker than descriptive approaches in dealing with the seven basic clinical assessment issues.

Regarding the *nature of the problem,* the psychometric approach virtually ignores this area whereas the descriptive approach defines the nature of a problem by presenting evidence of productive capacities via the use of patterns of behavior (preparation and attainment) and pertinent contexts (referential, linguistic, intentional). Moreover, different criteria reveal different assessments. For example, Damico, Oller, and Storey (1983) showed that a syntactic analysis identified a different group of so-called language disordered children than a pragmatic analysis.

Curiously, *individual differences* are abrogated by the psychometric approach. There is a strange logic surrounding the use of psychometric tests and developmental profiles and the issue of individual differences. According to this logic, if a test is used to assess one person at a time, an *individualized* assessment has been accomplished. This logic does not hold up because under such circumstances no effort is made to inventory an individual's repertoire of skills;

rather, test performance is obtained and compared to a gauge, index, or norm. In this way individual differences effectively become subjugated to group performance. Yet, it is sometimes claimed that an individualized assessment has taken place.

> Individualized assessment is characteristically abrogated in psychometric approaches but it is preserved in descriptive approaches.

The descriptive approach does indeed address individual differences because it ascertains the individual's *repertoire* of skills in context. Moreover, individual strategies of learning can be identified (nominal/referential learner, impulsive/reflective learner, etc.)

Intervention implications are essentially outside of the purview of psychometric testing simply because such testing merely indicates to what extent an individual's performance falls within or outside of particular norms. Such information gives virtually no information about *how* to change the individual's behavior.

Descriptive approaches, on the other hand, provide evidence for launching intervention efforts. Assuming that one viable language intervention approach is to expand or enlarge the child's repertoire of skills, the descriptive approach provides appropriate evidence for intervention by defining (a) which aspects of verbal capacities are productive, (b) contextual influences, (c) readiness to learn via spontaneous loci of learning (Muma, 1983a), and (d) individual strategies of learning. Each of these provide direction for intervention.

> Descriptive assessment approaches provide information for enlarging the child's repertoire of verbal capacities.

Prognosis is a big problem for both psychometric and descriptive approaches. To paraphrase Brown (1973a), natural language learning occurs in spurts of unknown duration. This being the case, there is no way one can say in advance when a spurt of learning will occur, nor how much learning, nor which aspects of learning, will take place. Language learning is just too complex for such predictions. However, Bloom (1985) was able to predict spurts of word learning from evidence of affective changes, duration of neutral affect, and certain object constructions in play.

> Spurts of learning of unknown duration undermine prognostic capabilities.

This is an especially troublesome problem for the applied fields, notably special education, because P.L. 94-142 requires that prognostic statements in the form of IEPs be made for each child. Given that the literature on language learning does not support prognostic statements, the IEP statements are little more than *operational promises* or commissives (Searle, 1975, 1977) whereby the clinician states some kind of future intervention activity. The impact of such activity is quite a complex matter, substantively and ethically. Evidently, the architects of P.L. 94-142 were not sufficiently acquainted with the literature on language learning when they invented the IEP.

As Bartlett (1972) pointed out, much of what is done in language intervention is not supported by the literature on language learning. Teachers and clinicians are *operational,* but there are serious gaps between what is done and what is often *claimed.* Unfortunately, IEPs comprise a major mechanism for becoming operational in spite of the psycholinguistic literature on language learning. Coombs (1954) made a similar observation about assessment.

IEPs may be nothing more than operational promises.

Accountability is the extent to which the teacher or clinician can document the effects of intervention on the child. This is a very difficult task because there are always many factors acting upon the child in the course of growing older and interacting with the world. Who is to say that only the interaction of the teacher or clinician accounts for changes in the child?

Even though it is difficult to say for sure that certain intervention efforts have been effective, some arguments are more persuasive than others. Here again, the psychometric approach is not as strong in accounting for the impact of intervention as the descriptive approach, because the latter affords information about the child's repertoire of skills and relevant contexts.

Psychometrically, only *gross* changes of behavior—those large enough to be evidenced by a change in an individual's status as it relates to norms—are detectable. However, the descriptive approach provides *fine-grained* evidence because it can detect changes in patterns *within* the child's repertoire of skills. Another way of accounting for changes as a function of intervention is to document an expanded repertoire of skills in new *contexts*. A third way is to document *generalizability* to new instances. Changes of patterns *within* a child's repertoire occur when the child shifts from preparation to attainment of a system (e.g, a shift from relatively few instances that are context bound to many instances not bound to context). Use of skills in new *contexts* is when the child uses a previously learned skill in new contexts. For example, a person may use pronouns initially as objective pronouns *(him, her, them)* and then shift to their use as subjective pronouns *(he, she, they)*. *Generalizability* is when the child generates new instances that were not used in intervention but that are related to what was done in intervention. For example, a child may learn the use of *he/him* in intervention, and then generalize that knowledge to the use of *she/her*.

> Descriptive approaches provide fine-grained evidence of the
> impact of intervention.

Clinical judgments (Goldberg, 1968) could play a significant role in documenting progress or lack of progress. It is well known that: (a) regression effects occur (subsequent ratings tend to regress toward the middle of a rating scale); (b) discriminant judgments on one scale but regression effects on the other scales occur when multiple scales are used; (c) naive judges are more reliable than sophisticated judges; and (d) perceptual drift occurs (the perception of different points on rating scales fluctuates). Thus, the use of rating scales as evidence of the impact of language intervention is somewhat questionable.

To reiterate, in clinical assessment, the *psychometric* approach is weak in comparison to the *descriptive* approach (Muma, 1978a, 1981a, 1983b). A comparison of how the two approaches deal with the seven basic clinical assessment issues illustrates this point. Further, the contemporary psycholinguistic literature overwhelmingly supports descriptive assessment procedures. In short, there is no contest. The major psycholinguistic authorities rarely, if ever, use psychometric tests; descriptive assessments prevail.

The Psychometric Mentality at Work

Darley's (1979) review of published tests in speech-language pathology (including some language tests) has two major limitations. First, Darley did not consider descriptive assessment procedures. He stated that only published tests would be reviewed. This is somewhat surprising because the psycholinguistic literature over the past two decades has been oriented largely on descriptive approaches. Thus, by limiting his book to published tests, Darley effectively dismissed the largest and most substantial segment of language assessment.

Second, it is curious that only a few of the test reviews considered the issue of *construct validity*—the central issue of assessment. Moreover, only a very small number of tests had established construct validity. As Darley said,

> The tests here reviewed differ in the extent to which they are based upon some explicit theoretical system. Some tests are frankly atheoretical; they are pragmatic compilations of items or subtests which the authors have come to regard as important for the dimension being tested. Other tests are based on some more explicit theory or model of speech and language. It is generally more satisfying to have a theoretical basis for a test than not to have one, but to have one may lead to problems: the relationship between the test and the theory is often tenuous; the theory may not be a very good

one to start with; sometimes the attempt to fit a test to a theory involves little more than adjusting the name of the test; theories develop, wane, and are supplanted by new theories, leaving as residuals tests that have found their way into print. (1979, p. v)

Toward the end of the quotation, it sounds as if Darley were prepared to accept atheoretical tests. But, Messick (1980), Guion (1977a, 1977b, 1980) and others in the field of measurement and assessment pointed out that the problems are much more serious if construct validity is not considered (see also Muma, 1984, 1985). Darley also acknowledged that some tests did not establish construct validity which raises the possibility that just because a test is published does not mean it is useful. He (Darley, 1979, p. v) said,

> Some test makers have done superior work in selecting and refining items, testing for reliability, occasionally determining validity, and preparing materials that are attractive and durable. But we recognize that we may be overimpressed by the simple fact that a test has been put into print. Tests are relatively easy to create and to sell. As Buros has said, "No matter how poor a test may be, if it is nicely packaged and if it promises to do all sorts of things which no test can do, the test will find many gullible buyers" (*Sixth Mental Measurements Yearbook,* Buros, 1972, p. xxiv)

Many psychometric tests either ignore construct validity altogether or give it only passing consideration.

McCauley and Swisher (1984) provide a case in point. They reviewed several psychometric language assessment tests. In spite of the centrality of construct validity, they did not include such considerations. They said, "Because the evaluation of construct validity is difficult and somewhat subjective, it was not conducted for tests in this review" (p. 35). This is particularly surprising because only a few lines earlier they alluded to construct validity as well as content and criterion validity, "Although Messick (1980) has presented a compelling case for considering construct validity as the keystone of test development, these three kinds of validity have often been defined independently and evidence about them for a given test is weighed jointly." The three kinds of validity were the three in the 'Holy Trinity' problem (content validity, criterion validity, construct validity). Other problems with the McCauley and Swisher review exist as well (Muma, 1985).

A review of Semel and Wiig's (1980) Clinical Evaluation of Language Functions (CELF) test revealed that this test, as well as several others in special education, failed to establish construct validity. CELF lacked a theoretical base and used pejorative or bastardized terms.

In short, such professional activity eventually reveals a naked scarecrow (to borrow Bruner's, 1981, concept) resulting in many straw men. Semel and Wiig's CELF is a case in point. They have managed to stack together several straw men in the components of the CELF, and at the same time cite the conceptual nakedness of the field of learning disabilities. (Muma, 1984, p. 102)

Aram and Nation (1982) also provided a rather extensive summary and review of language assessment tests and procedures. With a few exceptions, their reviews and summaries merely showed which tests and procedures address which parameters. The central issue of construct validity was essentially not addressed.

Muma (1983c) reviewed eight widely used psychometric language tests. The pivotal inquiry was if these tests (PPVT, ITPA, PICA, CELF, ACLC, TACL, DSS, TOLD) were predicated on *construct validity*. A subordinate inquiry was to what extent they dealt with five criteria about construct validity (relativity, conditionality, complexity, dynamism, ecology) and six basic aspects of clinical assessment (problem/no problem, individual differences, nature of a problem, intervention implications, prognosis, accountability). Finally, the review inquired about whether the assessment process was vested in a priori or a posteriori evidence (Beckwith, Rispoli, & Bloom, 1984). Greenfield and Smith recognized the importance of discovering rather than imposing aspects of language in ascertaining the child's repertoire of skills. They said,

If we are to discover structure in, rather than to impose structure on, child language, it is useful to have a descriptive system which allows separate treatment of each element of the situation. In that way, we can trace the gradual development of a linguistic structure without assuming the presence of the total structure from the outset. (1976, p. 16)

In short, these tests were remarkably weak in dealing with (a) construct validity, (b) these five criteria about construct validity, (c) these six basic clinical assessment issues, and (d) a posteriori evidence. Assuming that such tests are representative of language assessment by many clinicians in the field, this survey gave reason to question seriously the adequacy and appropriateness of services rendered to many language impaired children. On the other hand, surveys of training in language (e.g., Muma, Pierce, & Muma, 1983; Muma, Webb, & Muma, 1979) show that there has been a shift toward psycholinguistically derived descriptive approaches.

> Many of the widely used approaches in language assessment are psychometric but there is evidence of a shift to descriptive approaches.

Descriptive Procedures

The psycholinguistically derived descriptive approaches are characteristically grounded in theory and appropriate criteria such as relativity (patterns of behavior), conditionality (contexts of behavior), ecology (natural environment), productivity (preparation, attainment, consolidation), and a posteriori evidence (evidence deduced from the data). Accordingly, the clinical competencies in recent years have become more adequate and *appropriate*.

Some clinicians may think that the descriptive approach is too time consuming to use with a large caseload. There are two responses: appropriateness and the standing challenge. *Appropriateness* is simply that the client is entitled to the most appropriate services. This is the basic tenet of Public Law 94-142. Even though descriptive procedures may take more time, the client is entitled to such service if it is appropriate. Too often, *expediency* replaces *appropriateness* of services. To make the point more direct, how would you feel if you had an appendicitis attack. You go to the doctor and he tells you it takes too much time to do the operation so I'll just give you some aspirin. This, of course, is not funny, but it is also not different in principle from the expediency position. It also brings home rather forcefully the ethics of expediency.

The *standing challenge* response is straightforward. Simply admit that descriptive assessments are time consuming. However, *trained* clinicians can substantially reduce the time needed for executing them. After admitting that such assessments are time consuming, establish the following standing challenge: Take as much time as is otherwise used in current practice with developmental profiles and psychometric tests, but invest this time in descriptive assessment. The challenge itself is that descriptive assessment in the same amount of time (even though it may be incomplete) as that previously used by psychometric tests will yield *more information that is more relevant to the individual and it is more useful for deducing intervention implications* than psychometric procedures.

Interestingly enough, parents appreciate *descriptive* evidence more then psychometric test scores because they relate to descriptions of their children better than to test scores. Moreover, contextually relevant comments and issues of productivity are more palatable. In short, descriptive assessment yields information about parents intuitively understand and appreciate. Moreover, such understanding defines the clinician as a truly competent professional in rendering appropriate services. There is, of course, a caveat: a descriptive assessment must not be shrouded in jargon. A sober parent in search of appropriate services does not appreciate a barrage of razzle-dazzle terms.

Some Psycholinguistic Models: Products of Description

Heterogeneity, or individual differences, has been recognized as a major problem in dealing with the language impaired (Bloom & Lahey, 1978; Craig, 1983; Fey & Leonard, 1983; Gallagher, 1983; Kirchner & Skarakis-Doyle, 1983; Leonard, 1981; Muma, 1973b, 1978a, 1981a, 1984; Prutting & Kirchner, 1983). It is virtually impossible to match individuals with language impairments in terms of the nature of their problems. The range and severity of problems are considerable. The best that can be done is a "molar analysis" (Prutting & Kirchner, 1983). Such results only help delineate types of language impairments, however, the troublesome issue of heterogeneity remains as a major threat to the viability of one intervention approach compared to another even within types of language impairments.

There are several models of language impairments reflecting a molar perspective. The psycholinguistically based models are generally compatible. Table 12.2 illustrates some of these models.

Bloom (1974) and Bloom and Lahey (1978) conceived the content-form-use psycholinguistic model. This is a very powerful and useful model. *Roughly* speaking, content pertains to cognition; form to linguistic structure, and use to pragmatics. Obviously, these are forced parallels, but they are essentially correct. The reason for forcing these parallels is to appreciate the fact that the psycholinguistic models applied to language impairments are compatible.

When considering psycholinguistic models, Muma (1981a) found it useful to return to a quote by Brown (1956, p. 247), who said that language acquisition is a "cognitive socialization process." This denotes two major components of language, cognitive and social. And, his statement subsumes a formal linking system—a linguistic system (semantic, syntactic, phonological). Thus, Muma (1978a) conceptualized the cognitive-linguistic-communicative systems and processes model (see also McLean & Snyder-McLean, 1978).

Table 12.2. Some Psycholinguistic Models

Content-Form-Use	Bloom & Lahey, 1978
Cognitive-Linguistic-Communicative Systems	Muma, 1978a
Cognitive-Linguistic-Social Systems	McLean & Synder-McLean, 1978
Cognitive-Linguistic-Pragmatic Deficits	Prutting & Kirchner, 1983
(Cognitive) Linguistic-General Pragmatic Impairments-Nonassertive Impairments	Fey & Leonard, 1983
Pragmatic Scaffold for Semantic-Syntactic-Phonological Systems	Bruner, 1981

Prutting and Kirchner (1983) took a different tack but arrived at a similar clinical model: cognitive-linguistic-communicative deficits. They devised a rather extensive pragmatic protocol organized according to Austin (1962) and Searle's (1969; 1977) views of speech acts, notably locution, illocution, proposition, and perlocution. Upon assessing many language impaired children and reviewing several studies of language-impaired children, Prutting and Kirchner concluded that language impairments fall into three primary categories: cognitive-linguistic-pragmatic.

Fey and Leonard (1983) also reviewed the literature on language impairments, and they found that these impairments fit into three categories: linguistic, general pragmatic, and nonassertive pragmatic impairments. Even though they did not indicate cognitive impairments related to language, Leonard (1976) had reviewed cognitive skills that were thought to be precursors of language acquisition (see also Bates, 1979; Bloom, 1973; Ingram, 1978).

Bruner (1981) did not consider clinical models but he nonetheless provided a viable psycholinguistic model centered on pragmatics. He held that well before the child has semantic, syntactic, or phonological capabilities he or she is actively involved in conveying messages pragmatically. Bruner held that the child's pragmatic repertoire provides a *scaffold* for acquiring semantic-syntactic-phonological systems. And, Bruner contended that these capacities are extensions of *symbolization* and *intentions,* both of which are cognitive in nature. Regarding symbolization, Bruner stressed the importance of the communicative point in regulating joint attention and action. Even in earlier reaching and grabbing, Bruner (1981, p. 166) suggested that an infant "becomes a giver of signals about objects desired." He indicated that the two great intentions are to *indicate* and *request;* the four basic innate intentions are (a) achieve and regulate joint attention with another, (b) instrumental, (c) affiliative, and (d) engage others in pretense and simulation.

Thus, there appears to be a consensus that clinical models of language assessment-intervention deal with cognitive-linguistic-pragmatic issues.

Common denominators of language intervention models are cognitive-linguistic-communicative systems and processes.

Summary

This is truly a new era in language assessment and intervention. Construct validity and its social consequences have become focal issues in the evaluation of assessment. *"All measurement should be construct referenced"* (Messick, 1980, p. 1,015).

Descriptive procedures are more adequate in dealing with the seven basic components of language assessment than psychometric normative approaches. These components are the clinical complaint, problem/no problem (power, precision, relevance), nature of the problem, individual differences, intervention implications, prognosis, and accountability. Prognosis is especially difficult because language learning occurs in spurts of unknown duration.

The clinical fields have evidenced a psychometric normative mentality in the past which invested the assessment process in a priori procedures. Such orientations have raised questions as to what extent the assessment process has been merely a *data game* as opposed to an *evidence game*. Many of the widely used language assessment tests lack adequate construct validity; thus, their use raises important ethical questions. The major psycholinguistic experts rarely, if ever, use psychometric normative tests; they use descriptive procedures. Surveys show that training programs are shifting toward a descriptive orientation in language assessment.

The substantive (content and procedures) issues in language assessment have been identified throughout the book. Some of the more important issues are recapitulated here. First, it is instructive to note that the true psycholinguistic models that have been used in the clinical arena boil down to essentially the same model: *cognitive-linguistic-communicative systems and processes.*

13

APPLICATIONS: INTERVENTION

It is one thing to assess the child to ascertain if a problem exists, but it is quite a different matter to ascertain the nature of the problem, individual differences, intervention implications, and accountability. These latter assessment issues provide the substantive bases of intervention.

It all ties together. Philosophical issues lead to theory. Theory provides motivation for empirical evidence and methodology. These provide the substantive bases of language assessment which, in turn, provide the substantive bases for intervention.

Communicative Payoff

Brown (1977, p. 26) usually deals with language acquisition but at one point he dealt with language intervention. He responsed to the question, "How can a concerned mother facilitate her child's learning of language?" His response was predicated on the assumption that intuitive knowledge that is focused on communication, rather than language per se, will facilitate language learning. Brown said:

> Believe that your child can understand more than he or she can say, and seek, above all, to communicate. To understand and be understood. To keep your minds fixed on the same target. In doing that, you will, without thinking about it, make 100 or maybe 1000 alterations in your speech and

action. Do not try to practice them as such. There is no set of rules of how to talk to a child that can even approach what you unconsciously know. If you concentrate on communicating, everything else will follow. (1977, p. 26)

Bruner (1978a, p. 255) said he wished to add to Brown's statement, "The best practice for mastering dialogue is to enter into it. Give the child a chance. And at that, you don't have to give much of a chance . . ." Bruner (1978c, p. 248) also said, "For language is the medium of dialogue, and it is in dialogue, that knowledge of language per se develops."

If you concentrate on communicating, everything else will follow.

Even though Bruner (1981) was not talking about language intervention, he made a similar statement regarding the mother's role in facilitating language learning. Bruner regarded the role of the mother in facilitating language learning as an active *partnership* oriented on pragmatic skills. These pragmatic skills compose a *scaffold* (Bruner, 1981) from which subsequent semantic-syntactic-phonological skills may be acquired. He cast the "tutorial" or facilitating role of the mother in terms of a language assistance system (LAS) that was compatible with Chomsky's language acquisition device (LAD). Referring specifically to the pragmatic cornerstone of language acquisition, Bruner made the following comments about language intervention:

This brings us directly to the heart of the problem relating to a pragmatic route into language. What is the role of the "tutor" in language acquisition? The pragmatician's greater stress on shared convention and presupposition and "intersubjectivity" requires a far more active role for the adult in the child's language acquisition than just being a "model." The pragmatic route requires that the adult be a partner. You need a partner to learn how to converse. (1981, p. 159)

Pragmatic skills are learned with an active partner negotiating messages.

Bruner went on to cite Brown (1977) on this matter. What is critical, of course, is *communication* that works as *intended* regardless of the linguistic adequacy of the message. As Bruner put it,

The mother . . . is very much more preoccupied with teaching the child how, when, and where to make appropriate utterances than she is with issues of syntax or meaning. In contrast, it is very rare to find any early instances of syntactic correction and there is even some suspicion . . . that semantic corrections may lead to the suppression of the lexical items that produced the difficulty. It suffices to note only that there is a large investment of time and energy during acquisition in helping the child learn how to say it in a fashion appropriate to the discourse, even if syntax is ragged and semantics hazy. (1981, p. 159)

> **What is critical is that communication works as intended.**

Drawing upon this literature, Muma (1981a) indicated that *communicative payoff* is potent in language learning. Accordingly, it should be a focal issue in language intervention. "When a child's language works as intended he becomes enticed into doing more (quantitatively and qualitatively) than he had done before. This is what I call *pay-off* in language learning" (Muma, 1981a, p. 49). The notion of communicative payoff appears to be the key to the facilitation of new word combinations for language impaired children (Schwartz, Chapman, Terrell, Prelock, & Rowan, 1985).

Behaviorism and Mentalism

Considerations such as communication rather than language per se, facilitation rather than instruction, and payoff rather than reinforcement have led to major shifts of perspectives on language intervention. These shifts of perspective have been documented as training programs have moved away from a *behavioristic* philosophy to a *mentalistic* philosophy (Muma, Pierce, & Muma, 1983).

Muma (1975b, 1977a, 1978a, 1981a) and Craig (1983) have compared behaviorism and mentalism in language intervention. Table 13.1 summarizes these comparisons. With the clinical fields incorporating communicative or pragmatic perspectives, major changes have begun to occur not only in assessment but also in intervention. Heretofore, the clinical fields based their intervention on a behavioristic philosophy, but a shift toward mentalism has taken place.

Behaviorism held that the child is a passive learner waiting to be taught and that stimulation is necessary and sufficient. The role of the clinician was to determine content, sequencing, pacing, mediation, and reinforcement for the learning processes. Thus, the learning processes were presumed to be under the control of the learning expert, the teacher or clinician. Moreover, the assessment process was predicated on normative tests and group instruction was provided. This logic led to the development of many a priori assessment practices and procedures that merely categorized and labeled children while saying virtually nothing about the nature of a problem.

Muma (1978a) held that this logic also begot a priori intervention of dubious value. Such intervention programs were addressed to learning vocabu-

Table 13.1. A Comparison Between Behaviorism and Mentalism

Behaviorism	Mentalism
Passive learner	Active Learner
Stimulation necessary and sufficient	Stimulation necessary but insufficient
Teacher readiness	Child readiness
Teacher criteria: content, sequence, pacing, mediation, reinforcement	Child criteria: content, sequence, pacing, mediation, reinforcement
Group performance	Individual performance
Assessment: immediate, direct, parcelled	Assessment: delayed, indirect, integrated

From *Pragmatic assessment and intervention issues in language* (p. 206) by T. Gallagher and C. Prutting (Eds.), 1983, San Diego: College-Hill. Reprinted by permission.

lary words and building sentences outside of a meaningful communicative context. The clinical fields had invented and perpetuated the notion that language training should be highly structured to overcome the so-called short attention span or distractability of learning disabled children. Such notions reflect a lack of professional insight about attention, memory, and language rather than insights into the actual learning problems of children. Chomsky (reported in Cazden, 1972) warned that highly structured a priori programs are potentially detrimental to natural learning processes. Both Piaget (1954) and Bruner (1964, 1975a, 1975b, 1978a, 1978b, 1981) had defined cognitive and language learning as active dynamic processes, yet the clinical fields' utilization of a behavioristic orientation ignored fundamental issues of active dynamic processing. Indeed, behaviorism became so institutionalized in the clinical fields that assessment and intervention policies have been cast in behavioristic terms, notably Public Law 94-142. The irony is that this law contains mentalistic issues such as individualized assessment and readiness. These issues, though, can become corrupted.

> Behaviorism begets a priori approaches.

Mentalism contrasts significantly with behaviorism in intervention. Mentalism holds that the learning processes are active and dynamic and that stimulation is necessary but insufficient. This means that it is inappropriate to subject the child to a normative assessment or an a priori "canned" intervention program. Mentalism holds that cognitive and language learning takes several different forms, therefore it is necessary to ascertain which strategies a given child is employing. Indeed, the literature shows that there are several strategies of cognitive and language learning (Muma, 1978a, 1981a). Because such strategies are available, intervention issues about content, sequence, pace, mediation, and reinforcement are, by definition, the primary province of the child rather than of the teacher or clinician. Thus, a mentalistic model for intervention contrasts with the instruction model of behaviorism.

In the mentalistic model, the goal is to *facilitate* learning by exploiting the child's natural predisposition for learning. This means that it is necessary to ascertain the child's strategies for learning, readiness to learn within developmental sequences for various systems or processes, and contextual influences and determinants. Issues such as these rest on relativity, conditionality, complexity, dynamism, and ecology. K. E. Nelson described the role of active partners in language learning as *facilitation* rather than teaching.

> Adults and older children do not directly teach young children to use syntactically well-constructed sentences; they do not know how to do such teaching, and they produce sentences that for the most part, play no essential role in the child's learning of syntax, although the sentences may be vital to acquisition of discourse and other skills (Shatz, 1978). Nevertheless, at certain points in development, particular kinds of adult replies to the child are crucial for the child's syntactic progress. (1981, pp. 229–230)

Mentalism begets a posteriori approaches.

It is noteworthy that while the learning disability teacher claims to have expertise in language learning, this expertise is defined in terms of an instruction model (Hammill & Bartel, 1978; Myers & Hammill, 1976; Reid & Hresko, 1981). Clearly, the behavioristic philosophy has prevailed at the cost of more appropriate mentalistic and interactionistic models (Bloom & Lahey, 1978; McLean & Snyder-McLean, 1978; Muma, 1975a, 1978b).

Impact of Language Intervention: A Cloudy Picture

Leonard (1981) reviewed the somewhat sketchy literature on language intervention. He titled the paper, "Facilitating Linguistic Skills in Children with Specific Language Impairment." In the psycholinguistic literature, the term "facilitation" usually means to make easy or less difficult the active learning already undertaken by the child (Bloom & Lahey, 1978; Brown, 1977; McLean & Snyder-McLean, 1978; Muma, 1978a, 1981a).

Teaching, training, or instruction contrast with facilitation because in the former, the child is told what to learn (content) as well as how, when, where, and why. The instructional model is vested mostly in the discretion of the teacher or clinician, whereas much of the acquisition process in facilitation is vested in active learning and the learner's readiness to learn. The reason for this discussion of facilitation is because Leonard was not using this term contrastively with instruction or teaching; many of the studies he reviewed were instructional in nature. Given this caveat, the following is a summary of Leonard's review.

Facilitation rather than instruction is more compatible with the psycholinguistic principles of language learning.

Leonard (1981) suggested that the language intervention literature should be viewed from three perspectives: (a) the degree of structure placed on the child, (b) the degree to which the child plays an active problem-solving role, and (c) the degree to which training tasks simulates regular speaking. Rather, Leonard indicated that these perspectives were usually discussed in terms of some of their more salient characteristics (e.g., imitation-based approaches, modeling approaches, expansion approaches, focused stimulation approaches, general stimulation approaches, comprehension-based approaches, etc.). Fey (1986) has a nice review of both training and facilitating approaches in language intervention. Leonard did not discuss communicative payoff or facilitative approaches. In a sense, Leonard was forced to limit his review to instructional approaches because the literature concentrated largely on instruction of linguistic forms.

The language intervention literature concentrates largely on the instruction of linguistic forms.

It is to Leonard's credit that he recognized this and other limitations of the language intervention literature. Table 13.2 summarizes limitations of the language intervention literature that threaten generalizations and comparisons of approaches. For one thing, there are relatively few studies directed at examining the intervention process. As Leonard (1981, p. 90) put it, "It is somewhat surprising to note so few studies directed at examining the intervention process." Also, most of the available studies are not with language-impaired individuals per se, but mentally retarded individuals and individuals with other clinical conditions as well as language impairments. Thus, the literature on language intervention is highly confounded with mental retardation and other clinical conditions such as hearing impairments. Further, most of the intervention studies deal with the linguistic domain, usually syntax. The relationships of syntax to other domains are largely unanswered, which greatly restricts generalization about language intervention approaches. In addition, most language intervention studies deal with production. As Leonard (1981, p. 90) said, "These represent the great majority of language training studies."

Table 13.2. Summary of Limitations of the Language Intervention Literature that Threaten Generalizations and Comparisons of Approaches

---

There are relatively few studies on language intervention.

Most language intervention studies are confounded with a clinical population (i.e., mental retardation, hearing impairment, etc.).

Most language intervention studies are on linguistic forms, especially syntax.

Most language intervention studies deal with production.

Most studies do not have sufficient means of insuring that the language gains can be attributed to intervention.

Many gains obtained in intervention either are not sustained or do not generalize.

Group gains (or losses) are not the same as individual changes in language intervention.

Content, context, sequencing, pacing, and motivation constitute major confounding issues.

Most approaches are a priori rather than a posteriori.

Heterogeneity is pervasive, even within categories of language impairment.

Intervention studies with comprehension are few and their results are equivocal. Moreover, the old adage that comprehension precedes production is too simplistic (Ingram, 1974). Worldly knowledge and presupposition have given better insight on the complexity of language as an active dynamic process in social commerce.

Most studies do not have sufficient means of insuring that the language gains can be attributed to intervention. That is, the research designs are inadequate or so highly confounded with other variables that it is virtually impossible to attribute specific gains to specific intervention efforts. There is some credence in attributing gains that are specific to the intervention activities either as products or generalized processes. But even then, other contributing factors could have played a significant role. *Replication* and *prediction* can be very useful in attributing gains to intervention but even these are seriously threatened by heterogeneity.

The various single-subject designs (McReynolds & Kearns, 1983; Ventry & Schiavetti, 1980) seem to have considerable potential, but there are serious problems with them as well. In short, the single-subject designs rely on *quantification* of behavior which itself can jeopardize findings. It appears that the "one-to-many" or "many-to-one" studies (Bates & MacWhinney, 1982; McCaffrey, 1977) have considerable potential for documenting intervention outcomes.

In language, *quantification* has always been a serious obstacle (Muma, 1973b, 1978a). Efforts in the 1960s revealed some of the problems involved in attempting to quantify verbal behavior (Bever, Lockner, & Kirk, 1969; Fodor & Bever, 1965; Johnson, 1965, 1966; Yngve, 1960). Even so, Lee (1966, 1974), Lee and Canter (1971), and Koenigsknecht and Lee (1971) attempted to quantify syntax without taking into account the hierarchical nature of sentences. Indeed, it is very risky business to quantify language, especially when satisfactory models of verbal complexity remain to be worked out.

Miller (1962, 1965), Clifton and Odom (1966), and Frank and Osser (1970) tried, without much success, to work out a quantitative model of complexity for syntax. Quantitative models of syntax have not worked out primarily because syntax operates in the service of verbal functions—content and intent. Thus, such models must address content and intent. Yet, these, especially content, operate within active dynamic contexts. Moreover, Fillmore (1981) indicated that contexts are both internal (presuppositional) and external (social events). Similarly, Ochs (1979, p. 3) said that context is very complex and that "language itself can count as context." Turning to Brown (1973b), he admonished that the models of semantic functions and relations should be regarded with caution because their psychological reality has yet to be demonstrated. Then, to quantify content is only to compound it further. In summary, the quantification of verbal behavior is itself a tenuous undertaking; yet, quantification is needed to make various single-subject designs work.

Quantification of verbal behavior is tenuous.

Rather than formal single-subject designs, it may be more propitious to undertake detailed descriptions of individuals' pre- and post-intervention performance. Such descriptions can utilize available models for intentions, content (propositions with attendant presuppositions), context, and criteria for productive acquisition (preparation, attainment, consolidation). Such evidence would be more in line with the contemporary psycholinguistic literature than quantification and formal research design. Connell, Spradlin, and McReynolds (1977) argued for formal research on intervention approaches but Muma (1978b) suggested that such research is premature and frought with problems in adequately accounting for verbal behavior, quantification, context, relativity, etc. Curiously, Connell, McReynolds, and Spradlin's (1979) response did not address any of the five basic issues raised by Muma (1978b). Prelock and Panagos (1981) raised issues on both sides.

Fortunately, the psycholinguistic literature has provided exemplary descriptive studies that have the capability of documenting change (Bloom, 1973; Bowerman, 1973; Greenfield & Smith, 1976). These studies are not about intervention but they nevertheless provide models from which intervention gains could be documented.

Continuing with the limitations of the language intervention literature, two common findings of these studies are that the intervention gains are not sustained or they do not generalize. These are difficult problems because gains have been obtained yet not sustained or generalized. Such problems raise serious questions about the actual value of intervention. In referring to these and other problems attendant to showing effectiveness of language intervention programs, Bartlett (1972) observed that such "gains" may merely reflect the *operational* quality of language intervention programs rather than *actual gains* in children. This, of course, sheds a different light on the picture. Thus, such gains may be nothing more than spurious findings. Referring to this problem, Leonard (1981, p. 103) said, "It is possible that such extensive gains represent only situational artifacts."

> **Data on intervention gains may merely be statistical artifacts about operationism.**

Another drawback of the intervention programs cited in the literature is that group gains (or losses) are not the same as individual changes. Group performance is an average (with its variance), but the individuals within the group perform in a variety of ways that may, or may not, be adequately reflected by the dependent variables. In this way, individual differences become subjugated to group performance. Whatever benefits of a given intervention approach that may accrue to an individual may not accrue to the whole group. Given that clinical groups are heterogeneous and recognizing the complexities of language, it is not unreasonable to expect some but not other individuals to realize gains; yet, on balance, a group may show little or no gain.

Content, context, rate, sequencing, pacing, and motivation constitute major confounding issues in language intervention. On the one hand, such issues could be systematically controlled, but it is likely that such controls would result in a fallow language intervention program. The gains are sure to be temporary, with little or no generalization. Such programs strip away the very essence of language—communication by intention.

On the other hand, language intervention can be vested in *facilitating* the child's active attempts for language learning. Here, content, context, sequencing, pacing, and motivation are largely within the province of the learner. Facilitation is essentially a matter of *exploiting* the child's efforts. As Muma (1978a, p. 7) put it, "The best we can do in intervention is to *describe an individual's command of various cognitive–linguistic–communicative systems and processes—to the extent possible—*

then exploit such behavior." Such facilitation is aimed at expanding and replacing capabilities in the child's repertoire. Yet, these issues remain highly confounded.

> Content, pacing, sequencing, and motivation should be largely invested in the learner.

Most intervention approaches are a priori rather than a posteriori. This means that most language intervention is set up before seeing the child. Thus, the child conforms to the intervention program rather than the other way around. Training programs, instructional programs, and teaching programs—in short behavioristic programs—are typically a priori. Facilitative approaches—mentalistic programs—are typically a posteriori.

> Facilitation is compatible with a posteriori approaches.

In summary, there are several limitations of the language intervention literature that threaten generalizations and comparisons of approaches. We must be exceedingly cautious about general claims of one approach over another. The "saving grace" in this matter is that it is possible to discuss *individuals* and their gains in the *context* of particular intervention efforts. This brings up the last of these limitations—individual differences or heterogeneity. Heterogeneity is pervasive, even with normal populations, and especially within clinical populations such as children with language impairments and learning disabilities. "Children with specific language impairment constitute a rather heterogenous population" (Leonard, 1981, p. 89).

> Heterogeneity is characteristic of clinic groups.

Viability of Normal Acquisition Principles

Another central issue of language assessment and intervention that is evidently implicated but rarely stated outright is the viability of the normal language acquisition literature to clinical endeavors. Baer (1974) argued that normal language acquisition principles may be inappropriate for language intervention. He reasoned that the language impaired had already failed in the normal language learning arena; therefore, it would be inappropriate to subject them to more of the same. On its face, this appears to be a legitimate argument but, unfortunately, it lacks an adequate appreciation of the roles of others and the complexities of normal language acquisition.

Consider the logical fallacies of Baer's position. He posited an either/or argument, for example, one either passes or fails language learning. Moreover, for those that had presumably failed—the language impaired—the only recommended recourse was to step out of the normal language learning arena. Such reasoning is patently false. Indeed, the recent literature on *learnability* (Wexler, 1982) and *discovery* (Bever, 1982) of language may actually show that the option to step outside of the normal language learning arena is simply not available. It would be exceedingly difficult to do.

Even so, the fallacy of Baer's position can be seen in the children themselves and in the complexity of language learning. Only a casual review of the verbal accomplishments of language impaired children easily dispels this either/or logic. These children have actually learned many aspects of language. Other aspects are yet to be learned, and still other aspects may be only partially acquired. In short, normal language learning principles have indeed worked for these children, but they have not realized the full fruition of language. Language learning is not an all-or-none or pass/fail proposition.

Language learning is an exceedingly complex undertaking laden with many prospects for error. Given this complexity, it is remarkable that more people do not have language impairments. Indeed, it is a common observation that transient errors occur; these errors become reconciled through overt and covert hypothesis testing. Thus, the normal learning process begets errors, albeit transient errors.

Even so, the empirical side of the question supports a normal language acquisition model for the language impaired. Van Kleeck and Frankel (1981) showed that language-impaired children are not qualitatively different from normal children. Prutting and Kirchner (1983) and Fey and Leonard (1983) arrived at a similar conclusion.

Baer's logic is based on the unwarranted assumptions that (a) the child has run the language learning gauntlet alone and whatever failings that accrued were his or her doing, (b) the language learning process is the same for everyone, (c) language intervention based upon normal language learning principles would be nothing more than a replication of previous learning—presumably strengthening prior learning, and (d) whatever gains could be obtained in the normal acquisition process had been obtained already. The psycholinguistic literature shows that all of these assumptions are unfounded.

The child does not run the language learning gauntlet alone. Rather, he or she operates within an active partnership—with mother or others—who can serve as potent facilitators in the acquisition process (Bruner, 1981; Snow & Ferguson, 1977). A well-qualified clinician in language intervention may prove to be a critical difference in utilizing normal language learning principles.

The language learning process is not the same for everyone. Bloom and Lahey (1978) and Muma (1977a, 1978a) have summarized several different strategies of language learning. Language intervention oriented on more appropriate acquisition strategies may be sufficient to overcome language impairments.

Given the complexities of cognitive–linguistic–communicative systems and processes, it would be virtually impossible to do more of the same or replicate prior learning. Moreover, if true *stages* of learning (Brown, 1973b; Gleitman, 1981; Piaget, 1952) are involved, the possibilities of replicating prior learning are nonexistent.

Regarding the notion that whatever gains could be obtained had been obtained, this could only be so under a behavioristic philosophy of intervention whereby the child is thought to be a passive learner. However, if the child is an active learner, as posited by mentalism (Craig, 1983; Muma, 1977a), such conjecture is patently false because active learning affords the child new opportunities within his or her range of acquisition. In summary, there are solid grounds for dismissing the argument that normal language learning principles should not be used in intervention for the language impaired. Indeed, such principles constitute viable content for language intervention.

The literature on normal language learning constitute a viable substantive base for language intervention.

Further Observations of the Intervention Literature

Leonard's (1981) review of the language intervention literature outlined several approaches (see Table 13.3). *Imitation-based* approaches usually use elicited imitation and stop this imitation quickly once the child reaches a criterion of performance. Studies of this approach dealt almost exclusively with a small set of syntactic issues. Generally, these studies evidenced gains (although not necessarily significant gains) over a comparison group.

A related intervention strategy is *induced modeling*. This is different from imitation because the child is not asked to imitate the modeled behavior.

> The rationale behind a modeling approach is that the problem-solving undertaken by the child in order to determine what form the utterance is expected to take is a particularly effective means of learning the linguistic form. Although this is a type of imitation, it is a 'rule' for combining and sequencing words that the child is imitating, not particular utterances spoken by the model. (Leonard, 1975, p. 93)

Studies by Leonard (1975a, 1975c), Wilcox and Leonard (1978), and Courtwright and Courtwright (1976, 1979) used induced modeling as opposed

Table 13.3. Various Language Intervention Approaches

Imitation-based: elicited imitation

Induced modeling: cohort model selected aspects of language which the child may model

Expansion: structural or topical expansion of the child's utterance

Focused stimulation: story-telling format aimed at selected aspects of language

Spontaneous modeling: child initiated, active learning in natural context

Comprehension-based: comprehend language

A posteriori linguistic context: natural co-occurrence

Expansion: repertoire enlarged and varied

Replacement: one capacity replaced by another

Ten techniques: five child initiated/five clinician initiated; all based upon the child's repertoire

---

to informal spontaneous modeling and vicarious learning. Leonard reported that impressive (although significance testing was usually not mentioned) gains were obtained when a cohort or clinician modeled syntactic forms. In short, modeling seems to be effective. However, a replication of the Courtwright and Courtwright (1979) study by Connell, Gardner-Gletty, Dejewsky, and Parks-Reinick (1981) failed to obtain comparable results. Modeling from a different perspective is discussed below.

> Modeling and imitation are different from informal spontaneous modeling and vicarious learning.

Brown and Bellugi (1964) identified an *expansion* as a normal parental mechanism that presumably fostered syntactic learning. Expansions are when someone expands the child utterance either structurally or topically. Cazden (1965) and K. E. Nelson (1977) attempted to demonstrate the potency of this mechanism. In the Cazden study, the expansions of structure were not significant in extending language learning; but expansions of child initiated topics did significantly improve learning. Brown (1973a) suggested that expansions of structure may not have worked as well as anticipated because the children may have been satiated by such expansions. Scherer and Olswang (1984) showed that maternal expansions contribute to child language acquisition.

Brinton and Fujiki (1984) showed that topical expansion or "shading" occurs in peer dyads.

Leonard (1981) suggested that a *focused stimulation* approach might be regarded as a variant of modeling. He credited Lee, Koenigsknecht, and Mulhern (1975) for devising a story-retelling format in which the story contains certain target structures (see also O'Donnell, 1967). The notion of story retelling as a means of having children deal with dimensions in a story was devised by Blank and Frank (1971).

Distinctions should be made between induced modeling, Leonard's notion of focused stimulation, and spontaneous modeling with vicarious learning. In *spontaneous modeling,* someone who is engaged in natural spontaneous interaction affords the child an exemplar of a particular loci of learning. For example, the child may be in the process of learning possessives and someone in the natural course of events provides some instances of possessiveness. It is possible that such modeling is more potent than induced modeling. Leonard and Schwartz (1981) and Culatta and Horn (1979) offered evidence that such modeling is effective. Indeed, Schlesinger (1977, p. 161) held that this kind of linguistic input has considerable potential for language acquisition. "The child utilizes linguistic input to draw in the borders between adjoining categories."

In the *parallel talk* strategy (which Leonard calls *general stimulation*), Whitehurst, Novak, and Zorn (1972) asked the mother to *prompt* naming by giving names of objects and people and by requesting names from the child. Also, she was asked to increase the degree of conversation with the child by talking about what she was doing. The child had a significant increase in new words. In a similar but more contrived study by Cooper, Moodley, and Reynell (1978) that employed expansions and open-ended questions, gains were made. Two other studies by Blank and Solomon (1968, 1969) demonstrated that children benefit particularly when probes about topics are made in spontaneous interaction.

Comprehension-based approaches are predicated on the logic that the child needs to comprehend language before producing it. Leonard reviewed studies by Winitz (1973), Ruder, Smith, and Hermann (1974), and Paluszek and Feintuch (1979); and Leonard (1981, p. 99) said, "The data from comprehension training studies are equivocal." Perhaps they are equivocal because the basic notion itself is too simplistic.

As indicated above, *verbal context* is an important issue in language acquisition. Yet, most of the language intervention studies pay little attention to verbal context—linguistic, referential, intentional. Spontaneous modeling incorporates context with the active loci of learning (Muma, 1983a). As for linguistic context, Ochs (1979, p. 3) pointed out, "language itself can count as context." Her comment was not confined to linguistic context, however. She was also referring to internal and external contextualization (Fillmore, 1981).

A posteriori linguistic context reveals co-occurring systems (Bloom, 1973; Bloom & Lahey, 1978; Bloom, Lifter, & Hafitz, 1980; Brown, 1973a, 1973b;

Harris, 1965; Klima & Bellugi-Klima, 1969; Muma, 1973a, 1978a) has considerable implications for intervention. In short, it means that in addition to the target or locus of learning a clinician should attend to the co-occurring dimensions of spontaneous speech. For example, if the child says, "I just tell ya. I just told ya," the locus of learning is the tense change on the irregular transitive verb within the co-occurring structures of /subject pronoun, intensifier, (target structure), object pronoun/. Early on, there is reason to believe that the child is selective about the linguistic contexts in which he or she will try something new. Thus, co-occurring structures define the linguistic context in which the individual strives to do something new. Linguistic input is apparently useful in identifying new loci of learning with their attendant co-occurring structures. As Schlesinger (1977, p. 160) said, "It is the linguistic input which shows the child whether or not to collapse these cognitively distinguishable relations into one."

> Co-occurrence is the linguistic context in which a person tries something new.

Expansion and Replacement Principles

In intervention, it is appropriate to expand not only the child's repertoire for the loci of learning, but also the linguistic contexts. This is accomplished by varying either loci or context while holding the other momentarily constant; then, vary the other. This is known as the *expansion principle* of language learning (Bates, 1979).

The *replacement principle* (Bates, 1979) states that earlier modes of expression become replaced by subsequent modes. Early on, the child uses a communicative point. As the child acquires verbal performatives and labels (conventional or phonetically constant forms (PCFs) (Dore, 1975), the communicative point becomes replaced by these indicatives. Eventually, both the point and indicative can be used together (Bates, 1979).

Both the expansion and the replacement principles are major issues in intervention. The former is aimed at an increased repertoire and the latter deals with newer means of social interaction.

> The expansion and replacement principles constitute major intervention issues.

Applications: Intervention 291

Ten Techniques

Muma (1971a, 1977a, 1978a, 1981a) reported ten techniques for *facilitating* language learning. It is important to appreciate that these techniques are based upon the child's own communicative efforts or repertoire of skills; thus they are not a priori but a posteriori. These techniques are aimed at exploiting the child's repertoire of skills. The first five are child initiated within the context of natural spontaneous communication. Thus, they have the features of intent, content, reference, and context. The second five are clinician initiated. The clinician initiates these techniques based upon the child's spontaneous speech sample so they are within the child's range of *active* language learning.

The techniques, which were culled from the literature, are summarized in Table 13.4.

Table 13.4. Salient Features of the Ten Techniques for Facilitating Language Learning

	Model	Syntax	Semantics	Language Functions
Child-initiated	Correction	Errors identified and corrected by completion	Errors of reference identified and corrected	
	Expansion	Utterance retained but syntactically completed according to child's current sentence structure and available referents		
	Expatiation (simple)		Semantic aspects featured while syntax is not	Utterance the locus of communication
	Expatiation (complex)		Semantic aspects featured but diffused in complicated syntactic structures	Utterance the locus of communication

Table 13.4. continued

Model		Syntax	Semantics	Language Functions
	Alternatives			Logical assumptions underlying utterance
Teacher-initiated	Completion	Constituent analysis and equivalence	Grammatical-conceptual classes	
	Replacement	Constituent analysis and equivalence	Grammatical-conceptual classes	
	Alternative-replacement	Constituent analysis and alternatives. Morphology: semantic markers	Grammatical-conceptual classes	
	Revision	Exploring alternatives	Generalizing and reorganizing concepts	
	Combination	Exploring alternatives	Generalizing and reorganizing	

From *Language handbook: Concepts, assessment, intervention* (p. 295) by J. Muma, 1978, Englewood Cliffs, N.J.: Prentice-Hall. Reprinted by permission.

Correction Model. In this behavioristic model, the clinician identifies aberrant behavior and tries to correct it, usually by pointing out and correcting the error. Mellon (1967) reviewed this model extensively because it has been widely used in American education, and concluded that it was not very effective. However, Goldstein (1984) found the correction model useful. Correction of syntax is not very potent. Brown and Bellugi (1964) indicated that corrections are unnatural and infrequent in the acquisition of syntax. However, corrections are rather common from parents for semantic or referential errors. If teachers or clinicians do much correcting of syntactic errors, children will become reticent. However, they will usually accept corrections of referential errors.

The correction model is illustrated by the following:

Syntactic Correction
Child: *Doggy runned.*
Clinician: *No, not Doggy runned. The doggy ran.*

Referential Correction
Child: *He ate supper.*
Clinician: *No. She ate supper. She is a girl.*

Expansion Model. Brown and Bellugi (1964) reported that in normal parent-child interactions, parental verbal responses to children learning language are occasionally syntactic expansions of child utterances. These are timely, because (a) they are based on the child's grammar at a particular point in time, (b) they pertain to the child's intent to communicate in a particular circumstance, and (c) they pertain to available references in the circumstance. Moreover, Brown and Bellugi reported that sometimes the child reduces parental utterances. These reductions are not just word deletions that shorten utterances. The deletions are at certain points in the utterances that correspond with the child's grammar. Thus, the deletions reflect the child's linguistic repertoire. Occasionally both the parent and the child have cyclic interchanges in which both parent and child verbalize back and forth, one expanding and one reducing. Evidently expansions are an important language-learning activity (Scherer & Olswang, 1984).

Cazden (1965) studied expansions by having teachers expand the utterances of preschool disadvantaged children. After 6 months, the expansion group exhibited greater gains in various measures of language learning than the control group. However, the gains were not significant. Brown (1973a) reasoned that significant gains were not obtained because the expansion model was used too much and not interspersed with other response patterns. He held that the expansion process seems to offer too many opportunities for learning and that the failure to obtain significant results may be the fault of an excessive application of expansions rather than the model itself. Scherer and Olswang (1984) found that children's spontaneous imitations increase as a function of maternal expansions and that these in turn lead to an increase in two-term relations.

The expansion model is illustrated in this exchange.

Child: *Doggy bark.*
Clinician: *The doggy is barking.*

Notice there is no attempt to tell the child, "Do it this way." An alternative model is provided. The child may or may not use the model and may or may not engage in cyclic interchanges. Ervin (1966) indicated that after two or three cyclic interchanges the child varies the utterance in the direction of the available maternal utterance. For example, the child says, "Ball," whereupon the mother expands, "Throw the ball." This interchange may be repeated. Then, the child says, "Throw ball" (see also Folger & Chapman, 1978; Seitz & Stewart, 1975; Slobin, 1968). The variation is considered the locus of learning for a given utterance in a given communicative context. It should be noted that these expansions have pragmatic significance by maintaining the topic and the child's turn while affording linguistic input for discovering grammatical relations (Schlesinger, 1977). Clinicians should take note of child utterances, parent expansions, child variations, and available references. Together they define the circumstances in which the child can learn something new about language.

Simple Expatiation Model. Using the simple expatiation model, Cazden (1965) had a different group of teachers respond to child utterances with simple sentences. She found that the children in this group made significantly more progress than those in the expansion or control group. McNeill (1966b) analyzed the data and found that the teachers had not merely used simple sentences but had enlarged or extended the children's topics. Extending the topic is apparently more productive than expanding the syntactic model. McNeill called this model "expatiation," which means to enlarge or broaden. It indicates that functions may have priority over forms in language learning. Brinton and Fujiki (1984) showed that expatiation or "topic shading" increases with age. The priority of functions over form was also manifested in the correction model. Correction of form is poorly tolerated by language learners, but correction of reference is accepted. The expatiation model is illustrated as follows:

Child: *Doggy bark.*
Clinician: *The doggy's hurt. Puppies whine sometimes. Sometimes they bark.*

Complex Expatiation Model. Complex expatiation is a syntactic variant of simple expatiation. As with simple expatiation, the child's utterance is the locus of communication. Semantic aspects are elaborated in complicated syntactic structures. The complex expatiation model is illustrated as follows:

Child: *Doggy bark.*
Clinician: *The black doggy is named Spotty. Of all the dogs I know, he barks most.*

Alternatives Model. The alternatives model is only one of several that Blank and Solomon (1968) devised for developing abstract thinking. This model deals with the role of language in the development of logic. The clinician inquires directly or indirectly about the underlying logic of a particular utterance. Such questions serve to make the speaker aware of alternative interpretations and motivations. Moreover, the questions provide a way of making underlying presumptions explicit. Obviously, this model must be used judiciously because it could disrupt the continuity of communication. It should not be confused with the replacement model presented in the section on clinician initiated models. It is illustrated as follows:

Child: *Doggy bark.*
Clinician: *Yes. Why do doggies bark? Is it a big doggy or a puppy?*

Completion Model. The completion model is the first of five clinician initiated models. Bandura and Harris (1966) had children and adults make sentences with various words and phrases. They were interested in whether or not children utilized syntactic models employed by the adults. The data indicated that they do. Moreover, studies by Snow (1972), Clarke-Stewart (1973), Shatz and Gelman (1973), and Schachter, Kirshner, Klips, Friedricks, and Sanders (1974) indicated that older children and adults "talk down" to young children so that the models available to the child correspond somewhat to the child's level. Leonard (1973, 1975a, 1975c) has incorporated this principle in language intervention.

In the completion model, an incomplete sentence is given. Children are supposed to analyze what is needed and supply the appropriate words. Thus, this model requires the ability to deduce constituent requirements and equivalencies. The sentences the clinician gives to the child to complete should be derived from the descriptive analysis of the target and co-occurring systems the child is already dealing with. The clinician omits the new structures. The child completes a sentence with any structure equivalent to the deleted slot. Moreover, the child should complete it in a variety of ways in order to realize constituent equivalencies and eventually deal with structures germane to the particular sentence. It is important that the child complete the sentences with elaborate phrases rather than simple one-word completions. One-word completions give simple realizations of constituent equivalencies, but elaborate completions (wild, silly sentences) provide abundant opportunities for discovering equivalencies and alternatives. The completion model is illustrated as follows:

Clinician: *Doggy _____.*
Child: *Doggy ran home.*
Clinician: *The doggy is _____.*
Child: *The doggy is black. The doggy is barking.*
Clinician: *The _____ is old.*
Child: *The doggy is old.*

Replacement Model. Gunter (1960) discussed the appropriateness of using proportional drill in altering children's syntax. In principle, the drill deals with various dimensions of a sentence except those for the missing constituent. The object is to complete the sentence on the basis of constituent analysis and contingencies of grammar. Thus, proportional drill is like the completion model. However, it appears to be more powerful as a replacement model because there are more alternatives that can be taken. By using a replacement rather than a completion model, children can choose the particular syntax that meet their needs.

The clinician says a sentence, instructing the child to take something out and replace it with something else. The sentence has been devised with grammatical systems known to the child. Clinicians should encourage a variety of replacements to foster language exploration of equivalencies.

Clinician: *The doggy is barking.*
Child: *My doggy is barking.*
Clinician: *My doggy named Spotty is barking.*

Alternative-Replacement Model. Among several behavior modification studies dealing with verbal behavior, Krasner (1958) reported a study by Toffel (1955) that dealt with an alternative-replacement model. The principle of the model is that alternatives can be made in syntactic linkage. Exemplars of one form class can be alternatively replaced with alternative exemplars of another form class, provided that the various exemplars share semantic attributes that constrain syntactic operations.

Operationally, the clinician outlines several alternatives from one form class (pronouns: *I, he, she, they;* animate nouns: *frog, goat, horse;* human nouns: *boy, girl, man, woman, lady,* etc.). Then the clinician outlines several alternatives from another class that could be syntactically linked to the first (transitive verbs: *open, carry, hit;* intransitive verbs: *fall, jump, run, sleep,* etc.). The child is asked to make alternative replacements with the various exemplars in these classes. The child should recognize which alternatives are legitimate and which are not, and also when certain conventions are needed. For example, *I sleep* is similar to *He sleeps,* but the /s/ on *sleeps* is an added linguistic convention. On the other hand, while *the tree* or *the rock* may be semantically-syntactically equivalent for some predicates to *he,* certain semantic constraints do not permit such things as *sleep.*

After the child has done a fair amount of replacements and the alternatives extend beyond single words, the clinician can change the activity to include negative exemplars—things that violate the rules. These serve to define the domain of a rule. Children in spontaneous language learning use negative exemplars intentionally.

The alternative replacement model is frequently used by behavior modificationists because it is oriented on class learning, explicitness, criteria of complete or near complete learning, and "reversal learning." Behavior modificationists assume that this kind of model offers a way of accounting for semantic-syntactic knowledge. The pivot-open grammars of the 1960s were based upon a similar premise, that privileges of occurrence of form classes are needed in language learning. The most elaborate argument for pivot grammars was developed by McNeill (1966b). A similar argument was developed by Braine (1963a, 1963b, 1965) for contextual generalization. Brown (1973b) has indicated that such approaches deal with superficial aspects of language learning distributional rather than rule-governed behavior. McNeill (1970) shifted away from a pivot-open or distributional analysis of early language learning. Braine (reported in Bowerman, 1976) has redefined his theory from a syntactic to a semantic one.

Combination Model. Using this approach, Mellon (1967) presented a series of sentences to junior high school children and asked them to combine the sentences in any way they wanted. The children worked in small groups, competed with their peers, and did not discuss parts of speech. They produced a large number and variety of sentences. The activity gave them the chance to explore their language by making new combinations of things. These children were compared with children in two other groups. One group was taught traditional English and the other was taught English literature. After 6 months, the children in the sentence combining activity were writing competitively with junior and senior high school students, whereas children in the other two groups remained at the junior high school level. The combination model is illustrated as follows:

> Clinician: *The dog is barking. The dog is old. The dog is in the street.*
> Child: *The old dog that is barking is in the street.*

Revision Model. O'Donnell (personal communication, 1967) prepared a series of one-paragraph stories loaded with certain linguistic systems. Students were instructed to revise the stories. This activity was useful diagnostically because the clinician could determine the systems the individual could work with in the context of other systems. From the intervention standpoint, this provided a way of playing, manipulating, and exploring selected linguistic systems. Subsequent model paragraphs include additional linguistic systems that reflect what the child learned on previously modeled paragraphs. The revision model is as follows:

> Clinician: *The dog is black. His name is Spotty. The dog eats popcorn.*
> Child: *Spotty, the black dog, likes popcorn.*

Additionally, some other considerations should be given to these techniques. First, they deal with different aspects of verbal behavior. Second, the selection of a technique is based on the linguistic needs of the child to deal with a particular domain—they are not determined by a clinical condition such as mental retardation, deafness, "delayed language," and so forth. Third, most of them can be done with both oral and written language. Fourth, they should be used in combination rather than alone. Fifth, the child should feel free to modify them. Sixth, negative or false exemplars provide a useful way of learning and can be incorporated into most of these techniques. Seventh, the child should think of silly and elaborate responses for the techniques, because that provides opportunities to explore alternatives in language. Finally, the linguistic materials employed should be derived from each child's speech rather than from a clinician's notebook of a priori activities.

Input Status

Relatively little has been written about the status of input as it relates to language learning. Yes, much has been said to the effect that language acquisition is remarkably impressive with input that is brief, fleeting, and piecemeal. But, the concern here is not for such global impressions. The concern here is about the integrity of input. That is, it has long been assumed that *positive* instances foster learning and *negative* or *erroneous* instances interfere with learning.

Recent literature on language learnability shatters such traditional thinking. Wexler (1982) showed that *positive* instances, *negative* instances, and *ambiguous* instances are all potentially useful in language learning. Muma (1978a) suggested that positive instances are useful in deducing rules and that negative instances are useful in delimiting the domain of rules. The inclusion of ambiguous instances opens the question of appropriate intervention considerably. Moreover, the role of ambiguity underscores the open dynamic nature of language learning and use. Indeed, these issues raise major questions as to the true value of highly structured a priori approaches. It is no wonder that Brown (1977, p. 26) chose to invest his answer about language intervention in active social commerce. "If you concentrate on communicating, everything else will follow."

Positive, negative, and ambiguous contacts with language support language learning in different ways.

Three Basic Intervention Components

A serious incorporation of the contemporary psycholinguistic literature into intervention would logically include peer modeling, parallel talk, and parent participation, as shown in Table 13.5.

Peer modeling entails the use of a peer's behavior as a model to induce positive change in the behavior of the target child. Thus, the target child who is having difficulties with the pronominal system could engage in activities with another child who does not have difficulties with the pronominal system. This child then provides spontaneous examples of the pronominal system from which information can be extracted either indirectly or with selective inducement by the clinician's parallel talk (Schlesinger, 1977). Berman (1981, p. 609) indicated that "pre-school acquisition is crucially affected by peer input." It is easier for the child to learn from a peer model than from an instructional model because language is used in a spontaneous natural way, with intent and available reference supporting it. This defines language as purposeful and contextually related (referential and linguistic). In this arena, the behavioristic notions of carryover

Table 13.5. Three Basic Intervention Components

PEER MODELING
    Target child-peer match
    Natural ongoing behavior: utility
    Selective

PARALLEL TALK
    Presumed attention
    Intent
    Tuned
    Action patterns
    Informativeness
    Ten techniques

PARENT PARTICIPATION
    Observational
    Active participant:
        produce activities
        clinician role
    Counseling and informative

From *Pragmatic assessment and intervention issues in language* (p. 207) by T. Gallagher and C. Prutting (Eds.), 1983, San Diego: College-Hill. Reprinted by permission.

or generalization become moot points, because they are inherent in peer modeling.

Parallel talk is a procedure whereby the clinician strives to be tuned (Bruner, 1975a, 1978b) to the cognitive-linguistic-communicative needs of the child as he or she uses language in social commerce. The clinician codes ongoing events in ways that correspond to the child's readiness to code (Bruner, 1975a, 1978b), action patterns (Bates, 1979; Greenfield & Smith, 1976), available reference (Olson, 1970), informativeness (Greenfield, 1980; Pea, 1979) rather than salience to an event (Macnamara, 1972), presumed attention (McCall & Kagan, 1969), and intent (Bruner, 1975b; Dore, 1975; Halliday, 1975). Parallel talk is predicated on an appropriate descriptive assessment that delineates the nature of the child's language in communicative contexts so the clinician can be tuned to the child's active learning most of the time. Gopnik (1981) discussed parental comments as *signposts* affording children assistance in grammatical and cognitive development. Gopnik said,

> The adult language provides a series of signposts that help the child find his way around uncharted cognitive territory. However, the child can only make use of the signposts that he is able to comprehend. As the child covers more cognitive ground, he can take advantage of new linguistic signposts. (1981, p. 104)

Similarly, Hirsh-Pasek, Treiman, and Schneiderman (1984) indicated that mothers provide subtle cues concerning grammaticality but it is up to the child to capitalize on them (see also Gleitman, Newport, & Gleitman, 1984). Schlesinger (1977) also suggested that linguistic input is potentially useful to the child. Indeed, Chapter 7, "Assistance," gives many suggestions on how clinicians can function as parents do in facilitating language acquisition.

The five child initiated and clinician response models previously reported (correction, expansion, simple expatiation, complex expatiation, and alternatives, Muma, 1971a) compose part of the parallel talk procedure. The other five models (completion, revision, combination, alternative replacement, and replacement) need to be predicated on the child's own target structures and co-occurring systems to realize their full potency.

Unfortunately, the clinical fields are not well versed in parallel talking. The prevailing attitude is behavioristic and instructional. Most clinicians talk too much or say the wrong things. They are insufficiently tuned to the active language learning needs of the child. They are seemingly ignorant of a fundamental principle of language learning—*payoff*. If an utterance works as intended, it gets paid off or is realized. When payoff occurs, the child talks more and with more variety. This, of course, is not reinforcement. With reinforcement the target behavior increases or decreases. But with *payoff*, the child not only does more with language, but also attempts *new* things. This is because the child's *intentions* have been realized. As Bruner (1978a) indicated, intention has replaced reinforcement.

Unfortunately, the instructional model, in which children are told to wait their turn and then perform in ways directed by a teacher, undermines the use of language for the child's intent as it relates to an event and opportunities for appropriate payoff. In short, much of the instruction in special education (learning disabilities, resource room, etc.) has been contradictory to fundamental language learning principles.

Parent participation is essential to language intervention. Parents want and are able to play an effective role. It is helpful to have parents begin by observing target behaviors, co-occurring systems, available reference, communicative intent, hesitation phenomena, and so on. Then they can begin to take an active role in intervention. Initially, parents can bring in relevant activities. This relieves the clinician of the mundane busy work, freeing time to observe, report, and evaluate performance. After several weeks, parents can play a more active role by selectively carrying out certain activities. The clinician can provide feedback so parents can legitimately extend intervention to the home. In the Preschool Language Clinic, Texas Tech University, a high percentage (80%-90%) of the parents participate in this way. Such participation constitutes a significant portion of a successful program.

Parent participation is also important for another reason—counseling. As parents become involved, they learn more about their child's problems and their role in improvement. In this way, they come to more fully appreciate the progress of their child as it may relate to the various efforts of clinicians. Parental involvement also gives clinicians considerable leverage in the schools for calling the shots about the nature of services.

The three *Ps* of language intervention are: peer modeling, parallel talk, and parent participation.

Metalinguistics and Play

Chapter 11 discussed metalinguistics. Although understanding of this field is only beginning, it appears that metalinguistic, indeed even metacognitive, activities will play an increasingly important role in language intervention. Clinical observation suggests that as individuals learn to reflect on and possibly comment on their language and/or intentionally play with language, large increments of acquisition ensue (Muma, 1978b). This is nothing new. Weir (1962) reported a similar observation. Metalinguistic play seems to be similar to the heuristic function reported by Halliday (1975). Muma (1977b) developed a game for playing with sentence construction; this game is an example of metalinguistic learning. Mellon (1967) provided evidence that metalinguistic activities are potent.

Summary

"If you concentrate on communicating, everything else will follow" (Brown, 1977, p. 26). *Communicative payoff* is a case in point. When the child's *intention* is realized or paid off, he or she will do more and attempt new things. Thus, the traditional notion of *reinforcement* has been replaced by *intention* (Bruner, 1978a, 1981).

Language intervention is shifting from behaviorism to mentalism. The child is an *active* learner. It is necessary to devise language intervention that *facilitates* active language learning efforts. This is done by describing—to the greatest extent possible—what the child is doing, then by exploiting such behavior. Parallel talk, spontaneous peer modeling in social commerce, and parent participation are potential means of facilitation. These might be called the three Ps of language intervention.

Serious limitations of the current language intervention literature make it very difficult to generalize results of studies comparing the various approaches. These same limitations prevent comparisons of language intervention procedures studied.

The normal acquisition literature provides a viable base for conceptualizing, formulating, implementing, and possibly evaluating clinical language intervention approaches. This approach too, has its faults, but all things considered it is viable. Indeed, if the current learnability theory holds, there is simply no other recourse than to use normal language learning as the base for intervention with clinical populations.

Leonard (1981) reviewed various models of language intervention. It is diffucult to assess the value of the various approaches not because the review is wanting, it is not, but because the literature itself is fragmented and disconnected. Modeling of one sort or another appears promising. In addition to Leonard's considerations, the ten techniques gleaned from the literature by Muma (1977a, 1978a, 1981a) have promise. Moreover, the *replacement* and *expansion* principles of language learning have been amply documented (Bates, 1979). And finally, metalinguistic activities and play were regarded as having an increasingly important role in language intervention.

14

EPILOGUE

The quests for information about language acquisiton are portrayed in Chapter 1 from three perspectives, descriptive information, explanatory information, and methodologies. *Descriptive* information is about *what* the child does in quest of adult capacities. *Explanatory* information is about language learning principles concerning *how* the child goes about language learning. *Methodological* considerations are related to both; indeed, methodologies themselves influence both descriptive and explanatory evidence.

Philosophically, the contemporary language acquisition literature seems to reflect on two themes, rationalism and empiricism. Both are considered necessary for an adequate account of language acquisition. Furthermore, innatism and environmentalism are currently viewed as compatible, each making major contributions to language acquisition. This is why Bruner (1981) indicated that LAD and LAS are complementary.

Brown (1977) suggested that if one concentrates on communication everything else will follow. Greenfield and Smith (1976) made a similar comment. In fact, the contemporary literature on language acquisition brings home quite solidly the centrality of communication. In this regard, the coin-of-the-realm of communication in social commerce is *informativeness* in whatever form it may take. Communication theory in general and informativeness in particular means that the study of language acquisition extends considerably beyond the actual utterances of the child. These utterances are merely the products of elaborate relationships concerning the child's working knowledge of the world and presuppositional structure; the presuppositional structure is the source of propositions that contain semantic categories that are the bases of grammatical relationships. All of these complex matters relate to *context*, both internal and external.

Given this complexity, it is no wonder that the study of language acquisition has evidenced some major methodological shifts. The primary shifts were the diary period followed by the empirical period and then the psycholinguistic-pragmatic period. In the contemporary literature, it has become increasingly important to establish criteria for crediting the child with *productive* capacities of one kind or another (Brown, 1973b; Gopnik, 1981; Greenfield & Smith, 1976).

The child is an *active* learner who hypothesizes (overtly and covertly) about the nature of language. This process has also been regarded as a *discovery process* (Bever, 1982). Contextual learning, partial learning, varied loci of learning, and operantly selected loci of learning are language learning principles attendant to hypothesis testing (Muma, 1978a).

An interesting question is: What impels the child to learn language, especially when existing communicative skills are already working? We do not know, but it appears that progressively fuller realizations of *intentions* are important.

A similarly intriguing question is: What keeps the child narrowly focused in language learning in the face of considerable influences against such learning? Again, we do not know but it is remarkable that the child stays the course even though errors occur. Yet, these errors are easily recoverable. Moreover, it appears that language learning operates not only on positive information but on negative and even ambiguous information as well. These observations implicate predispositions and learnability theory.

Much of language learning is "underground"—that is, inside the child's mind—requiring inferences to appreciate what is taking place. Therefore, it is imperative that inferential activity be grounded in theory on the one hand and operational rigor on the other; otherwise, the whole process can collapse. The contemporary psycholinguistic literature has invested its efforts in dealing with "rigor of inference" according to certain criteria such as patterns of behavior or relativity, contextual influences, natural spontaneous behavior, and predictability. Given that *readiness* to learn and *opportunities* for learning vary dramatically across children, and at a particular time, it is no wonder that *individual differences* are commonly reported in the language acquisition literature. Yet, the literature does report viable *sequences, stages,* and *alternative strategies*.

For some time now, there has been a search for the cognitive precursors of language acquisition. Studies in the early 1970s focused on sensorimotor skills, but the results were anything but clear. However, the study by Bates (1979) indicates that emergence of the child's knowledge of symbolic play, causality, imitation, and means-ends may be viable precursors of language development.

Gopnik's (1981) recent research puts a different slant on this question. Her research on non-nominal expressions points to a psychological distinction between these early expressions and other early expressions. Brown (1973b), Bowerman (1973), Bloom (1973), and Schlesinger (1971) all recognized a distinction between non-nominal expressions and other early expressions but, more recent literature shows that these expressions operate as *cognitive comments* whereas the others operate as *communicative comments*.

The emergence of *symbolization* is a primary precursor to language learning. Again, the Piagetian model of cognitive development is useful for language acquisition. Bates's (1976, 1979) notion of language as tool is also germaine; yet, Bloom (1985) contended that the instrumental view of language was too narrow, asserting that the intentional view of language is more appropriate. Bruner's (1981) notion of pragmatic format was also helpful. As he indicated, the pragmatic format provides a means for learning semantic-syntactic-phonological capacities.

Werner and Kaplan (1963) had proposed a three stage model for the acquisition of grammatical capacities: identification or indicative, predication or formalization, and attribution or modification. It should be noted that this model is compatible in large measure with the *four big issues* in language acquisition: cognitive categories, semantic categories, grammatical categories, and pragmatic categories. Indicative centers on word learning as well as on early phonology. Word learning deals with the question of how the child comes to categorize the world and then use these categories to learn words. There is considerable controversy about both. In phonology, the evidence is increasingly clear that the child does not approach the acquisition of the sound system in terms of phonemes; rather, the child is oriented on syllable structure and word acquisition (Ferguson, 1978; Ingram, 1976; Waterson, 1971, 1981).

Predication raises the two big issues: How does the child convert knowledge of the world into semantic categories; and How does the child convert semantic categories into grammatical categories? (Bowerman, 1982; Gleitman & Wanner, 1972). In the acquisition of basic semantic relations, the child seems to be geared toward the eventual achievement of SVO constructions. It appears that the prosodic envelope, then, provides an early framework for acquiring basic grammatical knowledge. Gleitman and Wanner's (1982) Three Bears proposal seems to be compatible with both. Schlesinger (1977) held that linguistic input is useful to the child in discerning the grammatical categories of language.

Is the child given assistance in language learning? Bruner (1981) detailed the kinds and apparent consequences of assistance provided by the mother. However, Gleitman and Wanner (1982) questioned whether the child may benefit from such assistance. The communicative context and intention are at the heart of the issue. Relatively little attention has been given to the socio-emotional state of the child in language acquisition. Brown (1977) and Bloom

(1985) suggested that this could be a major factor. Bates (1979) offered suggestive evidence concerning the child's attachment and use of security base as they relate to language acquisition.

In the attribution stage, the child modifies basic grammatical structures. The MLU was found to have a very narrow range of use as a developmental index. Sequence of acquisition is more useful. The contemporary psycholinguistic literature has identified several ways in which loci of learning for the child can be shown, usually within contexts.

After the preschool period, the child needs to learn subtleties of language and some relatively complex structures. In all, the child is becoming progressively more adept in the use of language. This adeptness includes the ability to deal with contingent queries and indirect messages. Furthermore, the child is becoming increasingly aware of verbal capacities. This awareness—metalinguistic abilities—provides a means to play with language and to learn to write and read.

Dialogue between researchers and clinicians is a major goal for the language acquisition field. It is heartening to see theorists such as Leonard (1981, 1983) entering the arena of applications. By the same token, it is good to see the reverse (e.g., Craig, 1983; Prutting, 1979; Prutting & Kirchner, 1983). In short, both researcher and clinician have much to contribute and should not indulge in what Bruner (1978a) called "corrosive dogma."

In clinical assessment, it is imperative that *construct validity* be established (Messick, 1980). The descriptive approach is much more appropriate than the psychometric normative approach in addressing the seven basic aspects of assessment. In intervention, communicative payoff is crucial. It should be emphasized that communicative payoff is *not* reinforcement. Utterances are motivated by *intention;* consequences are a different matter. This is why Bruner (1978a) indicated that reinforcement has been replaced by intention in language acquisition. Similarly, there has been a shift from behaviorism to mentalism. The normal language acquisition literature has been viewed as a viable resource for dealing with language-impaired individuals. Many limitations in the current language intervention literature greatly reduce the possibility of generalizing findings or comparing intervention approaches. The importance of the language intervention principles of expansion of repertoire and replacement of skills has been documented. The three *Ps* of recommended language intervention are the parallel talk strategy, peer modeling, and parent involvement. Finally, it appears that metalinguistic activities will play an increasingly important role in language intervention. To reiterate, "concentrate on communicating, everything else will follow." (Brown, 1977, p. 26)

REFERENCES

Ainsworth, M. (1973). The development of infant-mother attachment. In B. Caldwell & H. Ricciuti (Eds.), *Review of child development research 3.* New York: Russell Sage Foundation.
Ainsworth, M., & Bell, S. (1969). Some contemporary patterns of mother-infant interaction in the feeding situation. In J. Ambrose (Ed.), *Stimulation in early infancy.* London: Academic Press.
Ainsworth, M., Blehar, M., Waters, E., & Wall, S. (1978). *Patterns of attachment: A psychological study of the strange situation.* Hillsdale, NJ: Erlbaum.
Ainsworth, M., & Wittig, B. (1969). Attachment and exploratory behavior of one-year-olds in a strange situation. In B. Foss (Ed.), *Determinants of infant behavior,* (Vol. 4). London: Methuen.
Anderson, E. (1977). *Learning to speak with style.* Unpublished doctoral dissertation. Stanford University, Stanford, CA.
Anglin, J. (Ed.). (1973). *Beyond the information given: Studies in the psychology of knowing by Jerome S. Bruner.* New York: Norton.
Anglin, J. (1975). The child's first terms of reference. In S. Erlich & E. Tulving (Eds.), Special Issue, *Bulletin de psychologie in semantic memory.*
Anglin, J. (1977). *Word, object and conceptual development.* New York: Norton.
Aram, D., & Nation, J. (1982). *Child language disorders.* St. Louis: C. V. Moseby.
Ardery, G. (1980). On coordination in child language. *Journal of Child Language, 7,* 305-320.
Aungst, L., & Frick, J. (1964). Auditory discrimination ability and consistency of articulation of /r/. *Journal of Speech and Hearing Disorders, 29,* 76-85.
Austin, J. (1962). *How to do things with words.* New York: Oxford University Press.

Baer, D. (1974). Discussion summary—language intervention for the mentally retarded. In R. Schiefelbusch & L. Lloyd (Eds.), *Language perspectives—Acquisition, retardation, intervention.* Austin, TX: PRO-ED.

Bandura, A., & Harris, M. (1966). Modification of syntactic style. *Journal of Experimental Child Psychology, 4,* 341-352.

Bar-Hillel, Y. (1954). Indexical expressions. *Mind, 63,* 359-379.

Barrett, M. (1978). Lexical development and overextension in child language. *Journal of Child Language, 5,* 205-219.

Bartlett, E. (1972). Selecting preschool language programs. In C. Cazden (Ed.), *Language in early childhood education.* Washington, District of Columbia: National Association of Education of Young Children.

Bates, E. (1976). *Language and context: The acquisition of pragmatics.* New York: Academic Press.

Bates, E. (1979). *The emergence of symbols.* New York: Academic Press.

Bates, E., Camaioni, L., & Volterra, V. (1975). The acquisition of performatives prior to speech. *Merrill-Palmer Quarterly, 21,* 205-226.

Bates, E., & MacWhinney, B. (1979). A functionalist approach to the acquisition of grammar. In E. Ochs & B. Schieffelin (Eds.), *Developmental pragmatics.* New York: Academic Press.

Bates, E., & MacWhinney, B. (1982). Functionalist approaches to grammar. In E. Wanner & L. Gleitman (Eds.), *Language acquisition: The state of the art.* New York: Cambridge University Press.

Beckwith, R., Rispoli, M., & Bloom, L. (1984). Child language and linguistic theory: In response to Nina Hyams. *Journal of Child Language, 11,* 685-687.

Beckwith, L., & Thompson, S. (1976). Recognition of verbal labels of pictured objects and events by 17- to 30-month old infants. *Journal of Speech and Hearing Research, 19,* 690-699.

Bell, S., & Ainsworth, M. (1972). Infant crying and maternal responsiveness. *Child Development, 43,* 1,171-1,190.

Benedict, H. (1979). Early lexical development: Comprehension and production. *Journal of Child Language, 6,* 183-200.

Berko, J. (1958). The child's learning of English morphology. *Word, 14,* 150-177.

Berman, R. (1981). Language development and language knowledge: Evidence from the acquisition of Hebrew morphophonology. *Journal of Child Language, 8,* 609-626.

Bernstein, B. (1970). A sociolinguistic approach to socialization: With some reference to educability. In F. Williams (Ed.), *Language and poverty: Perspectives on a theme.* Chicago: Markham Publishing.

Bernstein, M. (1983). Formation of internal structure in a lexical category. *Journal of Child Language, 10,* 381-400.

Berthoud-Papandropoulou, I. (1978). An experimental study of children's ideas about language. In A. Sinclair, R. Jarvella, & W. Levelt, *The child's conception of language.* New York: Springer.

Bever, T. (1970). The cognitive basis for linguistic structures. In S. Hayes (Ed.), *Cognition and the development of language.* New York: Wiley.

Bever, T. (1982). Some implications of the nonspecific bases of language. In E. Wanner & L. Gleitman (Eds.), *Language acquisition: The state of the art.* New York: Cambridge University Press.

Bever, T., Lockner, J., & Kirk, R. (1969). The underlying structures of sentences are the

primary units of immediate speech processing. *Perception and Psychophysics, 5,* 225-234.
Billow, R. (1975). A cognitive developmental study of metaphor comprehension. *Developmental Psychology, 11,* 415-423.
Birdwhistell, R. (1970). *Kinesics and context.* Philadelphia: University of Pennsylvania Press.
Blank, M., & Frank, S. (1971). Story recall in kindergarten children: Effect of method of presentation of psycholinguistic performance. *Child Development, 42,* 299-312.
Blank, M., & Solomon, F. (1968). A tutorial language program to develop abstract thinking in socially disadvantaged preschool children. *Child Development, 39,* 379-390.
Blank, M., & Solomon, F. (1969). How shall the disadvantaged child be taught? *Child Development, 40,* 47-61.
Blehar, M., Lieberman, A., & Ainsworth, M. (1977). Early face-to-face interaction and its relation to later infant-mother attachment. *Child Development, 48,* 182-194.
Block, E., & Kessell, F. (1980). Determinants of the acquisition order of grammatical morphemes: A re-analysis and re-interpretation. *Journal of Child Language, 7,* 181-188.
Bloom, L. (1970). *Language development: Form and function in emerging grammars.* Cambridge, MA: MIT Press.
Bloom, L. (1972). *Cognitive and linguistic aspects of early language development; short course.* American Language-Speech-Hearing Association Convention, November, Chicago.
Hague: Mouton.
Bloom, L. (1974). Talking, understanding, and thinking. In R. Schiefelbusch & L. Lloyd (Eds.), *Language perspectives: Acquisition, retardation, and intervention.* Austin, TX: PRO-ED.
Bloom, L. (1984). Review: Atkinson, M. Explanations in the study of child language development. *Journal of Child Language, 11,* 215-222.
Bloom, L. (1985). *From infancy to language: Contributions from affect, cognition and intentionality.* American Speech-Language-Hearing Association Convention, November, Washington, D. C.
Bloom, L., Capatides, J., & Tackeff, J. (1981). Further remarks on interpretive analysis: In response to Christine Howe. *Journal of Child Language, 8,* 403-412.
Bloom, L., Hood, L., & Lightbown, P. (1974). Imitation in language development: If, when, and why. *Cognitive Psychology, 6,* 380-420.
Bloom, L., & Lahey, M. (1978). *Language development and language disorders.* New York: Wiley.
Bloom, L., Lahey, M., Hood, L., Lifter, K., & Fiess, K. (1980). Complex sentences: Acquisition of syntactic connectives and the semantic relations they encode. *Journal of Child Language, 7,* 235-261.
Bloom, L., Lifter, K., & Hafitz, J. (1980). Semantics of verbs and the development of verb inflection in child language. *Language, 56,* 386-412.
Bloom, L., Lightbown, P., & Hood, L. (1975). Structure and variation in child language. *Monographs of the Society for Research in Child Development, 40,* (Serial No. 160).
Bloom, L., Tackeff, J., & Lahey, M. (1984). Learning *to* in complement constructions. *Journal of Child Language, 11,* 391-406.
Bloomfield, L. (1933). *Language.* New York: Henry Holt.

Bolinger, D. (1961). Verbal evocation. *Lingua, 10,* 113-127.
Bornstein, M. (1979). Perceptual development: Stability and change in feature perception. In M. Bornstein & W. Kessen (Eds.), *Psychological development in infancy.* Hillsdale, NJ: Erlbaum.
Bower, T. (1977). *The perceptual world of the child.* Cambridge, MA: Harvard University Press.
Bower, T. (1974). *Development in infancy.* San Francisco: Freeman.
Bowerman, M. (1973). *Early syntactic development.* New York: Cambridge University Press.
Bowerman, M. (1974). Discussion summary: Development of concepts underlying language. In R. Schiefelbusch & L. Lloyd (Eds.), *Language perspectives: quisition, retardation, and intervention.* Austin, TX: PRO-ED.
Bowerman, M. (1976). Semantic factors in the acquisition of rules for word use and sentence construction. In D. Morehead & R. Morehead (Eds.), *Normal and deficient child language.* Baltimore: University Park Press.
Bowerman, M. (1978). Systemizing semantic knowledge: Changes over time in the child's organization of word meaning. *Child Development, 49,* 977-988.
Bowerman, M. (1982). Reorganizational processes in lexical and syntactic development. In E. Wanner & L. Gleitman (Eds.), *Language acquisition: The state of the art.* New York: Cambridge University Press.
Bowlby, J. (1969). *Attachment and loss. Vol. I: Attachment.* New York: Basic Books.
Bowlby, J. (1973). *Attachment and loss. Vol. II: Separation.* New York: Basic Books.
Braine, M. (1963a). The ontogeny of English phrase structure: The first phrase. *Language, 39,* 1-13.
Braine, M. (1963b). On learning the grammatical order of words. *Psychological Review, 70,* 323-348.
Braine, M. (1965). On the basis of phrase structure: A reply to Bever, Fodor, and Weksel. *Psychological Review, 72,* 483-492.
Braine, M. (1974). Length constraints, reduction rules, and holophrastic processes in children's word combinations. *Journal of Verbal Learning and Verbal Behavior, 13,* 448-456.
Braine, M. (1976). Children's first word combinations. *Monographs of the Society for Research in Child Development, 41* (Serial No. 164).
Braine, M., & Hardy, J. (1982). On what case categories there are, why they are, and how they develop: An amalgam of *a priori* considerations, speculation, and evidence from children. In E. Wanner & L. Gleitman (Eds.), *Language acquisition: The state of the art.* New York: Cambridge University Press.
Branigan, G. (1976). Syllabic structure and the acquisition of consonants: The great conspiracy in word formation. *Journal of Psycholinguistic Research, 5.*
Brenner J., & Mueller, E. (1982). Shared meaning in boy toddlers' peer relations. *Child Development, 53,* 380-391.
Brinton, B., & Fujiki, M. (1984). Development of topic manipulation skills in discourse. *Journal of Speech and Hearing Research, 27,* 350-358.
Brown, A., & DeLoache, J. (1978). Skills, plans and self regulations. In R. Siegler (Ed.), *Children's thinking: What develops?* Hillsdale, NJ: Erlbaum.

Brown, R. (1956). Language and categories. In J. Bruner, L. Goodnow, & G. Austin (Eds.), *A study of thinking*. New York: Wiley.

Brown, R. (1958a). How shall a thing be called? *Psychological Review, 65*, 18-21.

Brown, R. (1958b). *Words and things*. New York: Free Press.

Brown, R. (1965). *Social psychology*. New York: Free Press.

Brown, R. (1968). The development of wh- questions in child speech. *Journal of Verbal Learning and Verbal Behavior, 7*, 279-290.

Brown, R. (1973a). Development of the first language in the human species. *American Psychologist, 28*, 97-106.

Brown, R. (1973b). *A first language: The early stages*. Cambridge, MA: Harvard University Press.

Brown, R. (1977). Introduction. In C. Snow & C. Ferguson (Eds.), *Talking to children*. New York: Cambridge University Press.

Brown, R., & Bellugi, U. (1964). Three processes in the child's acquisition of syntax. *Harvard Educational Review, 34*, 133-151.

Brown, R., & Berko, J. (1960). Word association and the acquisition of grammar. *Child Development, 31*, 1-14.

Brown, R., Cazden, C., & Bellugi-Klima, U. (1969). The child's grammar from I to III. In J. Hill (Ed.), *Minnesota symposia on child psychology* (Vol. 2). Minneapolis: University of Minnesota Press.

Brown, R., & Gilman, A. (1960). The pronouns of power and solidarity. In T. Sebeok (Ed.), *The integration of a child into a social world*. Cambridge, England: University of Cambridge Press.

Brown, R., & Hanlon, C. (1970). Derivational complexity and order of acquisition in child speech. In J. Hayes (Ed.), *Cognition and the development of language*. New York: Wiley.

Brown, R., & McNeill, D. (1966). The "tip of the tongue" phenomenon. *Journal of Verbal Learning and Verbal Behavior, 5*, 325-337.

Bruner, J. (1957). On perceptual readiness. *Psychological Review, 64*, 123-152.

Bruner, J. (1964). The course of cognitive growth. *American Psychologist, 19*, 1-15.

Bruner, J. (1975a). The ontogenesis of speech acts. *Journal of Child Language, 2*, 1-19.

Bruner, J. (1975b). From communication to language—a psychological perspective. *Cognition, 3*, 255-288.

Bruner, J. (1977). Early social interaction and language acquisition. In H. Schaffer (Ed.), *Studies in mother-infant interaction*. New York: Academic Press.

Bruner, J. (1978a). Foreword. In A. Lock (Ed.), *Action, gesture and symbol*. New York: Academic Press.

Bruner, J. (1978b). Learning the mother tongue. *Human Nature*, 43-49.

Bruner, J. (1978c). The role of dialogue in language acquisition. In A. Sinclair, R. Jarvella, & W. Levelt (Eds.), *The child's conception of language*. New York: Springer.

Bruner, J. (1981). The social context of language acquisition. *Language & Communication, 1*, 155-178.

Bruner, J., Goodnow, J., & Austin, G. (1956). *A study of thinking*. New York: Science Editions.

Bruner, J., Jolly, A., & Sylva, K. (1976). *Play: Its role in developmental evolution* Harmondsworth, England: Penguin.
Bruner, J., Olver, R., and Greenfield, P. (1966). *Studies in cognitive growth.* New York: Wiley.
Bruner, J., & Sherwood, V. (1976). Early rule structure: The case of peekaboo. In J. Bruner, A. Jolly & K. Sylva (Eds.), *Play: Its role in developmental evolution.* Harmondsworth, England: Penguin.
Burger, R., & Muma, J. (1980). Cognitive distancing in mediated categorization in aphasia. *Journal of Psycholinguistic Research, 9,* 355-365.
Buros, O. (1972). *The seventh mental measurements yearbook.* Highland Park, NJ: Gryphon Press.
Carey, S. (1982). Semantic development. In E. Wanner & L. Gleitman (Eds.), *Language acquisition: The state of the art.* New York: Cambridge University Press.
Carr, D. (1979). The development of young children's capacity to judge anomalous sentences. *Journal of Child Language, 6,* 227-242.
Carter, A. (1978). From sensori-motor vocalization to words: A case study of the evolution of attention-directing communication in the year. In A. Lock (Ed.), *Action, gesture and symbol.* New York: Academic Press.
Cazden, C. (1965). *Environmental assistance to the child's acquisition of grammar.* Unpublished doctoral dissertation, Harvard University, Cambridge, MA.
Cazden, C. (1966). Subcultural differences in child language: An interdisciplinary review. *Merrill-Palmer Quarterly, 12,* 185-219.
Cazden, C. (1968). The acquisition of noun and verb inflections. *Child Development, 39,* 433-448.
Cazden, C. (1972). *Child language and education.* New York: Holt, Rinehart & Winston.
Cazden, C. (1975). Play with language and metalinguistic awareness: On dimension of language experience. In C. Winsor (Ed.), *Dimensions of language experience.* New York: Agathon Press.
Chafe, W. (1970). *Meaning and the structure of language.* Chicago: University of Chicago Press.
Chai, D. (1967). *Communication of pronominal referents in ambiguous English sentences for children and adults.* Unpublished doctoral dissertation, University of Michigan, Ann Arbor, MI.
Chalkley, M. (1982). The emergence of language as a social skill. In S. Kuczaj (Ed.), Language Development (Vol. 2). Hillsdale, NJ: Erlbaum.
Chomsky, C. (1969). *The acquisition of syntax in children from 5 to 10.* Cambridge, MA: MIT Press.
Chomsky, N. (1956). Three models for the description of language. Reprinted in R. Luce, R. Bush & E. Galanter (Eds.), *Readings in mathematical psychology* (Vol. 2). New York: Wiley.
Chomsky, N. (1957). *Syntactic structures.* The Hague: Mouton.
Chomsky, N. (1965). *Aspects of the theory of syntax.* Cambridge, MA: MIT Press.
Chomsky, N. (1968). *Language and mind.* New York: Harcourt Brace Jovanovich.

Chomsky, N. (1971). Deep structure, surface structure, and semantic interpretation. In D. Steinberg & L. Jakobovitis (Eds.), *Semantics.* New York: Cambridge University Press.
Chomsky, N. (1972). Note in C. Cazden (1972). *Child language and education.* New York: Holt, Rinehart & Winston.
Chomsky, N. (1975). *Reflections on language.* New York: Random House.
Chomsky, N. (1980). *Rules and representations.* New York: Columbia University Press.
Clark, E. (1973a). Non-linguistic strategies and the acquisition of word meanings. *Cognition: International Journal of Cognitive Psychology, 2,* 161-182.
Clark, E. (1973b). What's in a word? On the child's acquisition of semantics in his first language. In T. Moore (Ed.), *Cognitive development and the acquisition of language.* New York: Academic Press.
Clark, E. (1975). Knowledge, context, and strategy in the acquisition of meaning. In D. Dato (Ed.), *Developmental psycholinguistics: Theory and applications.* Washington, DC: Georgetown University Press.
Clark, E. (1977). Strategies and the mapping problem in first language acquisition. In J. Macnamara (Ed.), *Language learning and thought.* New York: Academic Press.
Clark, E. (1978). Awareness of language: Some evidence from what children say and do. In A. Sinclair, R. Jarvella & W. Levelt (Eds.), *The child's conception of language.* Berlin: Springer.
Clark, E., & Garnica, O. (1974). Is he coming or going? On the acquisition of deictic verbs. *Journal of Verbal Learning and Verbal Behavior, 13,* 559-572.
Clark, H., & Clark, E. (1977). *Psychology and language.* New York: Harcourt Brace Jovanovich.
Clark, R. (1977). What's the use of imitation? *Journal of Child Language, 4,* 341-358.
Clark, R., & Delia, J. (1976). The development of functional persuasive skills in childhood and early adolescence. *Child Development, 47,* 1,008-1,014.
Clarke-Stewart, K. (1973). Interactions between mothers and their young children: Characteristics and consequences. *Monograph: Society for Research in Child Development* (No. 153).
Clifton, C., & Odom, P. (1966). Similarity relations among certain English sentence constructions. *Psychological Monograph, 80* (Serial No. 613).
Collis, G., & Schaffer, H. (1975). Synchronization of visual attention in mother-infant pairs. *Journal of Child Psychology & Psychiatry, 16,* 315-320.
Cometa, M., & Eson, M. (1978). Logical operations and metaphor interpretation: A Piagetian model. *Child Development, 49,* 649-659.
Connell, P., Gardner-Gletty, D., Dejewski, J., & Parks-Reinick, L. (1981). Response to Courtwright and Courtwright. *Journal of Speech and Hearing Research, 24,* 146-148.
Connell, P., McReynolds, L., & Spradlin, J. (1979). Reply to John Muma. *Journal of Speech and Hearing Disorders, 44,* 397.
Connell, P., Spradlin, J., & McReynolds, L. (1977). Some suggested criteria for evaluation of language programs. *Journal of Speech and Hearing Disorders, 42,* 563-567.

Conti-Ramsden, G., & Friel-Patti, S. (1983). Mother's discourse adjustments to language-impaired and non-language-impaired children. *Journal of Speech and Hearing Disorders, 48,* 360-367.

Coombs, C. (1954). Theory and methods of social measurement. In L. Festinger & D. Katz (Eds.), *Research methods in behavioral sciences.* New York: Holt, Rinehart & Winston.

Cooper, J., Moodley, M., & Reynell, J. (1978). *Helping language development.* New York: St. Martin's Press.

Corrigan, R. (1978). Language development as related to stage 6 object permanence development. *Journal of Child Language, 5,* 173-189.

Corsini, D., Pick, A., & Flavell, J. (1968). Production deficiency of nonverbal mediators in young children. *Child Development, 39,* 53-58.

Cotton, E. (1978). Noun-pronoun pleonasms: the role of age and situation. *Journal of Child Language, 5,* 489-499.

Courtwright, J. & Courtwright, I. (1976). Imitative modeling as a theoretical base for instructing language-disordered children. *Journal of Speech and Hearing Research, 19,* 651-654.

Courtwright, J., & Courtwright, I. (1979). Imitative modeling as a language intervention strategy: The effects of two mediating variables. *Journal of Speech and Hearing Research, 22,* 389-402.

Cowan, P., Weber, J., Hoddinott, B., & Klein, T. (1967). Mean length of a spoken response as a function of stimulus, experimenter, and subject. *Child Development, 38,* 191-203.

Craig, H. (1983). Applications of pragmatic language models for intervention. In T. Gallagher, & C. Prutting (Eds.), *Pragmatic assessment and intervention issues in language.* San Diego: College-Hill Press.

Cromer, R. (1970). 'Children are nice to understand.' Surface structure clues for the recovery of deep structure. *British Journal of Psychology, 61,* 397-408.

Cromer, R. (1974). Receptive language in the mentally retarded: Processes and diagnositc distinctions. In R. Schiefelbusch & L. Lloyd (Eds.), *Language perspectives: Acquisition, retardation, and intervention.* Austin, TX: PRO-ED.

Cross, T. (1977). Mothers' speech adjustments: The contribution of selected child listener variables. In C. Snow, & C. Ferguson (Eds.), *Talking to children.* New York: Cambridge University Press.

Crowder, R. (1972). Visual and auditory memory. In J. Kavanagh, & I. Mattingly (Eds.), *Language by ear and by eye.* Cambridge, MA: MIT Press.

Crystal, D. (1978). The analysis of intonation in young children. In F. Minifie & L. Lloyd (Eds.), *Communicative and cognitive abilities: Early behavioral assessment.* Austin, TX: PRO-ED.

Culatta, B., & Horn, D. (1979). *A program for achieving generalization of grammatical rules to spontaneous discourse.* American Language-Speech-Hearing Association, Atlanta.

Dale, P. (1972). *Language development: Structure and function.* Hinsdale, IL: Dryden Press.

Dale, P. (1976). *Language development: Structure and function* (2nd ed.). New York: Holt, Rinehart & Winston.

Dale, P. (1980). Is early pragmatic development measurable? *Journal of Child Language, 7,* 1-12.

Dale, P., Cook, N., & Goldstein, H. (1981). Pragmatics and symbolic play: A study in language and cognitive development. In P. Dale, & D. Ingram (Eds.), *Child language: An international perspective.* Austin, TX: PRO-ED.

Dale, P., & Ingram, D. (1981). *Child language.* Austin, TX: PRO-ED.

Damico, J., Oller, J., & Storey, M. (1983). The diagnosis of language disorders in bilingual children: Surface-oriented and pragmatic criteria. *Journal of Speech and Hearing Disorders, 48,* 385-393.

Daniloff, R., & Hammarberg, R. (1973). On defining coarticulation. *Journal of Phonetics, 1,* 239-248.

Darley, F. (1979). *Evaluation of appraisal techniques in speech and language pathology.* Reading, MA: Addison-Wesley.

Deese, J. (1970). *Psycholinguistics.* Boston: Allyn & Bacon.

DeMaio, L. (1984). Establishing communication networks through interactive play: A method for language programming in the clinic setting. *Seminars in Speech and Language, 5,* 199-211.

deVilliers, J., & deVilliers, P. (1973). A cross-sectional study of the acquisition of grammatical morphemes. *Journal of Psycholinguistic Research, 2,* 267-278.

deVilliers, J., & deVilliers, P. (1978). *Language acquisition.* Cambridge, MA: Harvard University Press.

deVilliers, J., Flusberg, H., & Hakuta, K. (1977). Deciding among theories of development of coordination in child speech. *PRCLD, 13,* 118-125.

deVilliers, P., & deVilliers, J. (1972). Early judgments of semantic and syntactic acceptability by children. *Journal of Psycholinguistic Research, 1,* 299-310.

Dollard, J., & Miller, N. (1950). *Personality and psychotherapy.* New York: McGraw-Hill.

Donaldson, M. (1978). *Children's minds.* New York: W. W. Norton.

Donaldson, M., & McGarrigle, J. (1974). Some clues to the nature of semantic development. *Journal of Child Language, 1,* 185-194.

Donnellan, K. (1966). Reference and definite descriptions. *Philosophical Review, 75,* 281-304.

Donnellan, K. (1981). Intuitions and presuppositions. In P. Cole (Ed.), *Radical pragmatics.* New York: Academic Press.

Dore, J. (1974). A pragmatic description of early development. *Journal of Psycholinguistic Research, 3,* 343-350.

Dore, J. (1975). Holophrases, speech acts, and language universals. *Journal of Child Language, 2,* 21-40.

Dore, J., Franklin, M., Miller, R., & Ramer, A. (1976). Transitional phenomena in early language acquisition. *Journal of Child Language, 3,* 13-28.

Drachman, G. (1973). Some strategies in the acquisition of phonology. In M. Kenstowicz, & C. Kisseberth (Eds.), *Issues in phonological theory.* The Hague: Mouton.

Duchan, J., & Lund, N. (1979). Why not semantic relations? *Child Language, 6,* 243-251.

Dunn, L. (1965). *Peabody Picture Vocabulary Test.* Circle Pines, MN: American Guidance Service.

Eckerman, C., & Whatley, J. (1977). Toys and social interaction between infant peers. *Child Development, 48,* 1,645-1,656.

Edwards, D. (1973). Sensory-motor intelligence and semantic relations in early child grammar. *Cognition, 2,* 395-434.

Edwards, M. (1974). Perception and production in child phonology: The testing of four hypotheses. *Journal of Child Language, 1,* 205-219.

Eimas, P., Siqueland, E., Jusczyk, P., & Vigorito, J. (1971). Speech perception in infants. *Science, 171,* 303-306.

Eisenberg, R. (1970). The organization of auditory behavior. *Journal of Speech and Hearing Research, 13,* 453-471.

Elkind, D. (1979). The figurative and the operative in Piagetian psychology. In M. Bornstein & W. Kessen (Eds.), *Psychological development from infancy.* Hillsdale, NJ: Erlbaum.

Emerson, H., & Gekoski, W. (1976). Interactive and categorical grouping strategies and the syntagmatic-paradigmatic shift. *Child Development, 47,* 1,116-1,121.

Emslie, H., & Stevenson, R. (1981). Pre-school children's use of the articles in definite and indefinite referring expressions. *Journal of Child Language, 8,* 313-328.

Entwisle, D. (1966). Form class and children's word association. *Journal of Verbal Learning and Verbal Behavior, 5,* 558-565.

Entwisle, D., Forsyth, D., & Muuss, R. (1964). The syntagmatic-paradigmatic shift in children's word associations. *Journal of Verbal Learning and Verbal Behavior, 3,* 19-29.

Erreich, A. (1984). Learning how to ask: Patterns of inversion in *yes-no* and *wh-* questions. *Journal of Child Language, 11,* 579-592.

Ervin, S. (1961). Changes with age in the verbal determinants of word association. *American Journal of Psychology, 74,* 361-372.

Ervin, S. (1966). Imitation and structural change in children's language. In E. Lenneberg (Ed.), *New directions in the study of language.* Cambridge, MA: MIT Press.

Ervin-Tripp, S. (1971). Social backgrounds and verbal skills. In R. Huxley & E. Ingram (Eds.), *Language acquisition: Models and methods.* New York: Academic Press.

Ervin-Tripp, S. (1973). Some strategies for the first two years. In T. Moore (Ed.), *Cognitive development and the acquisition of language.* New York: Academic Press.

Fagan, J. (1979). The origins of facial pattern recognition. In M. Bornstein, & W. Kessen (Eds.), *Psychological development from infancy.* Hillsdale, NJ: Erlbaum.

Fenson, L., Kagan, J., Kearsley, R., & Zelazo, P. (1976). The developmental progression of manipulative play in the first two years. *Child Development, 47,* 232-236.

Ferguson, C. (1977a). New directions in phonological theory: Language acquisition and universals research. In R. Cole (Ed.), *Current issues in linguistic theory.* Bloomington: Indiana University Press.

Ferguson, C. (1977b). Baby talk as a simplified register. In C. Snow, & C. Ferguson (Eds.), *Talking to children.* New York: Cambridge University Press.

Ferguson, C. (1978). Learning to pronounce: The earliest stages of phonological development in the child. In F. Minifie, & L. Lloyd (Eds.), *Communicative and cognitive abilities— early behavioral assessment.* Austin, TX: PRO-ED.

Ferguson, C., & Farwell, C. (1975). Words and sounds in early language acquisition. *Language, 51,* 419-439.

Festinger, L. (1957). *A theory of cognitive dissonance.* New York: Harper & Row.
Fey, M. (1986). Language intervention with young children. San Diego, CA: College-Hill Press.
Fey, M., & Leonard, L. (1983). Pragmatic skills of children with specific language impairments. In T. Gallagher, & C. Prutting (Eds.), *Pragmatic assessment and intervention issues in language.* San Diego: College-Hill.
Fillenbaum, S. (1966). Memory for gist: Some relevant variables. *Language & Speech, 9,* 217-227.
Fillmore, C. (1968). The case for case. In E. Bach, & R. Harms (Eds.), *Universals in linguistic theory.* New York: Holt, Rinehart & Winston.
Fillmore, C. (1972). Subjects, speakers, and roles. In D. Davidson, & G. Harman (Eds.), *Semantics of natural language* (2nd ed.). Boston: Reidel Publishing.
Fillmore, C. (1977). The case for case reopened. In P. Cole, & J. Sadock (Eds.), *Syntax and semantics, vol. 8: Grammatical relations.* New York: Academic Press.
Fillmore, C. (1981). Pragmatics and the description of discourse. In P. Cole (Ed.), *Radical pragmatics.* New York: Academic Press.
Flavell, J. (1968). *The development of role-taking and communicating skills in children.* New York: Wiley.
Flavell, J. (1970). Concept development. In L. Mussen (Ed.), *Handbook of child psychology.* New York: Wiley.
Flavell, J. (1977). *Cognitive development.* Englewood Cliffs, NJ: Prentice-Hill.
Fodor, J., & Bever, T. (1965). The psychological reality of linguistic segments. *Journal of Verbal Learning and Verbal Behavior, 4,* 414-420.
Folger, J., & Chapman, R. (1978). A pragmatic analysis of spontaneous imitations. *Journal of Child Language, 5,* 25-38.
Foppa, K. (1978). Language acquisition—A human ethological problem? *Social Science Information, 17,* 93-105.
Foster, S. (1981). Review: McNeill, D.: The conceptual basis of language. *Journal of Child Language, 8,* 660-663.
Fox, B., & Routh, D. (1975). Analyzing spoken language into words, syllables, and phonemes: A developmental study. *Journal of Psycholinguistic Research, 4,* 331-342.
Francis, H. (1972). Toward an explanation of syntagmatic-paradigmatic shift. *Child Development, 43,* 949-958.
Frank, S., & Osser, H. (1970). A psycholinguistic model of syntactic complexity. *Language & Speech, 13,* 38-53.
Freedle, R. (1972). Language users as fallible information-processors: Implications for measuring and modeling comprehension. In J. Carroll, & R. Freedle (Eds.), *Language comprehension and the acquisition of knowledge.* New York: Wiley.
Freeman, N., Sinha, G., & Stedmon, J. (1981). The allative bias in three-year-olds is almost proof against task naturalness. *Journal of Child Language, 8,* 283-296.
Frege, G. (1892). On sense and reference. In P. Geach, & M. Block (Eds.), *Translations from the philosophical writings of Gottlob Frege.* Oxford, England: Blackwell (1952).
Fudge, E. (1969). Syllables. *Journal of Linguistics, 5,* 253-286.
Furrow, D. (1984). Young children's use of prosody. *Journal of Child Language, 11,* 203-213.
Furrow, D., & Nelson, K. (1984). Environmental correlates of individual differences in language acquisition. *Journal of Child Language, 11,* 523-534.

Furth, N. (1984). *A school for thinking for deaf children.* Paper presented at the Spring Conference. Texas Tech University, Lubbock.

Gaer, E. (1969). Children's understanding and production of sentences. *Journal of Verbal Learning and Verbal Behavior, 8,* 289-294.

Gagne, R., & Smith, E. (1962). A study of the effects of verbalization on problem solving. *Journal of Experimental Psychology, 63,* 12-18.

Gallagher, T. (1977). Revision behaviors in the speech of normal children developing language. *Journal of Speech and Hearing Research, 20,* 303-318.

Gallagher, T. (1981). Contingent query sequences with adult-child discourse. *Journal of Child Language, 8,* 51-62.

Gallagher, T. (1983). Pre-assessment: A procedure for accommodating language use variabiity. In T. Gallagher, & C. Prutting (Eds.), *Pragmatic assessment and intervention issues in language.* San Diego: College-Hill.

Gallagher, T., & Craig, H. (1984). Pragmatic assessment: Analysis of a highly frequent repeated utterance. *Journal of Speech and Hearing Disorders, 49,* 368-377.

Gallagher, T., & Darnton, B. (1978). Conversational aspects of the speech of language disordered children: Revision behaviors. *Journal of Speech Hearing Research, 21,* 118-135.

Gardner, H. (1974). Metaphors and modalities: How children project polar adjectives onto diverse domains. *Child Development, 45,* 84-91.

Gardner, H., Kirchner, M., Winner, E., & Perkins, D. (1975). Children's metaphoric productions and preferences. *Journal of Child Language, 2,* 135-141.

Gardner, H., & Lohman, W. (1975). Children's sensitivity to literary styles. *Merrill-Palmer Quarterly, 21,* 113-126.

Gardner, H., Winner, E., Bechofer, R., & Wolf, D. (1978). The development of figurative language. In K. Nelson (Ed.), *Children's language, Volume 1.* New York: Gardner Press.

Garmiza, C., & Anisfeld, M. (1976). Factors reducing the efficiency of referent-communication in children. *Merrill-Palmer Quarterly, 22,* 125-136.

Garner, W. (1962). *Uncertainty and structure as psychological concepts.* New York: Wiley.

Garner, W. (1966). To perceive is to know. *American Psychologist, 21,* 11-19.

Garnica, O. (1977). Some prosodic and paralinguistic features of speech to young children. In C. Snow, & C. Ferguson (Eds.), *Talking to children.* New York: Cambridge University Press.

Garvey, C. (1975). Requests and responses in children's speech. *Journal of Child Language, 2,* 41-63.

Garvey, C. (1977). The contingent query: A dependent act in conversation. In M. Lewis, & L. Rosenblum (Eds.), *Interaction, conversation, and the development of language.* New York: Wiley.

Garvey, C. (1979). Continuent queries and their relations in discourse. In E. Ochs, & B. Schieffelin (Eds.), *Developmental pragmatics.* New York: Academic.

Gentner, D. (1975). Evidence for the psychological reality of semantic components: the verbs of possession. In D. Norman, & D. Rumelhart (Eds.), *Explorations in cognition.* San Francisco: Freeman.

Gentner, D. (1977). If a tree had a knee, where would it be? Children's performance on

simple spatial metaphors. *Papers and Reports on Child Language Development* (Stanford University), *13*, (157-164).
Geschwind, N. (1965a). Disconnexion syndromes in animals and man. *Brain, 88,* 237-294.
Geschwind, N. (1965b). Disconnexion syndromes in animals and man. *Brain, 88,* 585-644.
Gibson, E. (1969). *Principles of perceptual learning and development.* New York: Appleton-Century-Crofts.
Gleitman, L. (1981). Maturational determinants of language growth. *Cognition, 10,* 103-114.
Gleitman, L., Gleitman, H., & Shipley, E. (1972). The emergence of the child as grammarian. *Cognition, 1,* 137-164.
Gleitman, L., Newport, E., & Gleitman, H. (1984). The current status of the motherese hypothesis. *Journal of Child Language, 11,* 43-80.
Gleitman, L., & Wanner, E. (1982). Language acquisition: The state of the art. In E. Wanner, & L. Gleitman (Eds.), *Language acquisition: The state of the art.* New York: Cambridge University Press.
Glucksberg, S., & Krauss, R. (1967). What do people say after they have learned how to talk? Studies of the development of referential communication. *Merrill-Palmer Quarterly Behavior Development, 13,* 309-316.
Glucksberg, S., Krauss, R., & Higgins, E. (1975). The development of referential communication skills. In F. Horowitz (Ed.), *Review of child development research.* Chicago: University of Chicago Press.
Gold, E. (1967). Language identification in the limit. *Information & Control, 10,* 447-474.
Goldberg, L. (1968). Simple models or simple processes? Some research on clinical judgments. *American Psychologist, 23,* 483-496.
Goldin-Meadow, S., & Mylander, C. (1984). Gestural communication in deaf children: The effects and noneffects of parental input on early language development. *Monographs: The Society for Research in Child Development* (Serial No. 207).
Goldstein, H. (1984). Effects of modeling and connected practice on generative language learning of preschool children. *Journal of Speech and Hearing Disorders, 49,* 389-398.
Golinkoff, R. (1975). Semantic development in infants: The concept of agent and recipient. *Merrill-Palmer Quarterly, 21,* 181-193.
Golinkoff, R. (1980). The influence of Piagetian theory on the study of the development of communication. In I. Sigel, D. Brodzinskim & R. Golinkoff (Eds.), *Piagetian theory and research: New directions and applications.* Hillsdale, NJ: Erlbaum.
Golinkoff, R. (1981). The case for semantic relations: Evidence from the verbal and nonverbal domains. *Journal of Child Language, 8,* 413-438.
Golinkoff, R., & Harding, C. (1978). *Infants' perceptions of filmed events portraying case role concepts.* Paper presented at the International Conference on Infant Studies, Rhode Island.
Golinkoff, R., & Harding, C. (1980). *The development of causality: The distinction between animates and inanimates.* Paper presented at the International Conference on Infant Studies, Connecticut.

Goodson, B., & Greenfield, P. (1975). The search for structural principles in childrens' play: A parallel with linguistic development. *Child Development, 46,* 734-746.

Gopnik, A. (1981). Development of non-nominal expressions in 1-2-year-olds: Why the first words aren't about things. In P. Dale, & D. Ingram (Eds.), *Child language.* Austin, TX: PRO-ED.

Gopnik, A. (1982). Words and plans: Early language and the development of intelligent action. *Journal of Child Language, 9,* 303-318.

Gopnik, A. (1984). The acquisition of *gone* and the development of the object concepts. *Journal of Child Language, 11,* 273-292.

Gopnik, A., & Meltzoff, A. (1984). Semantic and cognitive development in 15- to 21-month-old children. *Journal of Child Language, 11,* 495-514.

Gratch, G. (1976). On levels of awareness of objects in infants and students thereof. *Merrill-Palmer Quarterly, 22,* 157-176.

Greenberg, J. (Ed.). (1963). *Universals of language.* Cambridge, MA: MIT Press.

Greenfield, P. (1980). Going beyond information theory to explain early word choice: A reply to Roy Pea. *Journal of Child Language, 7,* 217-221.

Greenfield, P., & Smith, J. (1976). *Communication and the beginnings of language: The development of semantic structure in one-word speech and beyond.* New York: Academic Press.

Grice, H. (1967). William James Lectures, Harvard University. [Published in part as "Logic and conversation."] In P. Cole, & J. Morgan (Eds.), *Syntax and semantics;* vol. 3, *Speech acts.* New York: Seminar Press.

Gruendel, J. (1972). Referential extension in early language development. *Child Development, 48,* 1,567-1,576.

Guion, R. (1977a). Content and validity—the source of my discontent. *Applied Psychological Measurement, 1,* 1-10.

Guion, R. (1977b). Content validity: Three years of talk—What's the action? *Public Personnel Management, 6,* 407-414.

Guion, R. (1980). On trinitarian doctrines of validity. *Professional Psychology, 11,* 385-398.

Gunter, R. (1960). Propositional drill as a technique for teaching grammar. *Language Learning, 10,* 123-134.

Hakes, D. (1980). *The development of metalinguistic abilities in children.* New York: Springer.

Halliday, M. (1975). Learning how to mean. In E. Lenneberg, & E. Lenneberg (Eds.), *Foundations of language development: A multidisciplinary approach.* New York: Academic Press.

Hammill, D., & Bartel, N. (1978). *Teaching children with learning and behavior problems.* Boston: Allyn & Bacon.

Hammond, D. & Summers, D. (1972). Cognitive control. *Psychological Review, 79,* 58-67.

Harris, Z. (1965). Co-occurrence and transformation in linguistic structure. In J. Fodor, & J. Katz (Eds.), *The structure of language: Reading in the philosophy of language.* Englewood Cliffs: Prentice-Hall.

Hayhurst, H. (1967). Some errors of young children in producing passive sentences. *Journal of Verbal Learning and Verbal Behavior, 6,* 634-639.

Heider, E. (1971). "Focal" color areas and the development of color names. *Developmental Psychology, 4,* 447-455.

Hirsh-Pasek, K., Gleitman, L., & Gleitman, H. (1978). What did the brain say to the mind? A study of the detection and report of ambiguity by young children. In A. Sinclair, R. Jarvella, & W. Levelt (Eds.), *The child's conception of language.* New York: Springer.

Hirsh-Pasek, K., Treiman, R., & Schneiderman, M. (1984). Brown and Hanlon revisited: Mothers' sensitivity to ungrammatical forms. *Journal of Child Language, 11,* 81-88.

Hood, L., Lahey, M., Lifter, K., & Bloom, L. (1978). Observational descriptive methodology in studying child language: Preliminary results on the development of complex sentences. In G. Sackett (Ed.), *Oberving behavior, vol. 1: Theory and applications in mental retardation.* Baltimore: University Park Press.

Horgan, D. (1978). How to answer questions when you've got nothing to say. *Journal of Child Language, 5,* 159-165.

Horgan, D. (1981). Learning to tell jokes: A case study of metalinguistic abilities. *Journal of Child Language, 8,* 217-224.

Howe, C. (1976). The meanings of two-word utterances in the speech of young children. *Journal of Child Language, 3,* 29-48.

Howe, C. (1981). Interpretive analysis and role semantics: A ten-year mesalliance? *Journal of Child Language, 8,* 439-456.

Howe, H., & Hillman, D. (1973). The acquisition of semantic restrictions in children. *Journal of Verbal Learning and Verbal Behavior, 12,* 132-139.

Hudson, J., & Nelson, K. (1984). Play with language: Overextensions as analogies. *Journal of Child Language, 11,* 337-346.

Hunt, K. (1964). Grammatical structures written at three grade levels. *National Council of Teachers of English* (Research Report No. 1).

Huttenlocher, J. (1974). The origins of language comprehension. In R. Solso (Ed.), *Theories in cognitive psychology: The Loyola symposium.* New York: Wiley.

Hymes, D. (1972). Introduction. In C. Cazden, V. John, & D. Hymes (Eds.), *Functions of language in the classroom.* New York: Teachers College, Columbia University.

Ingram, D. (1971). Transitivity in child language. *Language, 47,* 888-910.

Ingram, D. (1974). The relationship between comprehension and production. In R. Schiefelbusch, & L. Lloyd (Eds.), *Language perspectives: Acquisition, retardation, and intervention.* Austin, TX: PRO-ED.

Ingram, D. (1976). *Phonological disability in children.* New York: Elsevier.

Ingram, D. (1978). Sensori-motor intelligence and language development. In A. Lock (Ed.), *Action, gesture and symbol.* New York: Academic Press.

Ingram, D. (1979). *Early patterns of grammatical development.* Paper presented at Santa Barbara conference: Language behavior in infancy and early childhood.

Ingram, D. (1981). *Procedures for the phonological analysis of children's language.* Austin, TX: PRO-ED.

Ingram, D. (1984). *Language issues.* Paper presented at the Spring conference, Texas Tech University, Lubbock.

Ingram, D. (in press). *Child language acquisition: Method, description, and explanation.*

Jakobson, R. (1941/1968). *Child language, aphasia and phonological universals* (translations of 1941 edition). The Hague: Mouton.

Johnson, N. (1965). The psychological reality of phrase structure rules. *Journal of Verbal Learning and Verbal Behavior, 4,* 469-475.
Johnson, N. (1966). The influence of associations between elements of structural verbal responses. *Journal of Verbal Learning and Verbal Behavior, 5,* 369-374.
Kagan, J. (1969). Continuity in cognitive development during the first year. *Merrill-Palmer Quarterly, 15,* 101-119.
Kagan, J. (1970). The determinants of attention in the infant. *American Scientist, 56,* 298-306.
Kagan, J. (1971). *Change and continuity in infancy.* New York: Wiley.
Kagan, J., & Lewis, M. (1965). Studies of attention in the human infant. *Merrill-Palmer Quarterly, 11,* 95-127.
Kamhi, A. (1981). Nonlinguistic symbolic and conceptual abilities in language-impaired and normally developing children. *Journal of Speech and Hearing Research, 24,* 446-453.
Kamhi, A. (1982). Overextensions and underextensions: How different are they? *Journal of Child Language, 9,* 243-247.
Kaplan, A. (1964). *The conduct of inquiry: Methodology for behavioral science.* San Francisco: Chandler.
Kaplan, E., & Kaplan, G. (1970). The prelinguistic child. In Journal of Eliot (Ed.), *Human development and cognitive processes.* New York: Holt, Rinehart & Winston.
Karmiloff-Smith, A. (1979). *A functional approach to child language.* Cambridge, England: Cambridge University Press.
Karmiloff-Smith, A., & Inhelder, B. (1975). If you want to get ahead, get a theory. *Cognition, 3,* 195-212.
Kasl, S., & Mahl, G. (1965). The relationship of disturbances and hesitations in spontaneous speech to anxiety. *Journal of Personal and Social Psychology, 1,* 425-433.
Katz, E., & Brent, S. (1968). Understanding connectives. *Journal of Verbal Learning Verbal Behavior, 7,* 501-509.
Katz, J. (1967). Recent issues in semantic theory. *Foundations of Language, 3,* 124-194.
Keenan, E. (1971). Two kinds of presupposition in natural language. In C. Fillmore, & D. Langendoen (Eds.), *Studies in linguistic semantics.* New York: Holt.
Keller, M. (1976). Development of role-taking ability. Social antecedents and consequences for school success. *Human Development, 19,* 120-132.
Kessel, F. (1970). The role of syntax in children's comprehension from ages six to ten. *Monographs: The Society for Research in Child Development, 35* (No. 139).
Kessen, W. (1979). Introduction. In M. Bornstein, & W. Kessen (Eds.), *Psychological development from infancy.* Hillsdale, NJ: Erlbaum.
Kiparsky, P., & Menn, L. (1977). On the acquisition of phonology. In J. Macnamara (Ed.), *Language learning and thought.* New York: Academic Press.
Kirchner, D., & Skarakis-Doyle, E. (1983). Developmental language disorders: A theoretical perspective. In T. Gallagher, & C. Prutting (Eds.), *Pragmatic assessment and intervention issues in language.* San Diego: College-Hill.
Klima, E., & Bellugi-Klima, U. (1969). Syntactic regularities in the speech of children. In D. Reibel, & S. Schane (Eds.), *Modern studies in English.* Englewood Cliffs, NJ: Prentice-Hall.

Knapp, M. (1972). *Nonverbal communication in human interaction.* New York: Holt, Rinehart & Winston.

Koenigsknecht, R., & Lee, L. (1971). *Validity and reliability of developmental seentence scoring: A method for measuring syntactic development in children's spontaneous speech.* American Language-Speech-Hearing Association, Chicago.

Kohlberg, L. (1969). Stage and sequence: The cognitive developmental approach to socialization. In D. Goslin (Ed.), *Handbook socialization theory and research.* Chicago: Rand McNally.

Kopp, C. (1979). Perspectives on infant motor system development. In M. Bornstein, & W. Kessen (Eds.), *Psychological development from infancy.* Hillsdale, NJ: Erlbaum.

Krasner, L. (1958). Studies of the conditioning of verbal behavior. *Psychological Bulletin, 55,* 148-170.

Kretschmer, R. (1984). Metacognition, metalinguistics, and intervention. In K. Ruder, & M. Smith (Eds.), *Development language intervention.* Austin, TX: PRO-ED.

Kripke, S. (1972). Naming and necessity. In D. Davidson, & G. Harman (Eds.), *Semantics of natural language.* Boston: Reidel Publishing.

Kuczaj, S. (1981). Factors influencing children's hypothetical reference. *Journal of Child Language, 8,* 131-137.

Kuhn, D. (1983). On the dual executive and its significance in the development of developmental psychology. In D. Kuhn, & J. Meacham (Eds.) *On the development of developmental psychology.* Basel, Netherlands: Karger.

Kulikowski, S. (1981). Possible worlds semantics for early syntax. *Journal of Child Language, 8,* 633-640.

Kuno, S. (1973). *The structure of the Japanese language.* Cambridge, MA: MIT Press.

Labov, W. (1972). *Language in the inner city.* Philadelphia: University of Pennsylvania Press.

Lahey, M. (1972). *The role of prosody and syntactic markers in children's comprehension of spoken sentences.* Unpublished doctoral dissertation, Teachers College, Columbia University.

Lahey, M. (1974). Use of prosody and syntactic markers in children's comprehension of spoken sentences. *Journal of Speech and Hearing Research, 17,* 656-668.

Laila Khan, L. (1982). A review of 16 major phonological processes. *Language, Speech and Hearing Services in the Schools, 13,* 77-85.

Lamb, M. (1977). The development of mother-infant and father-infant attachments in the second year of life. *Developmental Psychology, 13,* 637-648.

Lee, L. (1966). Developmental sentence types: A method for comparing normal and deviant syntactic development. *Journal of Speech and Hearing Disorders, 31,* 311-320.

Lee, L. (1974). *Development sentence analysis: A grammatical assessment procedure for speech and language clinicians.* Evanston, IL: Northwestern University Press.

Lee, L., & Canter, S. (1971). Developmental sentence scoring: A clinical procedure for estimating syntactic development in children's spontaneous speech. *Journal of Speech and Hearing Disorders, 36,* 315-340.

Lee, L., Koenigsknecht, R., & Mulhern, S. (1975). *Interactive language development teaching.* Evanston, IL: Northwestern University Press.

Lees, R. (1965). *The grammar of English nominalizations.* Bloomington: Indiana University Press.

Lenneberg, E. (1967). *Biological foundations of language.* New York: Wiley.
Leonard, L. (1973). Teaching by the rules. *Journal of Speech and Hearing Disorders, 38,* 174-183.
Leonard, L. (1975a). Modeling as a clinical procedure in language. *Language, Speech and Hearing Services in Schools, 6,* 72-85.
Leonard, L. (1975b). The role of nonlinguistic stimuli and semantic relations in children's acquisition of grammatical utterances. *Journal of Experimental Child Psychology, 19,* 346-357.
Leonard, L. (1975c). Developmental considerations in the management of language disabled children. *Journal of Learning Disabilities, 8,* 232-237.
Leonard, L. (1976). *Meaning in child language.* New York: Grune & Stratton.
Leonard, L. (1981). Facilitating linguistic skills in children with specific language impairment. *Applied Psycholinguistics, 2,* 89-118.
Leonard, L. (1983). Normal language acquisition: Some recent findings and clinical implications. In A. Holland (Ed.), *Language disorders in children.* San Diego: College-Hill.
Leonard, L. (1985). Unusual and subtle behavior in the speech of phonologically disorderd children. *Journal of Speech Hearing Disorders, 50,* 4-13.
Leonard, L., Fey, M., & Newhoff, M. (1981). Phonological considerations in children's early imitative and spontaneous speech. *Journal of Psycholinguistic Research, 10,* 123-133.
Leonard, L., & Schwartz, R. (1981). *Factors influencing lexical acquisition in children with specific language disability.* Boston: Society Research Child Development.
Lewis, M. (1967). The meaning of a response or why researchers in infant behavior should be oriental metaphysicians. *Merrill-Palmer Quarterly, 13,* 7-18.
Lewis, M. (1970). *Attention and verbal labeling behavior: A study in the measurement of internal representations.* Princeton, NJ: Educational Testing Service.
Lewis, M., & Brooks, J. (1975). Infants' social perception: A constructionist view. In L. Cohen, & P. Salapatek (Eds.), *Infant perception: From sensation to cognition: Perception of space, speech, and sound* (vol. 2). New York: Academic.
Lewis, M., & Goldberg, S. (1969). Perceptual-cognitive development in infancy: A generalized expectancy model as a function of the mother-infant interaction. *Merrill-Palmer Quarterly, 15,* 81-100.
Lewis, M., Kagan, J., & Kalafat, J. (1966). Patterns of fixation in infants. *Child Development, 37,* 331-341.
Lewis, M., & Rosenblum, L. (1977). *Interaction, conversation, and the development of language.* New York: Wiley.
Liles, B. (1985). Cohesion in the narratives of normal and language disordered children. *Journal of Speech and Hearing Research, 28,* 123-133.
Limber, J. (1973). The genesis of a complex sentence. In T. Moore (Ed.), *Cognitive development and the acquisition of language.* New York: Academic Press.
Limber, J. (1976). Unraveling competence, performance and pragmatics in the speech of young children. *Journal of Child Language, 3,* 309-318.
Loban, W. (1963). The language of elementary school children. *National Council of Teachers of English* (No. 1).
Loban, W. (1966). Problems in oral English. *National Council of Teachers of English* (No. 5).

Lock, A. (1978). The emergence of language. In A. Lock (Ed.), *Action, gesture and symbol.* New York: Academic Press.
Locke, J. (1979). Homonymy and sound change in the child's acquisition of phonology. In N. Lass (Ed.), *Speech and language: Advances in basic research and practice.* New York: Academic Press.
Locke, J. (1983). Clinical phonology: The exploration and treatment of speech sound disorders. *Journal of Speech and Hearing Disorders, 48,* 339-341.
Longhurst, T., & Berry, C. (1975). Communication in retarded adolescents: Response to listener feedback. *American Journal of Mental Deficiency, 70,* 158-164.
Longhurst, T., & Sigel, G. (1973). Effects of communication failure on speaker and listener behavior. *Journal of Speech and Hearing Research, 16,* 128-140.
Loveland, K. (1984). Learning about points of view: Spatial perspective and the acquisition of 'I/you.' *Journal of Child Language, 11,* 533-556.
Lowe, M. (1975). Trends in the development of representational play in infants from one to three years—An observational study. *Journal of Child Psychology Psychiatry, 16,* 33-47.
Lust, B., & Mervis, C. (1980). Development of coordination in the natural speech of young children. *Journal of Child Language, 7,* 279-304.
Lyons, J. (1968). *Introduction to theoretical linguistics.* Cambridge, England: Cambridge University Press.
Lyons, J. (1969). *Introduction to theoretical linguistics.* Cambridge, England: Cambridge University Press.
Maccoby, E., & Bee, H. (1965). Some speculations concerning the lag between perceiving and performing. *Child Development, 36,* 367-378.
Macken, M. (1979). Developmental reorganization of phonological: A hierarchy of basic units of acquisition. *Lingua, 49,* 11-49.
Macnamara, J. (1972). Cognitive basis of language learning in infants. *Psychological Review, 79,* 1-13.
Macrae, A. (1979). Combining meanings in early language. In P. Fletcher, & M. Garman (Eds.), *Language acquisition.* Cambridge, England: Cambridge University Press.
MacWhinney, B. (1975). Pragmatics patterns in child syntax. *Papers and Reports on Child Language Development, 10,* 153-165.
MacWhinney, B. (1978). The acquisition of morphophonology. *Monographs: The Society Research in Child Development,* (Serial No. 174).
MacWhinney, B. (1981). Basic syntactic processes. In S. Kuczaj (Ed.), *Language development: Syntax and semantics.* Hillsdale, NJ: Erlbaum.
Main, M. (1976). Security and knowledge. In K. Grossman (Ed.), *Soziale grundlagen des lernens.* Munich: Kinderverlag.
Mandler, J. (1979). Commentary: A trialogue on dialogue. In M. Bornstein, & W. Kessen (Eds.), *Psychological development from infancy.* Hillsdale, NJ: Erlbaum.
Maratsos, M. (1973). Nonegocentric communication abilities in preschool children. *Child Development, 44,* 697-700.
Maratsos, M. (1976). *The use of definite and indefinite reference in young children: An experimental study in semantic acquisition.* Cambridge, England: Cambridge University Press.
Maratsos, M. (1982). The child's construction of grammatical categories. In E. Wanner,

& L. Gleitman (Eds.), *Language acquisition: The state of the art.* New York: Cambridge University Press.
Markham, E. (1977). Realizing that you don't understand: A preliminary investigation. *Child Development, 48,* 986-992.
Marshall, J., & Newcombe, F. (1973). Patterns of paralexia: A psycholinguistic approach. *Journal of Psycholinguistic Research, 2,* 175-199.
Mattingly, I. (1972). Reading, the linguistic process, and linguistic awareness. In J. Kavanagh & I. Mattingly (Eds.), *Language by ear and by eye.* Cambridge: MIT Press.
McCaffrey, A. (1977). Talking in class: A non-didactic approach to oral language in the elementary classroom. *Quebec Francais, 25.*
McCall, R., & Kagan, J. (1967a). Stimulus-schema discrepancy and attention in the infant. *Journal of Experimental Child Psychology, 5,* 381-390.
McCall, R., & Kagan, J. (1967b). Attention in the infant: Effects of complexity, contour, perimeter, and familiarity. *Child Development, 38,* 939-952.
McCall, R., & Kagan, J. (1969). Individual differences in the infant's distribution of attention to stimulus discrepancy. *Developmental Psychology, 2,* 90-98.
McCarthy, D. (1954). Language development in children. In L. Carmichael (Ed.), *Manual of child psychology* (2nd ed.). New York: Wiley.
McCartney, K., & Nelson, K. (1981). Children's use of scripts in story recall. *Discourse Processes, 4,* 59-70.
McCauley, R., & Swisher, L. (1984). Psychometric review of language and articulation tests for preschool children. *Journal of Speech and Hearing Disorders, 49,* 34-42.
McCune-Nicolich, L. (1981). The cognitive bases of relational words in the single word period. *Journal of Child Language, 8,* 15-34.
McGhee, P. (1974). Cognitive mastery and children's humor. *Psychological Bulletin, 81,* 721-730.
McGhee, P. (1977). A model of the origins and early development of incongruity-based humour. In A. Chapman, & H. Foot (Eds.), *It's a funny thing, humour.* Oxford, England: Pergamon Press.
McGhee, P. (1979). *Humor: Its origin and development.* San Francisco: Freeman.
McLean, J., & Snyder-McLean, L. (1978). *A transactional approach to early language training.* Columbus, Ohio: Merrill.
McNeill, D. (1966a). A study of word association. *Journal of Verbal Learning and Verbal Behavior, 5,* 548-557.
McNeill, D. (1966b). Developmental psycholinguistics. In F. Smith, & S. Miller (Eds.), *The genesis of language.* Cambridge, Mass.: MIT Press.
McNeill, D. (1970). *The acquisition of language: The study of developmental psycholinguistics.* New York: Harper & Row.
McNeill, D. (1973). Comments. In J. Bruner, & K. Connolly (Eds.), *The development of competence in early childhood.* New York: Academic Press.
McNeill, D. (1975). Semiotic extension. In R. Solso (Ed.), *Information processing and cognition.* Hillsdale, IL: Erlbaum.
McNeill, D. (1982). Explicating the conceptual basis of language. *Journal of Child Language, 9,* 521-526.
McReynolds, L., & Kearns, K. (1983). *Single-subject experimental designs in communicative disorders.* Austin, TX: PRO-ED.

McShane, J. (1980). *Learning to talk.* Cambridge, England: Cambridge University Press.

Mead, G. (1934). *Mind, self and society.* Chicago: Aldine-Atherton.

Menn, L. (1980). Phonological theory and child phonology. In G. Yeni-Komshian, Journal of Kavanagh, & C. Ferguson (Eds.), *Child phonology* (vol. 1). New York: Academic Press.

Mellon, J. (1967). Transformational sentence combining: A method for enhancing the development of syntactic fluency in English composition. *Harvard Research & Development Center on Educational Differences* (Report No. 1). Harvard University, Cambridge, MA.

Menig-Peterson, C. (1975). The modification of communicative behavior in preschool-aged children as a function of listener's perspective. *Child Development, 46,* 1,015-1,018.

Menn, L. (1979). *Towards a psychology of phonology: Child phonology as a first step.* Paper presented at the Conference on Applications of Linguistics Theory in the Human Sciences, Michigan State University, East Lansing, MI.

Menyuk, P. (1963). Syntactic structures in the language of children. *Child Development, 34,* 407-422.

Menyuk, P. (1964a). Alternation of rules of children's grammar. *Journal of Verbal Learning and Verbal Behavior, 3,* 480-488.

Menyuk, P. (1964b). Syntactic rules used by children from preschool through first grade. *Child Development, 35,* 533-546.

Menyuk, P. (1969). *Sentences children use.* Cambridge, MA: MIT Press.

Menyuk, P. (1974). Early development of receptive language from babbling to words. In R. Schiefelbusch, & L. Lloyd (Eds.), *Language perspectives: Acquisition, retardation, and intervention.* Austin, TX: PRO-ED.

Messick, S. (1975). The standard problem: Meaning and values in measurement and evaluation. *American Psychologist, 30,* 955-966.

Messick, S. (1980). Test validity and the ethics of assessment. *American Psychologist, 35,* 1012-1027.

Miller, G. (1962). Some psychological studies of grammar. *American Psychologist, 17,* 748-762.

Miller, G. (1965). Some preliminaries to psycholinguistics. *American Psychologist, 20,* 15-20.

Miller, G. (1974). Toward a third metaphor for psycholinguistics. In W. Weimer, & D. Palermo (Eds.), *Cognition and the symbolic processes.* New York: Wiley.

Miller, P., Kessel, F., & Flavell, J. (1969). Thinking about people thinking about people thinking about . . . : A study of social cognitive development. *Child Development, 41,* 613-623.

Mitroff, I., & Sagasti, F. (1978). Epistemology as general systems theory: An approach to the design of complex decision-making experiments. *Philosophy of Social Science, 3,* 117-134.

Moely, B., Olsen, F., Halwes, T., & Flavell, J. (1969). Production deficiency in young children's clustered recall. *Developmental Psychology, 1,* 26-34.

Moerk, E. (1972). Principles of interaction in language learning. *Merrill-Palmer Quarterly, 18,* 229-258.

Moerk, E. (1975). Piaget's research as applied to the explanation of language development. *Merrill-Palmer Quarterly, 21,* 151-170.

Moerk, E. (1977). *Pragmatic and semantic aspects of early language acquisition.* Austin, TX: PRO-ED.

Moerk, E. (1980). Relationships between parental input frequencies and children's language acquisition: A reanalysis of Brown's data. *Journal of Child Language, 7,* 1,105-1,181.

Moerk, E. (1981). To attend or not to attend to unwelcome reanalyses? A reply to Pinker. *Journal of Child Language, 8,* 627-631.

Montague, R. (1972). Pragmatics and intensional logic. In D. Davidson, & G. Harman (Eds.), *Semantics of natural language.* Boston: Reidel.

Moore, M., & Meltzoff, A. (1978). Imitation, object permanence and language development in infancy. In F. Minifie, & L. Lloyd (Eds.), *Communicative and cognitive abilities: Early behavior assessment.* Austin, TX: PRO-ED.

Morehead, D., & Morehead, A. (1974). From signal to sign: Piagetian view of thought and language during the first two years. In R. Schiefelbusch, & L. Lloyd (Eds.), *Language perspectives: Acquisition, retardation, and intervention.* Austin, TX: PRO-ED.

Morse, P. (1974). Infant speech perception: A preliminary model and review of the literature. In R. Schiefelbusch, & L. Lloyd (Eds.), *Language perspectives: Acquisition, retardation, and intervention.* Austin, TX: PRO-ED.

Moskowitz, A. (1970). The two-year-old stage in the acquisition of English phonology. *Language, 46,* 426-441.

Moskowitz, A. (1973a). On the status of vowel shift in the acquisition of English phonology. In T. Moore (Ed.), *Cognitive development and the acquisition of language.* New York: Academic Press.

Moskowitz, A. (1973b). The two-year-old stage in the acquisition of English phonology. In C. Ferguson, & D. Slobin (Eds.), *Studies in child language development.* New York: Holt, Rinehart & Winston.

Mowrer, O. (1954). The psychologist looks at language. *American Psychologist, 9,* 660-694.

Mueller, E., & Brenner, J. (1977). The origins of social skills and interaction among playgroup toddlers. *Child Development, 48,* 854-861.

Mueller, E., & Lucas, T. (1975). A developmental analysis of peer interaction among toddlers. In M. Lewis, & L. Rosenblum (Eds.), *Friendship and peer relations.* New York: Wiley.

Muma, J. (1971a). Language intervention: Ten techniques. *Language, Speech, and Hearing Services in Schools, 5,* 7-17.

Muma, J. (1971b). *Parent-Child Development Center. Conceptualization, program, evaluation.* Birmingham, AL.

Muma, J. (1973a). Language assessment: The co-occurring and restricted structures procedure. *Acta Symbolica, 4,* 12-29.

Muma, J. (1973b). Language assessment: Some underlying assumptions. *Asha, 15,* 331-338.

Muma, J. (1975a). The communication game: Dump and play. *Journal of Speech and Hearing Disorders, 40,* 296-309.

Muma, J. (1975b). (Review of *Language perspectives: Development, retardation, and intervention*). *Asha, 18,* 371-373.

Muma, J. (1977a). Language intervention strategies. *Language, Speech, and Hearing Services in the Schools, 8,* 107-125.

Muma, J. (1977b). *Make-change: A game of sentence sense.* Austin, TX: Learning Concepts.

Muma, J. (1978a). *Language handbook: Concepts, assessment, intervention.* Englewood Cliffs, NJ: Prentice-Hall.

Muma, J. (1978b). Connell, Spradlin and McReynolds: Right but wrong! *Journal of Speech and Hearing Disorders, 43,* 549-552.

Muma, J. (1981a). *Language primer for the clinical field.* Austin, TX: PRO-ED.

Muma, J. (1981b). *Muma Assessment Program (MAP).* Austin, TX: PRO-ED.

Muma, J. (1983a). Assessing loci of linguistic learning. *Australian Journal of Human Communication Disorders, 11,* 37-50.

Muma, J. (1983b). Speech-language pathology: Emerging clinical expertise in language. In T. Gallagher, & C. Prutting (Eds.), *Pragmatic assessment and intervention issues in language.* San Diego: College-Hill.

Muma, J. (1983c). Language assessment: How valid is the process? American Speech-Language-Hearing Association Convention (double miniseminar), Cincinnati.

Muma, J. (1984). Semel and Wiig's CELF: Construct validity? *Journal of Speech and Hearing Disorders, 49,* 101-104.

Muma, J. (1985). No news is bad news. *Journal of Speech Hearing Disorders, 50,* 290-293.

Muma, J., Lubinski, R., & Pierce, S. (1982). A new era in language assessment: Data or evidence. In N. Lass (Ed.), *Speech and Language, 7,* 135-147.

Muma, J., & Pierce, S. (1980). Language intervention: Data or evidence? In Panagos (Ed.), *Topics in Learning and Learning Disabilities, 1,* 1-11.

Muma, J., Pierce, S., & Muma, D. (1983). Language training in ASHA: A survey of substantive issues. *Asha, 25,* 35-40.

Muma, J., Webb, P., & Muma, D. (1979). Language training in speech pathology and audiology: A survey. *Asha, 21,* 467-473.

Muma, J., & Zwycewicz-Emory, C. (1979). Contextual priority: verbal shift at seven? *Journal of Child Language, 6,* 301-311.

Munson, J., & Ingram, D. (1985). Morphology before syntax: A case study from language acquisition. *Journal of Child Language, 12,* 681-684.

Mussen, P., Conger, J., & Kagan, J. (1969). *Child development and personality.* New York: Harper & Row.

Myers, P., & Hammill, D. (1976). *Methods for learning disorders.* New York: Wiley.

Nakazima, S. (1962). A comparative study of the speech developments of Japanese and American English in childhood. *Studies in Phonology, 2,* 27-39.

Neimark, E. (1970). Development of comprehension of logical connectives: Understanding of 'or.' *Psychonomic Science, 21,* 217-219.

Nelson, K. (1973a). Some evidence for the cognitive primacy of categorization and its functional basis. *Merrill-Palmer Quarterly, 19,* 21-39.

Nelson, K. (1973b). Structure and strategy in learning to talk. *Monographs: The Society for Research in Child Development, 38,* (Serial No. 149).

Nelson, K. (1974). Concept, word, and sentence: Interrelations in acquisition and development. *Psychological Review, 81,* 267-285.

Nelson, K. (1975). The nominal shift in semantic-syntactic development. *Cognitive Psychology, 7,* 461-479.

Nelson, K. (1976). Some attributes of adjectives used by young children. *Cognition, 4,* 13-30.

Nelson, K. (1979). The role of language in infant development. In M. Bornstein, & W. Kessen (Eds.), *Psychological development from infancy.* Hillsdale, NJ: Erlbaum.

Nelson, K. (1981a). Social cognition in a script framework. In J. Flavell, & L. Ross (Eds.), *Social cognitive development.* New York: Cambridge University Press.

Nelson, K. (1981b). Individual differences in language development: Implications for development and language. *Developmental Psychology, 17,* 170-187.

Nelson, K., & Brown, A. (1978). The semantic episodic distinction in memory development. In P. Ornstein (Ed.), *Memory development in children.* Hillsdale, NJ: Erlbaum.

Nelson, K., & Gruendel, J. (1979). At morning it's lunchtime: A scriptal view of children's dialogues. *Discourse Processes, 2,* 73-94.

Nelson, K., Rescorla, L., Gruendel, J., & Benedict, H. (1978). Early lexicons: What do they mean? *Child Development, 49,* 960-968.

Nelson, K. E. (1977). Facilitating children's syntax acquisition. *Developmental Psychology, 13,* 101-197.

Nelson, K. E. (1978). *Theories of language acquisition.* Paper presented to the New York Academy of Sciences, New York.

Nelson, K. E. (1981). Toward a rare-event cognitive comparison theory of syntax acquisition. In P. Dale, & D. Ingram (Eds.), *Child language.* Austin, TX: PRO-ED.

Nelson, K. E. (1982). Experimental gambits in the service of language acquisition theory: From the Fiffin Project to operation input swap. In S. Kuczaj (Ed.), *Language development: Syntax and semantics.* Hillsdale, NJ: Erlbaum.

Newport, E. (1977). Motherese: The speech of mothers to young children. In N. Castellan, D. Pisoni, & G. Potts (Eds.), *Cognitive theory* (Vol. 2). Hillsdale, NJ: Erlbaum.

Nicolich, L. (N. D.). *Beyond sensori-motor intelligence: Assessment of symbolic maturity through analyses of pretend play.* Unpublished paper, Douglass College, Rutgers University, Rutgers, NJ.

Nicholich, L. (1975). *A longitudinal study of representational play in relation to spontaneous imitation and development of multiword utterance* (Final report). Washington, DC: National Institute of Education.

Nicholich, L. (1981). Toward symbolic functioning: Structure of early pretend games and potential parallels with language. *Child Development, 52,* 785-797.

Ninio, A., & Bruner, J. (1978). The achievement and antecedents of labeling. *Journal of Child Language, 5,* 1-15.

Nooteboom, S. (1967). The tongue slips into patterns. In *Nomen, Leyden studies in linguistics and phonetics.* The Hague: Mouton.

Ochs, E. (1979). Introduction: What child language can contribute to pragmatics. In E. Ochs, & B. Schieffelin (Eds.), *Developmental pragmatics.* New York: Academic Press.

Odom, P., & Corbin, D. (1973). Perceptual salience and children's multidimensional problem solving. *Child Development, 44,* 425-432.

Odom, P., & Guzman, R. (1972). Development of hierarchies of dimensional salience. *Developmental Psychology, 6,* 271-287.

O'Donnell, R., Griffin, W., & Norris, R. (1967). Syntax of kindergarten and elementary school children: A transformational analysis. *National Council of Teachers of English Research,* Report No. 8.

Olds, H. (1968). *An experimental study of syntactic factors influencing children's comprehension of certain complex relationships.* Cambridge, MA: Harvard University Press.

Olson, D. (1970). Language and thought: Aspects of a cognitive theory of semantics. *Psychological Review, 77,* 257-273.

Olswang, L., & Carpenter, R. (1982a). The ontogenesis of agent: Cognitive notion. *Journal of Speech and Hearing Research, 25,* 297-306.

Olswang, L., & Carpenter, R. (1982b). The ontogenesis of agent: Linguistic expression. *Journal of Speech and Hearing Research, 25,* 306-314.

Olver, P., & Hornsby, R. (1966). On equivalence. In J. Bruner, & P. Olver (Eds.), *Studies in cognitive growth.* New York: Wiley.

Osgood, C. (1968). Toward a wedding of insufficiencies. In T. Dixon, & D. Horton (Eds.), *Verbal behavior and general behavior theory.* Englewood Cliffs, NJ: Prentice-Hall.

Palermo, D. (1971). Is a scientific revolution taking place in psychology? *Science Studies, 1,* 135-155.

Palermo, D. (1982). Theoretical issues in semantic development. In S. Kuczaj (Ed.), *Language development* (Vol I). Hillsdale, NJ: Erlbaum.

Palermo, D., & Eberhart, W. (1968). On the learning of morphological rules: An experimental analogy. *Journal of Verbal Learning and Verbal Behavior, 7,* 337-334.

Palermo, D., & Molfese, D. (1972). Language acquisition from age five onward. *Psychological Bulletin, 78,* 409-428.

Paluszek, S., & Feintuch, F. (1979). Comparing imitation and comprehension training in two language impaired children. *Working Papers in Experimental Speech-Language Pathology and Audiology, 8,* 72-91.

Panagos, J. (1974). Persistence of the open syllable reinterpreted as a symptom of language disorder. *Journal of Speech and Hearing Disorders, 39,* 23-31.

Panagos, J., & Hofmann, J. (1971). Some linguistic parameters of children's unintelligible speech. *Journal of Australian College of Speech Therapists, 21,* 68-72.

Pea, R. (1979). Can information theory explain early word choice? *Journal of Child Language, 6,* 397-410.

Peirce, G. (1932). In C. Jartshorne & P. Weiss (Eds.), *Collected Papers,* Cambridge, MS: Harvard University.

Perfetti, C. (1972). Psychosemantics: Some cognitive aspects of structural meaning. *Psychological Bulletin, 78,* 241-259.

Peters, A. (1977). Language learning strategies: Does the whole equal the sum of the parts? *Language, 53,* 560-573.

Petrey, S. (1977). Word associations and the development of lexical memory. *Cognition, 5,* 57-71.

Piaget, J. (1945, 1951, 1962). *Play, dreams and imitation in childhood.* New York: Norton.

Piaget, J. (1952). *The origins of intelligence in children.* New York: International Universities Press.

Piaget, J. (1954). *The child's construction of reality.* New York: Basic Books.
Piaget, J. (1955). *The language and thought of the child.* New York: New American Library.
Piaget, J. (1970). *Genetic epistemology.* New York: Columbia University Press.
Pick, H., Yonas, A., & Rieser, J. (1979). Spatial reference systems in perceptual development. In M. Bornstein, & W. Kessen (Eds.), *Psychological development from infancy.* Hillsdale, NJ: Erlbaum.
Pinard, A., & Laurendeau, M. (1969). "Stage" in Piaget's cognitive developmental theory: Exegesis of a concept. In D. Elkind, & J. Flavell (Eds.), *Studies in cognitive development.* New York: Oxford University Press.
Pinker, S. (1981). On the acquisition of grammatical morphemes. *Journal of Child Language, 8,* 477-484.
Prelock, P., & Panagos, J. (1981). The middle ground in evaluating language programs. *Journal of Speech and Hearing Disorders, 46,* 436-437.
Priestly, T. (1980). Homonymy in child phonology. *Journal of Child Language, 7,* 413-427.
Prutting, C. (1979). Process. *Journal of Speech and Hearing Disorders, 44,* 3-30.
Prutting, C. (1983). Scientific inquiry and communicative disorders: An emerging paradigm across six decades. In T. Gallagher, & C. Prutting (Eds.), *Pragmatic assessment and intervention issues in language.* San Diego: College-Hill.
Prutting, C., & Kirchner, D. (1983). Applied pragmatics. In T. Gallagher, & C. Prutting (Eds.), *Pragmatic assessment and intervention issues in language.* San Diego: College-Hill.
Quine, W. (1973). *The roots of reference.* LaSalle, IL: Open Court.
Ramer, A. (1976). Syntactic styles in emerging language. *Journal of Child Language, 3,* 49-62.
Ratner, N., & Bruner, J. (1978). Games, social exchange and the acquisition of language. *Journal of Child Language, 5,* 391-402.
Read, C., & Schreiber, P. (1982). Why short subjects are harder to find than long ones. In E. Wanner, & L. Gleitman (Eds.), *Language acquisition: The state of the art.* New York: Cambridge University Press.
Reeder, K. (1980). The emergence of illocutionary skills. *Journal of Child Language, 7,* 13-28.
Reich, P. (1976). The early acquisition of word meaning. *Journal of Child Language, 3,* 11-23.
Reid, D., & Hresko, W. (1981). *A cognitive approach to learning disabilities.* New York: McGraw-Hill.
Renfrew, C. (1966). Persistence of the open syllable in defective articulation. *Journal of Speech and Hearing Disorders, 31,* 370-373.
Rescorla, L. (1980). Overextension in early language development. *Journal of Child Language, 7,* 321-33 6.
Rescorla, L. (1981). Category development in early language. *Journal of Child Language, 8,* 225-238.
Retherford, K., Schwartz, R., & Chapman, R. (1981). Semantic roles and residual grammatical categories in mother and child speech: Who tunes into whom? *Journal of Child Language, 8,* 583-608.

Rice, M. (1983). Contemporary accounts of the cognition/language relationship: Implications for speech-language clinicians. *Journal of Speech and Hearing Disorders, 48,* 347-359.
Riegel, K. (Ed.). (1975). The development of dialectical operations. *Human Development, 18* (Parts I & II).
Ringel, R., Trachtman, L., & Prutting, C. (1984). The science in human communication sciences. *Asha, 26,* 33-37.
Rocissano, L., & Yatchmink, Y. (1983). Language skill and interactive patterns in prematurely born toddlers. *Child Development, 54,* 1,229-1,241.
Rodgon, M. (1977). Situation and meaning in one- and two-word utterances: Observations on Howe's 'The meanings of two-word utterances in the speech of young children.' *Journal of Child Language, 4,* 111-114.
Rosch, E. (1973a). On the interval structure of perceptual and semantic categories. In T. Moore (Ed.), *Cognitive development and the acquisition of language.* New York: Academic Press.
Rosch, E. (1973b). Natural categories. *Cognitive Psychology, 4,* 328-350.
Rosch, E., & Mervis, C. (1975). Family resemblances: Studies in the internal structure of categories. *Cognitive Psychology, 7,* 573-605.
Rosch, E., Mervis, C., Gray, W., Johnson, D., & Boyes-Braem, P. (1976). Basic objects in natural categories. *Cognitive Psychology, 8,* 382-439.
Rosembaum, P. (1967). *The grammar of English complement construction.* Cambridge, MA: MIT Press.
Rosenberg, S., & Cohen, B. (1966). Referential processes of speakers and listeners. *Psychological Review, 73,* 208-231.
Rubin, D. (1975). Within word structure in the tip-of-the-tongue phenomenon. *Journal of Verbal Learning and Verbal Behavior, 14,* 392-397.
Ruder, K., Smith, M., & Hermann, P. (1974). Effect of verbal imitation and comprehension on verbal production of lexical items. *Asha Monographs, 18,* 15-29.
Russell, B. (1905). On denoting. *Mind, 14,* 479-493.
Rutter, M. (1972). *Maternal deprivation reassessed.* Harmondsworth, Middlesex: Penguin.
Rutter, M. (1979). Maternal deprivation, 1972-1978; new findings, new concepts, new approaches. *Child Development, 50,* 283-305.
Sachs, J., & Devin, J. (1976). Young children's use of age-appropriate speech style in social interaction and role-playing. *Journal of Child Language, 3,* 81-98.
Sack, H., & Beilin, H. (1971). *Meaning equivalence of active-passive and subject-object first cleft sentences.* Paper presented at the Developmental Psycholinguistics Conference, State University of New York, Buffalo, NY.
Saltz, E. (1971). *The cognitive bases of human learning.* Homewood, IL: Dorsey.
Saltz, E., Soller, E., & Sigel, I. (1972). The development of natural language concepts. *Child Development, 43,* 1,191-1,202.
Salus, P., & Salus, M. (1974). Developmental neurophysiology and psychological acquisition order. *Language, 50,* 151-160.
Sameroff, A., & Harris, A. (1979). Dialectical approaches to early thought and language. In M. Bornstein, & W. Kessen (Eds.), *Psychological development from infancy.* Hillsdale, NJ: Erlbaum.

Sapir, E. (1921). *Language*. New York: Harcourt, Brace & World.
Schacter, F., Kirshner, K., Klips, B., Friedricks, M., & Sanders, K. (1974). Everyday preschool interpersonal speech usage: Methodological, developmental, and sociolinguistic studies. *Monographs: The Society for Research in Child Development* (No. 156).
Schaffer, H. (1979). Acquiring the concept of the dialogue. In M. Bornstein, & W. Kessen (Eds.), *Psychological development from infancy*. Hillsdale, NJ: Erlbaum.
Scherer, N., & Olswang, L. (1984). Role of mothers' expansions in stimulating children's language production. *Journal of Speech and Hearing Research, 27,* 387-395.
Schiff-Myers, N. (1983). From pronoun reversals to correct pronoun usage: A case study of a normally developing child. *Journal of Speech Hearing Disorders, 48,* 394-401.
Schlesinger, I. (1971). Production of utterances and language acquisition. In D. Slobin (Ed.), *The ontogenesis of grammar*. New York: Academic Press.
Schlesinger, I. (1974). Relational concepts underlying language. In R. Schiefelbusch, & L. Lloyd (Eds.), *Language perspectives: Acquisition, retardation, and intervention*. Austin, TX: PRO-ED.
Schlesinger, I. (1977). The role of cognitive development and linguistic input in language acquisition. *Journal of Child Language, 4,* 153-170.
Schlesinger, I. (1978). *The acquisition of words and concepts*. Unpublished manuscript, The Hebrew University, Jerusalem.
Schnur, E., & Shatz, M. (1984). The role of maternal gesturing in conversations with one-year-olds. *Journal of Child Language, 11,* 29-41.
Scholl, D., & Ryan, E. (1975). Child judgments of sentences varying in grammatical complexity. *Journal of Experimental Child Psychology, 20,* 274-285.
Scholnick, E., & Wing, C. (1983). Evaluating presuppositions and propositions. *Journal of Child Language, 10,* 639-660.
Schwartz, R., Chapman, K., Terrell, B., Prelock, P., & Rowan, L. (1985). Facilitating word combination in language-impaired children through discourse structure. *Journal of Speech and Hearing Disorders, 50,* 31-39.
Schwartz, R. & Leonard, L. (1982). Do children pick and choose? An examination of phonological selection and avoidance in early lexical acquisition. *Journal of Child Language, 9,* 319-336.
Scollon, R. (1976). *Conversations with a one year old: A case study of the developmental foundation of syntax*. Honolulu: University Press of Hawaii.
Searle, J. (1969). *Speech acts: An essay in the philosophy of language*. Cambridge, England: Cambridge University Press.
Searle, J. (1972). Chomsky's revolution in linguistics. *The New York Review of Books, 18,* 16-24.
Searle, J. (1975). Indirect speech acts. In P. Cole, & J. Morgan (Eds.), *Syntax and semantics* (Vol. 3). New York: Academic Press.
Searle, J. (1977). A classification of illocutionary acts. *Language in Society, 5,* 1-23.
Seitz, S., & Stewart, C. (1975). Expanding on expansions and related aspects of mother-child communication. *Developmental Psychology, 11,* 763-769.
Semel, E., & Wiig, E. (1980). *Clinical evaluation of language functions*. Columbus, OH: Merrill.
Shantz, C., & Wilson, K. (1972). Training communication skills in young children. *Child Development, 43,* 693-698.
Shatz, M. (1978). On the development of communicative understandings: An early

strategy for interpreting and responding to messages. *Cognitive Psychology, 10,* 271-301.
Shatz, M. (1982). On mechanisms of language acquisition: Can features of the communicative environment account for development? In L. Gleitman, & E. Wanner (Eds.), *Language acquisition: The state of the art.* Hillsdale, NJ: Erlbaum.
Shatz, M. (1984). *Bootstrap operations in child language.* Third International Congress for the Study of Child Language, Austin, TX.
Shatz, M. & Gelman, R. (1973). The development of communication skills: Modifications in the speech of young children as a function of listener. *Monographs: The Society for Research in Child Development* (No. 152).
Shibamoto, J., & Olmsted, D. (1978). Lexical and syllabic patterns in phonological acquisition. *Journal of Child Language, 5,* 417-456.
Shriner, T. (1969). A review of mean length of responses as a measure of expressive language development in children. *Journal of Speech and Hearing Disorders, 34,* 61-67.
Shultz, T. (1976). A cognitive-developmental analysis of humor. In A. Chapman, & H. Foote (Eds.), *Humor and laughter: Theory, research, and applications.* New York: Wiley.
Shultz, T., & Pilon, R. (1973). Development of the ability to detect linguistic ambiguity. *Child Development, 44,* 728-733.
Shuy, R. (1970). The sociolinguists and urban language problems. In F. Williams (Ed.), *Language and poverty: Perspectives on a theme.* Chicago: Markham.
Sigel, I. (1970). The distancing hypothesis: A causal hypothesis for the acquisition of representational thought. In M. Jones (Ed.), *Miami symposium on the prediction of behavior, 1968: Effect of early experiences.* Coral Gables, FL: University of Miami Press.
Sigel, I. (1971). Language of the disadvantaged: The distancing hypothesis. In C. Lavatelli (Ed.), *Language training in early childhood education.* Urbana, IL: University of Illinois Press.
Sigel, I., & Cocking, R. (1977). Cognition and communication: A dialectic paradigm for development. In M. Lewis, & L. Rosenblum (Eds.), *Interaction, conversation, and the development of language.* New York: Wiley.
Sinclair, H. (1970). The transition from sensory-motor behavior to symbolic activity. *Interchange, 1,* 119-126.
Sinclair-de-Zwart, H. (1969). Developmental psycholinguistics. In D. Elkind, & J. Flavell (Eds.), *Studies in cognitive development.* New York: Oxford University Press.
Slobin, D. (1966). Grammatical transformations and sentence comprehension in childhood and adulthood. *Journal of Verbal Learning and Verbal Behavior, 5,* 219-277.
Slobin, D. (1968). Imitation and grammatical development in children. In N. Endler, & H. Osser (Eds.), *Contemporary issues in developmental psychology.* New York: Holt, Rinehart & Winston.
Slobin, D. (1973). Cognitive prerequisites for the development of grammar. In C. Ferguson, & D. Slobin (Eds.), *Studies of child language development.* New York: Holt, Rinehart & Winston.
Slobin, D. (1977). Language change in childhood and in history. In J. MacNamara (Ed.), *Language learning and thought.* New York: Academic Press.
Slobin, D. (1978a). Cognitive prerequisites for the development of grammar. In L. Bloom & M. Lahey (Eds.), *Readings in language development.* New York: John Wiley.
Slobin, D. (1978b). A case study of early language awareness. In A. Sinclair, R. Jarvella, & W. Levelt (Eds.), *The child's conception of language.* New York: Springer-Verlag.

Slobin, D., & Welch, C. (1971). In C. Lavatelli (Ed.), *Language training in early childhood education*. Urbana, IL: University of Illinois Press.

Smith, F., & Miller, G. (1966). *The genesis of language*. Cambridge, MA: MIT Press.

Smith, N. (1973). *The acquisition of phonology: A case study*. New York: Cambridge University Press.

Snow, C. (1972). Mother's speech to children learning language. *Child Development, 43,* 549-566.

Snow, C. (1979). The role of social interaction in language acquisition. In A. Collins (Ed.), *Children's language and communication*. Hillsdale, NJ: Erlbaum.

Snow, C. (1981). Social interaction and language acquisition. In P. Dale, & D. Ingram (Eds.), *Child language*. Austin, TX: PRO-ED.

Snow, C., & Ferguson, C. (Eds.). (1977). *Talking to children*. New York: Cambridge University Press.

Snow, C., & Goldfield, B. (1983). Turn the page please: Situation-specific language acquisition. *Journal of Child Language, 10,* 551-570.

Snow, C., Perlman, R., & Nathan, D. (1985). Why routines are different. Harvard University, Graduate School of Education (manuscript), Cambridge, MA.

Sroufe, L., & Waters, W. (1976). The ontogenesis of smiling and laughter: A perspective on the organization of development in infancy. *Psychological Review, 83,* 173-189.

Stalnaker, R. (1972). Pragmatics. In D. Davidson, & G. Harman (Eds.), *Semantics of natural language* (2nd ed.). Boston: Reidel.

Stampe, D. (1973). *A dissertation on natural phonology*. Unpublished doctoral dissertation, University of Chicago.

Stark, R. (1980). Stages of speech development in the first year of life. In G. Yeni-Komshian, J. Kavanagh, & C. Ferguson (Eds.), *Child phonology* (Vol. 1). New York: Academic Press.

Stemmer, N. (1971). Some aspects of language acquisition. In U. Bar-Hillel (Ed.), *Pragmatics of natural languages*. Berlin: Reidel.

Stemmer, N. (1973a). *An empiricist theory of language acquisition*. The Hague: Mouton.

Stemmer, N. (1973b). Semantic approaches to language acquisition. *Language Sciences, 26,* 4-6.

Stemmer, N. (1978). Similarity, creativity, and empiricism. In F. Peng, & W. Von Raffler-Engel (Eds.), *Language acquisition and developmental kinesics*. Hiroshima: Bunka Hyoron.

Stemmer, N. (1981). A note on empiricism and structure-dependence. *Journal of Child Language, 8,* 649-663.

Stoel-Gammon, C. (1983). Constraints on consonant-vowel sequences in early words. *Journal of Child Language, 10,* 455-457.

Stoel-Gammon, C., & Cooper, J. (1984). Patterns of early lexical and phonological development. *Journal of Child Language, 11,* 247-272.

Strawson, P. (1950). On referring. *Mind, 59,* 320-344.

Strawson, P. (1959). *Individuals*. London: Methuen.

Strawson, P. (1964). Identifying reference and truth-values. *Theoria, 30,* 96-118.

Sugarman, S. (1973). A description of communicative development in the prelanguage child. In I. Markova (Ed.), *The social context of language*. New York: Wiley.

Sullivan, J., & Horowitz, F. (1983). The effects of intonation on infant attention: The role of the rising intonation contour. *Journal of Child Language, 10,* 521-534.

Tanz, C. (1977). Learning how "it" works. *Journal of Child Language, 4,* 225-236.
Tanz, C. (1980). *Studies in the acquisition of deictic terms.* Cambridge, England: Cambridge University Press.
Templin, M. (1957). *Certain language skills in children: Their development and interrelationships.* Minneapolis: University of Minnesota Press.
Terrell, B., Schwartz, R., Prelock, P., & Messick, C. (1984). Symbolic play in normal and language-impaired children. *Journal of Speech and Hearing Research, 27,* 424-429.
Toffel, C. (1955). Anxiety and the conditioning of verbal behavior. *Journal of Abnorn. Soc. Psychol., 31,* 496-501.
The Santa Cruz Special Education Management System (SEMS). (1973). Superintendent of Schools, Santa Cruz County, California.
Thomson, J., & Chapman, R. (1977). Who is 'Daddy' revisited: The status of two-year-olds's over-extended words in use and comprehension. *Journal of Child Language, 4,* 359-375.
Tomasello, M., & Farrar, M. (1984). Cognitive bases of lexical development: Object permanence and relational words. *Journal of Child Language, 11,* 477-494.
Trevarthen, C. (1979). Communication and cooperation in early infancy: A description of primary intersubjectivity. In M. Bullowa (Ed.), *Before speech.* New York: Cambridge University Press.
Tulving, E. (1972). Episodic and semantic memory. In E. Tulving, & W. Donaldson (Eds.), *Organization of memory.* New York: Academic Press.
Turner, E., & Rommetveit, R. (1967a). The acquisition of sentence voice and reversibility. *Child Development, 38,* 549-660.
Turner, E., & Rommetveit, R. (1967b). Experimental manipulation of the production of active and passive voice in children. *Language & Speech, 10,* 169-180.
Turnure, C. (1971). Response to voice of mother and stranger by babies in the first year. *Developmental Psychology, 4,* 182-190.
Tyler, S. (1969). *Cognitive anthropology.* New York: Holt, Rinehart & Winston.
Ungerer, J., Zelazo, P., Kearsley, R., & O'Leary, K. (1981). Developmental changes in the representation of objects in symbolic play from 18 to 34 months of age. *Child Development, 52,* 186-195.
Uzgiris, I., & Hunt, J. (1975). *Assessment in infancy: Ordinal scales of psychological development.* Urbana, IL: University of Illinois Press.
VanKleeck, A., & Frankel, T. (1981). Discourse devices used by language disordered children: A preliminary investigation. *Journal of Speech and Hearing Disorders, 46,* 250-257.
Ventry, I., & Schiavetti, N. (1980). *Evaluating research in speech pathology and audiology.* Reading, MA: Addison-Wesley.
Vihman, M. (1981). Phonology and the development of the lexicon. *Journal of Child Language, 8,* 239-265.
Vygotsky, L. (1962). *Thought and language.* Cambridge, MA: MIT Press.
Wales, R. (1979). Deixis. In P. Fletcher, & M. Garman (Eds.), *Language acquisition.* Cambridge, England: Cambridge University Press.
Wallace, J. (1972). On the frame of reference. In D. Davidson, & G. Harman (Eds.), *Semantics of natural language.* Boston: Reidel.
Wanner, E., & Gleitman, L. (Eds.). (1982). *Language acquisition: The state of the art.* New York: Cambridge University Press.

Warden, D. (1976). The influence of context on children's use of identifying expressions and references. *British Journal of Psychology, 67,* 101-112.
Waterson, N. (1971). Child phonology: A prosodic view. *Language, 7,* 179-211.
Waterson, N. (1981). A tentative developmental model of phonological representation. In T. Myers, J. Laver, & J. Anderson (Eds.), *The cognitive development of speech.* Amsterdam, North Holland.
Waterson, N. (1984). *Phoneme segments in child phonology: How valid is the concept?* Paper presented at the Third International Congress for the Study of Child Language, Austin, TX.
Weber-Olsen, M., Putnam-Sims, S., & Gannon, J. (1983). Elicited imitation and the oral language sentence imitation screening test (OLSIST): Content or context? *Journal of Speech and Hearing Disorders, 48,* 368-378.
Wechsler, D. (1975). Intelligence defined and undefined: A relativistic appraisal. *American Psychologist, 30,* 135-139.
Weir, R. (1962). *Language in the crib.* The Hague: Mouton.
Weiss, A., Carney, A., & Leonard, L. (1985). Perceived contrastive stress production in hearing-impaired and normal hearing children. *Journal of Speech and Hearing Research, 28,* 26-35.
Weist, D. (1982). Verb concepts in child language: Acquiring constraints on action role and animacy. *Ars Linguistica, 12,* 5-124.
Wells, G. (1974). Learning to code experience through language. *Journal of Child Language, 1,* 243-269.
Wells, G. (1981). *Learning through interaction.* New York: Cambridge University Press.
Werner, H., & Kaplan, B. (1963). *Symbol formation.* New York: Wiley.
Wexler, K. (1982). A principle theory for language acquisition. In E. Wanner, & L. Gleitman (Eds.), *Language acquisition: The state of the art.* New York: Cambridge University Press.
Wexler, K., & Culicover, P. (1980). *Formal principles of language acquisition.* Cambridge, MA: MIT Press.
Wheeler, M. (1983). Context-related age changes in mothers' speech: Joint book reading. *Journal of Child Language, 10,* 259-263.
White, S. (1965). Evidence for hierarchical arrangement processes. In L. Lipsitt, & C. Spiker (Eds.), *Advances in child development and behavior.* New York: Academic Press.
Whitehurst, G., Novak, G., & Zorn, G. (1972). Delayed speech studied in the home. *Developmental Psychology, 7,* 169-177.
Whorf, B. (1956). *Language, thought and reality.* Cambridge, MA: MIT Press.
Wilcox, M., & Leonard, L. (1978). Experimental acquisition of wh- questions in language-disordered children. *Journal of Speech and Hearing Research, 21,* 220-239.
Wilkinson, L., Wilkinson, A., Spinelli, F., & Chiang, C. (1984). Metalinguistic knowledge of pragmatic rules in school-age children. *Child Development, 55,* 2,130-2,140.
Wing, C., & Scholnick, E. (1981). Children's comprehension of pragmatic concepts expressed in 'because,' 'although,' 'if,' and 'unless.' *Journal of Child Language, 8,* 347-366.
Winitz, H. (1973). Problem solving and the delaying of speech as strategies in the teaching of language. *Asha, 10,* 583-586.
Winner, E. (1979). New names for old things: The emergence of metaphoric language. *Journal of Child Language, 6,* 469-492.

Winner, E., Engel, M., & Gardner, H. (1980). Misunderstanding metaphor: What's the problem? *Journal of Experimental Child Psychology, 30,* 22-32.

Winner, E., McCarthy, M., Kleinman, S., & Gardner, H. (1979). First metaphors. In H. Gardner, & D. Wolf (Eds.), *Early symbolization: New directions for child development* (Vol. 4). San Francisco: Jossey-Bass.

Winner, E., Rosenthiel, A., & Gardner, H. (1976). The development of metaphoric understanding. *Developmental Psychology, 12,* 289-297.

Witkin, H., Dyk, R., Faterson, H., Goodenough, D., & Karp, S. (1962). *Psychological differentiation* . New York: Wiley.

Wittgenstein, E. (1953). *Philosophical investigations.* New York: Macmillan.

Yngve, V. (1960). A model and an hypothesis for language structure. *Proceedings of the American Philosophical Society, 108,* 275-281.

Yussen, S., & Bird, J. (1979). The development of metacognitive awareness in memory, communication, and attention. *Journal of Experimental Child Psychology, 28,* 300-313.

Zaporozhets, A., & Elkonin, D. (1971). *The psychology of preschool children.* Cambridge.

Zimmerman, G. (1984). Knowledge and service: Does the foundation of our science need shoring? *Asha, 26,* 31-32.

AUTHOR INDEX

Ainsworth, M. 204, 205, 206(4), *307*(4), *308, 309*
Anderson, E. 255, 256, *307*
Anglin, J. 106, 107, 130, 137, 138, 144, 144, *307*(3)
Anisfeld, M. 244, *318*
Aram, D. 271, *307*
Aungst, L. 150, *307*
Austin, G. 130, 133, *311*
Austin, J. 14, 23, 24, 27, 31, 45, 119, 274, *307*

Baer, D. 285, 286(3), *307*
Bandura, A. 295, *308*
Bar-Hillel, Y. 21, 164, *308*
Barrett, M. 143, *308*
Bartel, N. 280, *320*
Bartlett, E. 268, 284, *308*
Bates, E. xii, xv, 4, 14, 15(3), 16, 16, 17, 17, 18, 18, 19, 19, 20, 22, 25, 26, 48(3), 49, 58, 58, 66, 76, 80, 93, 109, 109, 110(4), 111(6), 112, 115, 117(3), 123, 126, 126, 127, 144, 170, 173, 205(3), 206(3), 207(3), 223, 247, 251(3), 253, 253, 255, 274, 283, 290(3), 300, 304, 305, 306, *308*(5)
Bechofer, R. 253, *318*
Beckwith, L. 114, 266, *308*
Beckwith, R. 155, 163, 271, *308*
Bee, H. 135, 255, *325*
Bell, S. 206, 206, *307, 308*
Bellugi, U. 35, 70, 81, 201, 218, 288, 290, 292, 293, 293, *311, 311, 322*
Beilin, H. 256, *333*
Benedict, H. 108, 115, *308, 329*
Berko, J. xi, 237, 256, *308, 311*
Berman, R. 299, *308*
Bernstein, B. 90, *308*
Bernstein, M. 144, *308*
Berry, C. 244, *324*
Berthoud-Papandropoulous, I. 255, 256, 256, *308*
Bever, T. 3, 15, 15, 35, 83, 86, 163, 218, 283, 283, 286, *308*(3), *317*
Billow, R. 253, *309*
Bird, J. 256, *338*
Birdwhistell, R. 243, *309*
Blank, M. 289, 289, 294, *309*(3)

Author Index

Blehar, M. 206, 206, *307, 309*
Block, E. 183, 188, *309*
Bloom, L. xv, 4, 11, 18, 25, 26, 26, 27, 27, 29, 33, 47, 48, 52, 53, 69, 70(5), 72, 74, 75, 79, 81, 81, 84, 92, 99, 99, 105, 108, 109, 110, 110, 131, 138, 143, 144, 145, 155(5), 157, 159, 161, 162, 163, 166, 166, 167, 167, 168, 168, 169(3), 171(3), 174, 174, 175(5), 178(4), 179, 179, 181, 183, 185, 196, 202, 203, 208, 214, 218(3), 219, 221, 222, 226, 228, 237(3), 239, 241, 244, 247, 252, 255, 265, 267, 271, 273(4), 274, 280, 284, 286, 289(3), 305(3), *308, 309*(12), *320*
Bloomfield, L. 12, 63, 64, 65(4), 66(3), *309*
Bolinger, D. 145, *310*
Bornstein, M. 106, 133, 165, *310*
Bower, T. 108, 120, 133, *310, 310*
Bowerman, M. 4, 18, 26(3), 27(4), 29, 34, 52, 59, 66, 68, 69, 92, 92, 93(4), 95, 117, 133, 136, 136, 137, 138, 144, 144, 145, 155, 156, 159, 159, 168, 171, 172(3), 177, 181, 185, 188, 210, 284, 297, 305, 305, *310*(5)
Bowlby, J. 205, *310, 310*
Boyes-Braem, P. 144, *332*
Braine, M. 29, 52, 137, 156, 158, 158, 159, 159, 161, 161, 168, 171, 171, 297, *310*(6)
Branigan, G. 153, 153, *310*
Brenner, J. 209(3), *310, 328*
Brent, S. 237, *322*
Brinton, B. 210, 281, 294, *310*
Brooks, J. 106, *324*
Brown, A. 48, 252, *329*
Brown, R. xi, xii, xv, 1(3), 2, 4, 16, 17, 18, 18, 21, 24, 25, 29, 30, 32, 33, 33, 34, 35, 37, 38, 39, 44, 48, 52, 53, 58, 64, 68, 69(3), 70, 70, 71, 75, 76, 80, 81, 85, 86, 88, 89, 90, 90, 92, 99, 108, 133, 138, 139, 145, 155(4), 156(3), 158, 166, 167, 169, 169, 170, 170, 171, 171, 174, 175, 182, 183(5), 184, 185, 185, 186, 186, 188, 188, 189, 192, 201, 201, 202, 203, 204, 204, 210, 211, 212, 213, 213, 214, 215, 221, 224, 228, 237, 237, 241, 244, 245, 255, 267, 273, 276, 277, 277, 280, 287, 288, 288, 289, 292, 293(3), 297, 298, 301, 302, 303, 303, 304, 305, 305, 306, *311*(14)
Bruner, J. xv, 1, 2, 3, 3, 4, 13, 13, 14, 15, 15, 16, 16, 19, 19, 20, 21, 27, 33, 34, 35, 38, 42, 44, 45, 48(3), 49(4), 56, 58, 64, 68, 71, 74, 79(3), 91, 91, 92, 92, 94, 97, 98, 105, 106, 107, 107, 109, 110, 113, 114, 117(3), 118, 119, 120, 120, 124, 126(4), 128, 129, 130(2), 132, 133, 136, 159, 166, 180, 180, 186, 187, 190, 190, 192, 192, 193, 194(4), 199, 200, 201, 201, 203, 206, 208, 208, 211, 218, 224, 241(3), 242, 246, 251, 252, 273, 274(3), 277(5), 279, 285, 286, 300(3), 301, 302, 303, 305, 305, 306, *311*(10), *312*(3), *330, 332*
Burger, R. 114, *312*
Buros, O. 269, *312*

Camaioni, L. 110, *308*
Canter, S. 283, *323*
Capatides, J. 155, 155, 157, *309*
Carey, S. 135, 177, 185, *312*
Carney, A. 180, *337*
Carpenter, R. 202, 288, 293, 293, *330, 330*
Carr, D. 255, *312*
Carter, A. 115, 115, 283, *312*
Cazden, C. 91, 141, 160, 183, 185, 185, 198(4), 202, 202, 206, 211, 214, 221, 249, 249, 250, 279, 288(4), 293, 294, *311, 312*(5)
Chafe, W. 53, 155, 193, *312*
Chai, D. 235, *312*
Chalkley, M. 48, *312*
Chapman, K. 53, 54, 57, 120, 121, 193, 193, 196, 278, *332, 334*
Chapman, R. 145, 145, 294, *317, 336*
Chiang, C. 49, *338*
Chomsky, C. 234(4), 235, *312*
Chomsky, N. xi, xii, 12, 12, 13, 13, 15(4), 19, 26, 26, 40, 49, 63, 64(3), 65(4), 66(3), 67(5), 91, 91, 155, 180,

198(3), 200, 221, 277, 279, *312*(5), *313*(3)
Clark, E. 2, 23, 26, 40, 49, 74, 80, 119, 143, 144(3), 145, 193, 220, 234, 244, 250, 252, 255, *313*(6)
Clark, H. 2, 23, 74, 119, 145, 193, 220, 244, 250, *313*
Clark, R. 244, *313*
Clarke, Stewart, K. 295, *313*
Clifton, C. 283, *313*
Cocking, R. 59, 84, 94, 113, 223, *335*
Corbin, D. 283, *330*
Cohen, B. 242, *333*
Collis, G. 191, *313*
Cometa, M. 253, *313*
Conger, J. 135, *329*
Connell, P. 283, 283, 288, *313*(3)
Conti-Ramsden, G. 248, *313*
Cook, N. 123, 123, 124, 124, *314*
Coombs, C. 268, *313*
Cooper, J. 86, 99, 146, 153, 153, 289, *314, 336*
Corrigan, R. 108, *314*
Corsini, D. 145, *314*
Cotton, E. 222, *314*
Courtwright, I. 287, 288, *314, 314*
Courtwright, J. 287, 288, *314, 314*
Cowan, P. 183, 214, *314*
Craig, H. 40, 74, 86, 99, 273, 278, 287, 306, *314, 318*
Cromer, R. 234, 234, *314, 314*
Cross, T. 192, *314*
Crowder, R. 127, *314*
Crystal, D. 181, *314*
Culatta, B. 289, *314*
Culicover, P. 198, *338*

Dale, P. 34, 114, 123, 123, 124, 124, 125, 183, 213, 214, 233, *314*(3), *315*
Damico, J. *315*
Daniloff, R. 152, 152, 219, *315*
Darley, F. 269(4), 270(3), *315*
Darnton, B. 39, 90, *318*
Deese, J. 4, 200, 200, *315*
Dejewski, J. 288, *313*
Delia, J. 244, *313*
DeLoache, J. 252, *310*

DeMaio, L. 124, *315*
deSaussure, 63
deVilliers, J. 160, 188, 211, 236, 252, 255, *315*(4)
deVilliers, P. 160, 188, 211, 252, *315, 315*
Devin, J. 256, *333*
Dollard, J. 20, 140, *315*
Donaldson, M. 25, 25, 108, 143, 144, 234, *315, 315*
Donnellan, K. 20, 21, *315, 315*
Dore, J. 26, 27, 27, 33, 48(6), 49, 100, 128, 159, 174(3), 193, 290, *315*(3)
Drackman, G. 149, *315*
Duchan, J. 155, 156, 157, 158, *315*
Dunn, L. 266, *315*
Dyk, R. 98, *338*

Eberhart, W. 160, 185, 211, *331*
Eckerman, C. 209, *315*
Edwards, S. 29, 53, 108, *315*
Eimas, P. 127, *316*
Eisenberg, R. 127, 127, *316*
Elkind, D. 109, 247, *316*
Elkonin, D. 48, *338*
Emerson, H., 237, *316*
Emslie, H. 186, 187, *316*
Engel, M. 146, *338*
Entwisle, D. 237, 237, *316, 316*
Erreich, A. 224, *316*
Ervin, S. xi, 241, 293, **316, 316**
Ervin-Tripp, S. 18, *316, 316*
Eson, M. 253, *313*

Fagan, J. 106, *316*
Farrar, M. 111, 112(3), 113, 113, *336*
Farwell, C. 152, *316*
Faterson, H. 98, *338*
Feintuch, F. 289, *331*
Fenson, L. 123, 124, *316*
Ferguson, C. 49, 88, 128, 146, 148(5), 152, 153, 160, 192, 203, 203, 204, 286, *316*(4), *335*
Fetsinger, L. 243, *316*
Fey, M. 86, 99, 148, 273, 273, 281, 286, **17, 317, 323**
Fiess, K. 228, *309*
Fillmore, C. 29, 30, 31, 31, 53, 59, 68,

Fillmore, C. (cont'd)
    68, 74, 154, 155, 155, 158(3), 183,
    218, 219, 283, 317(4)
Flavell, J. 130, 135, 145, 145, 240, 242,
    242, 244, 257, 314, 317(3), 327, 327
Flusberg, H. 236, 315
Fodor, J. 283, 317
Folger, J. 294, 317
Foppa, K. 255, 317
Forsyth, D. 237, 316
Fox, B. 255, 317
Francis, H. 237, 238, 317
Frank, S. 283, 289, 309, 317
Frankel, T. 286, 337
Franklin, M. 33, 315
Freedle, R. 95, 317
Freeman, N. 80, 227, 317
Frege, G. 19, 20(4), 21, 317
Frick, J. 150, 307
Friedricks, M. 333
Friel-Patti, S. 248, 313
Fudge, E. 152, 317
Fujiki, M. 210, 289, 294, 310
Furrow, D. 86, 99, 317, 317
Furth, H. 94, 220, 222, 318

Gaer, E. 237, 318
Gagne, R. 139, 318
Gallagher, T. 39, 39, 72, 72, 73, 73, 74,
    74, 90, 90, 242, 247, 248, 264, 273,
    279, 299, 318(5)
Gannon, J. 337
Gardner, H. 146(3), 253(3), 256, 256,
    318(4), 338(3)
Gardner-Gletty, D. 288, 313
Garmiza, C. 244, 318
Garner, W. 43, 106, 135, 243, 318, 318
Garnica, O. 80, 193, 203, 313, 318
Garvey, C. 39, 90, 242, 247, 318(3)
Gekoski, W. 237, 316
Gelman, R. 241, 295, 334
Gentner, D. 234, 283, 318, 318
Geschwind, N. 211, 211, 319, 319
Gibson, E. 130, 135, 319
Gilman, A. 44, 90, 170, 311
Gleitman, H. 66, 192, 197, 199, 300, 319,
    319, 320

Gleitman, L. 17, 24, 33, 33, 59, 65, 66,
    66, 92, 93, 113, 156, 157, 158(5), 159,
    160(3), 161, 161, 163(3), 169, 177(4),
    180, 188, 192, 197(4), 198(4), 199(4),
    210(3), 211, 211, 255, 287, 300,
    305(3), 319(4), 320, 337
Glucksberg, S. 242, 242, 244, 319, 319
Gold, E. 66, 319
Goldberg, L. 194, 269, 319
Goldberg, S. 78, 130, 324
Goldfield, B. 120, 335
Goldin-Meadow, S. 202, 319
Goldstein, H. 123, 123, 124, 124, 292,
    314, 319
Golinkoff, R. 58, 108, 109, 139, 155, 156,
    157, 319(3)
Goodnow, J. 27, 98, 130, 133, 311, 338
Goodson, B. 24, 319
Gopnik, A. 25, 25, 47, 47, 108(3),
    112(3), 139(3), 140, 175, 176(5), 196,
    300, 300, 304, 305, 319(4)
Gratch, G. 108, 320
Gray, W. 144, 332
Greenfield, P. xv, 1, 4, 5, 22, 24, 29, 29,
    33, 33, 34, 38, 42, 43, 43, 44, 47, 48,
    52, 53, 53, 55(5), 57, 58(3), 60, 67,
    69, 76(3), 80, 84, 92, 92, 97, 98, 109,
    115, 129, 130, 131, 137, 137, 138,
    142, 154, 159, 160, 164, 164, 165,
    165, 166, 168, 168, 170(4), 171, 172,
    172, 174, 174, 175, 176, 178, 179(3),
    185, 201, 201, 215, 219, 223, 224,
    263, 266, 284, 300, 300, 303, 304, 312,
    319, 320, 320
Grice, H. 14, 23, 119, 119, 320
Griffin, W. 214, 232, 330
Gruendel, J. 48, 108, 320, 329, 329
Guion, R. 262(3), 270, 320(3)
Gunter, R. 296, 320
Guzman, R. 283, 330

Hafitz, J. 70, 131, 161, 169, 172, 218,
    221, 289, 309
Hakes, D. 91, 320
Halwes, T. 145, 327
Hakuta, K. 236, 315

Halliday, M. 46(3), 47, 48, 48, 176, 251, 300, 301, *320*
Hammarberg, R. 152, 152, 219, *315*
Hammill, D. 280, 280, *320, 329*
Hammond, D. 239, *320*
Hanlon, C. 192, *311*
Harding, C. 58, 109
Hardy, J. 159, 159, *310*
Harris, A. 91, *333*
Harris, M. 295, *308*
Harris, Z. 66, 70, 161, 173, 237, 290, *320*
Hayhurst, H. 235, 237, *320*
Heider, E. 137, *320*
Hermann, P. 289, *333*
Higgins, E. 242, 244, *319*
Hillman, D. 255, *321*
Hirsh-Pasck, K. 35, 256, 257, 300, *320, 320*
Hoddinott, B. 183, *314*
Hoffman, J. 152, *331*
Holland, A. 51
Hood, L. 81, 99, 99, 105, 202, 219, 222, 228, 236, 236, 239, *309*(3), *320*
Horgan, D. 120, 252, *321, 321*
Horn, D. 289, *314*
Hornsby, R. 256, *330*
Horowitz, F. 191, 192, *336*
Howe, C. 29, 155, 158, 158, 159, 159, 160, *321, 321*
Howe, H. 255, *321*
Hresko, W. 280, *332*
Hudson, J. 144, 146, 146, 147(3), 253, *321*
Hunt, J. 25, 108, 108, 110, 111, 112, *337*
Hunt, K. 214, 214, *321*
Huttenlocher, J. 138, *321*
Hymes, D. 239, *321*

Ingram, D. xiii, 4, 25, 53, 92, 108, 108, 125, 127, 145, 148, 148, 149(3), 150, 152, 172, 211, 254, 265, 274, 282, 305, *315, 321*(8), *329*
Inhelder, B. 11, 14, *322*

Jakobson, R. 149, 152, 153, *321*
Jenkins, J. 4
Johnson, D. 144, *332*

Johnson, N. 283, *321, 321*
Jolly, A. 124, *312*
Jusczy K, P. 127, *316*

Kagain, J. 79(4), 120(5), 123, 130, 130, 135, 300, *321*(4), *324, 325*(3), *329*
Kalafat, J. 79, *324*
Kamhi, A. 143, *321, 322*
Kaplan, A. 13, 263, *322*
Kaplan, B. xv, 5, 6, 6, 29, 38, 115, 129, 130(3), 142, 154, 205, 213, 253, 253, *316, 337*
Kaplan, E. 127, *322*
Kaplan, G. 127, *322*
Karmiloff-Smith, A. 11, 14, 47, *322*
Karp, S. 98, *338*
Kasl, S. 243, *322*
Katz, E. 237, *322*
Katz, J. 155, *322*
Kavanagh, J. 256
Kearns, K. 282, *327*
Kearsley, R. 123, *316, 337*
Keenan, E. 22, 43, *322*
Keller, M. 244, *322*
Kessel, F. 183, 188, 234, 242, *309, 322, 327*
Kessen, W. 78, 79, 165, *322*
Kiparsky, P. 160, *322*
Kirchner, D. 86, 99, 273(4), 274, 286, 306, *332*
Kirk, R. 283, *308*
Kirshner, K. *333*
Kirshner, M. 295, *318, 322*
Klein, T. 183, *314*
Kleinman, S. 146, *338*
Klima, E. 218, 290, *322*
Klips, B. 295, *333*
Knapp, M. 243, *322*
Koenigsknecht, R. 283, 289, *322, 323*
Kohlberg, L. 210, *322*
Kopp, C. 105, 120, *322*
Krasner, L. 4, 296, *322*
Krauss, R. 242, 242, 244, *319, 319*
Kretschmer, R. 91, 250(3), 251, 251, 252, 252, 257, *322*
Kripke, S. 20(3), 136, *322*
Kuczaj, S. 124, 185, *323*

Kuhn, D. 11, *323*
Kulikowski, S. 220, 220, *323*
Kuno, S. 17, 173, 173, *323*

Labov, W. 243, *323*
Lahey, M. 70, 72, 74, 79, 168, 169, 179(3), 180, 196, 218, 237, 247, 252, 265, 273(3), 280, 286, 289, *309*(3), *320, 323, 323*
Laila Khan, L. 150, *323*
Lamb, M. 208, *323*
Laurendeau, M. 59, *331*
Lee, L. 283(3), 289, *323*(4), *322*
Lees, R. 132, *323*
Lenneberg, E. 46, *323*
Lenneberg, E. 28, 46, 133, 211, 211, *323*
Leonard, L. 25, 29(3), 30(3), 33, 53, 55, 67, 79, 86, 146, 146, 148, 150, 154, 157, 158, 180, 273(3), 274, 274, 280, 281(7), 284, 285, 286, 287(4), 288, 289(6), 295, 302, 306, *317, 323*(8), *324, 334, 337, 338*
Lewis, M. 79(4), 106, 120, 130, 130, 205, *321, 324*(6)
Liberman, A. 206, *309*
Lifter, K. 70, 131, 161, 169, 172, 218, 221, 289, *309, 309, 320*
Lightbown, P. 29, 81, 99, 99, 202, 222, 228, *309, 309*
Liles, B. 248, *324*
Limber, J. 58, 213, 224, 255, *324, 324*
Lloyd, L. 141
Loban, W. 246, *324, 324*
Lock, A. 90, 117, 204
Locke, J. 62, 150, 150, *308, 324, 324*
Lockner, J. 283
Lohman, W. 256, *318*
Longhurst, T. 244, 244, *324, 324*
Loveland, K. 227, *324*
Lowe, M. 124, *324*
Lubinski, R. 262, *329*
Lucas, T. 209, *328*
Lund, N. 29, 155, 156, 157, 158, *315*
Lust, B. 236
Lyons, J. 29, 53, 136, *325*

Maccoby, E. 135, 255, *325*
Macnamara, J. 21, 84, 92, 96, 97, 97, 251, 300, *325*
Macrae, A. 29, 155, 156, 157, 158, *325*
MacWhinney, B. xii, xv, 4, 14, 15(3), 16, 17, 17, 18, 18, 19, 19, 40, 152, 170, 173, 173, 222, 228, 228, 265, 283, *308, 308, 325*(3)
Mahl, G. 243, *322*
Main, M. 206, 206, 207, *325*
Mandler, J. 25, 40, 80, 110, *325*
Maratsos, M. 161, 161, 186, 186, 244, 256, *325*(3)
Markham, E. 255, 257, *325*
Marshall, J. 84, 114, *325*
Mattingly, I. 249, 250, 257, *325*
McCaffrey, A. 283, *325*
McCall, R. 79, 120, 130, 300, *325*(3)
McCarthey, M. 146, *338*
McCarthy, D. 63, *325*
McCauley, R. 270, 270, *326*
McCune-Nicolich, L. 108, 112, 112, 139, 175, *326*
McGarrigle, J. 143, 144
McGhee, P. 122(3), *326*(3)
McLean, J. 73, 74, 79, 273, 273, 280, 280, *326*
McNeill, D. 66, 89, 92, 145, 173, 179, 226, 237, 250(3), 294, 294, 297, 297, 311, *326*(6)
McReynolds, L. 282, 283, 283, *313, 313, 326*
McShane, J. 50, *326*
Mead, G. 205, 242, *326*
Meltzoff, A. 108, 108, 112(3), 139, 139, *319, 327*
Mellon, J. 292, 297, 302, *326*
Menig-Peterson, C. 256, *326*
Menn, L. 146, 148, 148, 160, *322, 326*
Menyuk, P. xiii, 73, 92, 127, 127, 159, 210, 229, 230, 237, 240, *326, 326, 327*(3)
Mervis, C. 130, 144, 236, *324, 332, 332*
Messick, C. 124
Messick, S. 13(3), 261(3), 262(9), 270, 270, 274, 306, *327, 327, 336*

Author Index   347

Miller, G. 181, 283, 327(3), *335*
Miller, N. 20, 25, 42, 140, 177, *315*
Miller, P. 242, *327*
Miller, R. *33, 315*
Miller, W. xi
Mitroff, I. 13, 263, *327*
Moely, B. 145, *327*
Moerk, E. 88, 108, 113, 113, 114, 183, 188, 188, *327*(5)
Molfese, D. 214, 214, 234, 235, 235, 246, *331*
Montague, R. 21, 164, *327*
Moodley, M. 289, *314*
Moore, M. 108, *327*
Morehead, A. 108, *327*
Morehead, D. 108, *327*
Morse, P. 127, 127, *327*
Moskowitz, A. 148(3), 160, *328*(3)
Mowrer, O. 200, *328*
Mueller, E. 209(4), *310, 328, 328*
Mulhern, S. 289, *323*
Muma, D. 263, 263, 271, 271, 278, *329, 329*
Muma, J. xii, xiii, 16, 23, 35, 39, 39, 58, 67, 69, 70, 71, 72(3), 73, 74, 74, 79, 81, 82, 83, 84, 85, 85, 86(3), 90, 114, 114, 196, 197, 198, 200, 218, 218, 220, 222, 225, 228, 237, 238, 238, 241, 242, 244, 245, 249, 251, 262(3), 263(7), 267, 269, 270, 270, 271(4), 273(3), 278(5), 280(3), 283(3), 284, 286, 287, 289, 290, 291, 292, 298, 300, 301, 301, 302, 304, *312, 328*(16), *329*(6)
Munson, J. 254, *329*
Mussen, P. 135, *329*
Muuss, R. 237, *316*
Myers, P. 280, *329*
Mylander, C. 202, *319*

Nakazima, S. 127, 127, 179, *329*
Nathan, D. 199, *335*
Nation, J. 271, *307*
Neimank, E. 237, *329*
Nelson, Katherine xv, 4, 28, 48(3), 66, 86, 88, 99, 99, 106, 108, 108, 130, 133, 136(3), 137, 137, 138, 140, 144(4), 145, 146(3), 147, 147, 164(6), 165, 194, 194, 228, 228, 240, 246, 253, *317, 321, 325, 329*(11)
Nelson, Keith 86, 89, 89, 196, 280, 288, 329, *330*(3)
Newcombe, F. 84, 114, *325*
Newhoff, M. 148, *323*
Newport, E. 66, 192, 192, 197, 199, 300, *319, 330*
Nicholich, L. 122, 123(5), 124, *330*(3)
Ninio, A. 56, 58, 194, 194, *330*
Nooteboom, S. 145, *330*
Norris, R. 214, 233, *330*
Novak, G. 289, *338*

Ochs, E. 68, 283, 289
Odom, P. 283, *313, 330, 330*
O'Donnell, R. 214, 232, 233, 289, 297, *330*
Olds, H. 237, *330*
O'leary, K. *337*
Oller, J. *315*
Olmstead, D. 155, *334*
Olsen, F. 145, *327*
Olson, D. 44, 84, 300, *330*
Olswang, L. 202, 288, 293, 293, *330, 330, 333*
Olver, R. 92, 129, 256, *312, 330*
Osgood, C. 200, *330*
Osser, H. 283, *317*

Palermo, D. 4, 4, 14, 21, 37, 65, 68, 98, 134, 135, 185, 200, 211, 214, 214, 234, 235, 235, 241, 246, *330 331*(3)
Paluszek, S. 289, *331*
Panagos, J. 152(3), 153, 153, 283, *331*(3)
Parks-Reninick, L. 288, *313*
Pea, R. 137, 170, 174, *331*
Peirce, G. 253, 253, *331*
Perfetti, C. 28, 30, 131, 173, 177, *331*
Perkins, D. 146, *318*
Perlman, R. 199, *335*
Petry, S. 48, *331*
Piaget, J. 21, 47, 67, 74, 75, 79, 80, 84, 84, 93, 97, 106, 107, 110, 113, 117, 122, 123(5), 124(3), 135, 151, 159,

Author Index

Piaget, J. (cont'd)
  205, 215, 240, 242, 279, 287, 305, 331(5)
Pick, H. 106, 107, 107, 145, *314, 331*
Pierce, S. 262, 262, 263, 271, *329*(3)
Pilon, R. 256, 257, *334*
Pinard, A. 59, *331*
Pinker, S. 183, 188, *331*
Prelock, P. 124, 278, 283, *331, 334, 336*
Priestly, T. 149, 150, 151, *331*
Prutting, C. 12, 64, 85, 86, 99, 264, 265, 273(3), 274, 279, 286, 299, 306, 306, *331, 331, 332, 332*
Putnam-Sims, S. *337*

Quine, W. 193, *332*

Ramer, A. 33, 99, 187, *315, 332*
Ratner, N. 126, *332*
Read, C. 180, *332*
Reeder, K. 49, *332*
Reich, P. 143, *332*
Reid, D. 280, *332*
Renfrew, C. 152, 153, 153, *332*
Rescola, L. 86, 99, 108, 132, 132, 142, 144, 145, 146, *329, 332, 332*
Retherford, K. 53, 54, 54, 57, 120, 121, 193, 193, 196, *332*
Reynell, J. 289, *314*
Rice, M. 26, *332*
Riegel, K. 32, 240, *332*
Rieser, J. 106, 107, *331*
Ringel, R. 12, *332*
Rispoli, M. 155, 163, 271, *308*
Rocissano, L. 196, *332*
Rodgon, M. 155, 156, 157, 158, *332*
Rommetveit, R. 235, 235, *336, 336*
Rosch, E. 96, 130, 137, 144, *332*(4)
Rosenbaum, P. 132, *333*
Rosenberg, S. 242, *333*
Rosenblum, L. 205, *324*
Rosenthiel, A. 146, *338*
Routh, D. 255, *317*
Rowan, L. 278, *334*
Rubin, D. 145, *333*
Ruder, K. 257, 289, *333*
Russell, B. 19, *333*

Rutter, M. 204, 205, *333, 333*
Ryan, E. 256, *333*

Sachs, J. 256, *333*
Sack, H. 256, *333*
Sagasti, F. 13, 263, *327*
Saltz, E. 130, 135, 135, *333, 333*
Salus, M. 127, *333*
Salus, P. 127, *333*
Sameroff, A. 91, *333*
Sanders, K. 295, *333*
Sapir, E. 24, 42, 251, *333*
Schachter, F. 295, *333*
Schaffer, H. 40, 80, 119, 138, 191, 205, *313, 333*
Scherer, N. 202, 288, 293, 293, *333*
Schiavetti, N. 12, 282, *337*
Schiefelbusch, R. 141
Schiff-Myers, N. 222
Schlesinger, I. 2, 4, 15, 24, 26, 26, 27, 27, 29, 33, 33, 34(5), 35, 47, 53, 58, 66, 67, 80, 81, 83, 84, 109, 109, 134(4), 135, 135, 138, 140, 140, 141, 144, 155, 155, 159, 166, 168, 168, 169, 170, 175, 193, 199, 218, 219, 289, 290, 294, 299, 300, 305, 305, *333*(4)
Schneiderman, M. 35, 300, *320*
Schnur, E. 191, *333*
Scholl, D. 256, *333*
Scholnick, E. 237, 237, *334, 338*
Schreiber, P. 180, *333*
Schultz, T. 120, 256, 253, 257
Schwartz, R. 53, 54, 57, 120, 121, 146, 146, 193, 193, 196, 278, 289, *324, 332, 334, 334, 336*
Scallon, R. 255, *334*
Seatle, J. 14, 31(3), 42, 45(3), 47, 49, 64, 268, 274, *334*(4)
Seitz, S. 294, *334*
Semel, E. 270, 271, *334*
Shantz, C. 244, *334*
Shatz, M. 15, 191, 198, 198, 241, 280, 295, *333, 334*(4)
Sherwood, V. 126, *312*
Shibamoto, J. 155, *334*
Shipley, E. 192, *319*
Shriner, T. 183, 214, *334*

Shultz, T. 256, 257, *334, 334*
Siegel, I. 59, 84, 94, 94, 113(3), 130, 135, 223, *333, 334, 335, 335*
Sigel, G. 244, *324*
Sigueland, E. 127, *316*
Sinclair, H. 25, 108, *335*
Sinclair-de-Zwart, H. 24, *335*
Sinha, G. 80, 227, *317*
Skarakis-Doyle, E. 273, *322*
Slobin, D. 18(3), 29, 52, 58, 59, 74, 97, 168, 177, 201, 235, 252, 294, *335*(7)
Smith, E. 139, *318*
Smith, F. 181
Smith, J. 1, 5, 22, 29, 29, 33, 33, 34, 38, 42, 43, 44, 47, 48, 53, 53, 54(4), 57, 58(3), 67, 69, 76(3), 80, 92, 98, 109, 115, 129, 130, 131, 137, 138, 142, 152, 159, 160, 164, 164, 165, 165, 166, 168, 170(5), 171, 172, 172, 174, 175, 176, 178, 179(3), 185, 201, 201, 215, 223, 224, 263, 266, 284, 300, 303, 304, *320*
Smith, M. 257, 289, *333*
Smith, N. 255, *334*
Snow, K. 88, 115, 115, 120, 126(3), 192, 194, 199, 203, 286, 295, *335*(6)
Snyder-McLean, L. 73, 74, 79, 273, 273, 280, 280, *327*
Soller, E. 130, 135, *333*
Soloman, F. 289, 289, 294, *309, 309*
Spinelli, F. 49, *338*
Spradlin, J. 283, 283, *313, 313*
Sroufe, L. 120, 204, 205, *335*
Stalnaker, R. 21(5), 22, 22, 23, 28, 28, 34, 98, *335*
Stampe, D. 149, *335*
Stedman, J. 80, 227, *317*
Stemmer, N. 13, *336*(5)
Stevenson, R. 186, 187, *316*
Stewart, C. 294, *334*
Stoel-Gammon, C. 86, 99, 146, 152, 153, 153, *336, 336*
Storey, M. *315*
Strawson, P. 14, 20, 20, *336*(3)
Sullivan, J. 191, 192, *336*
Summers, D. 239, *320*
Swisher, L. 270, 270, **27**
Sylva, K. 124, *312*

Tackeff, J. 155, 155, 157, 169, *309, 309*
Tanz, C. 221, 227, *336*
Templin, M. 63, 63, *336*
Terrell, B. 124, 278, *334, 336*
Thompson, S. 114, *308*
Thomson, J. 145, 145, *336*
Toffel, C. 296, *336*
Tomasello, M. 111, 112(3), 113, 113, *336*
Tractman, L. 12, *332*
Treiman, R. 35, 300, *320*
Trevarthen, C. 120, *336*
Tulving, E. 48, *336*
Turner, E. 235, 235, *336, 336*
Turnure, C. 127, *337*
Tyler, S. 27, 34, 134, *337*

Ungerer, J. 124, *337*
Uzgiris, I. 25, 108, 108, 110, 111, 112, *337*

Vankleek, A. 286, *337*
Ventry, I. 12, 282, *337*
Vigorito, J. 127, *316*
Vihman, M. 92, 100, 100, 149, 150, *337*
Volterra, A. 110, *308*
vonHomboldt, 63
Vygotsky, L. 47, 136, 242, 249, *337*

Wales, R. 80, 130, 138, 227, *337*
Wall, S. 206, *307*
Wallace, J. 60, *337*
Wanner, E. 17, 24, 33, 59, 65, 66, 66, 92, 93, 113, 157, 158(4), 159, 160, 160, 161, 161, 163(3), 169, 177(4), 180, 197(3), 198(4), 199, 199, 205, 210, 211, 305(3), *319, 337*
Warden, D. 187, *337*
Waters, E. 206, *307*
Waters, W. 120, 204, 205, 305, *335*
Waterson, N. 148(3), 149, 149, *337*(3)
Webb, P. 263, 271, *329*
Weber, J. 183, *314*
Weber-Olson, M. *337*
Wechsler, D. 24, *337*
Weir, R. 74, 81, 85, 220, 255, 301, *337*
Weiss, A. 180, *337*
Weist, D. 80, 162, *337*

Author Index

Welch, C. 74, *335*
Wells, G. xv, 23, 31, 45, 45, 96, 97, 119(3), *337, 337*
Werner, H. xv, 5, 6, 6, 29, 38, 115, 129, 130(3), 142, 152, 213, 253, 253, 305, *337*
Wexler, K. 67, 162, 163(3), 198, 286, 298, *338, 338*
Whatley, J. 209, *315*
Wheeler, M. 194, *338*
White, S. 159, 211, 239, *338*
Whitehurst, G. 289, *338*
Whorf, B. 24, 42, 251, *338*
Wiig, E. 270, 271, *334*
Wilcox, M. 287, *334*
Wilkinson, L. 49, *334, 338*
Wilson, K. 244, *334*
Wing, C. 237, 237, *334, 338*

Winner, E. 91, 146(4), 253(3), *318, 318, 338*(4)
Witkin, H. 98, 130, 136, *338*
Wittgenstein, E. 21(3), 164, 193, 193, *338*
Wittig, B. 206, *307*
Wolf, D. 253, *318*

Yatchmink, Y. 196, *332*
Yngve, V. 283, *338*
Yonas, A. 106, 107, *331*
Yussen, S. 256, *338*

Zaporozhets, A. 48, 247, *338*
Zelazo, P. 123, *316, 337*
Zimmerman, G. *338*
Zorn, G. 289, *338*
Zwycewicz-Emory, C. 85, 238, 238, *329*

SUBJECT INDEX

Action based learning (see Sensorimotor skills) 105–106, 107–109, 110–113, 113–114, 115–116, 126, 129, 137–138, 300
Active learning 78–79, 81–83, 83–89, 89–95, 87, 106, 107, 132, 137, 218, 236, 277, 279, 282, 287, 291, 302, 304
Adeptness 7, 232–247, 247–249, 257
Affect 93, 105, 120, 203–204, 205–208, 212, 243, 267
Allative bias 80, 138
Anaphoric reference 226–227, 231, 265
Animateness 80, 109, 138, 140–141, 162, 173, 296
Appropriate 33, 85, 185, 197, 240, 240–241, 266, 272, 278.
A priori/a posteriori 71, 163, 218, 264, 266, 271, 275, 278, 279, 284–285, 298, 304
Assistance 6, 86–89, 190–212, 300, 305
Attachment 205–208, 212
Attributing psychological reality 29–30, 55, 155–158, 188, 283
Attribution 5, 38, 132

Behaviorism xv, 3–4, 15, 78, 278–280, 297
Bootstrap theory (see Learnability) 15
Buildup 74, 85–86, 171, 220–221
Buttressing 222, 223, 229, 231

Capacity 84, 92, 145–146, 160, 171, 221, 224, 242, 246
Categorization 26, 27–28, 34, 132–139, 139–142, 153
Categorization problem 2, 26–28, 34–35, 134, 135
Celebration of learning 94, 220
Clinicianship xiii, 12
Cluster concept theory of names 20
Code matrix 38, 170, 243Codification processes 16–19, 42, 44, 87–88, 170, 178, 242, 243–247, 300
Cognitive bases xii, xv, 1, 2, 3, 23–28, 36, 37, 40, 60, 105, 109, 116, 122, 133–138, 166, 207, 244, 251, 273–274, 305
  General cognitive capacities 1, 2, 24, 26–27, 97, 113, 135, 139, 169, 170, 175–176

351

Subject Index

Substantive dimensions 2, 24, 26–27, 28, 34–35, 97, 135
Codification processes 2, 24, 26, 97, 170
Metalinguistics 2, 24, 36, 91, 146–147, 249–257, 301–302, 306
Cognitive distancing 84, 94, 113–114, 223
Cognitive-linguistic—communicative systems 1–2, 4, 6, 16, 22–23, 26, 34–35, 40, 48, 85, 95, 120
Cognitive precursors 24, 25, 33, 67, 97, 105, 108
Cognitive socialization xv, 1, 24, 37, 40, 80, 133, 273
Coin-of-the-realm (see Informativeness) 182, 219
Communication xv, 1, 3, 16, 60, 87, 94, 115, 116, 126, 139, 153, 164, 175, 188, 201, 202–203, 207, 242, 245, 246, 273–274, 276–277, 278, 290, 291, 295, 303, 306
Communication game 23, 39, 115, 241, 243–247, 247–249
Communicative payoff 200, 211, 276–278, 281, 300, 302, 306
Competing influences 16–19
Content 29, 71, 283
  Explicit 19, 29, 38–39, 52–60, 63, 90, 132, 213, 219, 249, 283
  Implicit 29, 38–39, 60, 63, 219, 283
Context xv, 19, 20, 21–22, 30, 36, 37, 55, 63, 65, 68, 71, 74, 76, 81–83, 83–85, 89, 93, 97, 100, 127, 143–144, 152, 160, 164, 178, 194, 218, 237–239, 241, 244, 247, 251, 265, 267, 280, 282, 283, 285, 289, 297, 300, 304
Context bound 48, 142–144
Contextrealization (internal, external) 31
Convention 80, 105, 117, 129, 142, 148, 153, 190, 195, 290
Co-occurrence 38, 70, 74, 84, 161–162, 188, 218–219, 220, 231, 237, 289, 290, 295, 301
Cooperative principle 118, 119
Criteria for productivity 33, 55, 76, 155, 157, 283
  Attainment 59, 75, 77, 88, 266, 272, 283

Consolidation 59, 75, 77, 88, 214, 265, 272, 283
Preparation 59, 75, 77, 88, 266, 272, 283
Crossover 47

Data 13, 14, 72, 86, 262–263, 264, 275
Decontextrealization 48, 223, 247
Deduction 12, 20
Descriptive evidence 4, 65, 263–269, 271, 272, 275, 284, 295, 300, 303
Designation 20
Developmental profiles 69–72, 218, 272
Dialogue 16, 119, 164, 165–166, 194, 201, 223, 242, 247–248, 277, 306
Diary studies 63
Direct stimulation 107
Discrepancy learning 79, 87, 138, 294

Empirical base 6, 11, 12, 62, 276
Empiricism 6, 12–14, 36, 63–64
Envelope 178–181
Evidence 13, 72, 86, 262–263, 264, 275
Expansion 26, 111, 112, 285, 288, 290, 302
Explanatory evidence 4, 303
Expressive function 176, 203, 204, 212

Facilitate 79, 196, 197, 199, 205, 208, 211, 227, 277, 278, 280–281, 284, 286, 291–298, 300
Fallibility 95–96
Formal 1, 54, 80, 117, 120, 129, 159, 190, 194–197, 232, 246
Formal knowledge 105, 129, 154, 157, 161, 181, 188, 190, 229, 248, 273–274
Four big issues 32, 34–35, 36, 166–167, 177, 199, 305
Function 6, 37, 68
  Content 29, 39, 71
  Expressive 176, 203, 204, 212
  Intent 29, 39, 71
  Mathetic 3, 16, 47, 176
  Pragmatic 3, 16, 47, 176
Functional attributes (also Dynamic features) 144–145
Function over form xv, 3, 16, 37, 39, 39–44

Subject Index 353

Generalization 268
Generative semantics 28–30, 67, 154
Given/new information 106, 164, 186, 191, 224
Glossing 162, 221–222
Grammatical knowledge 3, 24, 26–27, 34–35, 154–166, 166–173, 167, 168–172, 218, 294, 296, 305
Grammatical systems 1, 2, 132, 223–230, 232–237

Hesitation phenomena 74
Highlighting 191
Homology 25, 111, 112–113, 149–151
Homonymy 100, 149–151
Humor 120–127, 253
Hypothesis testing (also Discovery theory) 35, 81–83, 83–89, 100, 163, 180

Impelled learning 89–95, 111, 112, 181
Impose 266
Indexical expression 21–22
Indicative (labelling) 5, 39, 49, 56, 58, 61, 132, 133, 142–143, 274
Indirect speech acts 42
Individual differences 72, 86, 98–100, 101, 153, 266, 271, 272, 275, 282, 284, 285, 286, 304
Individualized assessment 71, 266–267
Inductive generalization 66
Inference 3, 96–98, 157, 265
Inflectional system 183–188, 215–217
Informativeness 5, 6, 38–39, 40, 42, 43–44, 52, 60, 68, 80, 132, 137, 162, 164, 168, 170, 173–174, 181, 189, 219, 224, 225, 239, 240, 244, 300, 303
Initial dubbing ceremony 20, 192
Input 34, 35, 66–67, 87, 134, 188, 202, 290, 298
Intentionality (intent) 3, 4, 28, 29, 31–32, 36, 37, 38–39, 42, 45–52, 60, 67, 71, 74, 80, 85, 90, 93, 100, 101, 105, 109, 115, 117, 200, 211, 244, 274, 277, 301, 302, 304, 306
Interpretation of data 13

Interpretation problem 2, 26, 34, 134, 155, 199
Interpretative semantics 30–36, 67
Intersubjectivity 117, 118, 119, 128, 129
Intervention
　Impact 198, 280–285
　3 Ps 299–301, 306
Intonation 191, 223

Knowledge of language 27–28, 29
Knowledge of the world (also Theory of the World) 1, 2, 22, 25, 26, 27, 29, 32, 37, 40, 97, 98, 105, 132, 133, 134, 135, 158, 282

Language Acquisition Device (LAD) 13, 19, 65, 66, 67, 79–80, 91, 97, 190, 195, 277, 303
Language Assistance System (LAS) 13, 19, 79–80, 91, 97, 190, 277, 288, 303
Language learning 12, 29, 48, 88, 99, 116, 119, 124, 126, 134, 190, 221, 240, 286, 300, 301
Language sampling xi–xii, 72–75
Learnability (also Discovery theory) 3, 15, 83, 91, 162–163, 188, 254, 286
Learned distinctiveness 20, 140
Learned equivalence 20, 140
Line-of-regard 118
Linguistic context (see Co-occurrence) 84, 144, 170, 220, 237–239, 290
Linguistic determinism 24, 42
Loci of learning 81, 83, 85, 86, 94, 145, 171, 217–223, 231, 267, 290, 294
Locution 38–39
Looming 191

Mean length of utterance (MLU) 34, 70, 99, 182–183, 213, 214, 230, 306
Mentalism 6, 79, 278–280
Message-of-best-fit 16, 39, 182–183, 242–243
Methodology 5, 6, 62–77, 78–101, 303
Modelling 209–210, 287–290, 299–300, 302, 306

354 Subject Index

Mothese 66, 121, 163, 197–199, 199–202, 203–204

Narrowly focused learning 94, 95–96, 97
Nativism xii, 14–19, 36
New era xi
New forms, old functions; new functions, old forms 29–30, 59, 60, 111
Non-nominal expressions 25, 111–113, 140, 169, 175–176
Normal language acquisition: substantive base xiii, 6, 285–287

Objectivity 12, 64, 76
Operational promise 268
Overextension 143–147

Parallel talk 289, 299–301
Parent-child relationship 86–89
Parent participation 81, 86–89, 190–196, 208, 248, 277, 299–301, 302, 306
Partial learning 85
Passive learning 78–79
Perception 106–107, 128, 133
Perceptual attributes 144–145
Performative 55–56
Perlocution 38–39
Phonetically consistent form (PCF, also vocables) 49, 128, 153, 193, 290
Phonetic inventory 145
Philosophical base 6, 11, 36, 276
Philosophy of language 14, 65
Phonetic inventory 149
Phonological avoidance 146
Phonology 81–83, 127–128, 148–153, 160, 180, 218, 305
Power 264
Pragmatic ambiguity 21
Pragmatic domain 2, 17, 19, 35, 42, 59, 80, 120, 246, 251
Pragmatic function 3, 16, 18, 47
Precision 265
Predication 5, 38, 132, 152, 154–189
Presupposition 21, 22–23, 29, 36, 37, 38–39, 40, 43, 59, 60, 68, 136, 154, 183, 237, 282, 283, 304

Process 3, 24, 26, 64, 65, 68, 70, 97, 280
Productivity (see Criteria for) 30, 55, 59, 75–56, 100, 142, 265, 266, 272, 283, 304
Products 64, 65, 70
Proposition 21, 22, 28, 29, 38–39, 40, 52–60, 116, 171, 237, 250, 283, 304
Prosody 118, 148, 178–181, 184, 189, 191, 203, 204, 223
Prototype 25, 114
Psycholinguistics xv, 3, 15, 16, 42, 63, 65, 154, 269, 271, 272, 273–274, 275, 283
Psychology of language 14, 37
Psychometrics 263–269, 269–272, 275

Quantification 282–283

Raising the ante 192–193
Rationalism 12–14
Readiness 33, 79, 196, 217, 267, 300
Recontextualization 48, 247
Reductionism 168, 171
Reference 19–21, 36, 84, 97–98, 115, 118, 242, 300, 301
Referential display 118
Referential meaning 48, 84
Reinforcement 3, 4, 42, 78, 200, 278, 302, 306
Relational meaning 139, 154–166, 167, 175–176, 178
Relativity (patterns) xii, 266, 271, 272
Reorganization 92–93, 159, 160, 188, 211, 239, 240
Repertroire 33, 34, 58, 135, 139, 159, 181, 201, 267, 268
Replacement 26, 111, 112, 179, 285, 290, 302
Replication 282
Representativeness 72–73, 77, 107–109, 114, 128, 188, 203, 241
Request 49, 61, 274
Robustness 91, 95–96, 159, 190, 202–203, 212
Rule learning 88, 92, 148–152, 154–157, 163, 164, 167, 169, 174–175, 180, 228, 296, 297

Salience 52, 80, 137, 168, 300
Scaffold (also Lattice) 19, 120, 241
Scientific learning 136
Selectivity 37, 81, 170, 174, 219, 224, 301
Semantic domain 17, 19, 26–27, 28–31, 34–35, 59, 67, 154–156, 157, 160, 162, 166–167, 168
Sense 19
Sensorimotor skills 25, 105–106, 107–109, 110–113, 119, 120, 128, 135, 137
Sequence 29, 55, 59, 69, 183–188, 215, 228, 230, 231, 232–237, 280, 304, 306
Simplification processes 149, 150–152, 203
Social commerce xv, 3, 5, 6, 35, 37, 39–44, 60, 68, 74, 76, 105, 90, 95, 109, 115, 132, 161, 199, 201, 219, 230, 282, 300, 303
Socialization (see Cognitive Socialization) 40, 80, 105, 110, 115, 164–166, 176, 204, 209, 212, 246
Socio-emotional development 106, 205–208, 212
Spontaneous imitation 35, 81, 99, 202, 222, 231, 289
Spontaneous learning 136
Spontaneous rehearsal 35, 81, 86, 94, 222, 231
Spurts of learning 69, 108, 208, 214, 254, 267
Stages xii, 24, 32–34, 36, 46, 59, 84, 85, 89, 92, 93, 100, 112–113, 122–127, 154, 158, 159, 160–161, 182–183, 188, 190, 210–211, 225, 232–233, 287
Standard condition 74
Standing challenge 272
Stimulus-Response (S-R) theory 3, 4, 45, 200

Strategies 98–100, 150, 228, 267, 280, 286, 304
Subject–Verb–Object (SVO) constructions 91, 92, 99, 100, 167, 168–173, 173–175, 177–178, 178–181, 181–182, 188–189, 213, 215–217, 223, 224–226, 229, 230, 233, 305
Symbolic play 114, 116, 117, 120–127, 206, 302
Symbolization 108, 110, 113, 116–118, 164, 190, 274, 305
Syntagmatic–paradigmatic shift 237–239

Technicianship 12
Ten techniques 291–298
Theoretical base xi, xiii, 6, 11, 12, 13, 36, 77, 78, 160, 276
Three Bears theory 15, 177–178, 189
Three primary domains (cognitive, grammatical, communicative) 1, 273–274
Tools 109–110
Tuning 192–196, 197, 199, 203

Validity 69, 72, 135, 155, 261–263, 269–272, 274, 306

Werner and Kaplan model xv, 5, 6, 38, 115, 129, 154, 213, 305
Words 44
  Early word functions 139–142, 166–167, 175
  Lures to cognition 139–140
  First word 142–143, 148, 153
  Overextension 143–147, 218
  Invented 147, 218
  Phonology 148